RUYSBROECK THE ADMIRABLE

RUYSBROECK
THE
ADMIRABLE

BY

A. WAUTIER D'AYGALLIERS

KENNIKAT PRESS, INC./PORT WASHINGTON, N. Y.

TO MY WIFE

RUYSBROECK THE ADMIRABLE

First published 1923
Reissued 1969 by Kennikat Press

Library of Congress Catalog Card No: 68-26207
Manufactured in the United States of America

TRANSLATOR'S NOTE

THE author of *Ruysbroeck the Admirable* is Professor of the History of Philosophy at the Faculté de Théologie protestante de Paris.

He is also *pasteur* of the Foyer de l'Âme, Église réformée évangélique libérale, which continues in Paris—and spreads throughout France—the tradition of emancipated Protestantism, with which are connected the names of Athanase Coquerel fils and Jean Réville, as well as that of Charles Wagner whose books *Jeunesse, Vaillance* and *La Vie Simple* have exercised so profound an influence upon the present generation. M. Wautier d'Aygalliers is the son-in-law of Charles Wagner, whom he succeeded in 1918.

A pupil of François Picavet, late Professor of the Collège de France, our author has made a special study of the questions which deal with the influence of Hellenism upon Christianity.

That Neoplatonism constituted a sort of under-current to speculative mysticism through which it feeds the whole of modern philosophy, including Bergsonism, is the general idea of this work on the fourteenth-century Flemish mystic. Regarding it, Edouard Schuré, the famous author of *The Great Initiates*, uses the following words: "Livre admirable de solidité et de clarté, de profondeur et d'élévation."

In addition to numerous sermons our author has published an *Étude critique des Sources de la Vie de Ruysbroeck* (1909) and *Les Sources du Récit de la Passion* (1920).

As the text of the French volume was the thesis presented by M. Wautier d'Aygalliers for the degree of Doctor of Philosophy of the University of Paris, various notes and a critical investigation into the sources of information have, with his approval, been omitted from this English edition.

Ruysbroeck the Admirable was crowned by the *Académie française* in 1925, winning the *Prix Marcelin-Guérin*, which is devoted to works of history of serious social value and moral purpose.

F. R.

TABLE OF CONTENTS

FIRST PART

HISTORICAL INFLUENCES AND THE LIFE OF RUYSBROECK

CHAPTER I

SOCIETY IN THE FOURTEENTH CENTURY AND THE DEMOCRATIC REVIVAL—

     The democratic revolution takes place simultaneously on the social,
     the political and the religious ground, p. 3.

CONTENTS

CHAPTER IV

CHAPTER V

CHAPTER VI

SECOND PART

PHILOSOPHICAL SOURCES

CHAPTER X

CHAPTER XI

CHAPTER XII

CHAPTER XIII

PREFACE

We are living in serious times.

As is the case in all periods of transition, we are confronted with the great question of life and death, of the spirit and the flesh.

Disenchanted and embittered, incapable for the most part of discerning the right and essential directions without which life becomes a failure, present-day humanity, between the past from which it expects nothing and the future which it dreads, has come to a halt, like a traveller in the night. . . .

Many have wrapped themselves about in their wretchedness as in a shroud: what though death does come, if, to their mind, it is to end everything!

We are wretched, not because we have shut ourselves up in cloisters or subjected the flesh to the harsh discipline of hermit or recluse, but because we have profaned life, because we did not see it as duty, not as enjoyment.

We have quenched the spirit. And now we find ourselves on roads full of bogs and quagmires, some of us wringing our hands, others in a state of besotted stupefaction, all incurably sad.

Any voice that makes itself heard in this darkness and solitude, any voice in which a higher humanity speaks, is a friendly and welcome voice.

It is such a voice that we wish to sound forth, the voice of an old monk of the Middle Ages, utterly forgotten except by a few ardent souls, a few scholars, who believe that the past, when questioned by history, may still throw light on the present.

A monk! many will say in accents of mingled pity and

scorn. Yes, but one beneath whose rough garment beat the heart of a man, one who found himself in conditions almost identical with our own.

To those who suffered and wandered astray he spoke words of life. In an age sunk in the lowest depths of materialism, he succeeded in awakening the divinely human soul, immortal daughter of God, slumbering in its tomb.

It may be that the solution he propounded is so especially adapted to his own far-away times that we cannot pretend to apply it, as it stands, to our own. For there are forms that die, as in a garden die the stalks of the previous season.

The root, however, is still alive, and the problem which, at various periods of human history, inspires so many different solutions is fundamentally the same: man confronted with the mystery of his destiny, man seeking, behind the shifting curtain of his days, a Will that is good and a Thought that will direct him aright.

Do not, therefore, say of the following pages: "This doctrine has no longer anything to do with us." Everything has to do with you, since you no longer have anything — or scarcely anything — though you must live a true and noble life, in accordance with the dignity of your humanity.

Do not say it is nothing to you, that bold motto which Ruysbroeck gave as a *viaticum* to two students of· Paris, logic-proud and rich maybe in many things, poor only in hope and in good-will: " Vos estis tam sancti sicut vultis."

Pick up the phrase, as you would a crumb of good bread, without taking umbrage at the grave and erudite apparel in which it is attired.

For myself, whose rôle is that of a modest transmitter, I say in the words of Olivétan, when issuing his translation of the Bible:

"Je n'ay point honte, comme la veusve évangélique, d'avoir apporté devant vos yeuls mes deux petites quadrines en valeur d'une maille, qui est toute ma substance. Aulcuns viendront après qui pourront mieulx."

INTRODUCTION

THE MEDIÆVAL PHILOSOPHIES AND HISTORY

I

THE present work on Ruysbroeck the Admirable is neither a book of history nor one of philosophy: it comes under that well-defined domain of scholarship which we call the history of philosophy.

By this we mean that, while retaining its own distinctive character, it nevertheless keeps in close contact with history, properly so called, as well as with philosophy.

Though tributary to those two scientific provinces, the history of philosophy is subject to the same rules of research, of criticism and exposition. It applies to ideas, though it cannot lose interest in events, which determine and condition ideas. Besides, what value could it give to these ideas did it not previously secure to itself the resources of psychology, of dialectics, and of metaphysics?

And so the history of philosophy, as regards its special purpose, harmonises with the clearly-marked predilection manifested by our times for historical reconstitutions. Indeed, no age has worked so diligently in keeping track with a humanity that has disappeared and in applying to the present the lessons of the past.

This century, so generous in spite of all its troubles, could not resign itself to leave so many heroes sunk in oblivion, without a soul to lament, or a poet to sing their praises. In applying this filial piety, it has shown such sturdy integrity as will remain one of its finest characteristics. Perseverance in effort, foresight in research, a scrupulous conscientiousness in the use of documents: such is a brief summary of the progress effected in the domain of history.

It is not simply the machinery that has been improved by the creation of special schools in which real laboratories have helpfully supplied the various disciplines connected with history. Suffice it to mention in France the *École des Chartes* and the *École pratique des Hautes-Études*. Progress, however, is still—and mainly—connected with the working out of a method that has definite rules and with the conception of the educational rôle of history.

All the same, historians have been found to depreciate this extremely delicate task. "Alas, what mountains of dead ashes, wreck and burnt bones, does assiduous Pedantry dig up from the Past Time, and name it History, and Philosophy of History." [1]

It is no doubt right that the historian should be aware of the limits imposed on his task. Turning towards the past, he knows beforehand, as Gabriel Monod says, that "historical reality is never known to us in the absolute and precise truth of its endless complexity."

The exact sense of our limitations, however, is a different thing from the scepticism of the toiler overwhelmed by his impotence. Still, this form of scepticism, like all others, is an injustice. Is not the workman greater than his tools? And though the historian works under more unpromising conditions than, for instance, a chemist, he is able nevertheless, through a series of minute approximations, gradually to lessen the risks of error and almost grasp *facts* themselves in all their throbbing life.

Thus the question of method makes itself imperiously felt at the very outset of every historical undertaking.

History is made up from documents: manuscripts, inscriptions, or figured documents such as the works of architecture, of painting and sculpture, objects of every kind: arms, costumes, coins, etc. But even in the most favourable cases, discovered documents are always nothing

[1] Carlyle, *Past and Present*, book II. chapter ii.

more than ruins, the flotsam and jetsam left from the great shipwreck of time.

Of all scientific workers, then, the historian, at first sight, is the most imperfectly equipped, for his vision of facts is indirect and fragmentary. He would thus be reduced to nothing more than the barren preserver of the vast necropolises of bygone ages, did not precise methods enable him to go back from *traces* to *facts*.

The collected material should first be interpreted, weeded out and verified by a series of critical processes: criticism regarding scholarship, origin, and interpretation. Then it is advisable to group together this material into cadres that press home the reality we would grasp, a reality which still exists only in the mind.

In such groupings there are always gaps, all the greater owing to the paucity of documents. Then reasoning comes in. Trusting to the law of analogies which places past humanity in the same category as the present, the historian goes back from deduction to deduction right to the time he has undertaken to reconstruct. The exactness of his reconstruction is in direct ratio to the certainty and foresight of reasoned processes. Thus he connects facts with facts, links together the separate rings in order to obtain a continuous outlook upon events. He cannot grasp the truth all at once. He rises, however, from one level to another, like a traveller climbing the side of a mountain, until he reaches the top, whence his glance takes in as a whole the world in which men move and have their being.

Here science should precede art. To collect testimonies, to test them, to correct them if they have been distorted by passion or apologetics: such is the task of the scholar—an arduous and thankless as well as prolonged task, though one that constitutes the very condition of success. Unless he has lived long in the atmosphere of his origins, the historian is building on sand, and his labours, neither solid nor conscientious, are soon proved to be valueless. Nothing but prolonged contact with the springs of knowledge gives that

xxii   RUYSBROECK THE ADMIRABLE

vivid illumination in which lines and features stand clearly outlined and the framework is fittingly arranged. This enthralling work, which makes a historian the amazed witness of a veritable renaissance, is one that he both suffers from and enjoys alone. Like the stones that form the foundation of a structure, it does not appear in broad daylight, though constituting the solid bottom which is to sustain the edifice.

Of itself alone, however, the work of criticism would be inadequate. This work has even been called idle play: *ignavia critica.* To documents—those mute witnesses—we shall find it necessary to give contemporary speech. Art follows on science in breathing upon these dry bones, collecting events in striking epitomes, dashing off a silhouette with a pencil-stroke, and setting up the harmonious balance of the parts in the wide stretch of the *ensemble.* The historian must now be able to forget his own period, to assimilate the soul of past ages, and to make up his mind—as against the protesting scholar—to sacrifice in order to acquire that conciseness which alone contains the one thing needed.

Now, in this dual task, what is the historian's claim? Erudition for its own sake is egoism. No longer does history, as Augustin Thierry vigorously expresses it, "interest itself in the fortunes of princes, it now deals with the destinies of men who lived and suffered like ourselves."

Crime-proving articles, whether the deeds of Philippe-Auguste or the altar-screen representing the Elders adoring the Lamb by Hubert and Jan van Eyck, are now expressed in terms of the human soul. For it is the soul that interests us; its griefs and hopes are our own. Time has not parcelled it out into arbitrary categories. It is *one,* "in such fashion that the whole sequence of men should be regarded as the same man ever subsisting and continually learning," as Pascal says. This soul, like the Sleeping Beauty, lies slumbering in documents: it is for the historian to wake it with a kiss. For history is indeed a work of love.

What have we to do with these dusty archives, these broken columns which daily crumble away, these worn-out costumes, unless we bring back life? " History," says Michelet, "has nothing to do with these heaps of stones. History deals with the soul, original thought, fruitful initiative, the heroism of action and creation. It teaches that a soul weighs infinitely more than a kingdom, an empire, a state system—sometimes more than the human race itself."

Herein lies the greatness of history, its distinctive objective. History is a *morale*. To know what the human soul has believed, thought and suffered during the various ages of mankind is a source of grave joys, a task that carries one far. This is the supreme educational value of history.

We are sometimes surprised to find how far men, even quite intelligent, may fall short of sane judgment in their appreciation of contemporary tendencies and facts. On inquiring into the reason, we almost invariably discover that it is based on a total or a partial ignorance of history. This lack contains the germ of all pride and vanity as well as of the gravest deviations of thought. The man who has not instinctively grasped the inextricable interlinking of generation with generation, and the indefatigable renewal of life, cannot really understand his own age, in which survivals of the past and novelties of the present are both to be found. History is perhaps the only school in which tolerance and justice are taught, the only one that forbids absolute judgments, because it knows that every sentence is subject to perpetual revision.

In this pathetic drama which unrolls itself as the ages pass, the historian assuredly finds a place. He has his sympathies and his antipathies. Still, while attempting to create a truth that satisfies him, he does not regard as false what he has been unable to appropriate from the vast stores of the past. He knows that the gods die, as do the stars. Still, he does not forget that these cold thoughts, whose vitality has run out, were once living and invigorating. And he loves them for their past accomplishments, though himself removed from them by all the distance of his more recent acquisitions.

In these pacific heights, everything becomes passionately

interesting and concurs most effectively to the utility attributed to history: the understanding of the present. *Incessu
patuit dea.* The human soul has passed by, and its regal outline has stamped itself on the dust of vanished centuries.

The few pages of a well-directed monograph on some
forgotten character may shed illuminating brilliance. The
deciphering of an inscription on a stone in the desert may
serve as a link to bind together the broken chain of a tradition.

Does this mean that all reconstituted facts are of like
importance? No, indeed. If history is to be a *morale*, it must
effect a sorting-out process. It expresses itself by distinguishing good from evil. It either brands or exalts, without
taking sides, simply inviting man to learn from repeated
demonstrations that show forth the beauty of effort, the
persistence of hope, and the greatness of human misery.
It dashes to the ground the pride of conquerors and goes
seeking a pensive monk in some forgotten monastery. It
attaches less importance to the victor's blood-stained laurel
wreath than to the last cry of the Crucified on an arid
eminence of Judaea. Thus does it ordain and compute, compare and proportion, restore to their right place the haughty
ones whose stormy personality filled the entire stage of their
period, whilst shedding radiance upon the only individuals
worthy of the unanimous acclaim of mankind.

And so history prefers to dwell upon such characters as
are truly great, whether in work, in sanctity, or in martyr-
dom. "The only thing that makes history worth writing,"
says H. de la Gorce, "is the spectacle of a soul superior to
the peril that confronts it." Doubtless crowds also are
great, whether worked up by some strong ferment, or, as
they quietly pass their lives in common, unconsciously
moving forward beneath the urge of thousands of obscure
and—one might think—useless lives. But the hero, the great
man, the saint: these constitute the very voice of this confusion, this agitation. In such a soul all the stirrings of the
crowd find an echo. They give an expression to the unconscious thought, a will to men's aspirations. Here essentially

is the historical individual, the one through whom history becomes both instruction and creation.

For it is the living alone who propagate life. By setting the great man or the saint in strong relief, history reveals the splendid possibilities slumbering within each of them. The great man is a guarantee that any man may acquire the same energy and capacity that made up his own greatness. The magic wand of a master is capable of arousing these slumbering powers. And it is this wand that the historian wields.

II

If such, indeed, be the object of history: "to teach man to man," we can understand the extraordinary development of certain branches almost entirely neglected a century or two ago: the history of ideas, for instance, or the history of philosophy.

If man's greatness lies mainly in the effort he makes to understand himself and his destiny, then religious history should arouse more justifiable interest than any other phase of general history.

This consideration has not been a matter of indifference in the choice of our subject. In undertaking to study the life and work of a fourteenth-century monk, Ruysbroeck the Admirable, whose very name is scarcely known in France, it has been our purpose to revive a moment of the religious evolution of mankind, on the eve of one of the greatest spiritual transformations recorded in history. For this man apprehends and expands, by his thought, the aspirations of his generation; he also enables us, in his person, to repudiate the unjustifiable discredit still hanging over the Middle Ages.

We are accustomed to give this name to the period extending from the fall of the Western Roman Empire in 476, or even from the separation of the Eastern Empire and the Western Empire in 395, to the capture of Constantinople in 1453. But can life be so easily circumscribed? Like the ocean waves, it passes over the frail chronological barriers whereby man opposes its fury, and covers with its smooth even surface lands whose confines have been too carefully fixed.

The very term Middle Ages implies an intermediate period. This intermediate stage, however, can be justified only from the philological point of view.

The *aetas media* marks one phase of the development of the Latin tongue. It is the epoch when Latin is no longer the noble classical language which, up to the reign of Constantine the Great, was the vehicle of ancient thought, and when, gradually permeated with Germanic idioms, it had not yet been transformed to the point of retaining only the traces of its ancient nobility (*infima latinitas*). The humanists, who flattered themselves upon having resurrected elegant latinity, came to blend the *aetas media* and the *aetas infima* into one single philological period; between the past glory and the restored splendour the language was enveloped in a zone of shadows.

But this division, arbitrary in the case of language, was extended by the humanists to history itself. The favourable reception of this preconceived idea gave birth to a veritable historical distortion.

If, according to the humanists, the Middle Ages constitutes a period of opposition to the great classical civilisation in the two forms it has assumed—the Græco-Roman antiquity and the Renaissance—it was natural to regard the period as one bristling with error of every kind. Illumination was monopolised by Rome and Athens, and, after a prolonged eclipse, a radiant dawn began to gild the domes of the Renaissance. The pride of life is reborn in pagan art and literature; mankind shakes off its wrappings and comes out of its long lethargy.

What could the night bring forth? Fear, nightmares, crimes. Is not night still the symbol of ignorance? Hence that sombre phrase which Voltaire so imprudently coined.

Speaking of the "temps grossiers qu'on nomme le moyen âge," the sceptical philosopher of Ferney in all probability gave expression to his scorn of Christianity by a systematic depreciation of the Middle Ages. The historian who penetrates into the Middle Ages, he wrote, "is like a traveller who, on leaving some proud city, finds himself in a wilderness covered with brambles." Thus was credit gained for legends which have not withstood the critical investigations of the nineteenth century: the repulsive filth of the Middle Ages, the baths of blood, the *jus primae noctis* of libidinous lords, the intellectual lethargy lasting ten centuries, etc. Historians like Michelet and Taine vied with each other in circulating formulas which continued to spread such foregone conclusions. Michelet is fond of speaking of "la gigantesque moisissure," of "la nuit de mille ans." Taine, though brilliantly acknowledging how deeply the modern world was indebted to the Middle Ages, occasionally forgets his own arguments and regards this period as nothing but a "fosse noire," "une époque maladive et détraquée."

It might be easy to summon arguments, to bring forward incontrovertible authorities in favour of such a picture. Nor is it to no purpose that the sluggish blood of the Barbarians runs in the veins of an almost utterly transformed humanity. It is true that morals were coarse, passions violent, poverty and misery widespread. This was an age of shocks and collisions, of strong clashing forces, in which soul and flesh vie with each other, and the latter only too often obtains undoubted mastery. Still, are we impartial in applying to different times a common standard of measurement, in judging with our own contemporary mentality things which were then widely tolerated? There can be no just comparison between dissimilar terms. And it would be equally easy to give chapter and verse for a contrary generalisation, altogether on the bright side, though quite as unfair as the other.

Indeed the times were barbarous, though the barbarity was wholly permeated with idealism, through which the mastery of the spirit was slowly but surely making itself felt.

Strict historical methods have been needed to give historians a more correct outlook upon mediæval times. Manifestly the Middle Ages was above all else creative, the matrix which was to shape the whole of our modern civilisation. Stupendous evocation of a world thought to be dead, a world which, owing to the deciphering of a great number of charters and the publication of a host of monographs, shakes itself free of the dust of ages! We see the awakening not only of the individual but of the national consciousness. When the Roman eagles which hitherto had guaranteed the imposing unity of the ancient world were conquered, patriotism becomes a reality, fragile perhaps, though destined to become consolidated. There are heard the first feeble stammerings of tongues which are still our own. Ancestral brutality is compelled to recognise external authority, whose sway extends from lord to peasant. A great process of domestication is then carried on by the Church, and the iron discipline it exercises over the Western world right on to the twelfth century—a discipline particularly severe upon princes—alone prevents this world from perishing in anarchy. In the councils we see the first faint outlines of parliamentary life, wherein the decisions of a group may find expression; the corporative franchises of the thirteenth and fourteenth centuries have their origin in these well-filled assemblies, dominated by ideals of order and goodwill. The vanquished and the oppressed acquire new rights. To all comes a revelation of the moral, no less than material, necessity for work. The undisciplined energies of the people are directed into methodical occupations. And, sloughing off the thick layer of slime which northern torrents had deposited upon the Gallic soil, we see the world burst into flower: the first farm and the first *scriptorium* are decisive pledges of a reparative future.

While the material task is of necessity the first in order of time, it is speedily followed by a wonderful intellectual activity. Compilations are made of the ancient acquisitions of the human race, fragments of pagan literature and science, patristic literature. Then, under the direction of Charlemagne and his collaborators, we see the faint outlines of a contemporary science and theology.

The Roman Church, which suggested the idea of calm majesty, of firmly established power, undergoes a gradual transformation. The solid architecture befits the age of the famous nineteenth-century controversies stoutly based on arguments from which mysticism is almost wholly absent. These were the days of Scotus Erigena and Hincmar, of Gerbert and Fulbert, of Bérenger and Lanfranc. The early Gothic churches coincide with contemplative poetry, which imbues with hitherto unknown sweetness the intellectualism of the doctors. There is a desire to attain to God, but thought must be firmly buttressed before venturing forth. This dual movement or impulse, which appears both in architecture and in speculation, may be perceived in the entire line of great thinkers up to the fifteenth and sixteenth centuries: Guillaume de Champeaux, Saint Bernard and Abélard, his opponent, the great Victorins on to Albertus Magnus and Saint Thomas, and the mystic school which crowns the Scholasticism of the thirteenth century.

It is scarcely possible to form any idea of the intellectual progress which extends throughout six centuries, produces veritable encyclopædias and evolves thinkers whose powerful originality in certain directions has never been surpassed, any more than has the *Sainte-Chapelle*, the *Divina Commedia*, or the *Adoration of the Lamb*.

After this, can we still affirm that the Middle Ages was a period of barrenness, of sombre savagery?

In a true concatenation of the ages, the Renaissance, with which the modern world is generally linked up, far from being a triumphant resurrection from death, is nothing but the magnificent culmination of a lengthy process, the flowering of a venerable tree. The old ancestor, however, has been forgotten, the slow uprising of the sap, and the very root which had to seek its sustenance in the land where Jesus was born.

If mention of an intermediary is to be made, it is rather to the Renaissance that the terms should be applied; for what are the ideas that have survived, in the patrimony bequeathed to us? Have glory and voluptuousness remained the end of life? Have we maintained the principle of Germanic right: *cujus regio hujus religio*? Have we not preferred democratic regimes and social solidarity to royal absolutism? And where are to be found the germs of emancipation, of internal reform and social progress, if not in the Middle Ages, and more particularly in the fourteenth century?

Again, if the predominance of spiritual over material interests has been firmly established in history, when did the Christian soul utter a finer chant than in the *Imitation of Christ*: "And what have we to do with genus and species? . . . Let all the learned hold their peace . . . speak Thou alone unto me"?[1] At what period has there been found such passionate interest in the life of the spirit? The cry of Italian students when their professors entered the lecture-hall: "Tell us of the soul, tell us of the soul!" is not a solitary cry; it spreads over an entire period.

By reason of its generous efforts and accomplishments, its aspirations and that broad spirit which attempted to combine in one imposing synthesis Christianity, Neoplatonism, Aristotelianism and Arabic philosophy, because of its disinterestedness and enthusiasm, the Middle Ages cleared the paths along which we are still travelling.

It constitutes the modern age in its infancy, at a time when the flesh rebels against the constraint of the spirit. And, in the glad return of man to the independent years of his childhood, we may rightly see the reason why our own generation eagerly devotes itself to the study of mediæval times.

[1] Book I. chapter iii.

III

The long and traditional misunderstanding of Middle-Age civilisation has had its repercussion on the history of philosophy.

In university instruction, the entire interest is centred upon ancient philosophy, which ends in 529 with the closing of the school of Athens, and upon modern philosophy, inaugurated by Descartes. According to this conception, humanity lay sunk in leaden slumber until the time came when the clarion call of the Renaissance announced the awakening of human thought.

As people have not taken the trouble to study such men as Thomas Aquinas or Duns Scotus, they are regarded somewhat as logic-choppers, repeating old theological arguments over and over again, as men out of touch with the world of reality and so devoid alike of originality and of interest. Is it right, we should ask ourselves, thus to rend asunder the evolution of human thought? Even admitting that the philosophical processes of mediæval thinkers are utterly different from our own, do not these thinkers represent a stage of the human mind ever advancing towards an elusive truth? There is nothing in Roger Bacon's alchemy resembling our detailed laboratory experiments; still, it is not on that account neglected in the history of science. There is nothing in the evolution of mankind altogether devoid of interest, no single conception that has not assimilated to itself something of the past, that has not supplied something of itself to the patrimony handed down to one another by the following ages. Simply from this point of view, the history of philosophy, in suppressing ten centuries of speculation, offers humanity a truncated image that is absolutely illegitimate.

From another point of view, the history of philosophy is lacking in the great joy of associating with really powerful and original thinkers. The problem to which the great speculatives of the thirteenth century and the mystics of the fourteenth applied their resources is an ever-present problem. It is ours, as it was that of Plato, Plotinus and Leibniz. There have been few attempts in history so gigantic as the effort to solve it. The broad sweep of the system of Thomas Aquinas, the soaring heights attained by such mystics as Ruysbroeck or Meister Eckhart, have seldom been equalled. Now, if human thought is a heritage handed down to us, with the obligation to pass it on to our children in nobler and grander form, we are indebted to the philosophers of the Middle Ages just as we are to the Greek thinkers: this, too, in a degree that we are only just beginning rightly to estimate.

Modern philosophy, preoccupied about its links with the past, has gone beyond Descartes and halted before the door of the cathedrals of Strasbourg and Cologne or at the threshold of the cells of fourteenth-century monks. "That the moral consciousness is a method, that we are authorised to regard as certain the theories we need for right action, even if we find ourselves incapable of explaining and developing them, of incorporating them with science, is a fruitful thought which Kant certainly borrowed from no one; it was the peculiar inspiration of his generous heart; all the same, he might have found its germ in Pascal, its development, perhaps too audacious and confident, in the despised mysticism of the Middle Ages, according to which the progress of knowledge has for its condition and standard the fidelity of the thinker in regulating his conduct by previously known truth." [1]

The idealistic school which succeeded Kant is reproduced, along with Hegel and Schelling, in the mysticism of Meister Eckhart and Saint-Victor. Far from being a rootless—and therefore lifeless—tree, mediæval thought drew its best elements from Hellenism. It continues the philosophical tradition of antiquity, modifies it by its own temperament and hands it on to successors who bring it right down to

[1] Ch. Secrétan: *La Civilisation et la Croyance*, p. 7.

the present time. Here, indeed, after the failure of the materialistic school, modern tendencies, along the lines of psychology and material science, proceed to a conception of the Divine, the striking relationship of which to mediæval speculation is manifest, "that is to say, to the vision of God regarded as immanent in the universe . . . and also of human life regarded as forming part of this profound reality."

If this be the case, we can no more destroy ten centuries with a stroke of the pen than we can isolate the Middle Ages as a sort of watertight historical period. Indeed, these centuries form the very links for establishing the continuity of our intellectual patrimony.

IV

The only convincing arguments in favour of this general position are to be found in closely correlated texts.

What is the great fact to which this examination leads? That the Middle Ages had another master than Aristotle; that the dominating influence must be attributed to Plotinus and Neoplatonism.

The Aristotle of the Middle Ages is himself a Neoplatonist. As the original texts were lacking, the Middle Ages knows the Stagirite only in fragmentary fashion, through Neoplatonist commentaries. The copious influx of ideas introduced by Jewish and Arabic philosophers is wholly imbued with Neoplatonism, quite as much as the Greek and Latin Fathers. We cannot forget that the two great spiritual leaders of the Middle Ages, Saint Augustine and Scotus Erigena, were in touch—the one directly and the other indirectly—with Neoplatonism.

If therefore we had to give a chronological frame or scheme to the Middle Ages, we should have to extend the conventional limit beyond the years 476 or 395 and go back to the third century, to the very origins of mediæval spirituality. We ought likewise to go beyond 1453, for Neoplatonism is the principal factor—along with Marsilio Ficino—in the Florentine Renaissance.

The Middle Ages is mainly characterised by the predominance of religious unrest and the supremacy of theology. We cannot understand this general unrest if we know nothing of the seething conditions in which third-century Christianity was involved, seriously imperilling it, until the hypocritical opportunism of Constantine determined once for all the establishment of Christianity.

This official Christianity, however, contrary to general opinion, did not come about as a substitute for pagan civilisation. Just as victorious Rome assimilated vanquished Hellenism—*Graecia capta ferum victorem cepit*—so Christianity was profoundly influenced by its environment. It is in the third century—in the popular aspirations which spring up simultaneously in pagan syncretism, in agnosticism, followed by Manichæism, and in Platonic mysticism, in the universally experienced need for pardon and expiation, in that *élan* towards invisible things which is common to so many races then blended in the ferment of Rome—that we must seek the germs of mediæval thought.

In the third century, Neoplatonism, Gnosticism and Christianity have almost equal influence. The balance, however, is soon to be disturbed, and the struggle limited to the philosophy of Plotinus and to Christianity: Gnosticism can meet the erudition of an Origen and the speculations of a genius like Plotinus only with the lucubrations of the *Pistis Sophia* or the books of *Jeû*. It continues to degenerate, and, in proportion as life fades away, formulas and rites increase, as happens with all dying religions. And so it dies, though not until it has bequeathed something of itself to Christianity. Indeed, it was Gnosticism which handed down to the Church the sacramental idea, the theory of a rite working solely by its own virtue (*opus operatum*).

Afterwards Manichæism is seen to revive in the heresies of the Middle Ages, which change their name though not their tendency. On the other hand, we find the mystical ferment of the philosophy of Plotinus, after Iamblichus and Porphyry, working out systems, encouraging the contemplative habit, and finally, among the people, culminating in a veritable pantheism.

On the Christian side, this is the time for laying firm foundations. Confronted with such a medley of ideas and aspirations, Saint Cyprian and Origen aspire to provide the religious soul of humanity with a unique refuge; and this, not only in a spiritual conception, but also in a universal ecclesiastical organism. Obedient to an intuition of genius, these great organisers offer the world the very thing that pagan syncretism lacked. This mighty organism was to assert itself with all the more power, seeing that in so vast a structure was found the very thing that the restless soul of the period was seeking: contact with God, the touching sacrifice of a Mediator whose saving death was evoked in a glow of mystery well suited to initiates. When therefore, in the fourth century, the Edict of Milan gave official sanction to the universal religion, the world of antiquity found itself ready to enter, without either repugnance or regret, the vaults of the Church.

The third century has another important claim on our attention. Not only is it, historically and psychologically, connected with the Middle Ages, but it also gives evidence of striking correspondences with the present state of things.[1]

From the strictly philosophical point of view, it is possible, *grosso modo*, to mark off the various stages which connect Neoplatonism and the third century with the thought of the Middle Ages.

The closing of the school of Athens disperses the official masters of Neoplatonism. Its spirit, however, can neither be exiled nor recovered. Already Saint Augustine had utilised the theories of Plotinus dealing with exemplarism and the purification of the soul. Boëtius, the unfortunate minister of Theodoric, found great inspiration in the *De Consolatione*

---

[1] See W. R. Inge, *The Philosophy of Plotinus*, London, 1918, v. II. pp. 219 ss.

of Porphyry, nor did he fear to justify by Neoplatonic arguments the mysteries of the Trinity and the Incarnation.

After 529, the condemned philosophy is reduced to the point of presenting itself as Christian. The Pseudo-Dionysius is a true disciple of Proclus, and Scotus Erigena, by circulating a translation of Dionysian treatises in the ninth century, ensures for Neoplatonism a renewed — though hidden — vitality. In addition, Scotus Erigena relies upon the doctrine of the Pseudo-Dionysius in elaborating his great work on the divisions of nature.

With Scotus Erigena determining the main trend of the intellectual life of the Middle Ages, it is not surprising that we are continually finding survivals of Neoplatonism. Scholasticism itself, hitherto regarded as under the patronage of Aristotle, has become assimilated both with Neoplatonism and with Aristotelian Peripateticism. Along with the Pseudo-Dionysius, it divides questions by stating positive arguments on one side and negative arguments on the other; crowning its important synthesis with a mystical method derived direct from Plotinus. And so the distinction set up between the great Scholastics and the speculative mystics of the fourteenth century does not exist: the latter do but complete the work of the former.

It is quite evident, then, that the Middle Ages showed no anxiety to confine the mind within rigid formulas or to embark along false paths. The profound idealism of the philosopher of Lycopolis flows like a subterranean stream beneath the foundations of the Church, gushing up to the surface, now in such personalities as Scotus Erigena, Hugues de Saint-Victor, Meister Eckhart, and again in the Protestant movements of the twelfth or the fourteenth century.

Carinthia and Ukraine are traversed by a very winding stream. At its source it is called Poik. After a time, it disappears in a crevice and continues underground. Very soon it emerges, swollen with the waters it has encountered in subterranean darkness. It is now called Unz. It disappears a second time, and, on coming to the surface, is called Laibach. The water is still the same, though it changes name after each visit underground.

This stream supplies us with a good analogy for the history of Neoplatonism. It does not always appear visibly, though supplying sustenance for ten centuries of philosophy. And though it frequently has no name, it is always there, at the very heart both of Scholasticism and of Mysticism, in the palace schools with Scotus Erigena as in the peaceful retreat of the abbey of Saint-Victor. It is Neoplatonism that arouses in the mind of the people those uneasy longings whose manifestation exposed the steel corslet with which, in knightlike fashion, it was clothed. It was Neoplatonism that made the Middle Ages, not the period of quibbling and logic-splitting, but pre-eminently the spiritual age, wherein the problem of religion dominates all others, seeks expression, lisps the principles of the religion of the spirit, and is resolved into the very bosom of God, after having superseded all forms and intermediaries.

V

A view so different from the usual conception of things calls for proof. It is our purpose to supply this proof in Ruysbroeck the Admirable. Great historical syntheses have become increasingly difficult. Henceforth they can only be undertaken with the aid of numerous specialists.

Thus limited, our work aims at being no more than a chapter in the history of philosophy. We have confined ourselves exclusively to unravelling the springs of Ruysbroeck's thought. Whence come its essential elements? How far is it influenced, and how far original? Does this thought, culminating in different intellectual currents, consist of a single stream, after a previous stage of incubation? Or rather has it become expanded by successive impulses, themselves determined by the accidents of life? Such, strictly, is our plan.

This inquiry, difficult enough though passionately instruc-

tive, has not hitherto tempted any of the scholars who have
dealt with the speculative mysticism of the fourteenth century. Is it presumptuous of us to undertake to fill up the gap?

In order not to lose himself in such an investigation,
however, the historian should trace out for himself beforehand a plan, with a well-defined method.

While the study of the texts—with all that it involves
in combining and collating, examining manuscripts, showing their connections and interdependence—is the main concern, of itself alone it is insufficient. The inner or spiritual
development of the ideas, the very formation of the thought,
largely depend on external facts. In this direction our task
is closely connected with history and psychology.

We must make acquaintance with the man and his
surroundings. Genius itself is conditioned by time, race and
environment. The combined effect of various influences,
exercising outward pressure, models and shapes the personality, as does the thumb of a sculptor. This it is that
gives stability to genius, disciplines the inner powers by
compelling them to function within determined limits.
Would a Savonarola, a Luther, a Dante have been what
they were had the political and religious conditions of their
age been different? It is not very probable.

As the tree draws its sap from the soil, so the historical
individual feeds his ardour on the aspirations and the sorrows
of his times. He gives them greater expression, though they
must mainly be sought in that laboratory made up of the
life of a nation, or in the collective consciousness of the crowd.

This history is more than the picture of all the developments whereby nation or man assert or organise themselves,
oppose their enemies. Modern historiography has reinstated
the naïve chroniclers who scrupulously told of ruined crops
and floods, attributing to these events—which were outside
the sphere of the human will—an importance at least equal
to that of the death of a prince, or the promulgation of a
charter. In Brussels, in the year 1315, a violent insurrection
was found to have originated in a terrible cattle-plague.

The enhanced price of food, followed by famine, provoked a series of disturbances which, ten years later, caused John the Third to make important concessions. In 1314, a deluge of rain arrested Louis X. le Hutin, who was making ready to invade Flanders, and the destruction of crops in the army zone compelled him to dismiss his troops. We may also note the direct connection between the plague epidemic of 1348-9 and the itinerant manifestations of the Flagellants.

And so we should leave no stone unturned in penetrating to the very heart of the everyday life of the times. The description of the toilet of a *grande bourgeoise* and the scale of wages received by the weavers are quite as important elements of historical reconstruction as are the martial deeds of a prince. Ruysbroeck plays an active part in the religious agitation that characterises the first half of the fourteenth century. This effervescence, as we shall see, is so intimately linked with social and political vicissitudes that these latter cannot be neglected with impunity.

Before therefore attempting a sketch of this highly intellectual figure, if we would have it complete, we must have recourse to history. It is impossible not to wonder how such a personality was moulded, what impressions made themselves felt in his soul, especially when the youth was emerging into manhood. What was his family, and what did school teach him? What was the condition of Flanders and the Duchy of Brabant, slowly being squeezed on the one side by the king of France and on the other by the king of England? What were the hopes and the miseries of the populace and those material and spiritual disturbances which rise and disappear, like bubbles on the surface of still water?

So vast and complex is the subject that we have frequently been compelled to keep to the main lines, those we regarded as indispensable to the *ensemble*. The biographers of old represented Ruysbroeck as humbly submissive to the inspiration of the Holy Ghost. Of this *nescio quid divinum* the historian can have but a very distant vision. Still, he is fortunate if he can keep it steadfastly before his eyes, for it is that which, at bottom, constitutes the entire value of history.

The sole recommendation by which this work can profit is that it was undertaken on the advice of François Picavet, of the Collège de France, Professor at the École pratique des Hautes-Études.

In it he saw the realisation of a wish expressed in his *Esquisse des philosophies médiévales*, when he asked students "to determine as exactly as could be expected . . . that which, in the work of each thinker, comes from his predecessors and contemporaries, and that which he has found out for himself and handed on to his successors. . . . The time is past," he added, "when one man could study, as did Aristotle and Descartes, almost every subject which human intelligence undertakes to investigate: each one should devote himself wholly to a definite line of research if the field of the unknown is to become smaller and smaller."

The eminent master who thus expressed himself was good enough to examine with us, during the last few days of his life, the main theories of this work and their textual justifications. We shall not forget those conversations, solemnised by the approach of death, nor that ascetic face, lit up by the glow of thought and meditation. It is with keen emotion that we tender the homage of profound gratitude to the memory of the learned mediævalist.

And it would be ungrateful not to mention in this place those whose works have cleared the way for us. The book of Dr. A. A. Van Otterloo,[1] which constituted an extremely remarkable initiative for this period, unfortunately follows the biography of Surius, of no personal value, and does not enter into questions of criticism. Canon A. Auger is far better informed.[2] In a general review of the Netherland

[1] *Johannes Ruysbroeck, een bijdrage tot de kennis van den ontwikkelingsgang der Mystiek*, Amsterdam, 1874.

[2] *Étude sur les mystiques des Pays-Bas au moyen âge*, pp. 157–264 (in *Mém. couronnés de l'Académie royale de Belgique*, t. XLVI., 1891.—*De doctrina et meritis Joannis van Ruysbroeck*, in *Thèses de doctorat* of the University of Louvain, 1892).

mystics of the Middle Ages, he devoted to Ruysbroeck a hundred pages, so well documented that they undoubtedly merit the esteem of scholars. In addition, he wrote a Latin thesis on the teachings of our mystic. Undoubtedly these early works inspired later ones, which could but develop, with occasional rectifications of detail, the theories of the regretted Canon.

And we should like to mention the learned works of Professor W. L. De Vreese, and of Père Van Mierlo, S.J., both of considerable scientific standing.

Professor De Vreese, formerly head librarian of the University of Gand, first published some ancient documents on the life and work of Ruysbroeck in a series of articles in the review *Het Belfort* (Gand, 1895-6).[1] Pursuing his investigations in several libraries throughout Europe, he subsequently issued in two volumes a list of the principal manuscripts of Ruysbroeck's works, thus affording an extremely important working basis for future editors of the text.[2] Finally, we are indebted to him—in the *Biographie nationale*, published by the Royal Academy of Belgium—for a note which not only takes into account the works of Van Otterloo and Canon Auger, but also contains a number of personal hypotheses deserving of being taken into consideration.

For the most complete study of Ruysbroeck, however, which has appeared so far, we are indebted to Père Van Mierlo, a Flemish Jesuit scholar. In a series of articles which appeared in 1909-10 in a review entitled *Dietsche Warande en Belfort*, Père Van Mierlo presented a very fine critical essay on the great mystic. By inserting Ruysbroeck's works into the life of the author, Van Mierlo was the first to lay emphasis on the regular advance of Ruysbroeck's thought, which, in a way, was moulded first on the career of the priest, then on that of the monk. Like his predecessors, Van Mierlo has not touched upon the question of the springs

---

[1] Collected in a pamphlet entitled: *Bijdragen tot de kennis van het leven en de werken van Jan van Ruusbroec*, Gand, 1896.

[2] *De Handschriften van Jan van Ruusbroec's werken*, Gand, 1900, 1902.

xlii   RUYSBROECK THE ADMIRABLE

of the mystic's thought. Still, he refers to his dependence on Scholasticism.

In the preparation of this work frequent journeys have been necessary to Belgium and Holland, for the verification of sources of information, in the various university and other libraries. Special mention should be made of days spent, in August 1922, in Holland, at the abbey Saint-Paul de Wisques, a place in which Ruysbroeck is loved more than anywhere else in the world.

With what intelligent understanding of the task, with what goodness of heart did the learned Benedictine Fathers place at our disposal the wealth of their library! There we worked, in a humble cell, identifying ourselves, so to speak, with the Admirable. One of the Fathers would come and seat himself at the work-table; in the refectory, with its red brick vaults, we shared their frugal repast, a Father meanwhile reading aloud some portion of a pious work from a stone pulpit, so that it might be continually borne in upon us that man does not live by bread alone. At night, before compline, we would walk about the garden or under the columns of the cloister with the hospitable monks. It was as though we had been carried back, far away from these harassed times of ours, to the very age in which Ruysbroeck lived.

If it is the historian's first duty to make himself contemporary with his hero, there can be no doubt but that the Benedictines of Saint-Paul made this duty easy. In their laborious solitude we breathed the very air that must have circulated beneath the vaults of the Brabantine monastery.

One evening, an aged monk, with emaciated face but impressively profound eyes, entered the cell, his arms laden with books. After laying down his burden, we began to talk —of Ruysbroeck, naturally.

Suddenly, with that energy which at times would seem to convert the monk into the soldier, the old Father, to whom we had set forth the main lines of our thesis, said: "This work must be done well, or not at all." The imperative tone of his voice betrayed the monk's veneration for the blessed Ruysbroeck, and the dread of seeing profaned so ancient and touching a figure. . . .

Alas! We do not know if we have done well; what we can say is, that this has been a labour of love and of unbounded respect. In contact with great souls, one must grow. Erudition, analysis and criticism do not exclude that mental attitude which allows itself to be permeated with heroic influences. For here, as at all times, to understand is to love.

FIRST PART

HISTORICAL INFLUENCES AND THE LIFE OF RUYSBROECK

RUYSBROECK THE ADMIRABLE

FIRST PART

HISTORICAL INFLUENCES AND THE LIFE
OF RUYSBROECK

CHAPTER I

SOCIETY IN THE FOURTEENTH CENTURY AND THE
DEMOCRATIC REVIVAL

JOHANNES RUYSBROECK belongs wholly to a century whose destiny it was to spread about the world the germs of emancipation without succeeding in freeing itself.

From beginning to end, the fourteenth century was shaken by the starts and upheavals of that giant, the people. The latter had suddenly roused itself at the beginning of the century, being threatened by two enemies, the king of France and the patriciate, whose causes were really one and the same. For eighty years, the struggle, waged on religious grounds, favoured now one side, now the other. When the century ended, however, all that remained of the popular victories was, to the vanquished, a painful memory. The battle of Roosebeke (1382) saw the breaking of looms, the rout of the "horribles tisserands" who, but a short time before, were picking up, on the plains of Courtrai, the golden spurs of French knights, as trophies of an antiquated regime and pledges of a more hopeful future.

The democratic revolution of the fourteenth century was essentially of an economical and social order. Still, it cannot be circumscribed within these narrow limits. Indeed, the interplay of alliances extends the field of conflict beyond the

3

theatre in which the drama is being played. Besides, the
political passions being born are not unrelated to the religious unrest silently working upon the masses. Questions of
social emancipation, of external politics and of spiritual
independence overlap one another, nor can they be separated
under penalty of distorting or mutilating history.

And so it is the story of a vanquished man that we have
undertaken to relate, though of one whose defeat was dearly
paid for and whose hopes survived disaster.

How these hopes came to birth; how they manifested
themselves; how and why they could not become facts: such
is the threefold question it is important to solve if we would
apprehend the *soul* of the century.

What, indeed, should we know of a period, if we were
content with giving a list of outstanding events? Centuries,
like trees, grow in concentric circles, but development could
not come about without the hidden action of the sap. This
it is that calls forth the thrust and urge of the sap-wood
towards the exterior. In like fashion, there is present in the
life of communities a secret and active element which does
not appear in chronicles but which it is important to seek
behind the letter of the documents.

This will enable us at the same time to establish the connections, the religious, national and political bonds whereby
Ruysbroeck is linked on to the history of his people and his
time. In a study of the origins of his thought, work of this
kind is absolutely necessary. In the condition of the country
are to be found the reasons of his vocation, the causes that
impel him along the path he is about to take.

I

Above all else, there is the social question.

There had been set up in Flanders and Brabant of the
twelfth century an oligarchical regime, known under the
name of the patriciate. At the moment, the patrician regime
is very powerful; but domination was accompanied by a

forgetfulness of the original tradition, which consisted in absolute devotion to public affairs. But in ascertaining the distinction between the original spirit and the present deviations therefrom, the historian must take into consideration the eminently civilising part played by the patriciate in the thirteenth century. By appointing the commons, endowing them with a liberal system of constitutions or *Keures*, distributing equally rights and obligations over the whole of the citizens, submitting all their doings to the jurisdiction of a tribunal, it was the patriciate which, in the midst of a feudal system, was the first to set up the image of the *patrie* and to confer on a group of men, united by common interests, a real moral personality.

The character of the commune, clearly democratic at first, was quickly to become modified—not by a sudden exhibition of force, but by that very action or interplay of social life for which absolute equality is but a claim impossible of realisation.

The varying fortunes of commerce, skill and intelligence, perseverance in work, credit: these are some of the factors which detached from the masses an ever increasing number of individuals whose professional competence ensured their ascendency over the rest. With this authority, and for the same reasons, corresponded financial superiority. Thus there came into being, by the very laws of social life, a veritable moneyed aristocracy, the *majores*, who exercised ever greater dominance over the masses, the *minores*.

No doubt the people would have accepted this dependence, had merit and the regulations of work alone continued to make it possible to draw upon this aristocracy. The working generation of the first patricians, however, was succeeded by a generation of unproductive heirs. The sons of many a bourgeois were content to enjoy, in idleness, the fortunes they had inherited. Stigmatised by the people as loungers or saunterers (*lediggangers*) or as *huiseux* (*otiosi*), they none the less took care to profit by the privileges attached to functions they no longer performed. The populace rightly

D

despises those who refuse to work because they have been born with a silver spoon in their mouth. The *mercatores*, in spite of their insolent ostentation, were never so bitterly hated as these proud idlers.

This scission in the population of the city was further aggravated by specialisation. Dealers or merchants were a class apart from the artisans. The latter in turn, through a spirit of professional vanity, became subdivided according to their special occupations: there were weavers and fullers, carders and furriers, dyers and tanners. The *Keures* of Bruges even make separate mention of black leather tanners (*zwartledertauwers*) and white leather tanners (*witlederverwerkers*). Thus split up, it is easy to see that the artisans, who, with all the naïveté of the simple-minded, regarded their narrow workshop rivalries as interests of vital importance, could not marshal their scattered forces against the well-ordered might of the *majores*.

In this state of things, the supremacy of money came to eclipse the old democratic spirit. Equilibrium, whilst literally remaining with the *Keures*, was disturbed to the detriment of the artisans. Having considerable economic power at their disposal, the rich patricians and the merchants joined in *gildes*, which thus retained in the hands of a few families the greater part of the city's fortune. Besides, it was almost exclusively from these families that the *échevins*, or aldermen, and other communal functionaries were recruited. The *bourgeoisie*, indeed, scorning the constitutions, directed the city life and contracted alliances with foreign princes who had recourse to patrician fortunes to maintain their own pomp and luxury. In 1276, a communal regulation formally excluded from the *échevinage* of Alost *tout homme de vilain mestier*.

Thus thwarted in their rights and subjected in their work to arbitrary jurisdiction, the artisans, determined to win the rights they were refused, in turn banded themselves together into professional confraternities. They were well aware that, more than any other party, they contributed to the prosperity of the city, and were the real providers of patrician wealth.

Herded in wretched huts built of wood or of a mortar made of loam and straw, in unhealthy districts, they could not help comparing their lot with that of the rich owners in their proud châteaux (*steenen*). They could not help seeing that the harshness of the law was directed against themselves alone, and that the wealthy violated with impunity the very constitutions which they were pledged to maintain. While the members of the oligarchical clique scorned the fathers, they showed less disdain for their daughters. At night-time, the sons of the wealthy *bourgeoisie* organised regular razzias for the purpose of gratifying their lust. The *Keures* of Ghent tell of the shameless violence to which the wives and daughters of the artisans were daily subjected. And these disgraceful practices had entered so largely into the life and habits of the great, that the rape of a *filia pauperis* was less severely punished than the abduction of a high-born demoiselle.

The dependence in which the trades found themselves, relatively to the guilds, made difficult all attempt at emancipation. The masses had attempted by strikes to escape the many tyrannies of the rich. Their feeble efforts, however, but made their servitude heavier than before. As a certain number of artisans had evaded patrician domination by emigrating, workmen were forbidden to leave the towns with their tools. An industrial police, consisting of dependents of the *échevinage*, henceforth exercised a vexatious check upon the trades, controlling the hours of toil, fixing the amount of work to be done, setting up a scale of wages and of selling prices, and, by its spirit of unremitting interference, exasperating the smouldering hatred.

From the end of the twelfth century onwards, the artisans live in expectation of a better future. Deep in the human heart, repressed hate awaits its day. But there is a presentiment that this day will be a terrible one.

The avenging morrow towards which were directed the enraged desires of the people was generally looked upon as the day of divine vengeance. Socialism, it has been said, is the religion of those who have no religion. This is true, if we are to understand thereby that great popular movements readily assume a religious character. Besides, the fourteenth century was fully prepared to introduce an element of mysticism into its violent claims.

The soul of the Middle Ages had thrilled to the voice of Francis of Assisi. Are not the poor and disinherited nearer to the heart of God? Is not the scorn of riches one of the conditions for entrance into the kingdom of heaven? The artisans, by their very circumstances, thus felt themselves marked out to establish the kingdom of righteousness on the ruins of the former regime.

Justice! A magic word which will ever inflame the hearts of men. It is justice that stirs up immense hope in the soul of the simple-minded, and yet authorises, in their eyes, the most dastardly acts of violence. In the vicinity of the artisans were to be found men capable of nourishing this hope and of blending with it the spirit of piety. These were the Minor Friars, half laic and half religious, who went about the land preaching resignation and holy poverty. Uncultured, fanatical, and frequently coarse, they possessed one merit at all events: they loved the people. They shared the life of the poor, nursed and watched by the sick and wounded. Protected by their sacred mission, they were not afraid, on occasion, of raising their voice in favour of their brothers in misfortune.

To these men was largely due that strange blend of mysticism and violence which characterises the social tendencies of the fourteenth century.

II

The situation, nevertheless, was threatening to continue indefinitely when political events supplied the people with an opportunity of effecting their emancipation.

These events may all be summed up in the struggle with France, whose ambitions are directed both against opulent Flanders and against the States that originated in ancient Lotharingia.

Indeed, at the end of the thirteenth century, the centre of gravity of Europe became suddenly displaced.

The Empire, a purely nominal suzerain of the Lotharingian States, exhausted by its prolonged struggle with the popes, was divided against itself. Soon, in 1314, there happened the scandal of the dual consecration: Louis the Bavarian at Aix-la-Chapelle, and Frederick of Austria at Bonn.

The other "half of God," the papacy, is in no better case. The new situation finds complete expression in the sentence which, at the beginning of the century, Pierre Flotte puts into the mouth of Boniface VIII.: "The power of my master is real; yours is but verbal." From that time, a long series of bitter experiences begins for the pontiffs. Even if the tradition which states that Boniface VIII. was given a blow on the face by Nogaret has no solid foundation, it nevertheless reflects the policy adopted by the royal power towards the Holy See. Soon afterwards begins the Babylonish captivity.

Set free on both sides, the king of France devises a vast political development, aiming at attaching to the Crown, Flanders and the small Lotharingian States so badly supervised by the German suzerain.

It is not known how Philippe le Bel would have carried through his ambitious intrigues, had not popular disturbances opened to him the gates of Flanders.

What had taken place? The Flemish lion was aroused. He had already made trial of his strength in successive revolts all over Belgium. Riots followed in Brabant, Flanders, Liége during the years 1245, 1248, 1253, 1255 and 1267. These, however, were but skirmishes, fiercely repressed assaults. In 1280, there came about a veritable revolution, in which the artisans were united against the patricians. It spread like a conflagration from town to town, encouraged in Flanders by Count Gui de Dampierre, humiliated at finding himself ever

more and more under the sway of the *gildes*. The struggle
lasted over twenty years, and everything pointed to the
victory of the democratic masses when the patriciate, alarmed
for their privileges, called Philippe le Bel to their aid.

The popular conscience, however, cannot be prostituted.
Whilst the patriciate were shamelessly fêting the knights,
decked out in *fleurs-de-lis*, revenge is being organised. One
night, the plebeian wrath suddenly bursts forth: a terrible
morrow for Bruges is the result. French blood mingles with
that of the patricians. Then begins a thrilling epopee,
whose heroes consist of poor weavers, despised fullers: all
such artisans as have caught a momentary glimpse of freedom. The people, intoxicated by the odour of carnage and
favoured by disunion among the masters, hastens to complete its triumph. Armed with pikes, iron clubs, and dreadful
cudgels with bristling points, the artisans assemble on the
plain of Courtrai (1302). It is related that, before forming
in squares, they knelt on the ground and kissed the very
soil of their fatherland. That same night, the corpses of
proud knights lay scattered over a plain bespangled with
thousands of gold spurs.

The news of the French defeat sent a prolonged thrill
throughout Europe. Although ill, Boniface VIII. rose in the
middle of the night, for he regarded the defeat of his insulter
as a judgment direct from God. But nowhere had the democratic victory such important results as in the Duchy of
Brabant, where the conditions of the people were quite as
harsh and unpleasant as in Flanders.

An artisan having been wounded in Brussels by a
patrician, the various trades rose with one accord in 1305:
*fabri, textores, sutores, tabernarii, lanii atque omnis illa fax
civitatis.*

Victorious at first, the trades gain possession of the
common house and reorganise the *échevinage*. John II.,
Duke of Brabant, however, whose position as vassal of the
Empire did not prevent him from accepting payment from
the privy purse of Philippe le Bel, cut them in pieces a few

weeks afterwards on the plain of Vilvorde. In addition, the better to frighten them into a state of absolute obedience, he goes so far as to bury alive the ringleaders.

In Flanders, the people, supported by the sympathy of all the democracies of Europe, refuse to submit. The entire continent would appear to have become the field on which the fortunes of the smaller peoples are being decided.

Deluded by the fallacious peace of Athis, which had been concluded without their consent, the artisans hold the enemy in check by sudden revolts: the rising of maritime Flanders under Nicolas Zannekin was followed by the insurrection of 1324, characterised on both sides by such deeds of violence that, as an old chronicler says, "men conceived a distaste for life itself." In 1327, there raged a veritable red terror headed by Jacques Peit, until the exhausted rebels were crushed at Cassel by Philippe de Valois in 1328.

Is this the end? No, an unexpected ally on the side of Flanders enters on the stage: the king of England. Here again it is economic questions that determine external policy.

Unsuccessful in overcoming the hostility of the trades, Philippe de Valois had decreed the cessation of commerce with England. This decree (1336) meant ruin and famine for Flanders. English wool, indeed, which the butchers obtained from immense flocks in the Highlands, passed entirely into Flanders, where the artisans transformed it into those splendid scarlet striped materials which had carried the fame of Flemish workmanship into the farthest confines of Europe.

A prolonged cry of pain and hatred resounded throughout Flanders. Looms ceased working and men were seen wandering about in piteous groups, begging bread which no one could give them.

Once more rebellion is a consequence of the prevailing ruin. It is a patrician this time who espouses the cause of the poor: Jacques van Artevelde. He does not hesitate to summon Edward III. to his aid, by which alliance he succeeds in reopening the English markets. In addition, he obtains from France, directly menaced by the might of England, recognition of the neutrality of Flanders and—something altogether novel in those days—effects a community of interests between Flanders and Brabant by means of an economic partnership, for he thinks that *chil deus pays sont pleins de communauté de peuple ki soustenir ne se peuvent sans marcandise.*

The English, however, wholly occupied in waging a victorious war against France, rapidly forgot their allies. After the destruction of the French fleet, they besieged Tournai, this time with the aid of Jean III., Duke of Brabant. What happened? Was there treason on this occasion? Or was the old rivalry between Brabanters and Flemish rekindled? In any case, the allies had to raise the siege, the consequence being riot and revolt both in Gand and in Brussels.

Weavers and fullers come to blows, and the chief tribune in Gand is the first victim of these fratricidal struggles (1345). In Brussels, when the duke returns from the ill-starred siege of Tournai, he finds the place in open insurrection. For several days the revolt was on the point of succeeding: it was overcome only by the most pitiless measures. The list of banishments, confirmed by the duke in 1341, included several thousand names.

And, as though these misfortunes were not enough, the two countries, with common language, interests and aspirations, enter upon a ruthless war regarding the seigniory of Malines. The Flemish invade the duchy and cut to pieces the Brabanters on the day of the "fatal Wednesday." Hostile brothers were seen killing one another in the streets of Brussels. A bold attack by Éverard T'Serclaes drove the Flemish out of the town.

But from that day the destiny of the two countries follows the same path. Separated at a time when union would have been the guarantee of their common victory, they are about to be reunited in servitude. A foreign master is to establish that territorial unification which they found it impossible to realise in discord. So true is it that neither peoples nor individuals can with impunity sacrifice moral interests in favour of material ones.

The people have let their opportunity pass. In vain do they unite in Flanders and again rebel against the ruling patriciate in 1379. Their hour has struck, in spite of the valiant efforts of Philippe van Artevelde. Summoned a second time against the rebels, the king of France completes the destruction of the communes. This was the young Charles VI., nephew of Philippe le Hardi. The communers were unable to recover from the defeat of Westroosebeke (1382). And when the House of Burgundy annexed exhausted Flanders, nothing was left of the audacious dreams and aspirations that had risen from the plains of Courtrai at the beginning of the century.

In Brabant, a similar decline in popular expectations took place.

Under the reigns of Jean III. and of Wenceslas, riots followed (1356, 1357, 1359, 1368, 1370, etc.), without succeeding in guaranteeing the rights of the artisans. Here, the rebellion was strongly tinged with mysticism, owing to stimulation by the mendicant orders or by heterodox sects.[1] At other times, the misguided anger of the people turns upon the Jews. Then follow odious massacres, in which a spirit of madness, perverted from its true object, allows itself a free hand. In Brabant, the fourteenth century is perhaps the most grievous and sanguinary page in the book of the people's misfortunes. From 1350 onwards their cause is lost, they cannot indulge in the prolonged hopes which sustained the Flemish. The *Joyeuse Entrée*, solemnly sworn by the Duchesse Jeanne and her husband Wenceslas in 1356, really confirms the hegemony of the patriciate at the same time as the dependence of the ruling house. By this act, all the prince's initiatives—wars, alliances, coin-stamping—are

---

[1] When, in 1310, the Council of Vienna abolished the mendicant orders, the people manifested such violent opposition to the Dominicans, that Pope Clement V. was compelled, by brief, to revoke his first bull. Geldolphe A. Rijckel, *Vita S. Beggae*, p. 382.

made subject to the consent of the *commun-pays*. This *commun-pays*, however, has no room in it for artisans.

The new policy only ends in filling the streets with bloodshed and ensuring the dominance of the wealthy and the *haute bourgeoisie*. An unfortunate campaign against the Duc de Juliers ended by discrediting Wenceslas. The Brabanters were crushed at Bastweiler (1370). Seven thousand were slain in battle, two thousand, including Wenceslas, were taken prisoner.

Wenceslas died in 1383 without an heir, and a few years later the Duchesse Jeanne ceded her land in usufruct to Philippe le Hardi.

And now the House of Burgundy is to begin its amazing fortunes, like the conquerors of old, dragging behind its chariot the two vanquished provinces, this time linked together by the same chain.

III

The vanquished, however, are great; they have suffered for the future. We may say that the germ of all the contemporary social realisations was contained in the fourteenth century. The greatness of this age consisted in conceiving reforms, preparing freedom; its calamity, in being unable to translate into facts its bold and generous dreams. On the ruins of the feudal system it attempted to set up a new world, based on equality. It instilled in the heart of the artisan a pride in the perfection of his work. In particular, it thrilled with joy as it faintly glimpsed the indefeasible dignity of man as an individual.

But there comes a time of maturity for ideas as well as for the fruits of the earth.

When we inquire into the causes of this great repulse, we find something else than royal absolutism, which is too exclusively regarded as the destroyer of this ardent age.

First, there is the absence of a true national consciousness. What did fatherland mean during these troublous times? Perhaps it may have been faintly outlined in the commune: but from the thirteenth century the commune is no longer the mother, solicitous of the interests of all her children; indeed, it is no more than the property of an abhorred class. Again, the commune is a tiny world in itself, without spiritual cohesion with other communes. Though but a few miles away, such towns as Gand, Bruges, Ypres, engage in jealous strife with one another. And in the very heart of the communes, as we have seen, specialisation of work brings into conflict with one another the different trades, blind to their interdependence.

Nor does the sentiment of race exist, any more than the idea of fatherland. These men hate one another, though they speak the same language, are of the same blood and think the same thoughts. They hate one another because material interests dominate all other. The humble weavers, no less than the rich patricians, feel a grudge against the looms at work in the neighbouring town.

And in the revolts which rouse the people from time to time, is it simply the vision of a better world that enflames men's hearts and places weapons in their hands? We may doubt this. Certainly the lot of the people is a terrible one. When the historian finds them relegated to unhealthy districts, when he sees their poor houses burnt to the ground in those immense conflagrations which razed an entire district in a night, when he knows what a toll this unfortunate people pays to pestilence and epidemic, when he finds them cheated of their wages, and forced to idleness by the martial caprice of princes or the intrigues of alliances—he cannot help feeling sympathetic towards the poor and disinherited. Sympathy, however, cannot abolish clarity of vision.

Manifestly the people were ill prepared to understand an aim or objective too far ahead. A Van Artevelde, a Pierre Coutereel are really prophets, advocates of a cause that has been well thought out. The masses, ignorant of the laws that regulate social life, see in insurrection only an opportunity to gain possession of coveted goods, to know in their turn something of the enjoyments of the great. It is not simply domineering wealth, it is also the blind ignorance of the crowd that has doomed to failure the most ardent social aspirations.

Strength of muscle alone cannot ensure the greatness of a city; it must be allied with might of brain. So long as the intellectual level remains below human aspirations, nothing need be expected from the most legitimate developments. It is still worth while, at the present time, to learn the lesson of the fourteenth century.

But there is another lesson, also an instructive one, for our own sorely harassed age. Social reforms cannot be instituted without a corresponding development of the moral sense, without the approach of the individual to a spiritual dignity in accord with his civic dignity.

Now, the fourteenth century, like the whole of the Middle Ages, is deeply imbued with dualistic elements. While it transcends previous centuries in realisations and hopes, it does not rise above them in the domain of morals.

It is rent asunder by a prolonged antithesis. Of this, its art and architecture, morals and religion, are a proof. Along with economic power at its highest is found the most sordid wretchedness; intense external refinement accompanies the most repulsive vice, as does a noble humanitarianism unbridled violence. The culture of the purest ideal is one with the deification of the flesh and delight in all uncleanness.

This contrast was perfectly expressed by the painters of genius who appeared a few years later. With like masterly skill they depict an indecent orgy and the pure profile of a virgin. Inspiration is found in illuminated engravings or carvings of altar-screens. Such "imagiers" as Jean de Gand (1328), Beauneveu (1364), Hennekin de Bruges, Jean de Marville (1372), to quote only a few names, are the precursors of such delightful artists as van Eyck and his brother. Although belonging to the following century, they are really the offspring and the interpreters of the fourteenth. Born, the one in 1364 and the other about 1385, they follow the lines of the famous Haekendover altar-screen, which has already broken away from the affected symbolism of the Middle Ages in order to copy life exactly as it manifests itself. Through them we glimpse the continuity of a tradition which will be nothing else than the potent expression of *that which is*: we catch a faint vision of Memlinc and van der Goes, and, a century earlier, of Pierre Breughel and of Rubens, that artist so enamoured of pronounced flesh effects.

Now, from the middle of the fourteenth century, this tradition is a dual one. Look, for instance, at Jan van Eyck's portrait of Jean Arnolfini and his wife. Here the light does not come from without, in dazzling sheets falling from above, as in the case of Italian painters. It is created in the very room itself, from the shining pewter and copper or from the play of colour on silk or satin. Who has more admirably expressed the peace and quiet of the home or the splendours of a spiritual life shedding divine light upon the ecstatic brows of the "Anges chanteurs"?

Alongside of this we have the sleek poetry of super-abundant life, the glorification of carnality impudently obtruding itself on the gaze. Here is Eve, with marble flesh, and overflowing with vitality. And such, very shortly, will be the attraction of the real for these masters of colour, that they will endeavour to give a faithful interpretation even of the foul impurity of an orgy, with its overturned stools. . . .

This dissociation is also to be found in the clear-cut separation between the classes, in economic organisation, in literature, where we find some page of Boendale or of Ruysbroeck combining the most truculent realism with the most exquisite *finesse*. It expresses itself in the new buildings beginning to appear.

The markets, for instance, are half church and half citadel in style. They bring together the same crowds, not this time given up to the disinterested ecstasy of piety, but rather to positive material realities. By the side of the steeple, with its summons to God, rises the belfry, a lofty tower clearly symbolising the dominance of the civil power. Its brazen bell is indeed the voice of the laic city; it celebrates feasting and good cheer, or suddenly, with ardent clang, calls on the people to defend their threatened interests.

Mention may also be made of the obliteration of the moral sense, the practically general prevarication on the part of magistrates who do not fear to set themselves above the laws they so strictly enforce. Jean Boendale, our valuable chronicler, who knew what he was speaking about, seeing that he had for many years been secretary to the college of *échevins* at Antwerp, delivers himself on this matter without mincing his words:

He who takes a step towards buying the *échevinage* purchases hell, for scarcely one in ten *échevins* holds the scales evenly balanced. Friendship, a liking for presents, relatives, all these cause him to forsake justice at any hour of the day. So blind is he that he does not recognise what is right.

What must morality have been amid so general a state of disturbance and unrest? Among the poor, a secret hatred, champing at the bit and waiting its time. Among the rich, insolent luxury and the cruelest domination. Moral decay on every side, a lack of those sturdy virtues which alone warrant the safety of societies and individuals alike.

We have pointed to the wretched lot of the artisans, who were wholly dependent on political events. And yet, in periods of quiet, never had the wages of the workman risen so high in proportion to the cost of the necessaries of life. It has been calculated that a workman earning nine sols per day received the equivalent of eighteen loaves. A daily wage of three sols corresponded to three chickens, or one hundred and twenty eggs, or again, one hundred and fifty herrings. This meant that a workman could effect large economies in view of a rainy day. And when this latter comes along, if he complains, he should find fault with his own heedlessness quite as much as with external events. The simplicity of antiquity, however, no longer holds any charm, either for wealthy patricians or for negligent artisans.

The very stones are, as it were, racked by a sickly imagination. Consider the monumental *hostels* of the people in high quarters. On their façade, innumerable small columns, miniature grinning faces. Even the many-coloured window-panes seem bent on thwarting the light of day. All this is apart from simple, reliable humanity.

This extravagant inspiration creates fashions in which the bizarre vies with the immodest. The fourteenth century has been called *le siècle de la chemise*, because this undergarment was so generally worn. It would be more correct to call it the century of nudity.

Woman, abandoning her normal rôle, has become a flower *de luxe*. From the low-cut corset to the narrow tightfitting gown, everything contributes to enhance the lewd splendour of the flesh.

On this point listen to Ruysbroeck, who had seen these unveiled beauties in the streets of Brussels:

Women make themselves gowns so narrow as to be shameful. They ornament them within and without, devising numberless futilities to enflame the senses. If they imagine themselves of noble birth, they must have on their face twisting horns like those of a goat, so that they may resemble the Evil One. Thus bedizened, they go and look at themselves in a mirror to see if they are beautiful enough to seduce the devil and the world. In spite of all this finery, however, their body is none the less a foul and unclean sack. All the same, they make wide cuttings at the top of their gowns, so that one may contemplate at leisure this repulsive sack, full of vile dung.[1]

These are not the words of an ascetic inclined to excess. For Boendale, a layman, says the same thing:

Men wear coats so short as to be immodest. Women squeeze themselves so much that they give undue prominence to those parts of the body intended to remain veiled, thus arousing guilty desires.

Then appear the *hennin* and the *escoffion*, extravagant coiffures against which, at the beginning of the fifteenth century, there arose a veritable crusade directed by Thomas Connecte, a Carmelite friar. At Brussels, Wenceslas organised at court *farandoles* of semi-nude girls; the pleasure train was

[1] *The Tabernacle*, vol. II. pp. 175 ss.

one that never stopped. Respite from warfare was given up to feasting and good cheer. Listen to the lines in which the poet Eustache Deschamps expresses his adieux to this life of enjoyment and plenty:

> Adieu, beauté, liesse, tous déliz,
> Chanter, danser et tous esbatements!
> Cent mille foys à vous me recommans,
> Brusselle, adieu, où les bains sont jolys,
> Les estuves, les fillettes plaisans!
> Adieu, beauté, liesse et tous déliz,
> Belles chambres, vins du Rin, molz liz,
> Connins, plouviers et capons et fesans,
> Compaignie doulce et courtoises gens,
> Adieu, beauté, liesse et tous déliz.

Nor were the people much more moral. Deprived of sumptuous meals, they found compensation in ignoble beer-drinking and debauchery, as far as their means allowed. They were also fond of singing. The character of a race is perhaps most clearly expressed in its popular songs. In the present instance, we have mysticism and a cloying sentimentality, combined with truculence of expression which is almost invariably carried to the length of obscenity. The populace takes huge delight in licentious farces, *sotternijen*, public shows in which a deceived husband or mistress, or a shameless monk, excites the ribald jest and laughter of the masses.

Love has completely stripped itself of its chivalrous aspect; on the contrary, it is paraded in all its brutal immodesty from top to bottom of the social scale. The *étuves*, or bathing establishments, an innovation of the times, are really houses of prostitution, in which scantily clad *ancillae* place themselves at the service of the coarsest appetites. The prescriptions of the *Keures*, forbidding *ribauderie et niaise compaignie*, remain a dead letter. Sad-eyed matrons openly intervene to procure for the daughters of the people "gallants who will buy them fine gowns." "Youth is spent in health-destroying lewdness. Did not girls know the consequence of frailty, scarcely one would be found deserving the name of virgin. . . . Almost all men attempt to seduce girls, whom they afterwards abandon. Is there a single woman who, for money, would not sell herself, body and soul? Vice and shame are of little concern to them." [1]

The general vogue of abortion, moreover, makes it easy for them to indulge fearlessly in the most barefaced licentiousness.

In vain do the *Keures* inflict severe penalties against the general decline of morals, punishing with ban and fine rape adultery and *promenades immorales*.

You cannot check a raging torrent with paper dikes. The flesh has been given the rein, and not until the sixteenth century will the spirit regain some control and mastery over unfettered bodies.

---

[1] Boendale, *Dietsche Doctrinale*, édit. Jonckbloet, v. 907 ss., 1025 ss., 1163 ss.; Vanderkindere, *Le Siècle des Artevelde*, 2nd ed., Brussels, 1907, p. 311.

E

CHAPTER II

THE CHURCH IN THE FOURTEENTH CENTURY

MANIFESTLY this general rout and subversion of intellect can be traced to more than one cause. Various influences, which we have attempted to define, contributed to it. Of them all, however, too great importance could not be attached to theories of independence which tend to alienate the civil from the spiritual power.

I

For a moment let us forget this separation, now an actual and universally recognised fact, and try to imagine what the principle of spiritual authority meant in the Middle Ages. Societies were then included within the scheme of a single organisation, the hierarchy of which ensured intimate co-hesion between all parties. Even kings were subject to this supreme authority.

Now, in the fourteenth century, a blow was dealt at this principle. Attacks on the authority of the pope could not fail to have their repercussion from top to bottom of the social edifice, the very foundation of which was shaking.

In France there was the downfall of Boniface VIII. and immediately afterwards the "Babylonian captivity." The exile into Avignon is perhaps not, as is generally imagined, the period when the papacy came under subjection to the kings of France. All the same, papal authority cannot be exercised absolutely; with Clement V. it enters upon a policy of concessions and half-measures.

Among the popes who succeed one another in Avignon,

only one, John XXII., was really great. With indomitable energy he opposes alike the schism of the *spirituels* and the revolt of Italy, the King of England, Edward III., who is carrying on a devastating war in France, and Ludwig of Bavaria, whose victory at Mühldorf (1322) has just won for him the imperial throne.

In this formidable conflict, it is nothing less than the spiritual peace of Europe that is at stake. No single measure taken by the pope fails to provoke an immediate response on the part of the ambitious monarch. He openly welcomes at court the spiritual rebels. To the pontiff's interdict, in 1324, over all the territories of the empire, the emperor answers by a manifesto in which John XXII. is called an "oppressor of the poor, an enemy of Christ and his apostles, one who endeavours, by falsehood and treachery, to crush out dire poverty." The excommunicated Ludwig marches upon Rome, is crowned at Saint Peter's, and solemnly declares "the priest Jacques de Cahors, who assumes the name of Pope John XXII.," to have fallen from pontifical dignity.

The *Defensor pacis*, by Marsilius of Padua, a book destined to become widely read, deals with these happenings and constitutes itself the vehicle of the new theories of independence. It repudiates any difference *de jure divino* between pope, bishop and priest. It recognises that the entire ecclesiastical hierarchy has only a *potestas ordinis* for administering the sacraments, reserving for the State alone the *potestas juridictionis in fors externo*.

In vain do the popes subsequently attempt to restore their compromised authority. Men disappear, but ideas live and progress. Both the great combatants fall: John XXII. in 1334, Ludwig of Bavaria in 1347.

Clement VI. hopes to rally to his side the new emperor by ensuring his election. This tutelage, however, appears too onerous for Charles IV., who, in his famous *Golden Bull* (1356), definitely breaks the ancient bonds between papacy and empire.

On the other hand, in matters concerning Flanders, the

policy of the Avignonese popes, by upholding the claims of Philippe le Bel, is distinctly opposed to him. Benoît XII. uses the entire weight of his diplomacy to prevent the alliance of the communers with England.

Thus it is not surprising to find that the Flemish, at the time of the great schism, sided with Urban VI., the Roman pope, against Clement VII. in Avignon, and that they defended their choice on the battlefield. They did not give way before the crusade of the followers of Clement—a crusade headed by Charles VI. of France in person. Their tenacity, tested in many a fight, finally won for them recognition by Philippe le Hardi for their sympathy with the Urban party.

II

The general policy of the Avignonese popes, clearly opposed to national aspirations which John XXII. regarded as the work of a demon (*voce hostis iniqui*), could not fail to meet with a powerful echo in the soul—religious by nature —of the Flemish and the Brabanters.

These simple-minded men felt themselves abandoned by their spiritual pastors, who remembered them only for the purpose of laying them under an interdict or of excommunicating them. But though the spiritual interests of the Flemish were little considered by the pontiffs, their material resources had not escaped the notice of the treasurers of the court of Avignon.

John XXII. had inaugurated a vast fiscal system through whose fine meshes nothing was allowed to slip. The land was constantly being traversed by *collectores*. These emissaries levied many taxes: the *decimae*, the *annatae*, the *procurationes*, the *jus spolii*, the *subsidia caritativa*, the *vacantes*, etc.

In short, under cover of so high an example, the great religious establishments still exercised a veritable financial jurisdiction over wider and wider territories, not even hesitating to levy execution on them.

Documents are unanimous in pointing to the ravages of simony:

Cupidity [says Boendale] has fastened upon the whole of the clergy. Benefices are not given to poor and deserving priests. No longer dare the preachers speak of covetousness, for they are all implicated and would be condemning themselves. Have not priests been known to draw up the wills of their sick parishioners, wills which they compel them to seal before administering the Sacrament? Many begin to lament and moan if the dying man has bequeathed them nothing. I should never dare [he says] to appear before my Lord with such a will. This is how priests provide themselves with an income.[1]

The good priests use similar language. We find a canon of Ypres, Jan Weert, who died in 1362, stigmatising, in tones which recall the biting satires of Dante, the undue influence employed in testamentary dispositions:

Thus do pastors provide themselves with an income. They manufacture God in order to sell him, true Judases who would betray Jesus himself, were he still on earth. Preachers convert the word of God into traffic and merchandise, for they do not preach gratis. . . . Your prelates are Pilates. Sanctity consists not in appearances, in outer signs, but in really being saints. Tenderness of heart, soft speech, fervent prayer: this is what constitutes sanctity in the sight of God. Let priests and clergy, nuns and *beguines*, begin thus if they would lay claim to the title of saint. Let them know that convents and churches cannot bestow sanctity, for God is everywhere. And, as it is by purity of heart that we best serve God, we can serve him in all places: in the streets, on the mountains and in the valleys.

Pious Ruysbroeck echoes these stern words:

The rule, alas, is now observed in accordance with the glosses, not with the text. . . . Poverty has been changed into as much magnificence, opulence and comfort as possible. . . . Poverty is indeed extolled in words, but deeds are not in conformity therewith.[2] The religion which Christ and his disciples have instituted is destroyed by Satan. Christ and his apostles were poor in temporal and rich in spiritual goods, the prelates and priests who now govern the Church are rich in silver and poor in virtue. . . . Amongst the twelve only one was found to be a hypocrite, good outwardly and evil inwardly, whereas out of a hundred prelates and priests who govern the Church and live on the patrimony which Christ purchased with his precious blood, it might be possible to find one who, following the example of the apostles, imitates Christ within and without. . . . These sons of Judas who now govern the Church are hateful, greedy and rapacious. They have put on sale everything that is spiritual; if they had the power, they would sell to sinners both Christ and his forgiveness and eternal life, like their master who, for a fee, sold our Saviour to the quibbling Jews and hanged himself to his eternal damnation.[3]

---

[1] *Dietsche Doctrinale*, vv. 389–97. [2] *The Seven Cloisters*, chapter i.
[3] *The Twelve Beguines*, chapter lvi.

Again:

Annually the deans send into each parish visitors who make an inquisition upon serious and public sins. If they find any who are guilty, they exact a fine; this is the penalty and the satisfaction due to sin. When the fine is paid, all is over; one can live in peace, and spend the whole year in the service of Satan. Even though they were to beg their bread, they must pay, but if they are rich and the matter is serious, they are compelled to give a great deal; as much money as possible is extorted from them. When the money is paid, they look upon themselves as free and quits; yea, they are free until the devil comes for their soul and makes them do penance in eternal hell. Thus each has what he desires: Satan, the soul; the bishop, the money; the poor imbeciles, their momentary satisfaction.[1] These greedy shepherds go about the towns and villages; they preach in words, but very little in deeds. And that is why their words produce so little fruit. They are more solicitous for the fleece than for the sheep, i.e. they have in mind their own personal profit, not the salvation of souls.[2]

Abbots and monks, in the enjoyment of rich prebends, live idle, gluttonous lives:

They shut themselves in their homes, eating and drinking at their pleasure. They have to be asked at night-time what they desire for the morrow, and how it must be prepared.[3]

Luxury and extravagance go hand in hand:

To-day the devil and vain men have found out something new: that which ought naturally to be black becomes a brownish material imitating hair-cloth. Grey clothes turn to a brown tinged with blue, green and red. White cannot be adulterated, it has to remain as it is. But whatsoever the colour, care is taken to choose the best wool. . . . And when the cloth is prepared, no one knows what shape or fashion to give it, in order to afford greater pleasure to the world and Satan. Sometimes it is so wide and ample that two or three garments could be made from it; sometimes so narrow, that one would think it were sewn on to the skin. Nuns wear short dresses only reaching the knee, knotted in front like the clothes of madmen. Or else they are so long that they have to be turned up very high, otherwise they will trail in the mud. And another kind of adornment is worn, adding to the folly now prevalent in the cloisters. This consists of silver-wrought girdles on each side whereof hang various tinsel objects which sound when one moves, the result being that the virgin or nun sets the whole thing tinkling when she walks, like a goat with tiny silver bells round its neck. The monks ride on horseback fully armed, wearing long swords like knights. But when confronted with Satan, with the world and their own evil impure passions and desires, they remain weaponless. . . . There are nuns who show themselves outwardly adorned, desirous of pleasing the

[1] *The Spiritual Tabernacle* (David), t. II. p. 181.
[2] *Ibid.*, t. II. p. 191.
[3] *The Seven Cloisters*, chapter viii.

world rather than God; consequently, all that emanates from them is poison very pleasing to the devil, venom which they drink with him for all eternity in the foul dens of hell. In addition, the nuns must now adorn their cells with sumptuous beds, with carpets and luxurious quilts and cushions, just as though they still belonged to the world.[1]

Everywhere the original rule is given up. Pierre de Herenthals, prior of the abbey of Floreffe about the year 1350, bewails the fact in these terms:

Alas! it seems at present that in many monasteries is being verified the saying that an undisciplined house shall fall. In many religious communities there is no longer seen to be any order or observance of rules, but rather disorder and a frightful state of irregularity. Jealousy has taken the place of love. Where peace and charity ought to reign, there is found only bitterness and murmuring, anger and indignation, insult, fickleness and depraved morals.

Doubtless this depravity, this scandal of debauchery and impurity on the part of priests and nuns, dates back beyond the fourteenth century. It is known that Gregory VII. attempted to eradicate from within the Church the frightful licentiousness which prevailed. Sigismund, at the Council of Bâle, proposed to repeal celibacy, which he regarded as the main cause of the discredit into which monasticism had fallen.

Both in Flanders and in Brabant, however, the corruption of the clergy was far from equalling that of the Italian monks or the Avignonese cardinals. But it had overstepped the indulgence which the Middle Ages readily allowed for loose morals, if we are to judge by the Flemish chroniclers, both religious and laic. Boendale, Jean de Dixmude, Ruysbroeck, archive documents as well as popular *sotternyen*, agree in branding with infamy the frequent rapes and abductions, the habitual intercourse between concubines and priests.

A chronicler of 1367 relates that "prostitution was so general, both among the people and among the clergy, in the town of Gand, that the official of Tournoi ordered information of it to be given by aldermanic letters."

[1] *The Seven Cloisters*, chapter xx.

Gilles Li Muisis, abbé of Saint-Martin, in 1349, bewails the situation in these terms:

> The entire populace, clergy and laity, had fallen into such a state of unbridled licence that it was horrible to behold. . . . Unfortunately for the Church, it seemed as though the time had come for the fitting application of the common proverb: "Like people, like priest."

As a rule, honest priests entered into a civil marriage upon which the Church closed its eyes. These *papen die wijf hadden gesworen* were naturally more respected by the people than those who had taken a mistress: *die tamien hadden ghecoren.*

On this subject Boendale is very sarcastic. As aldermanic secretary, he had had occasion to register many a legacy made by priests to their children or their *focaria*.[1]

> These irregular households [he writes] are customary. The priests bring up their children, provide rich marriages for them in town or country, or, should they enter the Church, they procure for them fat livings; the seigneurs listen to their counsel, they become treasurers and receivers. . . . There are many of the priests who are not content with one wife, nor with two . . . nor with three. . . . If they think the moment favourable . . . whether she be married or not is of little consequence . . . they endeavour to win her, either by gifts or by entreaties. Yes, even if they were their own nieces, I fear they would have no conscientious scruples whatsoever.

Gérard de Groote devoted to these fornicators a whole sermon, preached in the chapter-house of Utrecht in 1383. In an impetuous burst of eloquence, he exclaims:

> My lords and beloved brethren, having to speak to you of the exclusion and the correction of fornicating priests, I should not wish anyone to imagine that I have neither affection nor esteem for the priesthood. Far be such a thought from me. For there are two things in this connection: priest and fornicator. Now, just as I love and esteem the priest, so I hate and abhor the fornicator. My lords, the more august the priesthood, the more scandalous the dissoluteness therein.

III

Is it any wonder that, in the conflict which is to bring face to face the spiritual and the mendicant orders with the ecclesiastical authority, the people take sides against revellers

---

[1] The glossary of Du Cange defines the *focaria* as *meretrix foco assidens.*

and spoilers and go to the extent of rioting in defence of their humble disinterested friends? They, at all events, had really taken the vow of poverty. They had linked on their cause to that of the people, accompanying the communers on the battlefield, nursing the sick, living and active witnesses to the goodness of God. These poor tramps, with their rough garments, were accused of propagating the heresies of the Beghards and the Lollards. A bull of John XXII. had given the authorities power to pursue them *ad extirpandos orthodoxae fidei inimicos et herbam tam noxiam pestiferam de horto dominico radiatus evellendam.* But were not these the true defenders of orthodoxy, of that evangelical orthodoxy which regards love and indifference to worldly possessions as the very conditions of religious life? The people had no wider vision.

Besides, these minor orders met a genuine need. Abandoned by their real shepherds, towards whom would the wretched people have turned? The interdict weighed heavily on Flanders, and, had it not been for the humble friars, the innocent crowd of believers, left to pay for the quarrels of the great, the emperors and the popes, would have felt themselves forsaken by God himself.

Their faith, however, amid sorrows and scandals, had remained intact. People seek solace in a refuge of peace, where souls can at last expand. With their innate good sense, the people refuse to associate religion with the vileness and turpitude of the monks. The necessity of an interior reform makes itself increasingly felt, and it is the purest and most devoted sons of the Church who raise their voices on behalf of such a reform.

Frequently this revolt of conscience finds a terribly ironical expression. Thus it is related that, in 1365, in full public consistory, a cardinal adroitly let fall a letter, taking care that it should be picked up and taken to the pontiff. This epistle, signed by the name of the prince of darkness, was addressed to Clement VI. The demoniacal writer assured the pope, "son vicaire," and the cardinals, "ses chers conseillers," of his esteem, exhorting them to merit it still more fully by their scorn of the holy and impoverished life of the apostles. The letter ended as follows:

Your proud and haughty mother salutes you, along with your sisters, avarice, immodesty and the rest of the vices, your relatives and friends, who boast that they are everywhere prosperous through your aid. Given in the centre of hell, in the presence of our chief officers.[1]

More and more distinctly are heard the rumblings, prophetic of awful—though purifying—days to come. Every one is convinced that, as Boendale says, the cowl does not make the monk, and glimpses are caught of the relations that unite the pure Gospel of Christ to secular sanctity.

Die cappe en maect niet den monc,
Noch die mutse den canonc.

The voices of the prophets ring out, proclaiming the imminent downfall of a faithless and corrupt Church, and their accents, like thunder in the valleys, grow louder and louder with the innumerable echoes to which they give rise in the hearts of men.

This was no separatist movement, as has been thought, no revolt against the Church itself. The harsh-voiced prophets all protest their attachment to the ancient faith; their indignation springs from their love. Therefore these protesting tendencies must not be regarded as preludes of the Reformation in the sixteenth century: it is from within that Ruysbroeck, Boendale, Li Muisis and their disciples aim at regenerating the Church. Still, one might be mistaken on this point when one reads such declarations as these:

It has been said in former days—That the clergy would be expelled—And that the Church will suffer—Wholly because of the clergy—So that popes and cardinals—Bishops and monks all together—Affrighted will hide their tonsure—And seek shelter everywhere—Otherwise the people would beat them.[2]

Guillaume Friesen, of Maestricht, foretells in 1360 that all the clergy will be humiliated, the monasteries destroyed and the monks reduced to abject poverty. Hounded by all, they will no longer be able to

[1] Altmeyer, Les précurseurs de la Réforme aux Pays-Bas, Brussels, 1886, p. 198. De Berault-Bercastel, Histoire de l'Eglise, t. XIV. pp. 129–30.
[2] Jan's Teestye, vv. 3682 ss.

find refuge anywhere. No longer will prelates go about in silk and purple. The Church of Rome will disappear. Popes, cardinals and bishops will be despoiled of everything, because of their pride, their avarice, and many other vices. Scarcely will they be left the wherewithal to cover their nudity. They will be the hue and cry of the masses, and will remain exposed to this terrible chastisement until they correct their mode of life, until, sincerely repentant, they confess their sins and ask God's forgiveness, promising to live in all the simplicity of the early Christian era.

This scandalous state of things and the complaints of the better element of the populace were bound to meet with a profound echo in the naturally religious soul of the Flemish and the Brabanters. Deep in the human conscience is being enacted an entire drama, on which light is not wholly forthcoming, and which really culminates, behind the imposing façade of the Church, in the disintegration of spiritual unity.

Fourteenth-century mysticism undoubtedly sprang from this interior crisis. It offers itself as a providential help to the state of widespread inanition into which the souls of men had fallen. By doing away with unworthy intermediaries between the soul and its God, it rescued religion from the general discredit that weighed it down, and offered piety a refuge into which the din of strife and scandal could not penetrate. We may state without exaggeration that, by satisfying the strong religious aspirations of the time, it ensured the continuity of the Gospel tradition . . . a tradition that threatened to be overwhelmed by the raging torrent.

Not all, however, were capable of following mysticism on to the heights to which it summoned the tempest-beaten masses, or of divorcing faith and Church, of gathering the perfume and leaving behind the mire. Hasty generalisers and the spiritually blind, as well as materialistic monks who regarded the rites and ceremonies of the Church as comprising the whole of religion, declared at once that all was lost. And, as secular support suddenly failed them, these despairing prelates fell into a condition of general laxity and decline.

Others, no longer finding light in doctrinal authority, communed with themselves and sought in their own conscience for a solution of their religious aspirations. It was just at this moment that the heterodox sects, in the decline of the principle of authority, responded wonderfully to this individualistic spirit. They abounded everywhere, gathering up the wrecks, which were astonishingly alive and active, and associating spirituality with the strangest moral distortions.

The rôle played by these sects in the religious drama being enacted throughout the fourteenth century is so important in dealing with the history of the thought of Ruysbroeck, that we must now examine it in detail.

CHAPTER III

I

THE historian who studies mediæval piety is especially struck by the extreme mobility of its manifestations. The empire of a doctrinal religion which directs the impetuous stream of religious feeling within the rigid banks of imposed belief seems to be abolished. Never has this feeling been stronger. Nor has it ever been less disciplined. The Middle Ages was pre-eminently the period of individualism, an individualism that must be connected with the sense of religious unrest which more or less torments the minds of all men.

It has been well said that the religious society of the Middle Ages "is not to be compared with a great peaceful stream flowing quietly between its appointed banks, but is rather a torrent in which stagnant water and whirling rapids alternate, and is with considerable difficulty held in by continually shaken and unsettled dikes."

Far from being submissive to the Church, the Middle Ages seeks a spiritual refuge apart from it. Unable to find, in the stormy present, any safe shelter, it constructs for itself its own faith. Or rather, despairing of finding without help the key to the great mysteries, the secret of destiny, nature and sin, in a bold revival of hope it makes appeal to the future.

In decadent Rome, *taedium vitae* was the venomous flower of corruption and luxury. Now, however, the "tired of life" feeling has a nobler origin. It was born of the desperate confronting of the Gospel ideal with imperfect human realisations, of the spectacle of a world given up to violence and disorder, a world from which it seemed that God had fled. And, as though the debauchery of men were not enough to overwhelm the soul, Nature in travail appeared, with terrible and unexpected phenomena, to ally herself with the work of terror and brutality.

A finibus terrae ad te clamavi dum anxiaretur! This despairing cry of Abélard is the wail of an entire epoch. But what God could listen to such a plaint?

The very face of God was veiled, hardened, as it were. Arms were extended towards the Lover of Justice, not towards the Comforter; towards the awful Avenger of the Apocalypse, not towards the pitying Host of the holy love-feasts. And the reason why life was still tolerated was because judgment, which would meet, once for all, the distracted longings after justice, seemed imminent.

In this respect the Middle Ages comes nearer to the early Christian centuries than does the present age. We have flung into the background all eschatological speculations and have given the place of honour to those moral exigencies, those broad claims of conscience, which we regard, in the Gospel, as the one eternal and unassailable element. But the Middle Ages could not yet liberate itself from the letter of things. The precise declarations of Christ, while justifying the sorrows and pains of history, afforded wider scope for the drama of salvation. The Cross left unfinished the Redemption, which was supposed to find its definitive fulfilment in the dissolution of all things. The Apocalypse, assiduously read—that stupendous book which was said to have been dictated by the Holy Spirit himself to the beloved disciple on a sea-beaten rock—spoke to the imagination differently from the Gospel records. In its highly-coloured imagery, its decisive dualism, its extremely vivid symbols, it was moulded, so to speak, on mediæval thought. Nor did successive disappointments permit of any authoritative statement of the hope which was kept alive by circumstantial calculations.

In addition to which, the great Doctors themselves shared in this kind of obsidional fever. Had not Augustine, while

distrusting the precise statements, continually being contradicted, in which paltry-minded individuals took delight,[1]
devoted two books of the *City of God* to a consideration
of the great day of wrath?

Of necessity, this materialistic view of things, beneath
the pressure of reiterated contradictions, was bound to
become spiritualised.

This was largely the work of Scotus Erigena. By sub-
stituting for cosmic revolution the Neoplatonist idea of the
return of creation in God, he set free the believing soul from
materialistic terrors, without robbing it of hope. By contemplation he opened for it the doors of the eternal and
invisible Church; though by doing so he laid stress upon
the inadequacy and the secondary rôle of the visible Church.

Such audacity of thought could have no other consequence than what has rightly been called *spiritual anarchy*.
The Church was not deceived on the matter. And when in
1205 it flung on to the same pile the writings of David de
Dinant and the *De divisione naturae* of Scotus Erigena, it
gave proof of a remarkable knowledge of the historical
filiation of heresy.

We will now on our side restore this filiation.

§ 1. Great developments of ideas do not come about in
a day. Their germ needs first a period of obscurity, the
symptoms of which will only at a much later date have
their true meaning. It would seem as though the spirit were
awaiting a propitious hour and were anxious in advance to
secure future reserves for itself. Sometimes its manifestations are timid and uncertain, imperfect outlines over which
silence speedily draws a veil. Then suddenly, and often
simultaneously in several places, it issues from its darkness,
this time endowed with a vitality and a power capable of
victoriously meeting hostile forces. The period of incubation
is followed by the militant era.

[1] *Quae omnia quidem ventura esse credendum est; sed quibus modis et quo
ordine veniant, magis tunc docebit rerum experientia, quam nunc ad perfectum
hominum intelligentia valet consequi. De Civit.*, lib. XX. cap. xxx.

The manifestation of spiritual anarchy in the Middle Ages followed no other law. After smouldering for two or three centuries, it first assumes form at the end of the twelfth century in the movement with which the name of Joachim de Flore is associated: the eternal Gospel.

In this doctrine, truth to tell, there was nothing particularly subversive. The popes who honoured the Calabrian monk with their friendship, Lucius III. and Clement III., shared the indignation of the seer against the corrupt state of the clergy. The prediction of the disappearance of the Church they could not regard as insubordination, for here the Church would but share in the lot that befell all things. Even the declarations of Joachim regarding the *misticus intellectus*, which alone was capable of grasping the eternal signification of the Gospel, but faintly skirted the fringe of insubordination and heresy. But the gentle prophet probably did not suspect this. Neither a tribune nor a revolutionary, he was mainly concerned with living the Gospel: ever the best way of converting men to it. More than once was he seen to share his garments with the poor, to nurse lepers and take the dying to his breast. His true disciple is not the restless and stormy heresiarch, but rather the *poverello* of Assisi. The saint, whom Dante placed in his *Paradise* between Saint Anselm and Saint Bonaventura, died in 1202, repeating the words: "Love one another, as the Lord Jesus has loved us."

How comes it, then, that the eternal Gospel must be looked upon as one of the most active ferments in the dissolution of Christianity? From the fact that enthusiastic disciples, thinking they are following in the lines of the master, generally go beyond him.

From the outset the *Fratricelli*, dissenters from the Order of Saint Francis, made use of the holy Calabrian's name against the popes who had sanctioned the successive extensions made in the rules.

Above all, however, the theoretical supporters of independence were able to draw unexpected consequences from the idyllic dream of a golden age which Joachim had indulged on his peaceful mountains.

Indeed, a little book appeared in 1254: *Liber introductorius in Evangelium aeternum*. In it could be read such propositions—which the humble Joachim de Flore would certainly have not recognised—as the following:

Jesus Christ and his apostles were not perfect in the contemplative life. The understanding of the spiritual meaning of the Scriptures has not been entrusted to the pope. What has been entrusted to him is but the understanding of the literal meaning. If he permits himself to decide upon the spiritual meaning, then his judgment is rash, no account must be taken of it. The doctrine of Joachim repeals both Testaments; the gospel of Christ has not been the real Gospel; it has not been able to build the true Church, it has led no one to perfection.

There was a great scandal, an echo of which may be found in the *Roman de la Rose*. Here Jean de Meung approves of the action of the University in burning the insolent volume:

> Ung livre de par le grant diable,
> Dit l'Évangile pardurable
> Que le Saint-Esperit ministre
> Si com il aparoit au tistre.

The principal author suspected, Gérard de Borgo San-Donnino, miserably perished in a subterranean dungeon, by order of Saint Bonaventura.

But ideas cannot be imprisoned. Driven back in one direction, they make a new channel underground and spring up in another place, sometimes far away from their source.

After all, ecclesiastical insubordination found soil for development ready prepared by the relics of the old oriental Manichæism. For this it is that survives under the common name of Catharism, uniting a number of variations. Heirs of the Paulicians and of the dualistic Bogomiles whom the Emperor Alexis was unable to subjugate, we find in restless motion throughout Europe, Albanenses, Concorrezanes, Arnoldists, Albigenses, Patarins, and others, who had all revolted against the hierarchy of the Church, and claimed, by virtue of a mysterious sacrament, the title and the prerogatives of initiates. They professed that souls were divine spirits

that had fallen from heaven into a material body made by
the Evil One: hence their fierce asceticism, the prohibition of
all carnal intercourse, abstention from meat and eggs, even
to the extent of suicide, whereby they broke through their
prison-house of flesh (*endura*).

§ 2. In France, a country favourable to systematisation,
the new spirit made its way into the very heart of the
University. It found philosophic expression in the writings
of two professors of the University of Paris: David de Dinant
and Amaury de Bène, who were teaching at the beginning
of the thirteenth century.

We can acquaint ourselves with the ideas of David de
Dinant only through Saint Thomas, who supplies a lengthy
refutation of them. David had set forth his heretical propositions in the form of quatrains, the *Quaternuli*. In attributing
to him another work, *De Tomis vel de Divisionibus*, Albertus
Magnus would appear to have gravely erred.

A study of the propositions raised by Saint Thomas
enables us to recognise the dual influence of Scotus Erigena
and the Arabic commentaries on Aristotle's physics and
metaphysics. It is impossible, however, to say how far
David carried his doctrines; does he even justify the accusation of pantheism? This could not be affirmed on the word
of Saint Thomas, who declares that David "was so mad as
to profess that God is nothing else than first matter." David,
in particular, would appear to have paid for the philosophical
authorities whose names he invokes. Albertus Magnus cites
a number of these authorities: Anaximenes, who taught the
essential unity of all things, the poet Orpheus, Lucan and
Seneca, whose proposition—*quid est Deus? Mens universi*—
David appears to have reproduced. The fact remains that the
unfortunate professor and fourteen of his pupils atoned for
their audacity in the flames, on the very spot which is now
occupied by the Halles, condemnation against them being
pronounced by the Council of Paris in 1210.

The name of Amaury de Bène is generally associated with

that of David de Dinant, though it is impossible to define clearly the relations between the two. Which was the master of the other? Was there even any connection between the two systems? Forced to recant, Amaury died heartbroken in 1204. His trial, however, was resumed in 1209, and, condemnation being ratified, his bones were exhumed and buried on the high-road.

The inculpation of pantheism seems indeed justified in the doctrine of Amaury: *nemo potest esse salvus nisi credat se esse membrum Christi.* Everything inclines us to the belief that the interpretation of the apostolic word by Amaury reduced to extreme limits the human personality. This doctrine, along with that of Scotus Erigena, led naturally to the identity of God and the universe. This was the sole motive of Amaury's condemnation.

So far we fail to see the relation between these doctrines and the development of the eternal Gospel. In the first place, chronology is opposed to it, and, again, the two systems move on altogether different planes: Joachimism is above all else realistic; the Parisian doctrines depend solely on speculation. It was the work of the disciples to combine the two teachings, and, by carrying to extremes the premises of the doctrine, to work out a real libertarian system.

§ 3. It is easy to glimpse the moral and religious consequences resulting from the propositions of Amaury and David. If matter is the universal principle, if God himself is but the essential form of matter, then individuality loses all consistency, good and evil lose all reality. The appetites, as emanations of matter made divine, are legitimate and must not be subjected to constraint. Further, the satisfaction of the passions can only facilitate the identification of the individual with the Deity.

Neither Amaury nor David had any idea of the far-reaching effects of their doctrine; but those who subsequently used the names of the condemned masters were better logicians.

The votaries found a scheme ready prepared for the
reception of this new system: the theory of the three ages
which the disciples who had deviated from Joachim de Flore
had popularised. Indeed, it is impossible to designate too
clearly the part played by apocalyptic preoccupations among
the Amalricians.

When Guillaume l'Orfèvre, the prophet of the sect, in
the year 1210, called upon Maître Rodolphe de Nemours, in
order to attract him to himself, he speculates on the stirring
drama of the latter days: *item prophetabat*, says Césaire
d'Heisterbach, *quod infra quinque annos istae quattuor plagae
evenire debent.* Fire from heaven will descend *super praelatos
ecclesiae qui sunt membra Antichristi. Dicebat enim quia Papa
esset Antichristus et Roma, Babylon.*[1] The era of the Son is
at an end; henceforth the Holy Spirit will control all things
on to the final consummation.

The kingdom of the Spirit, at all events during the early
years of the movement, does not appear to have implied
carnal freedom among the Amalricians. The fusion that had
come about at Lyons between the Cathari and our votaries
even previous to 1225 rather points to common ascetic preoccupations. Thus too much credit must not be attributed
to the accusations of Guillaume le Breton and Césaire
d'Heisterbach. A pretext for orgies is easily seen in the
secret meetings of the initiates. Even though the accusation
were justified, it would prove nothing against the doctrine.
It might be applied equally well against the accusers and
against Catholicism, if we are to believe Gerson, who violently
stigmatises the shameful profanations of the sanctuary.[2]

Documents, law-suit reports, registered confessions, etc.,
afford abundant proof that the disciples of Amaury afterwards degenerated very rapidly and that they became what

[1] *Dialogus miraculorum*, t. I. col. 1851, p. 305.
[2] Neither the presence of Jesus Christ nor respect for the altars prevented
ecclesiastics from indulging in shameful practices even in the cathedrals: *im-
pudentissima dissolutione ab ecclesiasticis talia fiunt qualia vel scribere horror est
vel etiam cogitare. Oper.*, I. pp. 121, 122; III. pp. 309, 310.

their accusers represented them to be. Still, it would not be right to anticipate history in this fashion. We will simply remember that these doctrines contained the germ of the most abominable deviations from a sense of morality. The *perfecti* readily imagine that the ideal lies in absolute liberty, and that complete detachment is realised not in the restriction but in the gratification of vice. To prove this, we need only go back to the licentious Gnostic sects, the Carpocratians and others.

In France the doctrine was mainly spread by small pamphlets, circulating from hand to hand. Doubtless the persecution to which the Amalricians were subjected brought about the disappearance of these precious testimonies, for not one circular has been found. Heresy, indeed, being vigorously combated, soon disappeared almost totally from the land. Nearly all its partisans seem to have taken refuge in the Rhine districts, for it is there that we shall find them and witness the transformation of the Amaury doctrine into a distinctly subversive system, one directed against the most elementary principles of Christian morals.

This licentious heresy is known as the doctrine of the *New Spirit*. Its filiation with regard to the Amalrician system is known to us through an anonymous compilation of the thirteenth century. Here we are informed that the Amalrician doctrine had been resumed at Strasbourg at the beginning of the thirteenth century by a certain Ortlevus or Ortlibus. Hence its votaries were called *Ortlibenses* or *Ortlibarii*, though this appellation speedily fell into oblivion. It was replaced by the name of disciples of the New Spirit.

The diffusion of this doctrine, favoured by troublous times that are propitious to religious risings, was extraordinarily rapid. Above all, the new ideas found a wonderful vehicle of propagandism: associations of Beghards, from Belgium, who, compelled by poverty and wretchedness, had constituted themselves distinct both from the laity and from the Church. Consisting almost wholly of women at first, these pitiful bands traversed the country crying out: Bread, for God's sake, bread! Thus did these mendicants give a name to their association. In English and in modern Flemish we have the expressions, to beg, *bedelen*, corresponding to the verb *beggen*.[1]

To these wretched starvelings wealthy citizens soon offered houses which were called *béguinages*. Here the women lived in common, after taking a vow of chastity, and devoted themselves to the nursing of the sick. At Louvain, in 1220, the men formed themselves into an association of laic brothers, spending their time in deeds of charity, such as keeping watch over contagious cases or burying the dead. They soon adopted the rope girdle of the Franciscans, for which they had to pay the price of attack by the *Fratricelli*. These new elements almost completely changed the character of these associations, which henceforth adopted a subversive attitude against the Church. Beghards and beguines were, above all, permeated with the doctrines of the New Spirit so completely, indeed, that the documents of the Inquisition make no distinction between the terms beghards, beguines, little brothers, and votaries of the New Spirit. A few years sufficed to bring all this about, as testified by the *Liber Manualis* of Albertus Magnus, a sort of inquisitorial formulary written in 1260, the chief propositions of which have survived in various manuscripts.

II

From this time we shall be confronted with a coherent system, whose applications, from the middle of the thirteenth century, are seen to be identical, in Swabia as in Rhenish soil and in Flanders.

[1] The derivation of *beghard* from Saint Begge or from Lambert de Bègue seems to us unjustified. The same may be said of the explanation given by Latomus and Hoybergius, who connect the term with the Flemish verb *beginnen*, to begin: *tanquamincipientes et aliquam viam religionis inchoantes qua deinde ad ordinem religiosum sub aliqua regula approbata militantentranseant. Corsendonca,* Antwerp, 1654, p. 67.

In retracing the main lines of this system in which the extreme consequences of the doctrines of Amaury are collected, we are no longer reduced to conjecture.

The documents are unanimous: the Free Spirit—for such is the name which the votaries of the New Spirit have adopted for their doctrine—is a moral and religious attitude which consists of nothing less than enfranchisement from all constraint. The Free Spirit brother claims absolute freedom towards any duty imposed by the moral and the social laws, or by religious authority. Equally does he repudiate private ownership and conjugal fidelity, the divine commands and the obligations of conscience.

"What is freedom of the Spirit?" Conrad Kannler is asked by Ebernard de Freyenhausen the inquisitor.

"It exists when all remorse of conscience ceases and man can no longer sin (*quod totaliter cessat remorsus conscientiae et quod redditur impeccabilis*)."

"Hast thou attained to this stage of perfection?"

"Yes, so much so that I can advance in grace, for I am one with God and God is one with me."

"Is a brother of the Free Spirit obliged to obey authority?"

"No, he owes obedience to no man, nor is he bound by the precepts of the Church. If any one prevents him from doing as he pleases, he has the right to kill him. He may follow all the impulses of his nature; he does not sin in yielding to his desires." [1]

Thus we are dealing with a veritable anarchist insurrection, set up against authority of every kind. All the same, we should be wrong in accusing of immorality all the brothers of the Free Spirit. Apart from those lost to all sense of shame, who regarded the doctrine as an opportunity to give free rein to all the cravings of the flesh, there were certainly pure disinterested apostles and ascetics who had reached a far different conclusion. If man is God, he should live like God, free himself from carnal affections by renunciation and the subjection of his passions, and give a predominant place to the spiritual element in his nature.

In this connection, Ruysbroeck, whom we are now about to bring on to the stage, was far more just than the majority of his contemporaries. The *freedom of the spirit*, which he so

[1] R. Allier, *Les Frères du Libre-Esprit*, in *Religions et Sociétés*, Paris, 1905, p. 135.

strongly opposed, appears to him almost exclusively as heresy, intellectual and religious error.

.   .   .   .

At the beginning of the fourteenth century the sect appears in Hainaut under the name of *Porretistes*, the disciples of a beguine, Marguerite Porrette. This enthusiast had written a book containing the following proposition: "The soul that has annihilated itself in the love of its Creator can accord to nature everything it desires." Such audacity cost the heresiarch her death by burning at Grève, on the 1st of June 1310. The Porretist doctrine, however, was resumed a few years later by the mysterious Bloemardinne, to whom we shall devote a special chapter.

It is possible to obtain, from information supplied by Ruysbroeck, a very consistent picture of the aberrations of the sect of the Free Spirit in Belgium during the fourteenth century.

First there was the penchant to idleness, scorn of all activity, and, as a consequence, a riotous abandonment to every passion. "For man to be perfect," they say, "it is sufficient that he follow the inclinations that God has implanted in his heart. That is the only way to return to a pure and natural life, to that close union with God which man possessed before the Fall." Next there was an irreducible opposition to the Church and to a constituted hierarchical society. Finally there was outright pantheism, without disguise of any kind. In *The Twelve Beguines* Ruysbroeck likens these four currents to the four sins against the Holy Spirit, against the Father, against the Son, and against the Church.

These men maintain outright that they are of the essence of God, superior to all distinctions, and that they realise a state of vacuity which is veritable non-being. This is why they do not work, for the primordial essence of God (*grondwesen*) is also inactive. But see in what manner they mean to practise this repose: they remain quietly seated, free of all activity, whether interior or exterior. Thus they are thrown back upon themselves. An unrestrained appetite attracts them wholly towards an interior delectation and a spiritual satisfaction that are purely natural. This is what is called spiritual lewdness, for it is an unrestrained propensity to natural love. Replete also with spiritual pride and self-will, these men sometimes propel themselves so passionately towards what they desire, that they frequently go astray and some of them fall under the power of Satan.

Imagining themselves God, nothing to them is either good or bad provided they can dispense with images, discover and possess their own being in a state of absolute void. Liberated from faith and grace, from the practice of every virtue, they claim to live superior to all modes, free of all, lost in the void as when they were non-existent, renouncing all knowledge, all love, all will, all desire, all virtuous practices, in order to be empty of all things. They also state that their soul is of the substance of God, and that at death this soul will return to divine substance, just as water drawn from the spring in a pitcher returns to the spring when the pitcher is emptied. Thus, in their folly, they imagine that all reasonable creatures, good or evil, angels or demons, will at the last day become a single modeless essence, and they assert that this essence will be God, of blissful nature, devoid of knowledge and will. They call this perfect poverty of spirit, though in very truth it is but an infernal and diabolical poverty. . . . Heathen and Jew, the most perverse of mortals can indulge in this vain idleness, if they succeed in crushing all remorse for sin, in isolating themselves from images and from activity of any kind. Then one falls into almost incurable spiritual pride and self-complacency, thinking one possesses that which one has never even approached.

The identity claimed by these heretics between themselves and God leads them into a repulsive pantheism. What, indeed, is it that they say?

Whilst I was in my eternal essence, I had no God. But that which I was I willed, and that which I willed I was. It is of my own will that I have become (*van minen vrien wille bin ic gheworden ende uutghegaen*). . . .

Without me, God would have neither knowledge nor will nor power, for it is I, with God, who have created my own personality and all things. From my hand are suspended heaven, earth and all creatures. And whatever honour is paid to God, it is to me that it is paid, for in my essential being I am by nature God. For myself, I neither hope nor love, and I have no faith, no confidence in God. I have nothing to pray for, nothing to implore, for I do not render honour to God above myself. For in God there is no distinction, neither Father nor Son nor Holy Spirit . . . since with this God I am one, and am even that which he is . . . and which, without me, he is not.[1]

They also say:

That which Christ is, we are; like him we are eternal life and wisdom, begotten with him of the Father in the divine nature, born with him in time, after the human nature. Accordingly we are one with him, God and man in every way. All that God has given to him he has given to us also, and that no less than to him. That he be now born of a virgin is a matter of indifference to us; it is an accident to which is attached neither sanctity nor happiness, which possesses no more importance than the fact that we others are born of ordinary women. In addition, Christ was sent only to devote himself to the practice of active life, in order to serve me, to live and die for me. I was sent for the contemplative life, which is superior to the active, a state which doubtless Christ, like myself, would have attained had he lived longer. Whatsoever honour is paid to him, it is also paid to me. In the Sacrament, when his body is raised on the altar, I too am raised. . . . For I am with him, flesh and blood, one single person who cannot be separated.[2]

There can be no doubt but that such doctrines led to moral depravation and insubordination; to a state of dissoluteness and licentiousness, first of all. No one, they say, not even God, is capable of giving them anything, or taking anything from them; for, in their opinion, they have transcended all religious practices, all virtues. . . . Hence they go so far as to say that, so long as man has a tendency to virtue and desires to do God's very precious will, he is still imperfect, being preoccupied with the acquiring of things. . . . Therefore they think they can never either believe in virtues, or have additional merit, or commit sins. . . . Consequently they are able to consent to every desire of the lower nature, for they have reverted to a state of innocence, and laws no longer apply to them. Hence, if the nature is prone to that which gives it satisfaction, and if, in resisting it, mental idleness must, however slightly, be either checked

[1] *The Twelve Beguines*, pp. 52–3.   [2] *Ibid.*, pp. 54–61.

or distracted, they obey the instincts of nature. They are all forerunners of Antichrist, preparing the way for incredulity of every kind. They claim, indeed, to be free, outside of commandments and virtues. To say what pleases them and never to be contradicted, to retain their own will and be in subjection to no one: that is what they call spiritual freedom. Free in their flesh, they give the body what it desires. . . . To them, the highest sanctity for man consists in following, without compulsion and in all things, his natural instinct, so that he may abandon himself to every impulse in satisfying the demands of the body. . . . They wish to sin and indulge in their impure practices without fear or qualms of conscience. Nevertheless, adds Ruysbroeck in fairness, such people are not met with in great numbers.

And now with regard to insubordination.

In their shameless licentiousness, they come to scorn all rules. Consequently they reject science, work, contemplation, love, property, Church practices and sacraments, the life, teaching, passion and death of Jesus, divine characters. . . . Eager for freedom, they will obey no one . . . neither pope nor bishop nor priest . . . for they are completely weaned of everything connected with holy Church. Superior to all the sacraments of the Church, they neither need nor want them. They ridicule and remember nothing as regards ecclesiastical practices and customs or the writings of the saints. In their own idea, they have transcended all things which they recognise as necessary only for the imperfect. Certain of them even are so bold and inveterate in their simplicity that they remain unoccupied and care naught for the works of God or for the Holy Scriptures, as though not a letter had ever been written. They will neither teach nor be taught by anyone, they wish to criticise but to accept no blame themselves, to command but never to obey.

It has been thought that in these characteristics were to be found four distinct heresies combated by Ruysbroeck, or rather separate currents of one and the same subversive heresy: a rationalistic current, a pantheistic current, and a

naturalistic current. But what Ruysbroeck teaches us coincides so nearly with what we know from other quarters of
the brothers of the Free Spirit, that we must not hesitate
to ascribe to one and the same sect the manifestations
observed by Ruysbroeck.

He would appear to have despaired of bringing these
ranters to saner views:

> They will die rather than retract a single point in what they put for-
> ward. But when death comes, they will see to what their base turpitude
> has brought them. They call themselves happy:
>
> > Happy like them is the sleeping dog,
> > Dreaming he has a morsel of meat in his mouth.
> > He wakes, and lo! he has nothing;
> > And that is what happens to them.[1]
>
> When the hour comes for them to be filled with bitter grief and mortal
> anguish, they are pursued by phantoms, they are terrified and dismayed
> within. Then they lose their calm tranquillity and fall into such a state of
> despair that they are inconsolable. And they perish like mad dogs.[2]

This heresy, which the mendicant Beghards, driven from
diocese to diocese, brought from Germany into Belgium,
became all the more rapidly acclimatised from the fact that
it tallied with the still active survivals of Tanchelm's doctrine.
This doctrine seems to have been of a particularly social and
revolutionary character. If, however, we are to believe a contemporary, we might find in it all the pantheistic tendencies
of the Free Spirit:

> Tanchelm said that if Christ was God because he was in possession of
> the Holy Spirit, he himself also was God by the same right, since he had
> received the fulness of the Holy Spirit. In this way he succeeded so well
> in taking possession of men's souls that he was worshipped as God by some
> of his partisans, and gave the stupid people to drink of the water in which
> he had bathed, which, he asserted, was a holier and more efficacious
> sacrament than the water of baptism.[3]

A century after the death of the heretic, who was assas-
sinated in 1115, his doctrine received a new lease of life

---

[1] *The Twelve Beguines*, p. 38.
[2] *The Highest Truth*, chapter iv.
[3] Letter of the canons of Utrecht to the archbishop of Cologne, quoted by
Gens, *Hist. de la ville d'Anvers*, pp. 33, 34. Regarding the doctrine of Tanchelm,
see a remarkable study by Janssen in the *Annales de l'Académie d'Archéologie
de Belgique*, t. XXIII. pp. 374 ss.

under Cornelis, a canon of Notre-Dame of Antwerp. Cornelis regarded poverty as the one supreme virtue, claiming that its possession gave man the right to sin with impunity. " As rust disappears beneath the action of fire, so all sin is dissipated by the virtue of poverty. A poor courtesan is more acceptable in the sight of God than a chaste person possessed of property." [1] He declared *omnes religiosos esse damnatos*, because of their opulent living, and these communistic ideas won him the favour of the people in spite of his condemnation by the bishop of Cambrai. Most of his partisans, in addition to the social ideas of their master, adopted the Manichæan or Albigensian heresy which Gondolphe, an Italian missionary, had introduced about the year 1025 into Belgium, where it had prospered greatly.

In the fourteenth century the heretical effervescence seems to have reached its highest point. Was it possible to surpass the eccentricities and the pride of the votaries of the Free Spirit? And yet new fanatics now appear. These are first the flagellants, and then the dancers, who are not heretics, though their practices were speedily to bring them into opposition with the Church.

III

Allusion to these practices may be found in the *Treatises of the Four Temptations*, wherein Ruysbroeck condemns those who think they can attain to genuine contemplation by means of ridiculous mortifications, absurd poses and contortions of the body. He connects them with the sect of the Free Spirit and adds that it is mostly the young and uncultured who follow along these lines.

The reason he alludes to them but briefly is doubtless because he came less directly in contact with them. Ruysbroeck had indeed entered Groenendael when, in the year

---

[1] Miraeus, *Tractatus de jurer egularium*, t. II. pp. 371 ss. Thomas de Cantimpré, *Bon. univ. vel de apib.*, t. II. p. 47.

1349, there appeared in Belgium the first bands of flagellants: *flagellatores* or *poenitentes* in Latin, *flagelleurs*, *batteurs*, *penans* in French, *geeselaars* or *cruusbroeders* in Flemish.

These strange penitents, who had had predecessors in Italy at the time of the plague of 1205, first appeared in Germany after the terrible *mort noire* of 1348–9: in *Hongaria*, in *Allemannia*, says their principal chronicler, Gilles li Muisis, abbé de Saint-Martin at Tournai. These bands were almost exclusively composed of men. Their garment consisted of a sort of blouse or surplice, back and breast ornamented with a red cross. They held in their hand the penitent's rod (*baculus poenitentiarius*).

Generally they proceeded as follows: They divided into small groups and entered the town, *cantando secundum suum idioma, Flamingi in flamingo, illi de Brabantia in theutonico et Gallici in gallico.* Reaching the market-place, they stripped themselves of their clothes, tied a girdle around the loins, so that they appeared, says the chronicler, like bakers in front of their ovens. Then "chantaient, en faisant leurs pénitences, cançons moult piteuses de la Nativité Nostre-Seigneur et de sa sainte souffrance." These songs, to which those members of the group who did not scourge themselves responded in chorus, were attuned to the rhythm of the arm which brandished the rod and inflicted the strokes. The flagellants mimicked all such indications as *alons, à genoulx . . . vos braz estandez . . . or nous relevons.* Thrice they flung themselves on to the ground, with arms outstretched crosswise. Then, rising, they whipped one another in kneeling posture, *sique le sanc de leurs espaules courait aval de tous costez* (Jehan le Bel). When they had finished, they remained on their knees until a priest gave them absolution, whereupon, *cantando de beata Virgine ibant ad se revestiendum.* Li Muisis states that among these penitents were a few women who, instead of undressing completely, bared only the back.

A number of French or Flemish songs were sung by these poor folk. The following are two of these, which seem to indicate the successive moments of the flagellation:

Or avant, entre nous tuit frère,
batons nos charoingnes bien fort
Ou nom de ce, *batons plus fort* . . .
Loons Dieu et *batons noz piz* . . .
Alons, à genoulx par penance
Loons Dieu. *Vos braz estandez,*
et en l'amour de sa souffrance,
Chéons jus en croix a tous lez . . .
Or tous *à genoulx* sans respit
rechéons en croix sans balance . . .
Or relevons de bon couraige
et devers le ciel regardons. . . .
Or rebatons nostre char villainne,
Or nous relevons. . . .
Batons noz pis, batons no face,
tendons nos bras de grant vouloir. . . .

Batons nos chars plaines d'envie,
batons d'orgueil *de plus en plus.* . . .
Enfin de nostre pénitence
nous fault *à genoulx* revenir.
Tous mourrons: c'est la remembrance;
qui nous fait tierce fois chéir.
Jhésu, ainsi comme devant
relevons nous la tierce fois,
et loons Dieu *à nuz genoulz*;
jointes mains, tenons l'escourgie.
Cremons Dieu, ayons le cuers doulx,
et *chantons* à la départie,
"Grace Dieu," car elle est en nous.
Prions pour l'humaine lignée.
Baisons la terre, levons nous.

These itinerant manifestations met with enormous success. The people vied with one another in lodging the exhausted penitents. To sensitive souls the sight of blood was so contagious that the groups always left the towns in greater numbers than when they entered. "It seemed to all," says Jehan le Bel, "that they were holy people and that God had sent them to offer an example to the masses to do penance and so obtain remission of sins."

Nevertheless, it would be wrong to dwell solely on these more or less morbid manifestations in judging the flagellants. Behind these extravagant practices were new aspirations, unsatisfied needs, evidently connected with the general effervescence already mentioned.

Li Muisis tells of a series of moral engagements to which aspiring flagellants were to subscribe before being admitted into the sect. *Item, recognoscendo quod omnes sumus ex una materia creati, redempti uno pretio, dotati uno dono, debemus unus alterum fratrem appellare. . . . Item, tu non portabis armaturas nec ibis in bellis pro quocumque, excepto tuo vero Domino. . . . Item, iu debes dare elemosynas pauperibus secundum posse tuum. . . . Item, tu te debes obligare ad totam abstinentiam carnis specialiter toto curso vitae tuae et custodire sancte tuum matrimonium, et non jurare in vanum.*

Then how was it that coercive power was rapidly brought to bear upon the sectarians? First, because the comparison

which the people made between them and the priests was
not favourable to the latter. Then, to constitute themselves a
confraternity, the flagellants had dispensed with all authorisation. The real grievance, however, was the danger that
popular enthusiasm, which everywhere accompanies men
bent on sacrifice, caused the Church to incur. Jehan le Bel
candidly confesses this.

The flagellants themselves protested their fidelity to the
Church and its institutions. Li Muisis recognises this himself
when he quotes a series of propositions to which the flagellants were to adhere *pro suo toto cursu vitae*. These propositions are the same as those which, in their ensemble, constituted the rules of the fraternity. A law-suit was none the
less begun. Had not a preacher, attached to a band of
flagellants from Liége, stated from the pulpit that the blood
of these fanatics was one with the blood of Jesus Christ?

In a similar line of ideas, Froissart relates that "auqunes
sotes femmes avoient drapelés apparilliés et requelloient ce
sanc et disoient que c'estoit sanc de miracle." This was
quite sufficient to justify the charge of heresy.

Pope Clement VI., circumvented by Jean du Fay, of the
University of Paris, launched against the flagellists, on the
20th of October 1349, a solemn bull enjoining the sectarians
to retract and dissolve: *et hoc sub poena perditionis corporum
et bonorum*. The King of France, Philippe VI., in a private
edict of the 13th of February 1350, applicable to Tournai,
reinforced the comminatory terms of the papal bull: ". . . con-
straignant à cesser et à la delaissier ceulx qui suivent la
secte, par impositions de peines temporelles, et par bans,
deffenses et autres voies et remèdes . . . en aidant sur ce à
Sainte-Église par le bras séculier et par main armée."

The persecutions against the flagellants, says Li Muisis,
roused *in populo murmur magnum*. The municipalities of
certain towns, such as Louvain, Tirlemont, Lierre, quite
openly sided with the condemned. The archives mention
that large sums were collected for them; when the wandering bands passed, straw was laid down in secret shelters to

ensure them repose, rich citizens poured out for them wine and beer. In time, however, violence dispersed these harmless penitents, and they seem to have completely disappeared after 1355.

They were seen again in 1400, but only for a short time, and nothing important is recorded of them.

IV

All the same, the religious exaltation beneath all these strange manifestations was maintained throughout the century. In 1374 it brought into being a new category of fanatics, who are first mentioned as appearing at Aix-la-Chapelle.

These were bands of men and women who, half-naked and wreathed with flowers, were suddenly transported out of themselves and danced about with streaming hair, shouting and singing all the while. The chroniclers looked upon these cries as diabolical invocations: *quaedam nomina daemoniorum nominabant, videlicet Friskes et similia.* This word *Friskes* is simply an exclamation intended to regulate the movements of the dance: *frisch, frisch auf, frisch op,* in French *debout, vivement.* Exhausted by their mad sarabands, the dancers rolled on the ground, a prey to violent pains which were relieved by placing girdles very tightly around the abdomen: *et in fine hujus chorizationis in tantum circa pectoralia torquebantur, quod nisi mappulis lineis a suis amicis per medium ventris fortiter stringerentur, quasi furiosi clamabant se mori.*[1]

In contradistinction from the flagellants, the dancers rose in open revolt against the Church. P. d'Herenthals says of the sect: *clerum habet odio, non curat sacramenta.* They traversed the country in large bands, soliciting alms, invading churches, propagating their special brand of neurosis. According to the chroniclers, they practised upon

[1] Pierre d'Herenthals, *Cronica episcoporum Leodiensium*, man. 3802–7 de la Bibliothèque royale de Bruxelles.

themselves unmentionable acts which can be transcribed in Latin alone: *noctis sub umbraculo ista perpetravit . . . cum naturali baculo subtus se calcavit.*

The people naïvely attributed these extravagances to the influence of fornicating priests who, in granting baptism to unworthy subjects, introduced demons into the bodies of children: *vulgus dicebat quod huius modi plaga populo contigisset eo quod populus male baptizatus erat maxime a presbyteris suas tenentibus concubinas.* Thus the sectaries were rather exorcists than inquisitors; perhaps this may be the reason why the dancers had had less suffering to endure than their predecessors, the flagellants. The chronicles are full of tales dealing with exorcism, and these throw a very curious light on the childlike credulity of the times. Where the practices of the priest failed, the magistrates inflicted the penalty of the ban.

In all probability these measures, along with the impossibility of maintaining for any length of time such a state of exaltation, rapidly brought these exhibitions of neurosis to an end. After a year the state of effervescence suddenly ceased. *Hec pestis infra annum satis invaluit, sed postea per tres aut quatuor annos omnino cessavit.*[1]

.   .   .   .

Such are the main currents which profoundly stirred the society in which Ruysbroeck lived. To judge impartially these wild impetuous manifestations, we must look beyond the things that shock and repel us in modern life.

There are ages that are cold and formal, in which religion is scarcely more than lifeless formalism. Quite different is the fourteenth century, whose mysticism is above all else a renaissance of enthusiasm. Religion has mostly ceased to be a duty or a function: it has become once again the expression of a vital need. Everywhere living intercourse with deity is sought; there is a wish to unite therewith, to love it and be loved by it, to experience materially, even in the emotions of the flesh, the continual presence of God.

[1] *Magnum chronicum Belgicum,* p. 147.

The germ of this mysticism must principally be sought in the survivals of Neoplatonism. Did not the philosophy of Plotinus culminate in his theory of ecstasy? Scotus Erigena and his disciples, in popularising the idea of a return to God and of the permeation of the human by the divine spirit, had cleared the path for all mystical initiatives. And the reason why these odd manifestations appear so frequently in the fourteenth century, is because the religious soul felt incapable of obtaining satisfaction in a Church where a great and inspiring message was no longer heard and a rapidly-spreading materialism had taken precedence of every other consideration.

Let us not, therefore, pass thoughtless or incautious judgment on these deviations from piety. Most assuredly a host of creditable instincts were blended with them.

There is one lesson, however, to be learned. Religion, if it is to develop normally, must be made up of the balance of two forces: feeling and reason. Should one of these two elements come to supplant the other, or to develop to the detriment of the other, then equilibrium is disturbed, and religion degenerates into either impotent rationalism or morbid exaltation. Now, ignorance is general throughout the century with which we are dealing. No one had yet dreamt of translating for the masses the lofty speculations of the great Scholastics. These men, nevertheless, had attempted to effect the synthesis between the claims of the heart and the requirements of the reason.

We are now about to see Ruysbroeck, warned by these very misfortunes, attempt this assuredly novel task. Religious enthusiasm will lose nothing, but he will be able to direct its impetuosity into the right channel and keep it within the limits of a steady doctrine. He will bring about a reconciliation between religion and virtue, between fervour and good sense, between faith and practice. And if, even in this world, communion is possible between man and God, he will show that only those can attain thereto who have disciplined their heart, their will and their thought.

CHAPTER IV

THE YOUTH OF RUYSBROECK

I

Two leagues to the south of Brussels, on the banks of the Senne, stands the market-town of Ruysbroeck. A manufacturing town in these modern times, it bears no resemblance to the country village from which Ruysbroeck takes his name.

In former days the forest of Soignes almost completely encircled it, except on the west, where the curtain of trees was rent to enable the vast stretch of Flemish plains gently to slope down towards the sea. Beneath the wild and rustling branches of the ash-trees flowed the little stream whose waters were soon to become fouled at Brussels by the weavers working there.

Here, in the year 1293, was born the man whom the piety of the ages designated the Admirable. His family name is totally unknown. As was the custom in the Middle Ages, it was his native village that gave him his name: *sic dictus a villa unde natalem traxit originem.*[1]

In some of the editions of Surius is to be found the following epigram intended to interpret the name of our mystic:

> *Hactenus in terris quasi gemma sepulta latebat,*
> *Ac velute paucis unio, notus erat*
> *Coelicus his doctor,* IEHOVAE *cui gratia nomen,*
> *Cognomen tribuit grande* SONORA PALUS. . . .

Ancient chroniclers make it possible for us to reconstitute the life of the villagers, which was even more wretched than that of the artisans in the large towns.

---

[1] Pomerius, lib. II. cap. iv. *Ruusbroec* is the mediæval spelling of the name. It is that of the most ancient documents, including the biography of Pomerius. We also find *Rusbroch, Rusbroek, Ruysebroek, Rusebruch, Reisbruch.*

Imagine a conglomeration of poor huts, made of clay or wood, grouped around a humble chapel. These primitive dwelling-places consisted mostly of a single room. There was no window, because of the high price of glass. The door served a double purpose: it allowed the smoke to leave the room and the light to enter. Here the people lived herded together, condemned at nightfall to utter darkness, mitigated in winter only by the ruddy glare of a wood fire. Candles were still a luxury, which the poor reserved for the altar when they attended church on special occasions.

The village itself was divided into lanes and tiny streets, filthy passages which a downpour of rain speedily transformed into pools of mud. As the prescriptions of the city *keures* did not extend to the country, filth and dirt of every kind still obstructed these lanes, the happy hunting-ground of swine and poultry.

The inhabitants all worked on the land. Very few of them had their own freeholds. The majority were subjected to a scarcely-disguised serfdom: emancipation for the peasant consisted mainly in freedom to exploit his land as he pleased. None the less was he attached to the soil—like the *metairie* or small farm on which he lived—whether as tributary to the churches or subject to prestations of every kind, payable to the seignior. Finally, at the foot of the social ladder was the unpaid labourer, the *cossaet*, the landless peasant forced to hire himself out to obtain a living.

Though these men were so harshly treated, they had nevertheless given considerable impetus to agriculture. Certain of them had become real masters in market-gardening or the cultivation of flowers, and their methods had spread far beyond the plains of Brabant.

From 1292 onwards we come across rural *échevinages*, similar to those of the towns. The guarantee, however, offered by these bodies was illusory in most cases: as a matter of fact, the peasant was the chattel of the seignior. If the latter took away his wife or daughters or imposed on him arbitrary prestations, there was no efficacious jurisdiction to protect him. In war-time, his crops were immediately ravaged, and himself, the very man who supplied town and country alike with food, was the first to fall victim to those terrible famines which form the blackest page in the history of the Middle Ages.

Against this unjust state of dependence, Boendale, who gave expression to the claims of the democratic spirit, often raised his voice:

> It is the tillers of the soil who feed the world; they supply all that life requires and yet have nothing themselves. Scarcely do they own a shirt, and yet they have to toil morning and evening. The world could better dispense with cardinals, bishops and monks, with lords and knights, than with the tiller of the ground.[1]

Priests and abbots were sometimes the strictest masters; a fact which explains the anti-clerical nature of certain village insurrections.

What kind of morality could there be in a state of servitude which had no place for human dignity? Family promiscuity gave rise to the most frightful immorality, for which less blame must be attached to the unfortunate peasants than to those who kept them in a most debasing serfdom. Drink and carnal sensations are the only joys of those whose lot scarcely rises above that of the brute creation.

II

Such was the state of things into which Ruysbroeck was born. Of his parents we know nothing. This silence, however, indicates that he was of humble extraction.[2]

The biographers, who speak at considerable length of his mother, do not say a word about his father: a fact which

---

[1] *Jan's Teestye*, chapter xxvii.
[2] At a later date the biographers claim that he was of noble parentage, *nobili familia natus*. Jan's family was related to a certain Gerelmus Hinckaert, who was *échevin* of Brussels from 1287 onwards (Henne and Wauters, *Histoire de la ville de Bruxelles*, t. II. p. 511). The biographers have made the most of this flattering cousinship. The family names Hinckaert and Ruysbroeck are found in the registers of N.-D. de la Chapelle in connection with the foundation, on the 28th of October 1396, of a *cantuarie* at the altar of Saint-Christophe.

has given rise to the supposition that Jan was an illegitimate child.[1] Mention has been made of a certain Arnoul de Ruse-brueck, who lived in 1264 and whose name is found in the deeds of the abbey of the Saint-Sépulchre de Cambrai, to which were ceded the tithes of Meghem-sous-Tourneffe on which was dependent the chapel of the village of Ruys-broeck. It is also thought he might have been the son of the *échevin* Gerelmus Hinckaert, Willem van Eleghem, brother of a canon of whom we shall soon read. These, however, are all gratuitous suppositions, and the wisest course is to accept the silence of Pomerius.

Of Jan's mother we have a moral portrait that justifies the exquisite tenderness lavished on her by her son: *ejus quotidie filialem habens in corde memoriam.*

Pomerius reproaches the good woman with having loved her son too well; this leads one to imagine that she might have been somewhat displeased at the religious vocation of Ruysbroeck. Surius dryly remarks—doubtless for the same reason—that she was not perfect in everything (chapter ii.).

Let us leave these clerical commentaries. If the impressions of childhood remain deeply graven in the mind, we must recognise the influence of this pious mother in moulding her son's nature. We may imagine the humble peasant woman, busied with household duties, solicitous about securing the daily supply of bread, of curds and of cheese, which made up the dietary of the poor. It was certainly by her side that little Jan had his first revelation of active life which, as he subsequently asserts, honours God quite as much as does worship in the sanctuary. The beauty of meekness, the sanctity of work, the sweet family devotion, all that he was later to extol in incomparable language—he saw in living radiance on the face of his mother.

Why must hagiographers distort reality when they illuminate and colour it? Is a man less great because angels have not folded their wings above his cradle? Pomerius

---

[1] K. Ruelens, introduction to the *Œuvres de Sœur Hadewyck,* edited by Prof. Vercouillie.

relates—and he says he was told it by those in Ruysbroeck's confidence—that the child, when only seven days old, stood upright, contrary to custom, in the basin in which his nurse was washing him, and that without anyone holding him. The pious chronicler adds:

> What else do these preludes indicate than that this babe, so frail and tiny, would some day rise superior to his own human nature and, with the eye of contemplation, look into the divine mirror, just as now his body stands upright, contrary to every natural law? (Lib. II. cap. i.)

Meanwhile, beneath the golden imagery of the legend, it is possible to learn something of the formation of the child's character.

We find him precociously stirred with an ardent desire after an intellectual life. He will have nothing to do with games that are noisy or of a commonplace nature.[1] An innate delicacy seems to have kept him from that precocious stigma which documents unanimously deplore in boys and girls. The turbulent gaiety of the villagers on festival days, with jugs of beer and tables laden with food, must have been obnoxious to him. His meditative mind looks far beyond these orgies: he sees how low man can descend when he forgets God, and he has a vision of the heights he may attain when he attempts to return to his source.

His first school was evidently the family home. Later on, when he delights to dwell on the analogy between religious life and family life, when, for him as for Jesus, man's relations with God remain principally a filial matter —do we not find in this a reminiscence of his pure and gentle youth?

There was but little instruction to be obtained in the country. Possibly the child received his first lessons from the village priest. At all events, he must have learnt to read and have picked up sufficient of the elements of grammar to be in a position, a few years later, to have his name

---

[1] *Puer juvenis non more communi carnales affectus, verum potius spirituales profectus pro suae aetatis modulo sectabatur.* Pomerius, lib. II. cap. ii.

enrolled on the registers of the schools of Brussels. His mother-tongue was the *thiois*, a Germanic dialect with softened inflections, from which modern Flemish is derived. In view of his ecclesiastical vocation, it is likely that he picked up some rudiments of Latin. Certainly it was in Latin that he said his first prayers, and that the echoes of the divine voice, in the Sunday services, reached him.

We find traces of these youthful emotions in his writings. Such fervour is never to be forgotten: when intellect is yet unable to question and faith is summed up in an *élan* of the entire being! In that stainless hour, God is apprehended as clearly behind the trembling stars as behind the florid and mysterious ceremonies of the Church. Indeed, the best part of man has its roots in that early piety so speedily followed by the torturing anxieties of practical matter-of-fact humanity which laboriously attempts to reconcile together a faith devoid of proof and a reason devoid of charm.

For the moment the child follows the promptings of his heart. He is sensitive as a lyre. It may be that, anticipating time by hope, he sees himself, clad in priestly adornments, raising aloft the chalice and touching it with his lips.

Most of his days are passed either in playing with children as quiet as himself or in watching some peasant or woodcutter at his work.

Through contact with the poor but gentle country-folk, he is first made acquainted with that great law of life which subjects man to toil and labour. He learns to discern, beneath the crude aspects of the particular trade or occupation, the sacred beauty of work. He becomes profoundly at one with his people, learning to know their needs, their miseries and their hopes. No doubt he must have sometimes felt that sudden flame of revolt which springs from pity and keeps man from becoming hardened at the spectacle of a world corroded by hatred and iniquity.

To all these influences we must add another.

The forest came right up to the outlying cottages of the village. Wide-spreading marshes, now converted into pastureland, cast a sort of moving wave beyond the river, bordered with gnarled willows. In the incomparable sunsets of Flanders this stretch of landscape shone like burning metal.

Saint Francis composed the canticle of the sun, but the entire work of Ruysbroeck is no more than a hymn to "Monseigneur frère Soleil." Later on he compares the whole of religious life, in the regularity of its progress, to the course of this magnificent orb.

Observation of the life of plants and animals, a profound intimacy with the mystery of forests and waters, will reveal to him that gracious Gospel which God writes on the corolla of the lily and the wing of the bird, and supply him with those marvellous images which adorn his whole work.

The forest in particular, which he has to traverse in every season, opens to him its shady or its sunlit refuges. With its straight-stemmed trees, it appears before him as the symbol of true life, firmly rooted in the depths of consciousness and spreading out its being to the heights. Most of the species he knows by name, as well as the variegated flora on the surface of the soil.

Sometimes, beneath sombre arcades, the child sees the dukes of Brabant gallop past in brilliant array, for they are fearless huntsmen. Indeed, so powerful were early influences upon him that, after years of practical ministry, Ruysbroeck returned to the woods to meditate beneath their shady walks, and to die not far from the spot where the waving foliage of the beeches had lulled him to sleep when a child.

III

And now Jan has reached his eleventh year.

Pomerius relates how, impelled by divine benevolence, the child tore himself away from the solicitous care of too loving a mother, and ran away from home.

There can be no doubt but that there is a legendary element in the episode as we find it related. The account has manifestly been influenced by the tradition regarding John the Baptist: *sicut ille civium turmas fugiens in deserto latuit.* Is it not in accordance with saintly tradition that he should flee from the world? Must not the saint regard as naught the affections of earth, and lose himself in that love and tenderness which alone is not subject to time? Good hagiographers would have thought they were detracting from their hero by subjecting him to the common laws of the heart. Indeed, a remark of Pomerius enables us to reconstruct the event: *casu veniens ad domum memorati canonici.* This little word *casu* informs us that young Ruysbroeck had the opportunity of visiting a relative of his, Jan Hinckaert, priest of Sainte-Gudule at Brussels.

In the course of this visit the boy must have shown himself, in all the ardour and spontaneity of his soul, already interested in the things of the spirit. Perhaps he spoke to the priest of his newly-conceived vocation. At all events, Jan Hinckaert welcomed him joyfully (*gaudenter suscepit*) and undertook his education

This was in 1304.

Here we must break into the story of Pomerius. The biographer relates that, affected by a sermon which he had heard, Hinckaert had completely shaken himself free from the vanities of the time, along with a friend of his, Franco de Coudenberg (*de Frigidomonte*). The two friends had formed a small mystical association, of which, evidently, young Ruysbroeck was a member. This story, in the place where it is inserted, anticipates the march of events. Indeed, we are aware through the *Necrologium Viridisvallis* that Coudenberg was born in 1296 and died in 1386. In 1304 he would have been only eight years of age. Now, at the time of his conversion, he is stated by Pomerius himself to be a *vir unus praecipuus famosus clericus.* Consequently we must antedate the event by at least fifteen years. Nevertheless, nothing authorises us to believe that Jan Hinckaert lived a dissolute life. Son of the *échevin* Gerelmus Hinckaert whose relationship with the Ruysbroeck family has been mentioned,

dowered with a rich patrimony, we can only think that
Hinckaert had not wholly detached himself from the life
of the world. He lived in a spacious house on the Sablon de
Sainte-Gudule, at the corner of the present rue du Marquis.
Neither better nor worse than other priests of his age, he
had not bid the world the *abrenuntio* of the ascetics.

Still, there can be no doubt but that the presbytery of
the Sablon Sainte-Gudule was the place in which the early
vocation of Ruysbroeck grew and developed.

Nothing has come down to us of the conversations
between uncle and nephew; so we will imitate the sobriety
of our documents. Still, in the pages subsequently written
by our mystic, we may find a sort of reminiscence of these
happy years. Certainly it is of them he is thinking when he
speaks of "the May month of the spiritual life," when man
as yet shows nothing more than promises and gives himself
up wholly to the divine influence which causes fragile hopes
to yield their fruit. As we read these pages, we are reminded
of Goethe's words: "What constitutes a beautiful life? A
dream of youth that has been realised in maturity."

But this life would be a mutilated imperfection if the
development of the soul were not accompanied by a corresponding development of the mind. If the soul infinitely
outstrips the possibilities of the intellect and oversteps the
barriers imposed by nature on this latter, there can be
no solid faith apart from sturdy intellectual culture. When
reason abandons its task of control and guidance, faith goes
astray. Then arise fanaticism, credulity, religious perversion.
In particular was this true of the century in which Ruysbroeck lived. Brussels was continually being disturbed and
upset by the fanatics of the Free Spirit.

Ruysbroeck was sent, from the very beginning, to the
Latin schools of Brussels, which he diligently attended for
four years.[1]

Let us visit these schools for a moment. At the outset

[1] . . . *quas* (*scholas*) *cum annis circiter quatuor Bruxellae docilis frequentasset.*
Pomerius, lib. II. cap. ii.

of the fourteenth century mention is made of a dozen establishments of secondary instruction. They were generally dependent on a chapter-house, and, as in all the schools of the Middle Ages, instruction was divided into two sections: an art section, or the *trivium*, and a scientific section, or the *quadrivium*. The complete cycle of study comprised grammar, dialectic, rhetoric, music, arithmetic, geometry and astronomy:

> *Gramm* loquitur, *Dia* verba docet, *Rhet* verba colorat,
> *Mus* canit, *Ar* numerat, *Geo* ponderat, *Ast* colit astra.[1]

In these schools the masters attached most importance to the teaching of grammar, on which subject such scholars as Évrard de Béthune and Michel de Marbais had written noteworthy treatises. At the termination of their studies young men were capable of writing Latin and of reading the language fluently. No mention is made of Greek: an omission which was not destined to be rectified much before the sixteenth century.

Fees were charged at these schools, so probably the wealthy Hinckaert personally supplied his nephew with the money required by the regulations. Consequently it was to this generous relative that Ruysbroeck was indebted for the solid basis of instruction manifest in the whole of his work. It is not definitely known if Ruysbroeck pursued his studies beyond the secondary stage. At that period Belgium was not supplied with those great universities which contributed to the renown of France, Italy and England. Young men desirous of studying theology or law had to leave the country, to betake themselves to Oxford, to Bologna, or to Paris.

It is possible—and even probable—that Ruysbroeck at Cologne became acquainted with the teaching of Meister Eckhart, and was initiated, also at Cologne, into the scholastic

---

[1] On the origin of this classification compare Hauréau, *La Philosophie scolastique*, Paris, 1850, t. I. pp. 19 ss. It probably dates back to Plato and Aristotle. Philo was acquainted with it, as was Saint Augustine. But the true theorist of this classification appears to be Martianus Capella in his *Satyricon, sive de Nuptiis inter Philologiam et Mercurium et de Septem artibus liberalibus.*

methods of Albertus Magnus. All the same, the biographers say nothing on this point.

But to what extent must we credit their assertions? According to Pomerius and Surius, Ruysbroeck showed no disposition whatsoever for study; his heart was better than his head. He had scarcely any acquaintance, says Pomerius, with the rudiments of grammar. We must seek, he adds, in supernatural instruction for the source of his marvellous knowledge: *non plane acquisita per suam industriam litterali scientia sed potius revelatione divina.*[1] Further on, however, Pomerius seems to amend his judgment. He shows us Ruysbroeck seeking in instruction for a rule of life and not for the realisation of vain ambition.[2] He even notes the progress he has made: *proficiens coram Deo et hominibus.*

It is important to remember the phrase. In the first place, it is traditional for hagiographers to regard their heroes as God-taught.[3] Again, such a presentation of things raises the writings of the saints above all human criticism. We must not forget that the works of Ruysbroeck were early suspected of pantheism. What better answer could be given to such accusations than to prove Ruysbroeck to have had little learning, to have received illumination only from on high? The good Surius himself, with all his pious wonder, gives a hint that Ruysbroeck not only surpassed in knowledge the dialecticians and the philosophers, but also that few of the theologians were capable of understanding his

---

[1] *De Origine . . .,* lib. I. cap. x. This legend has been repeated, unchecked by all the biographers. "He was ignorant," says Dionysius of Chartreux, "and scarcely acquainted with the elements of Latin" (*Serm. I. de conf. non pont.*). Again, "he was illiterate and without education (*illiteratus et idiota*), though after the fashion of the great apostles Peter and John . . . because his sole master was the Holy Spirit" (*Tract. de donis Spir. Sanct.,* ii. a. 13). Trithem calls him "*vir devotus sed parum literatus*" (*de Script. eccles.,* n. 672, édit. Fabric., p. 156); Valère André: "*vir divinae contemplationi addictissimus et sanctitatis majoris quam doctrinae*" (*Bibl. Belg.,* Lovanii, 1643, p. 555). It is astonishing to find such men as Altmeyer, Schmidt, Jundt, Bonet-Maury and J. Fabre accepting this judgment unchecked.

[2] *More beati Benedicti magis divinam sapientiam vita et moribus quam humanam scientiam vacantem honoribus adamavit* (lib. II. cap. ii.).

[3] Compare Thomas de Celano on Saint Francis (II. Vita, 3, 45): *quamvis homo iste beatus nullis fuerit scientiae studiis innutritus.*

works.[1] Here Surius is right, as against Pomerius. Our study of Ruysbroeck's thought will show not only the powerful originality of the thinker, but the many philosophical influences that were brought to bear upon him. We shall see that he has mastered the psychology and the physical sciences of his times, that he has adopted the method of the great Scholastics and the very *schema* of their speculations. He is acquainted with Saint Augustine and Saint Bernard, with Scotus Erigena and Albertus Magnus, and many others. The very close affinity of his doctrine with the system of Meister Eckhart can only be explained by the most singular open-mindedness.

Gerson, the chancellor of the University of Paris, was under no delusion. In the deed of accusation which he drew up against Ruysbroeck's pantheistic ideas, he declares:

It has been said that the man who wrote this book (the third book of *The Spiritual Marriage*) was illiterate and uneducated, and consequently an attempt has been made to regard it as inspired by the Holy Spirit, but the book gives evidence rather of human scholarship than of divine inspiration . . . and the style is somewhat laboured. Besides, in order to deal with such a subject, it is not sufficient to be pious, one must be a scholar.[2]

Lefevre d'Étaples also, in the introduction which precedes the Latin translation of *The Spiritual Marriage*, points to Ruysbroeck's profound knowledge of nature, astronomy, theology and medicine.

It may thus be regarded as historically certain that young Ruysbroeck rapidly and brilliantly assimilated the knowledge of his time. But he also soon discovered the vanity of all this scholastic logomachy (*logicorum fallacias . . . philosophorum vanas industrias*). And so, when his classes had come to an end, he gave up barren disputes about words to devote himself solely to theology, "that divine wisdom," *quae vitam ac mores pie componere docet.*

If we accept the data of Pomerius, Ruysbroeck must then have been about sixteen or seventeen years of age (1307–8). Now a period of silence intervenes. We know

[1] *Vita Rusbrochii*, cap. i.
[2] *Epistola . . . ad fr. Bartholomaeum*, in *Gersonii opera*, i. p. 59.

nothing of that time of intense preparation and of meditation during which he acquires by his own efforts a truth
capable of sustaining him. Reading Pomerius, we have the
feeling that a large blank has here been left in the story of
our hero's life. Did he form one of those bands of students
who went cheerfully each autumn to a famous European
university? History affords no means of answering the
question. None the less is it almost certain that the youthful scholar was very studious and that he had other masters
than those he might find at his uncle's, the canon Hinckaert.
It is likely that he then plunged into the writings of the
great mystics, whose influence is evident in his own work:
Dionysius the Areopagite, Saint Augustine, Gregory the
Great, Saint Bernard and the famous Victorines—Hugues,
Richard and Saint Bonaventura.

IV

Meanwhile the young student's mother came to live in
Brussels. The reputation of the pious and studious youth
had quickly reached the village, making the absence of
so gifted a son all the more intolerable to a mother's
heart.

And so the worthy peasant woman set off for Brussels,
after selling her scanty goods. Her wishes, however, fell foul
of the ecclesiastical rules which forbade a woman to dwell
beneath the same roof as a priest. She had to abandon the
idea of living with her son in the house of canon Hinckaert,
and so retired into a *béguinage*.

*Cum ejus non posset gaudere optato contubernio, statim
accessit ad beghuinagium* [1]: a melancholy phrase through and
through. It is the destiny of mothers to lose their children
more than once. No one like a mother, however, can content
herself with the crumbs of happiness. Deprived of the sweet
daily intimacy for which she had hoped, the good woman

[1] Pomerius, lib. II. cap. ii.

still regarded herself as fortunate in not being removed altogether from her son. Ruysbroeck frequently visited his mother at the *béguinage*. In the secret of her heart she marvelled at the special favours which Heaven was lavishing on the child of her flesh. Doubtless she must have been full of respect for this young scholar, who was still her child though she was making a sacrifice of him to God. And, by a prodigy of love, she succeeded in transmuting into gentleness her original feeling of bitterness: *materna plus viscera confortabat*, says the biographer, *quam si ejus carnali praesentia ad votum fuisset quotidie frequentata.*

Nor may we deny the influence of this feminine tenderness—more pure and disinterested than any other—in the formation of his character. In renouncing love, the saints renounce in particular the tumultuous stirrings of the heart and the sorrows of the flesh. Through the mother, however, they remain in communion with poor sorrow-burdened humanity which must ever be accorded the sweet tenderness of a kiss. We need not wonder at the place a mother holds in the biographies of the saints: Saint Monica, Pica, the mother of Saint Francis, Madame de Boisy, the mother of Saint François de Sales, will live in human memory as long as their sons.

Why is it that we do not value all the wealth of maternal love until it has been taken from us? When the old beguine died a few years afterwards, Ruysbroeck made acquaintance with his first and bitterest grief. Our biographer, who relates only the main lines of his life, insists on telling us that the young orphan did not spend a single day without dwelling in mind upon that cherished memory: *ejus quotidie filialem habens in corde memoriam.* No longer able to render to her any of those innumerable services whereby man imagines he repays the debts of childhood, he now commended his mother to the love and care of divine Pity. Son and mother thus exchanged mysterious visits in the spiritual realms. For it is impossible that those who have faithfully loved each other here below should no longer be anything to each

other once death has separated them. The dead we love
are eternally living.

Ruysbroeck, who probably delighted in meditation and
study, had postponed his priestly ordination beyond the
usual limits. He did not doubt that he was listening to his
mother speaking through that interior voice which re-
proached him for his continual delayings: *O mi fili dilectissime, quam longa adhuc mora temporis superest quousque
efficiaris presbyter!* [1] The image of the well-beloved departed
also appeared to him in his dreams, stimulating and encouraging him.

For some time past he had been assisting his uncle in
the services of the collegiate church. Thus, at least, must we
interpret the remark of Pomerius: *quem tam pro generis
affinitate quam vitae et morum probitate . . . effectum vicarium
ejusdem ecclesiae sanctae Gudilae.* [2] After filling this subordinate post for a few years, Ruysbroeck was ordained priest
in 1317, at the age of twenty-four.

He never received any other ecclesiastical dignity than
that of chaplain. In this capacity he was placed under the
direction of his uncle, Jan Hinckaert, *canonicus minor*, who
in 1328 was raised to be major canon of the fourth prebend
of Sainte-Gudule. [3]

On the morrow of his ordination the new chaplain celebrated mass for the first time.

At the moment his hands held aloft the chalice, a flood
of supernatural joy poured over him. He then knew that
his mother had entered into complete peace.

At a later date, when materialising these wholly interior
impressions, he often told the monks at Groenendael that,
on the day of his first mass, his mother visited him: *personaliter completo officio ipsum visitans.* Her countenance

---

[1] Pomerius, lib. II. cap. iii.
[2] Pomerius, lib. I. cap. x.
[3] We know through Miraeus and Foppens (*Opera diplom.*, t. I. pp. 57, 200) that
there were two chapters at Sainte-Gudule: one of twelve *major* canons, founded
in 1047 by Lambert, Count of Louvain and Brabant, and another of ten *minor*
canons founded by Duke Henri I. in 1226.

shone with joy and gratitude. And this vision clearly expressed that "by virtue of the divine sacrifice he had just offered, God had delivered his mother from purgatory."[1] And so, on the threshold of the new life of activity he was about to take up, Ruysbroeck was greeted with the same smile, the same tender affection, which had watched over his tottering footsteps as a child.

[1] Pomerius, lib. II. cap. iii. It may be that Ruysbroeck was thinking of this touching episode of his interior life when he wrote chapter xliii. of the second book of *The Spiritual Marriage*, on the granting of prayer.

CHAPTER V

BLOEMARDINNE

I

RUYSBROECK was no doubt still living with his uncle when the life of the latter underwent a sudden transformation.

The canon, a pious man, plentifully supplied with material possessions, in all probability conscientiously fulfilled the duties of his office, though without that utter consecration of heart and mind which alone marks the man of God. It was certainly owing to perplexity of soul that he once heard an interior voice saying to him: "Go at once to the church; there you will hear a preacher whose message will strongly move you and direct you along the path of salvation." Hinckaert gave heed to this voice. Hastening to the sacred edifice, he there saw, in the pulpit of Sainte-Gudule, a missionary priest, well known for a certain hesitancy in speaking. No sooner, however, did he perceive Hinckaert, than the preacher felt such a stream of eloquence pouring from his lips as he had never hitherto experienced. Amazed at the prodigy, he brought his sermon to a conclusion with the words: "I believe that this exuberance of speech to which you have listened has been given me because of one in your midst, in order that he may amend his ways and turn to righteousness." Hinckaert, considerably affected, said to himself: "You have spoken the truth. It was the grace of God that summoned me hither and gave you to utter these words, so that I may turn aside from the vanities of the age and secure salvation by changing my mode of life." [1]

From that day onward, the canon used his best endea-

[1] Pomerius, lib. I. cap. viii.

vours to lay aside the old Adam. So great was the change in him that this conversion speedily became, throughout the chapter, a potent germ of sanctification. Quite a number of priests and canons, some from *amour-propre* and others in a spirit of penance, also turned to the service of God alone. The one who most powerfully felt the contagion of example was a certain Franco de Coudenberg (*de Frigido-monte*), *famosus clericus, magister in artibus et ejusdem ecclesiae minor canonicus, dives proprio patrimonio, magnaeque reputationis et famae in populo.*[1]

The Groenendael *Nécrologe*, in which his death is registered *ad diem V Idus Julii anno Domini, MCCCLXXXVI.*, confirms the judgment of Pomerius. Such was the influence of Coudenberg, it is said, that neither the bishop of Cambrai, nor the duke of Brabant, nor the town of Brussels, undertook anything without previously consulting him. His moral guarantee alone ensured the due execution of wills and testaments.

A common desire for perfection so firmly united Hinckaert and Coudenberg that they set up house together under the same roof and distributed their goods to the poor, retaining for themselves only the bare necessaries of life.[2] Along with Ruysbroeck the two canons formed a veritable mystical association (*perfecto ternario*) in which the vocation of the young priest became very pronounced.

We can easily deduce the nature of this nucleus of spiritual life from the naïve expressions of the biographer: a house built on love and faith, enveloped in an atmosphere of humility and renunciation; in very truth, a laboratory of sanctity.

Even those who served participated in this general spirit of devotion. Pomerius complacently tells us of an aged domestic who, in a spirit of mortification, wore a dress of thin fustian, winter and summer alike. Whenever the wind

---

[1] Pomerius, lib. I. cap. ix.

[2] *Quidquid ultra sobrium victum et vestitum eis supererat liberaliter pauperibus erogarunt.* Pomerius, lib. I. cap. ix.

was too icy cold, she made for herself a *cilice* of plaited hay, or of some other material that was unpleasant to the skin (*corporis afflictiva*). Such piety did not fail to exasperate the eternal enemy of the human race. He tortured her in every possible way, especially with terrible and repulsive visions, though without being able to lead astray the humble *ancilla, confidens in Domino qui non derelinquit sperantes in se.*[1]

Ruysbroeck's experiences in such an environment were of a precise and definite character. In the person of his commensals he saw something of the beauty, the simplicity and heroism of the religious life. The flesh counted for nothing, and, in the subjection of the lower nature, the spirit blossomed forth magnificently. God spoke to him, not in the solitude of the desert, but through the voices of his friends. And doubtless their attention and care for this debutant in the mystic life prevented those gropings and hesitations, even those lapses from grace, that most great saints lament.

He endeavoured [says Surius[2]] to resemble Christ in his humility; he even showed this in his modest and reserved deportment and in his dress, about which he troubled so little that he appeared to all as a despicable and poverty-stricken creature.

Still, he did not give himself up wholly to the placid joys of solitary contemplation; he established a just balance between the peace of the cell and outside affairs (*forinsecas occupationes*).

While daily drawing upon the springs of the mystic life, he took an active part in the doings of the times. His books, indicative of a psychology of no ordinary type, prove that he shared in the warfare of ideas and of human life more than his biographer is willing to relate. Renown does not often seek out men, they must go to meet it. Several episodes, indeed, make it evident that the young priest soon became known to the masses.

One day, it is said, as he was walking the streets of Brussels absorbed in thought, some passers-by recognised

[1] Pomerius, lib. I. cap. xi., xii.   [2] *Vita Rusbrochii,* cap. iii.

BLOEMARDINNE 75

him and were struck by the simplicity of his bearing and of
his appearance. "How I should love to be as holy as this
priest now passing!" exclaimed one of them. "As for myself,"
answered his companion, "I would not change places with
him for all the gold in the world. What pleasure can one
find in such a state?" The saint, who chanced to hear
these words, said: "Oh! how little you know the delight
experienced by those who know something of the spirit
of God!" [1]

The soul, indeed, reveals itself in the countenance; and
the interior life radiates without, like the light of a night-lamp
through the translucent porcelain. Men are not for long
deceived as to real personality; tone of voice, rhythm of
gait and assurance of look express more than words. Gérald
Naghel has also borne witness to the extraordinary impression made by the chaplain of Sainte-Gudule:

> What edifying things might be written of him; one might speak of his
> serene joyful face, his humble benevolent speech, his external aspect of
> spirituality, his truly religious deportment, as expressed both in his
> raiment and in his every action.[2]

II

As we have seen, these were strangely troublous times.
Social tendencies, repressions accompanied with bloodshed,
and religious outbursts, kept Brussels in a state of continual
excitement. The artisans' revolt, brutally strangled in 1306,
had left behind in the heart of the conquered a tenacious
hatred which took advantage of every opportunity of
manifesting itself.

Large numbers of Beghards continually streamed from
Germany into Belgium, carrying everywhere the germs of
a pantheistic heresy. The people violently sided with these
pious tramps who seemed to be the genuine representatives
of the Gospel spirit.

No wonder, then, that we find, springing up with renewed

[1] Pomerius, lib. II. cap. iv.; Surius, cap. iii.
[2] *Prologue*, in De Vreese, *Bijdragen*, p. 12.

vitality, subversive systems, which from the outset may be connected with Marguerite Porrette, whose ideas continued quietly to make headway. Heresy, generally kept in check within the human consciousness, periodically acquires an increase of expression: real outbursts are related to have taken place in 1307 and 1316, and again between 1330 and 1335. It is to this latter manifestation that Pomerius alludes in chapter v. of his biography: *quomodo occultam haeresim et ejus fautricem dictam vulgariter Bloemardinne in oppido Bruxellensi famosam confutavit* (Ruusbroec).

This remark of Pomerius is the only document we possess regarding the prophetess. Is it possible to throw any light on the mystery shrouding her personality?

Let us first see what Pomerius says.

In Brussels, at the time when Ruysbroeck was a lay-priest, there lived a heretic (*mulier quaedam perversi dogmatis*) who was commonly called Bloemardinne.[1] Such was the fame of this woman that two seraphim were reported to accompany her whenever she appeared before the altar to receive the Communion. She had written numerous works *de spiritu libertatis*, in which she extolled seraphic love (*nefandissimo amore venereo quem et seraphicum appellabat*). Her doctrine had attracted numerous disciples. When teaching or writing she would sit on a silver seat. It was reported that this seat was offered, after her death, as a venerable relic, to the duchess of Brabant. When news of her death got abroad, numbers of the maimed and the halt drew near her bed, hoping to be healed by touching her dead body.

I affirm [adds Pomerius], from personal experience, that the writings of Bloemardinne, though excessively baleful, have such an aspect of truth and piety that no one could perceive in them any seed of heresy unless he receives help or special gifts from Him who teaches all truth.

Bloemardinne disappears after 1335. According to two valuable witnesses, however,[2] her doctrine is again to the

---

[1] Mastelinus (*Necrologium*, cap. vi. p. 91) assigns 1305–9 as the date of Bloemardinne's propaganda. This is evidently an error. Ruysbroeck was then no more than from twelve to sixteen years of age.

[2] Mastelinus (*Necrologium*, cap. vi.); Latomus and Hoybergius (*Corsendonca*, p. 84).

fore at the beginning of the fifteenth century. It is then called the sect of the Men of Intelligence, with Gilles le Chantre and Guillaume de Hildernissen at its head. The bishop of Cambrai, Pierre d'Ailly, delegated Hendrick Selle, the inquisitor, to exterminate the sectarians. Caught in an ambush, the inquisitor escaped only by flight. The trial of the Men of Intelligence was heard in 1411 by Pierre d'Ailly, and ended in the abjuration of Guillaume, who was condemned to perpetual detention in a convent.

This, in brief, is all that is known regarding Bloemardinne and her influence.

Who, in reality, is this mysterious prophetess?

Are we to identify her with Marie de Valenciennes of whom Gerson speaks? Reflecting on the danger of spiritual intimacy between the sexes, Gerson says:

In particular, Marie de Valenciennes must be avoided, for she applies to the burning passions of her soul things that relate to divine powers; she claims that he who attains to the perfection of divine love is liberated from all observance of law. . . . This woman, with incredible subtility, has written a book on the love of God.

In effect, the identity of doctrine between Bloemardinne and Marie de Valenciennes is very striking. Chronology, however, will not permit us to identify the two heretics. Gerson speaks of Marie as of a contemporary; now, the chancellor of Paris could not have written previous to 1390.

Two Belgian historians, Ruelens and P. Fredericq, think they recognise in Bloemardinne the poetess sister Hadewijck, who is generally regarded as a nun of the thirteenth century.[1]

The poetess calls herself Hadewijsk, Haywigis, Haywige, or Haduw. Now, the archives of the Brussels hospices mention between the years 1305-35 a certain *Domicella Heilwigis dicta Blommardinne*, daughter of *Wilhelmus, dictus Bloemart*. Still, the similarity of sound between Haywigis and Heilwigis would not, of itself alone, have been a sufficient argument

[1] Her works have been published in the collection of the Maatschappij der Vlaamsche Bibliophilen, the poetry (*ritmata*) by Heeremans and Ledeganck, 1875; the prose (*epistolae, visiones*) by J. Vercouillie, 1895.

to carry conviction. What causes Ruelens and Fredericq to identify the poetess and the heretic is the doctrine of sister Hadewijck herself, whose orthodoxy had hitherto seemed unassailable. Her sole theme, which she treats with unparalleled poetical ability, is the celebration of divine love to which she summons her co-religionists. Without proceeding to the extremes of which the Beghards and the brethren of the Holy Spirit are accused, this love nevertheless has a strict correlation with physical love; and sister Hadewijck expresses it in realism which is, at all events, daring.[1] She complacently describes her visions; they are always accompanied with physical suffering and with loss of consciousness. She calls her own her friends or the new (*die nuwe*), in opposition to the uninitiated, the strangers (*vremde*) or the old (*die oude*). She declares that love takes the place of all church services,[2] that she performs miracles and has received the gift of prophecy,[3] that she has raised the dead to life,[4] and that she has seen Christ himself come down from the altar to administer to her Communion with his own hand.[5]

The affinity of these passages with what we know of the doctrine of Bloemardinne does not appear of such a nature as to induce us to agree with Ruelens and Fredericq. We would advance a few objections to the reasoning of the two learned historians.

First, sister Hadewijck in all her works repeats the expression of her submission to the Church. She explicitly declares that Love must be served:

met woorden en werken
ende metter wet der Heileger Kerke.[6]

According to her own statements her partisans must have been very few: in the Duchy of Brabant the total

[1] Compare what she says of the kiss in her *Twee-vormich tractaetken*, in *Opera*, t. II. pp. 190–3.
[2] *Opera*, I., Gedichten, p. 209.   [3] *Opera*, II., Proza, p. 179.
[4] *Ibid.*, pp. 178, 195.   [5] *Ibid.*, p. 156.
[6] *Opera*, I., Gedichten, p. 190. Cf. also p. 72: *Wat ons orcondet de Heileghe Kerke,—hare meere, hare minderen, hare papen, hare klerke,—dat Minne es van den hoochste werken —ende edelst bi naturen.*

amounted to forty-three men, six maidens and six widows.[1]

But what is more important, we find in the work of Hadewijck a chronological argument which does not allow us to go farther back than the thirteenth century. In the fourteenth vision[2] Hadewijck gives a list of the *perfecti* who have attained to true love: *dit sijn die volmaecte, ghecleedt ghelijc Minnen, die Hadewich sach, elc met sinen seraphinnen.* Amongst the dead she names *Saint* Bernard, whose canonisation dates back to 1174, and she ends the list of deceased *perfecti* with "une béguine que *maître Robert* fit périr à cause de son amour parfait." Here reference is undoubtedly made to the Dominican Robert, surnamed le Bougre, a former Patarin, a grand inquisitor who entered upon his duties in 1233 and covered Flanders and Cambrai with stakes and funeral piles. Immediately after the mention of the ill-fated victim of Robert le Bougre, Hadewijck passes to the living *perfecti*. We know from another quarter that at the time when Thomas de Cantimpré ended his *Abeilles mystiques* (1262) Hadewijck was still living.[3]

Finally, the following argument seems to be of value. The writings of sister Hadewijck were certainly drawn upon by Ruysbroeck.[4] If sister Hadewijck is identical with Bloemardinne, can it be admitted that Ruysbroeck was inspired by the very person whose vigorous opponent he was? To ask the question is to answer it.

Still, would it not be possible to identify the heretic with the *Domicella Heilwigis dicta Blommardinne* mentioned in the archives of the Brussels hospices? Van Mierlo, impelled both by chronological reasons and by internal evidence, is tempted to do this. According to official documents this *domicella* was very wealthy, a fact which agrees with what Pomerius relates of the silver seat on which she sat. The consideration enjoyed by Bloemardinne (*tantae famae et opinionis*) might well extend to the prestige of her fortune. We know that

---

[1] *Opera*, II., *Proza*, pp. 180–8.   [2] *Ibid.*, pp. 183 ss.
[3] Van Mierlo, *Dietsche Warande . . .*, 1920–2, p. 84.   [4] *Ibid.*, p. 103.

Heilwigis bought several houses in Brussels between 1305 and 1306. She lent money to numerous ecclesiastics, including canons of Sainte-Gudule. The archives even mention the case of a certain Corneille Nieneve, a priest, to whom Heilwigis appears to have promised a sum of one hundred Flanders' *livres*. Not having kept her promise, she signed an acknowledgment of this sum in the presence of several witnesses, one of whom was Jan Hinckaert, on the 6th of July 1335. She died in the same year, and in 1336 a portion of her property was sold for the purpose of paying the debt.

We find it difficult to regard these rencontres as more than presumptions. To us the mystery of the personality of Bloemardinne remains unsolved. And we must resignedly content ourselves with the text of Pomerius alone. Moreover, this text is sufficiently explicit to enable us to recognise the doctrine of Bloemardinne as an offshoot from the sect of the Free Spirit. Ruysbroeck, indeed, never quotes the name of Bloemardinne, whereas he distinctly mentions, on several occasions, freedom of spirit (*vriheit des geestes*).

III

In Brussels Ruysbroeck found himself at the very heart of the spiritual uprising that took place in Belgium during the whole of the fourteenth century. While still young, he witnessed religious disturbances, caused in the latter half of the reign of Jean II. (1294–1312) by the masses being permeated with pantheistic ideas and by the more or less open opposition to the ecclesiastical authorities on the part of the Beghards, the Lollards and the beguines.

This uprising for the most part showed itself in serious cruelty practised upon the Jews, whom the people looked upon as responsible for all their troubles. In 1308 the anti-semitic outcry was so violent that the duke had to afford refuge in his castle of Genappe for the wretches who had escaped massacre. These violent scenes were repeated in 1315, because of the high cost of food subsequent on a terrible cattle-plague.

There can be no doubt but that these events, in which human brutality gave itself free play, made a deep impression upon Ruysbroeck. He at once grasped the relation between these disturbances and the spirit of religious individualism which nothing could check. As a result, when he found Bloemardinne making numerous proselytes (*multos haberet aemulos*), Ruysbroeck spoke strongly against the heresy (*illico perversae doctrinae opposuit*). He attacked Bloemardinne and unmasked her writings (*scripta fucata et haeretica . . . denudavit*) without troubling, adds the biographer, about the numerous enemies he made for himself by this opposition. It is likely that the polemic was fierce and ardently prosecuted on both sides. Songs were made up about Ruysbroeck and ridicule was poured on him in the streets of Brussels. Unfortunately the documents relating to this controversy have utterly vanished: both the pamphlets of Bloemardinne and the refutations of Ruysbroeck. This has led to the supposition that Ruysbroeck destroyed both alike. The substance of his replies, however, has passed completely into his polemical writings. There we can find a true account of these jousts in which the spirit of tradition and discipline was matched against individualism and moral anarchy.

The success of Bloemardinne and the sectarians of the Free Spirit was not so much due to the ideas propagated as to the fact that these ideas were presented in the vulgar tongue. It was thus necessary, in order to overcome subversive doctrines, to place within reach of the people the elements of true mysticism without committing oneself to an entirely negative refutation. Such is the character of Ruysbroeck's first works. His polemics are essentially positive: he relies on the attraction of truth to convert the masses, and it is with this end in view that he writes *The Book of the Kingdom of God's Lovers*.[1]

[1] David, t. IV. pp. 125-265: *Dat boec van den Rike der ghelieven*; Surius, pp. 389-430: *Liber insignis cujus titulus est Regnum Dei amantium*.

This work, written after the style of the great Scholastics Saint Thomas and Saint Bonaventura, proves Ruysbroeck already master of his language and of his expository method. The writer chooses from the sacred books a text, the words of which supply him with the main lines of development. Manifestly this process is bound to be subjective. Historical nature of the text, real meaning of words, exegesis: these are largely sacrificed. From the pedagogic point of view, however, this arbitrary division signally aided the memory by linking up the various parts of the book and referring them all to the central idea constantly being brought out by the text. In addition, the better to facilitate memorisation, at the end of the main divisions Ruysbroeck brings together the principal teachings in rhythmic form, which deals first with the positive ideal to be advanced and then with the obstacles, the errors to be avoided.

Here is an instance:

If one would possess the divine gift of knowledge along with all the discretion resulting therefrom,

> There is needed a tranquil spirit,
> One that, spite of tumult,
> Can maintain itself in perfect peace.
> And then ever bear with like dispassion
> Accusation, malediction and lamenting,
> Also the oddities of each man and woman;
> One that can judge all things righteously, etc., etc.

Obstacles, however, arise, preventing the full possession of the gift of knowledge:

> The great desires of virtue
> Without right discretion
> Are opposed to true knowledge.
> To blend disquietude of heart
> With every act of virtue,
> Is to impede discernment . . .
> To esteem oneself greatly
> And tolerate nothing in another
> Is to have no longer any self-knowledge, etc. . . . [1]

[1] Chapter xix. Van Mierlo thinks that the lines which break up the work of Ruysbroeck are due to the first copyist, but he recognises that this is only a personal impression. He cannot believe that a master-writer like Ruysbroeck could have composed such mediocre lines. "This maker of *bouts-rimés*," he says, "makes worse rhyme than a schoolboy of twelve." *Dietsche Warande* . . ., 1901, p. 274.

It will be to the purpose, as regards *The Book of the Kingdom of God's Lovers*, to examine carefully how Ruysbroeck cuts up his text, so as to find in it the main divisions of his task. The text is taken from the book of Solomon, chapter v. verse x.: *Justum deduxit Dominus per vias rectas et ostendit illi regnum Dei.*

(i.) *Dominus* explains the sovereignty of God in creation and incarnation (chapter i.).

(ii.) *Deduxit:* this is the return of the creature, separated from God, by means of the redeeming Christ and the seven sacraments (chapter ii.).

(iii.) *Justum :* by what signs is the righteous man known, and what are his prerogatives in the active life and in the contemplative life? (chapter iii.)

(iv.) *Vias rectas :* what are the true paths the upright man must follow to return to God? This is the whole of human psychology according to scholastic philosophy: the sensible and external path; the path of natural light with the virtues and the higher faculties; in a word, the path supernatural, i.e. the working of the Holy Spirit in the soul through his seven gifts (chapters iv.–xxxvi.).

(v.) *Ostendit regnum Dei.* Ruysbroeck distinguishes five kingdoms: the sensible kingdom or the universe; the natural kingdom, i.e. the universe seen in the light of grace; the kingdom of the Scriptures; the kingdom of grace; and lastly the kingdom which is God himself possessed by superessential contemplation (chapters xxxvii.–xlii.).

From beginning to end the book is a refutation of the false mystics, especially of Bloemardinne and of the supporters of the Free Spirit. Ruysbroeck's intention is to combat dangerous reveries by pointing to the true paths which lead to God. *The Kingdom*, then, is a veritable treatise of mysticism.

All the same, Ruysbroeck was not wholly satisfied with his work; only at a later date did he allow it to be published. At least, this is what the prologue of brother Gérard informs us. After saying that *The Kingdom* was Ruysbroeck's first treatise, Gérard states that he finds certain passages obscure.

I screwed up my courage [he relates], and, with a few of our brothers, we addressed Master Jan, praying him to enlighten us personally regarding certain profound passages we found in his books. Especially in his first work, where he dwells at length on the gift of counsel, there was much to perplex us. Therefore we begged him kindly to help us. In his great goodness and notwithstanding the inconvenience it must have caused him, he walked the five leagues that separated us. . . . When I spoke to him myself of the passages that had proved a stumbling-block . . . he answered with the utmost benevolence. He said he did not know that this book had reached us and that the fact of the work being known was displeasing to him. It was his first book. As a matter of fact, it was a priest—one who had been Master Jan's secretary (*die der Jans notarius gheweest hadde*)— who had secretly brought it to us, so that we might copy it. On hearing this, I proposed to return the book to him. He answered that he would write another book, to explain *The Kingdom*, and in it he would fully express himself and point out the doubtful words. This he did, and it is the fifth book on this list, a book beginning with the words: The Prophet Samuel.[1]

Ruysbroeck, however, did not wait until then before continuing the theme of *The Kingdom* and giving it a more satisfactory form.

Such was the occasion of the appearance of his great work, *The Adornment of the Spiritual Marriage*, written in all probability between the years 1335-40. Regarding this new book, Ruysbroeck declares to Gérard "that he considered it to be sure and good."[2] Like *The Kingdom*, it is a treatise on practical mysticism, though composed after a new plan and a considerably more concise method. Here the guiding text is a sentence taken from the parable of the Wise and Foolish Virgins: *Ecce . . . sponsus venit . . . exite . . . obviam ei* (Matt. xxv. 6). This text Ruysbroeck applies to the spiritual life as subdivided by the Pseudo-Dionysius: the active or beginning life; the intimate or illuminative life; the contemplative or unitive life. To each of these stages correspond the four movements indicated by the text: *ecce* is the vision, the indispensable principle of the spiritual life; *sponsus venit* is the object of the vision, the Christ who comes to meet the human soul into which he

---

[1] *Prologue*, in *Bijdragen* . . ., pp. 12–14.
[2] *Bijdragen* . . ., p. 15: *seide hi dat hi dat hielde over seker ende goet*.

inspires new virtues; *exite* is the determination of the soul which goes to meet the bridegroom; *obviam ei* is the mystic union, the consummation of the spiritual marriage.

The image of the mystic marriage was a frequent theme in the religious literature of the Middle Ages. In 1246 Thomas de Cantimpré made it the *schema* for his biography of Saint Lutgarde de Tongres. But nowhere has the subject been set forth in so harmonious and complete an ensemble as in Ruysbroeck's *chef-d'œuvre*. Böhringer rightly calls it *die Perle seiner Schriften, die kunstreichste mystische Schrift der germanischen Mystik, ein wahrhaft architektonisches Gebäude.* The symmetry of the parts is carefully arranged. The writer begins with a general statement of the main ideas he proposes to develop. Then he condenses and revolves them in his mind until they have yielded all they are capable of giving, to the least details. He never passes on to another division without summing up his conclusions in the previous one, so that the reader is constantly being carried along by the successive concatenation of ideas, without clash or rupture. The result really is, as has been said, a cathedral with broad and spacious arches; not a saint is missing from his niche of gold, and the voice of God alone is heard throughout the immense vaults.

In addition to these two great treatises, Ruysbroeck wrote several other works during his life as a lay-priest.

Let us take first *The Sparkling Stone*. Brother Gérard relates that

Ruysbroeck was one day conversing with a hermit on the spiritual life. Just as they were separating, the hermit earnestly begged him to write down the questions about which they had been speaking, in order that others, as well as himself, might be edified thereby. It was in answer to this request that Master Jan composed this book, which, of itself alone, contains sufficient instruction to lead man to the perfect life.[1]

This treatise is closely connected with *The Adornment of the Spiritual Marriage*, being a continuation of the same teaching. Its composition, however, is somewhat lax, and its development interrupted by frequent interrogations. It

[1] *Prologue*, in *Bijdragen* . . ., pp. 16–17.

may be that these questions form part of the conversation related by brother Gérard. The title is taken from a verse in Saint John's Revelation, chapter ii. verse 17: " To him that overcometh will I give a white stone."

Then comes *The Book of the Four Temptations*, manifestly inspired by the necessities of practical ministry. Ruysbroeck warns the faithful against four errors which appear to have been widespread in his day: the seeking after personal comfort, the pharisaical spirit, pride of intellect and in particular the quietism of the false mystics.

Some there are who think they have reached the highest point in the contemplative life and so despise all interior discipline. Nevertheless, had they passed a single moment in true contemplation, they would have understood that the very angels and saints are eternally engaged in love and desire, in actions of grace and praise, in will and knowledge. God himself is ever at work; without effort no one can attain to a state of beatitude. From neglect of all this comes every departure from freedom of spirit.

This book introduces nothing fresh. The temptations against which Ruysbroeck warns his readers he had already examined at greater length in his first two works. We must therefore look upon this tract as a work of vulgarisation in which our author brings within the reach of the faithful the doctrine he had already set forth in more explicit terms.

Finally we have a small catechism for popular use: *The Treatise of the Christian Faith*. If Christian faith is the only means which the soul possesses of uniting with God, it is important to know it well. It is contained in its entirety in the so-called Apostles' symbol. This tract is a paraphrase of all the articles of the symbol. Certain pages, those dealing with eternal life, for instance, are extremely fine. The list of celestial beatitudes and of infernal penalties forms a veritable anthology.

Gérard de Groote was particularly fond of this little book, which he calls: *ominologium aeternae sapientiae*. In a letter published by De Ram,[1] he expresses himself as

[1] *Bull. de la Commission royale d'Histoire*, II., 3rd series, pp. 106, 108. The same letter, published by Kist and Royaards in *Archief voor kerkgeschiedenis*, t. VIII. p. 255, bears the express mention: *libellum Ruesbroecs de fide*.

follows: *Rogo, gira oculum tuum ad me modicum et lege capitulum de arte moriendi quod habetur in Ominologio (Horologio) aeternae sapientiae. . . . Lege libellum, rogo, Rusebroec, ubi proponuntur tibi a gloria infinita factorum poenaque et mala malorum. Adverte quae poena in videndo, in audiendo, in tangendo in odorando et gustandomalis exhibeatur.*

Thus by his writings did Ruysbroeck enlarge his sphere of influence: *multis in seculo per suae conversationis eminentiam potioris vitae fuisset speculum et exemplar.*[1]

Still, he never allowed himself to become wholly engrossed in outside activities. He continually returned to the sources of his inspiration and questioned his God in the silence, content to repeat afterwards the whisperings of that mysterious voice.

It was soon to lead him to the heights where human speech and clamour die away.

---

[1] Pomerius, lib. II. cap. vi.

CHAPTER VI

CONVERSION

THERE is no writer so disinterested as to prevent something of his soul from appearing in his work, however apparently impersonal it may be. Is not the system of the most detached philosopher, of Spinoza, for instance, more than all else a sort of interior autobiography?

Thus one can only understand a man truly by applying to him the sole method which takes into account the development of life and the evolution of thought: the historical method. It alone is capable of explaining a man by those combinations which, in life, are set up between the various elements that make up a personality.

With an individual like Ruysbroeck, one can determine from childhood the permanent elements of this potent originality: the man is the outcome of the child. In the case of his spiritual development, however, these elements have not remained linked in the same way. For some there have been prolonged outshoots, for others strange retardations, both harmonised by a balanced and thoroughly sound nature. The soul is still the same, though its aspects change, like surface water which reflects the waving foliage of a tree or is suddenly stirred by a dropped stone or by the wing of a bird.

Beneath the outer complexity, therefore, our problem is to find the deep inner harmony between the man and his thought.

And in the solution of this problem the only known quantity that can be taken into consideration is the work itself, interpreted in the light of events.

For this purpose there is no document so important as *The Book of the Spiritual Tabernacle*.

Regarded as isolated and detached from life, this is but a long tiresome allegory, full of extravagant motives, a sort of mystic reverie in which the most extraordinary images and characters chase one another, as in a fevered brain. Related to external circumstances, however, the book becomes clear as a mirror. The symbols resolve themselves into realities, the allegory becomes the docile interpreter of truth. No longer have we a visionary stammering on the threshold of the infinity he has just glimpsed; we are in contact with a man revealing his secret.

I

How did Ruysbroeck come to leave the active ministry and his mission as a reformer and shut himself within the walls of the cloister? The answer is far less simple than Pomerius imagines: *jam dudum in vertice montis positus et radiis divinae contemplationis mirabiliter illustratus.* Here there is something more than the surrender of a soul naturally following the stream: the determination of a mind whose motives remain to be sought.

In our opinion, we shall find these motives concealed beneath the allegorical ornamentation of *The Tabernacle.*

This voluminous treatise is nothing else than a vast glorification of the mystic life within the bosom of the Church. Ruysbroeck may have been inspired by Hugues de Saint-Victor's book, *de Arca Noe morali.* Nevertheless, he treats the subject quite differently, the analogy being based not on the ark of Noah but on the ark of the Covenant.

The spiritual tabernacle is the goal to which the Christian life should tend, a life which Ruysbroeck describes as a race of love (*loep der minnen*), following Saint Paul's expression: "So run, that ye may obtain" (1 Cor. ix. 24). Before making a start, one must fulfil various conditions of a moral and religious order.

Here begins the building of the spiritual temple after the model of the tabernacle built by Moses (Exod. xxv.–xxviii.).

We will not pursue this complicated allegory, so foreign to the mentality of this age. With a profusion of detail Ruysbroeck describes the outer court, a symbol of the moral life in external works, the sacrificial altar, which typifies the sensible unity of the heart (*gevoellijke éénigheid des harten*); he mystically interprets the names of the architect Beleseel as the intellect, and of the joiner Oliab as the will.[1] There is not a detail of the furnishing or of the sacrifice without its mystical signification: the hangings, the columns, the curtain-rings, the six branches of the candlestick and the twelve stones on the high-priest's robe, the spices that make up the holy oil and the various categories of sacrificial beasts. For two hundred pages the parallel is followed without a break. It is also fatiguing for the reader. All the same, some of the pages are very fine. From his well-furnished palette, Ruysbroeck borrows the most dazzling tints, but the ever-changing effects tire the eye with the brilliance of the successive flashes of colour.

Besides, this compact work lacks unity. The thread of the narrative is frequently broken to make room for digressions that have no apparent connection with the subject. One would think the author had, time after time, abandoned his work to take it up at a later date, and then again had left it.

Nevertheless, Ruysbroeck had been careful at the outset to draw up a plan of his book. All this betrays extreme trouble, and the suppressions in the text are no less interesting psychologically than is the work as a whole.

The third degree of the spiritual life is included in the fourth part (ii. pp. 8–20). Instead of describing in the fifth part the holy place and showing that it prefigured the spiritual life in its second stage of development, the author

---

[1] To show Ruysbroeck's fondness for allegory, we will cite only the following incident. Beleseel's grandfather was named Hur, and his father Huri, meaning the grace of God. The Jews aspired after this grace, and this is indicated by the aspirate *H*. The Christians, having found this grace, write simply Uri.

introduces a veritable treatise on the Church and on the lives of ecclesiastics (ii. pp. 21–144). These digressions, devoted to the ideal Church, are full of invective against the disorderly lives of the clergy. It is evident that Ruysbroeck, moved by the profanation of the sanctuary, is here expressing his pain and sorrow. He is confronted with the question as to whether it is possible to find salvation in the Church as it revealed itself to be, faithless, rapacious and immodest. And yet, he adds,

the priesthood must be revered above all existing states in heaven or on earth: whosoever despises the priesthood despises Christ and his Apostles . . . for the loftier the state the deeper the fall; the more honours there are that accompany sin here below, the greater confusion and shame there will be above; the more pleasures and joys there are in this world, the more pains and torments there will be in the next.[1]

Brother Gérard tells us in his Prologue[2] that, when recopying *The Tabernacle*, he omitted everything that dealt with the ecclesiastical life.

Not without reason have I omitted to reproduce Ruysbroeck's account of the state of the holy Church. For he deplored the fact that it had fallen so low and that this fall had continued from its very beginning . . . besides, these invectives will be found in other copies of his book.

To the critic, these digressions, especially the one contained in chapters cxxv. to cxliv., have a greater value than the one dealing with the state of the Church: they are a revelation of unknown suffering, of a real spiritual crisis. From another quarter we know that the book was composed at two different times. Indeed the large manuscript A of Groenendael informs us that *hunc librum edidit Dominus Johannes Ruysbroeck pro magna parte adhuc presbyter secularis existens, residuum autem post ingressum religionis complevit.*

As the taking of the vows is dated the 10th of March 1349, an interval of seven or eight years elapses between the two parts of the book. The break is easily seen, for there is quite a different atmosphere at the end of the work, written in the sheltered peace of Groenendael. The invec-

---

[1] Chapter cxviii. [2] *Bijdragen . . .*, pp. 15–16.

tives certainly belong to the first period. At Groenendael, Ruysbroeck, now appeased, resumed his work and added Parts VI. and VII. He first describes the Holy of Holies, which symbolises the union of the soul with God, realised by adding the graces of God on to the works of man. Finally, in a short chapter (ii. pp. 243–5), Ruysbroeck shows us man peacefully enjoying the fruits of contemplation.

Such is this book which long remained Ruysbroeck's favourite, no doubt because he had put in it so much of himself. Gérard Naghel tells of the extraordinary favour it met with:

> As regards *The Tabernacle*, it speaks for itself; no one in the holy Church, from the Pope down to the humblest worshipper, could read it understandingly without receiving spiritual benefit thereby. Thus does it glorify its author, for it contains several truths grievously forgotten, drawn from the most difficult texts in Scripture, truths which, when they all unite in the soul, form one with it, as the tabernacle formed one with all that it contained.[1]

Some of the manuscripts have incorporated into the text glosses drawn from Flavius Josephus and from the *Historia scholastica* of Petrus Trecensis, alias Comestor. It is possible that Ruysbroeck may have utilised this history, which was famous in the Middle Ages; perhaps he alludes to it when he says: *die meester sprect in der Istorien,* or *Nu vent men in der historien.*[2] But the glosses are certainly not the work of Ruysbroeck. The manuscript D, of 1461, one of considerable authority, does not contain them. Moreover, brother Gérard says that he enriched his transcription of *The Tabernacle* with " glosses borrowed from other doctors, concerning the external form of the tabernacle, not in order to correct the author, but that his intelligent and prudent readers might learn something more." [3]

[1] *Bijdragen* . . ., p. 15.
[2] David, t. II. pp. 56, 100, 134, 148.
[3] *Bijdragen* . . ., p. 15; David, t. I. p. 11; De Vreese, *Biogr. nat.*, col. 532.

II

Can we obtain further light upon the events which drove Ruysbroeck to the cloister?

Pomerius refers to trifling episodes as influencing him. Surius briefly declares that "to devote himself more fully and profoundly to divine contemplation, Ruysbroeck forsook the world, along with a few companions. By divine illumination, he had seen that for him solitude would henceforth be more favourable to contemplation." [1] Gérard Naghel simply mentions his departure from Brussels. [2] Nowhere do the documents speak of a moral crisis, an interior change culminating in a sudden determination.

Though not clearly formulated, however, interior experience does exist; one may read between the lines, and it is possible to reconstitute its main developments.

Still, we must not expect to find here the illumination of a Saint Paul smitten on the road to Damascus, the cries of a Saint Augustine, the vigorous repudiation of the past of a Saint Francis, or the intellectual humiliations of a Pascal. The divine influence upon human souls cannot be referred to a single type, identically reproduced in every case. Only the character of this influence remains permanent: the fact that beneath the varying modalities a *drama* is being enacted.

Whether the soul engages in combat with the evil forces from which it would escape to take refuge in God, or whether it silently questions itself and confronts the ideal with the inadequate reality, a drama is always being enacted. Here it suddenly manifests, borrowing its fire and fury from passion, on which it is dependent. There, on the other hand, it abandons itself to silence, and expands, like subterranean water seeking an outlet. Here the struggle is with the world, the exacting and rebellious flesh. There the fight is confined to the heart and the intellect. But it has justly been

---

[1] *Vita Rusbrochii,* cap. v.   [2] *Bijdragen . . ., p. 8.*

remarked that, in the case of mystics, sudden crises are exceptional.

All, or almost all, have grown up beneath the shadow of the cloisters in which they are mostly to pass their lives; they have, if we may so express it, faith within their very blood. . . . Still, however united their lives, there will some time come a crisis that will tear them from the world, once for all, and fling them upon God, body and soul. This decisive crisis they call their conversion. Some insignificant and generally fortuitous circumstance apparently determines this conversion; really it is the culmination of prolonged interior processes.[1]

This interior leaven is not always perceptible to consciousness; it may rather be said to be connected with the subconscious life. Still, it is invariably a process of organisation. Divided within himself, man seeks after unity. He feels that the inexpressible discomfort from which he suffers is due to disharmony in his interior life. Long does the indecisive wavering *self* suffer and aspire, without yet being capable of self-realisation. During this period the same symptoms are uniformly to be encountered, until peace is established. Then in some we have a sudden irruption of a sense of deliverance (*crisis*), in others a gradual regeneration which may justly be compared to the path of an ascending spiral.

If we enter more fully into this interior process, we notice that the symptoms characterising it, a feeling of depression and imperfection, exaggerated scrupulosity, morbid self-analysis, etc., are due to the unstable centre of gravity of the moral life. In other terms, the group of ideas and feelings that dominate the thought of a man and determine his conduct is displaced. There are thus created what have been called various *fields of consciousness* which sometimes rapidly follow one another, like plates slipped one after another into the frame of a magic-lantern. Man lets himself go and regains possession of himself; it is these continual oscillations that constitute his pain. This suffering will cease only when a fresh centre of gravity has been deter-

[1] De Montmorand, *Psychologie des mystiques catholiques orthodoxes*, Paris, 1920, pp. 12–14.

mined, one towards which will converge all the thoughts, formerly scattered, though now grouped together.

Crystallisation gives the best idea of this grouping: if we plunge a crystal into a solution containing several bodies in process of saturation, from the depths of the solution, by a mysterious attraction, come the molecules of like nature with the crystal to combine with it. The *monoïdeism* of conversion is nothing else than a crystallisation around an ideal of those elements that possess the same tendency. So that we can say with H. Delacroix: "The convert is a man who reorganises his moral life around a new principle; in him there takes place a transformation, a recomposition, a reintegration of the self."[1]

Needless to say, this organisation of the moral life comes about in accordance with different coefficients, represented by environment, atmosphere, temperament. To arrive at the same result, the Catholic will attach greater importance to the efficacy of the sacraments than will the Protestant, who is rather dominated by a sense of sin. The *active* will use mighty efforts of will; the *meditative* will attach greater importance to the process of incubation. But the divers classifications set up by psychologists may all be referred to two quite distinct types: the one wherein conversion possesses the violent and decisive characteristics of a catastrophe; the other wherein regeneration comes about by a lengthy process.

. . . .

This granted once for all, is it possible to say to which of these two types may be referred the conversion of Ruysbroeck? To determine this, let us listen to Ruysbroeck himself:

When the righteous man continues in his poverty, recognising in himself nothingness, wretchedness, impotence; when he perceives himself to be utterly incapable of progress or perseverance; when he counts the multitude of his faults and neglected duties; when he appears to himself

---

[1] *La Religion et la Foi*, p. 331. William James also says: "To say that a man is 'converted' means, in these terms, that religious ideas, previously peripheral in his consciousness, now take a central place, and that religious aims form the habitual centre of his energy." *The Varieties of Religious Experience*, p. 196.

as he is in the reality of his indigence . . . then he knows his own misery. He acknowledges his distress, and exhibits it with groans and moanings before the mercy-seat of God.[1]

Again:

When man considers, in the depths of his nature, with eyes burning with love, the immensity of God and his faithfulness; when he reflects on his essence and his love, his benefits that can add nothing to his happiness; when man, at a subsequent time, has counted how often he has assailed his great and faithful Lord, he turns upon his own being with such indignation and scorn of self that he no longer knows what to do to express his horror. He knows no scorn profound enough to satisfy himself. He feels that the scorn he merits is greater than that of which he thinks. He falls into a strange astonishment, amazement, that he cannot despise himself deeply enough, and he remains undecided before the weakening of his powers. In this state of perplexity, the best thing to do is to complain to his God, his Lord and his friend, of the might of his disdain. . . . Man then resigns himself to the will of God, and, in strictest abnegation, finds true, invincible and perfect peace, the peace that nothing can disturb.[2]

These passages are characteristic. They confirm, as regards Ruysbroeck, the theory maintained by psychologists: that mystics, once their mind is made up, rely upon God for all the interior activity which is to lead them to conversion. They are types of conversion *by self-surrender*, as William James says. They surrender themselves into the hands of God, "like a rag in the mouth of a dog."[3]

This utter self-surrender to God, who, they know, can do that whereof they are incapable, then becomes the propelling idea which, acting by a process of incubation or *unconscious* cerebration, will bring them to that condition of inexpressible relief created by harmonisation of the *self*.[4]

III

It now remains for us to seek in the documents for arguments in support of our theory, to discover, if possible, the influences and interior developments which, in combining, led Ruysbroeck to this state of harmony.

[1] *The Spiritual Marriage*, book I. chapter vi.
[2] *Rusbrock*, by Hello, pp. 97–8. Compare *The Spiritual Marriage*, book I. chapter xiv.
[3] Suso, *L'Exemplaire*, chapter xxii., quoted by Montmorand, *op. cit.*, 16.
[4] Compare the remarkable analysis of Pascal's conversion by Emile Boutroux, *Pascal* (Col. des grands écrivains français), pp. 68 ss.

The disorderly composition of *The Tabernacle*, wherein preoccupations of professional *morale* constitute an ensemble disproportionate to the work and outside the object aimed at; the bitterness of tone, even the sarcasm; the sudden break we thought we could discern in the text itself: all these appear to indicate the line of thought which must have dominated the mind of Ruysbroeck, in Brussels, between the years 1340 and 1343.

We see both scrupulousness and dissatisfaction, the disharmony between the tendencies of the man and the possibilities offered by his environment. On the other hand, we have seen that the controversy between Ruysbroeck and Bloemardinne had not failed to rouse popular animosity against him. For here we must give only a modified credence to the biographer who dithyrambically extols the crushing out of heresy. This latter, on the contrary, by adapting itself to the popular aspirations after independence, daily increased in strength, and aimed at nothing less than the downfall of the ecclesiastical hierarchy. The clergy, discredited by their morals, had nothing to set against these vigorous outpourings of the revolutionary spirit.

Ruysbroeck evidently suffered from an environment ravaged by simony and cupidity, corrupt to the core and devoid of the true spirit of devotion. In mediocre circles, a person is but imperfectly understood; his intentions are suspected and his actions misconstrued by envy or stupidity.

Thus there grew up around Ruysbroeck an atmosphere of concealed hostility; it may be that ambushes were set for him by the less scrupulous. In these conditions, an active ministry must have seemed utterly opposed to the aspirations after spiritual purity that filled his soul.

These sorrows were shared by the other members of the small mystic circle that had collected round the canon, Jan Hinckaert. These pious priests endeavoured worthily to do their work.[1] They suffered, however, from the unedifying

---

[1] *Psalmis et hymnis Domino servientes, omni vigilantia horas canonicas solvere divinisque alacriter interesse satagebant.* Pomerius, lib. I. cap. xiii.

attitude of restless and officious chaplains, who had no respect for the holy place (*capellanorum inquietudines*). The faithful imitated the priests: they did not scruple to continue their disputings and conversations (*secularium strepitus et rumores*) during divine worship. Finally, there was a certain chanter, Godefridus Kerreken, whose common and guttural voice robbed the services of any possible solemnity.[1] This was so pronounced that on more than one occasion the pious celebrants had to break up the service and begin the mass over again in their own homes.[2]

Tired of the struggle (*victi taedio*), after enduring these evils for a number of years the two canons and their chaplain decided to try to find a mode of life more in conformity with their aspirations.

These details, carefully pointed out by Pomerius, indicate the characteristic feature of many mystics: lack of adaptation to their environment. The mystic feels incapable of self-realisation in the world of men.

This is expressed in the discourse—which has come down to us—of Franco de Coudenberg to Jan Hinckaert:

Mi pater, dilectissime et domine, quoniam devotioni nostrae nequimus ad plenum satisfacere, quamdiu fuerimus in hoc seculo : ad satisfaciendum nostro proposito unum videretur multum expediens, ut videlicet seorsum a communi hominum frequentia locum eligamus solitarium, in quo libere et absque scrupulo, juxta ordinis dignitatem, horas quiete solvere, devotioni vacare et conscientiis nostris juxta votorum exigentiam possimus fideliter providere.[3]

But if this discourse really expresses the feelings of the small circle of mystics in Brussels, there are reasons to doubt that it was actually delivered by Franco. At all events, Franco seems to have left Brussels for quite different motives. Indeed, his name appears on the banishment lists signed by Jean III. after the failure of the siege of Tournai (1340). The duke suspected that several of the inhabitants of Brussels had allowed themselves to be bought over by the king of France. On being arrested, they confessed and were con-

---

[1] *Habuit nimirum ipse vocem tubalem rudem et dissonam.*
[2] *Lecta relegere aut seorsum horas suas in privato dicere.*
[3] Pomerius, lib. I. cap. xiv.

demned to death. Franco de Coudenberg, accused though not convicted of treason, was compelled to leave the city.[1] Thus Franco's departure was but a disguised exile.

.   .   .   .

In the heart of the forest of Soignes the dukes of Brabant possessed an old shooting-lodge of Jean II., temporarily conceded to Lambert the hermit[2]: *Groenendael* or the *Vau-vert*.

The Vau-vert had been inhabited by three hermits in succession. The first, Jean des Bois, of the family of the dukes of Brabant, had gone there for penitential reasons at the beginning of the fourteenth century: *ibidem lacrimando pro suis vitiis sese viriliter emendaret.* The princely penitent constructed a primitive retreat, surrounded by a kitchen-garden and defended by fosses. The hermitage was ceded to Jean de Busco or des Bois in 1304, *on the Friday after Assumption*:

> *I quater et mille ter C, tunc floruit ille*
> *qui viridem vallem fundavit ad aethera callem.*

The deed of gift stipulated that, after the death of Busco, the hermitage must be occupied by another religious, *ad serviendum ibi Deo.*[3]

The second hermit, Arnold de Diest, was a holy man to whom numerous miracles were attributed. He lived an ascetic life at Groenendael, eating mouldy bread, drinking beer made of water slightly malted and into which crusts of this bread were dipped.[4] When approaching death, this

[1] Grammaye, *Bruxella*, p. 30; Henne and Wauters, *Hist. de la ville de Bruxelles,* t. I. pp. 105–6; III. p. 536.

[2] Pomerius, lib. I. cap. vii. *In nemore quodam dicta Zonia distante ab oppido Bruxellensi duobus fere milliaribus, vallem arboribus undique consitam et plus ferinis quam humanis usibus frequentatam.*

[3] Miraeus, *Opera diplomatica,* t. II. p. 779: *Nos Joannes . . . Joanni de Buscho eremitae domum nostram sitam in nostro nemore Zoniae in loco dicto Groenendael (gallice Vauvert) et fossatum quod hactenus de licentia nostra ibidem fecit, cum spatio intra fossatum dictum contendo, tenendam quamdiu vixerit conferimus. Ita ut, si eum alibi transferri vel mori contingat, ex tunc in posterum alter religiosus ad serviendum ibi Deo perpetuis temporibus morabitur. — Datum die Veneris post Assumpt. Virg. Mar.* 1304.

[4] Pomerius, lib. I. cap. iv.

pious anchorite had a vision. On being asked if he wished to
be buried at Hoelaert, his parish, he replied:

"No, wrap my body in my cloak and bury it in this cell."
"But this is not consecrated ground, brother Arnold!"
"Within a short time, my dear brethren, this place will be a monastery
in which will dwell devout and religious men who will honour God and
become the fruitful seed of a holy generation." [1]

Ruysbroeck, with the approval of his friends, betook
himself to Lambert, the hermit who had succeeded Arnold,
and begged him to give up the place to them. Lambert
agreed to do so (*cedit Lambertus non coactus sed libere*) and
himself settled down a distance of two leagues away, in the
solitary vale of Botendale.[2]

Permission had also to be obtained from the duke of
Brabant. Accordingly the three friends requested the authorisation of Jean III. to accept the assignment offered them by
Lambert. The deed of surrender of the Vau-vert, on the
territory of Hoelaert, was signed at Brussels on the fourth
day of the Easter festival, 1343, in favour of Franco Frigido
Montanus.[3] In addition to the hermitage, the duke conceded
the large pond close by and some additional land on condition there were erected on the spot a dwelling for five
religious, two of whom at least should be priests (*viventes
religiose*). The deed also stipulated that in the hermitage
there should be held services in honour of God, of Mary, of
the saints and the elect.

Ruysbroeck was now fifty years of age.[4]

Everything being in order, the three friends, followed
by Jean d'Afflighem, the good cook, left Brussels at the
beginning of the spring of 1343.

They were soon overshadowed beneath the lofty foliage
of the forest, as beneath the vaulted arches of a cathedral.

---

[1] Pomerius, lib. I. cap. vi.

[2] Sanderus, *Chorographia sacra Brabantiae*, t. II. p. 17; Pomerius, lib. I.
cap. vii.

[3] *Feria quarta in festis paschalibus anno Domini MCCCXI et III.* Miraeus,
Op. diplom., t. I. p. 781; *De Windesemensi Lateranensi Aroasiensi et aliis con-
gregationibus canonicorum regularium accessit vita et translatio corporis J. Rus-
broquii anno 1622. A. Miraeus publicabat*, cap. i.

[4] He was not sixty, as Pomerius says in error (*sexagenarius*), lib. II. cap. vi.

CHAPTER VII

GROENENDAEL (LE VAU-VERT)

I

THE vale of Groenendael, in which is mirrored a whole chaplet of ponds, lies in the heart of the forest of Soignes. It gathers the running waters from the three valleys tributary to the Yssche.

In the fourteenth century the forest group designated by the term of Zonia or Sonien, relics of the immense coal-bearing forest of primitive times, extended right to the first enceinte of the capital, the spot now occupied by the Place Royale and the Parc de Bruxelles. Even in those days it was an almost impenetrable barrier, an inextricable mass of undergrowth covered chiefly with oaks, beeches and firs; hardy species which found the requisite sap beneath the layer of pebbles washed down by the heavy rains. Except on the rough slopes of the fir-plantations, the soil almost entirely disappeared beneath the towering fern and bracken which still constitute the glory of the old forest.

From the most distant times this group of trees has been designated by various names which evidently have one common root: Sungia, Sonia, Zonia, Sonien. Are we to find here an echo of the solar cult celebrated, as Tacitus thinks, in the Belgian forest: *dicatum soli lucum dicebant?* In the Germanic languages the shining orb of day is, indeed, designated by such words as *sun, son, zon.* It is more likely that the forest obtained its name from the principal river running through it: the Senne, which in a deed of 1179 is called *Sonna.*

The history of the duchy of Brabant is inseparable from

K

the forest of Soignes. In the twelfth century the German suzerains had feoffed it to the dukes of Brabant, who obtained from it the greater part of their revenue. It was also overrun with game and thus a famous hunting-ground.

To preserve and protect their domain, the dukes had created a series of new dignities in favour of the nobility. There was the master of the hounds of Brabant (*opper-jaeger*), the *gruyer* or warren-master (*warant-meester*), the *comte d'eau* (*watergrave*), charged with protecting the fishing, the *comte de plume* (*plumgrave*), whose duty it was to attend to the feathered game. These chief officers, along with their assistants, composed the great ducal hunting-train, instituted at Boitsfort by Jean I., the victor of Woeringen.

The dukes scrupulously preserved the integrity of the forest; to no nobleman did they grant the right to build his dwelling in it. All the same, having respect for the sacred character of the forest, which was said to have been planted by the very hand of God, they willingly conceded to certain religious and monks plots of ground for building their hermitages.

Grammaye asserts that, at the time of Thomas de Cantimpré, the forest depths provided refuge for nearly a thousand anchorites.

When Ruysbroeck set up his hermitage at Vau-vert, there were already three convents in the forest of Soignes: a house of Cistercian nuns, founded in 1201 by Henri Premier, who granted to sister Gisle a site named Pennebeek, to build thereon a monastery in honour of God and of the Virgin; a convent of Benedictine nuns, at Forest, founded by the chevalier Gilbert de Gand and transferred into the forest of Soignes in 1107; and the Val-Duchesne, a cloister of Dominican sisters, the foundation of which in 1262 was due to the generosity of the duchess Aleyde, widow of Henri III. le Débonnaire. In addition to these important buildings were numerous hermitages which subsequently became the priory of Groenendael, the monastery of Rouge-cloître, the convent of Sept-fontaines, etc.

No wonder the forest speedily became the cradle of innumerable pious legends. It was said that Saint Hubert had come there to die, that his fast-closing eyes might gaze upon the sylvan splendour. In the thirteenth century Thomas de Cantimpré told of the benign appearance of Christ to Elisabeth de Gravia.[1] Ruysbroeck was certainly acquainted with this incident, and must frequently have reflected on it when sunk in meditation beneath the murmuring beechgroves.

In Brabant the very devout Elisabeth de Gravia was one day accompanied by another sister of like virtue and devotion, going from Nivelle to Leulos, about two leagues distant. Finding themselves near a wood, and having lost their way, there being no one at hand from whom they might inquire, . . . they began to shed tears. A young man of rarest beauty approaches, greets them and asks where they wish to go. . . . They ask the way to Leulos and he says he will lead them there. They follow him with the utmost joy and gladness, and with such a feeling of reverence that they could not find courage to address him further. Then, when the village came in sight, he suddenly disappeared, and they experienced great regret at not having further questioned this celestial guide. . . .

Such was the refuge which the three friends had chosen for themselves.

No cloister rivals with the open forest, not only for bringing absolute peace and calm to the disillusioned heart, but for looking up to God with eyes that seek him beyond the moving tree-tops. A desert is too empty and its barrenness too oppressive; there, man feels driven back upon himself, confined within his own soul by a scorching and pitiless sky. The God he there discovers has not a smile for him. The cravings of the flesh, too, instead of being appeased, become intensified in that vast solitude, so void of living beings though peopled with visions. The forest is truly religious: its slender shafts, its vaporous mists lying like scarves on the leafy branches, the solemn or plaintive moaning of the breezes, the never-silent hum of a formidable swarm of tiny lives, and the broad patches of daylight made by the sun which stands out in the heavens like some glorious rose-window: all this recalls the sanctuaries of stone whose

[1] *Les Abeilles mystiques*, *trad.* Willaert, 1650, p. 395.

primal motives are here in all their eternal novelty. In the forest the soul springs aloft, as though urged onward by all these up-shooting trees. God appears to it not only with smiling visage but in all his might, which, on stormy nights, bows giant oaks as well as human hearts. Then does man know himself to be feeble and empty-handed, though one with that universal life which throbs with the infinite. He experiences that mysterious sense of brotherhood which unites him with tiny plants and grasses, with the shimmering waters peacefully embedded in the shell-like ponds as innumerable lives lie enfolded within the great All, with the reddish-brown insects scuttling to and fro in the gravel, busy as human beings, and on which the finger of death has already been laid. . . .

It is here that we must look for the secret of Ruysbroeck's meditations; here that he glimpsed, with startling clearness, the vast cycle of creation ever returning to its source and origin.

II

The first thing for the monks to do was to build a chapel. To this object Franco devoted his allodial land and hereditary possessions. After obtaining the consent of Guy de Ventadour, archbishop of Cambrai, the religious set to work with such energy (*agentes viriliter*) that on the 17th of March 1344, the chapel, which possessed two altars, was ready to be consecrated by Matthias, bishop of Trébizonde and suffragan of Cambrai. On the same day Matthias appointed Franco vicar of the new chapel, entrusting to him full control over the monks and the servants.[1]

Our pious anchorites might now hope to devote themselves quietly to a life of contemplation. But they had not

---

[1] Pomerius, lib. I. cap. xv.; *Necrolog. Viridisval.*, fol. 5 v°: *iidemque vicarii eodem anno et die contulerunt Domino Franconi curam fratrum, familiarum et servientium. Praefectus est eis idem Dominus Franco jam dictus in patrem et curatum.*

taken into account the ever-watchful animosity of their former enemies.

The biographer naïvely states: *coepit zizania in agrum Dominicum hostis nequissimus seminare.*[1] The departure of the two canons and their chaplain had deeply perturbed the clergy of Brussels: some approving and the rest blaming the cenobites. There was quite a storm in this small ecclesiastical community: *tempestas valida et vehemens valde.*

All this disturbance excited the monks of the abbey of Saint-Victor. Pierre de Salicibus, their prior, consequently addressed a long letter to the hermits of Groenendael, severely (*non modicum*) reproaching them for living apart from all rules and for not having submitted their association to the approval of the ecclesiastical authority.[2] Lastly, the new congregation, unprovided with any princely or ecclesiastical immunity, was daily disturbed by the duke's huntsmen who carried on "des chasses infernales" in the neighbourhood. There were the barkings of the pack of hounds, the sounding of horns, the demands of hunters for food and drink (*expensas quotidianas*), without mentioning the brutalities (*molestias*) of valets and whippers-in.

Tired and worn out by these difficulties, Franco, *vir prudens et circumspectus*, assembled his friends to deliberate as to the best way of avoiding these disturbances of every kind. The entire difficulty arose from their independent situation. The violence of the huntsmen might any day occasion a conflict, and they would have no protection of any kind. On the other hand, so long as the house was not attached to a regular order, it could not benefit by the fiscal privileges attached to mortmains (*per debitam amortisationem*).

Our religious therefore determined to place themselves under the protection of some old-established order. They

---

[1] Pomerius, lib. I. cap. xvi.

[2] The documents do not agree as to the date of this epistle. The *Necrologium Viridisval.* and Petrus Impens date it as far back as 1365 or 1366. But as the monks placed themselves under rules in 1349, its preparation and publication must be placed previous to that date. Pomerius appears to be quite right in this detail.

chose that of the regular canons of Saint Augustine after consulting with a friend of Franco, Pierre André, at that time bishop of Cambrai.

On the 10th of March 1349, they received the habit of the regular canons from the hands of Pierre André himself: *assumpto habitu Canonicorum Regularium quem idem episcopus eis tradidit, curam mutans in praeposituram.*

Franco was appointed provost, and Ruysbroeck prior. Owing to his advanced age, Hinckaert was enabled to retain his amice and his title as prebendary. While differing from his companions in dress and mode of life, he joined in all their religious practices, preferring, says the biographer, to do penance with his brethren in solitude rather than to return *ad vomitum seculi.*[1] He was with them as a father with his children. But in order not to trouble them, he had built for himself a small hut in the vicinity.

On resuming their regular canons' habit, the recluses, according to brother Gérard, were eight in number, if not more. The small band shortly afterwards had their numbers increased by the addition of a few sympathetic souls, belonging both to the clergy and to the laity.

For his own part, Ruysbroeck would have preferred to remain alone with his two friends. Franco, however, felt urged to bring many souls to God, and so Ruysbroeck humbly yielded to so excellent a reason, for, adds Gérard Naghel, to whom we are indebted for this detail, "he knew that he could attend to things of this world and at the same time find rest in God."

The regularity of their situation soon procured valuable privileges for the new religious, both from the bishop of Cambrai and from the duke of Brabant, *qui sibi eos adoptavit in spirituales dilectos filios.* Death was not long before visiting the peaceful hermitage; aged and infirm, Jan Hinckaert fell asleep on the 18th of May 1350, leaving the monastery not only a blessed memory but an income in perpetuity of twelve florins.[2]

[1] Pomerius, lib. I. cap. xviii.   [2] *Necrologium Viridisval.*, ad 18 Maii.

III

After the death of the aged canon, Franco took over the control of the monastery. Being a man of action rather than of contemplation, it was he who brought the priory into that amazingly flourishing condition which evokes the admiration of the chroniclers. Supervising everything, encouraging the construction of new buildings, stimulating the carpenters at their work, he was the real founder of the splendour of Groenendael.

Ruysbroeck, but little adapted to practical life, gave himself up to meditation. In solitude, writes Pomerius, his youth was renewed as the eagle's, and as the king of the air fixes his gaze upon the sun, so did our mystic fix his ardent gaze upon truth alone.[1]

Far from delighting, however, in selfish contemplation, he was also eager to set an example to the brethren in the various duties of the convent. He found satisfaction for his deep humility by accepting and performing the most repulsive tasks. He loved to wheel away the contents of the dungheap, or to carry them off in a basket slung over his back.[2] In fasting and watching, in manual work of every kind, he surpassed all the rest. Unfortunately his strength was not always equal to his willingness. His candid innocence made him rather a hindrance than a help to the gardener, for, unable to distinguish vegetables from weeds, he rooted up both alike.[3] Such holy simplicity and candour afforded no cause for indulgent smiling on the part of the brethren, but rather one for abasement and humiliation!

When thus working, a halo of divine light enveloped him. Never did he allow himself to be disturbed or diverted from his interior contemplation. He would always toil with one hand whilst telling his beads with the other. Often would

---

[1] Pomerius, lib. II. cap. vi.

[2] *Ibid.*, lib. II. cap. xx.: *portans scilicet fimum cum gerula vel aliqua alia magis vilia ducens humiliter cum moniga.*

[3] Pomerius: *Nimirum qui malas a bonis minus dijudicans, eradicando herbas mortiferas, bonas similiter exterpavit.*

he assure his brethren that it was easier for him to raise his soul to God in contemplation than to raise his hand to his forehead.

It was his great joy to be with the brethren; then he would freely unbosom himself. His piety and his knowledge of things divine would overflow like a generous wine from the goblet into which it has been poured. At times these delightful conversations would last the whole night long, from compline to matins. At other times inspiration proved lacking, whereupon the saint would say, with touching modesty: "My dear children, to-day I have nothing to say to you."

Certain features of his life recall to mind the gentle Saint Francis, who spoke to the birds, or Saint Bernard, who once hid in his cloak a hare that was being hunted.[1] He was so compassionate, says Pomerius, that his love extended not only to reasoning beings but even to suffering beasts. When the north wind was blowing, the brethren, who knew him well, would slily remark: "Father, it is snowing, what will the poor little birds do?" Thereupon his countenance would express real sorrow and chagrin. And he would give to the birds of heaven, in so far as place and time permitted, that whereof they had need.[2]

The grace of God formed his sole adornment. It transfigured with beauty his entire person. He preferred to wear filthy and worn-out garments, being above all solicitous after spiritual ornaments: devotion, patience, obedience.

He endeavoured to celebrate mass every day: it was a keen grief to him when some important reason prevented him from doing so. Such interior gentleness did he experience before the altar that very often he had not sufficient strength to complete the holy sacrifice: *tanta dulcedine est liquefactus ut vivacitas exteriorum sensuum pene deficiens prae dulcore naturae subsidium denegaret.* The assistant, in dismay, would hurry away to look for another priest.[3]

[1] "This love, this knowledge of animals is found in all mystics, and more generally in all saints." Montmorand, *op. cit.*, p. 24.
[2] Pomerius, lib. II. cap. xxi.
[3] *Ibid.*, cap. xxvii.

As age advanced, his eyesight began to fail, and it was difficult for him to distinguish the form of the Host. It occasionally happened that, at the elevation, the image of the Christ was seen by the worshippers upside down, *pedibus sursum et capite deorsum.* As this weakness of sight became more frequent, and as the devout prior one day remained motionless before the altar, utterly unable to move his limbs, the provost forbade him to officiate in future, through fear of a scandal.

"Father, I beseech you," sorrowfully answered Ruysbroeck, "do not on this account prevent me from celebrating the holy sacrifice; this physical infirmity, which appears to you the result of old age, is caused by the merciful plenteousness of grace divine (*non propter senium ; magis est divinae gratiae collatum desuper mihi xenium*). This very day, the Lord Jesus Christ has again come to visit me, filling me with his grace benign and saying to me: 'Thou art mine and I am thine.'" [1]

His patience, too, was as great as his piety. One day, finding himself grievously ill in the infirmary, he requested the brother nursing him to give him drink, to calm his fevered thirst. The sub-prior, on being consulted, refused to allow the drink, dreading lest it might make his condition worse. Although his mouth was quite parched, Ruysbroeck submitted with utmost resignation, *cupiens per bonum obedientiae se Deo magis offerre sacrificium quam carnis concupiscentiae obtemperare.* Shortly afterwards, however, feeling utterly faint, and being more perturbed by the grief his death would have caused than anxious for his own health: "Father prior," he humbly murmured, "unless I drink now, I shall never recover." The prior, affrighted, replied: "Drink, brother; drink as much as you please." [2]

Gérard Naghel relates another instance of the saint's profound obedience and humility. Summoned to spend a few days at the charterhouse of Hérinnes, where the friars desired information on certain passages of *The Kingdom of God's Lovers,* he hurried to the spot.

How much might be told [says Gérard] of his strong, manly face, all lit up with joy, of his speech so meek and affectionate, of the spirituality

[1] Pomerius, lib. II. cap. xxviii. [2] *Ibid.,* cap. xxii.

emanating from his entire person, and of his deeply religious demeanour, even in the way he wore his garments. . . . Though we were eager that he should speak of himself, he would never do so, but contented himself with expounding certain lessons from the holy Epistles. . . . Two or three of us told him that we had assiduously studied and copied out his books; he proved himself as devoid of vainglory as though he had never written them. The three days he spent with us seemed all too short. . . . Consequently we strongly urged him to prolong his stay somewhat. "My dear brethren," he replied, "above all else we must be obedient. I have told my superior, my provost, that I expected to be back on a certain day, whereupon he permitted me to absent myself for that definite length of time. This is why I must leave in good time, to fulfil my vow of obedience." [1]

Such virtue, however, exasperated Satan, ever bent upon preventing the salvation of men. The more successfully the prior's devoted life defeated his ingenious artifices, the more determined did Satan become to persecute the holy man. He tried to affright him by appearing, leaping along the paths, under the form of a hideous toad or some other repulsive creature. But the inventive enemy was unsuccessful, for all his evil devices. When the prior was asked if these apparitions did not terrify him, he simply answered: No. He only felt humiliated by the fact that the diabolical perverter of mankind was thus able to come so near to him. However, he had a presentiment of these attacks, and took care to arm himself against him with spiritual weapons. As he was one night sharing the cell of the provost, the latter heard him exclaim: *Pater, ecce venit, ecce venit.*[2]

Indeed, the holy prior accused himself of affording the devil the opportunity of tormenting him. Pomerius relates one of these incidents, the fault for which Ruysbroeck, with scrupulous conscientiousness, attributed to himself.

It was the custom, in a convent, to read out the anniversaries of the deceased in the chapter-house, each one separately, according to the order in which they were enrolled in the obituary (*divisim*). Certain monks asked permission of the prior to read these services all at one time (*conjunctim*). Absorbed in meditation, Ruysbroeck imprudently

---

[1] *Bijdragen* . . ., pp. 12, 13, 14.   [2] Pomerius, lib. II. cap. xxiv.

acceded to their request. This resulted in the demons visiting him in most terrible fashion.[1]

May this be a lesson to you, monks of the present time [concludes Pomerius]; it is so easy for you to fall into such breaches and infractions. And if sometimes Satan does not chastise you immediately here below, rejoice not on that account; rather dread the stern Judge of all men who punishes all the more severely in proportion to the patience he has exercised.

All the same, God did not abandon his child; amid all his sorrows and trials, he favoured him with ineffable visions. Often did Jesus Christ come to visit him, bestowing signal favours on his faithful servant. One day he appeared visibly before him, surrounded by his mother Mary and all the saints in the heavenly places. The Lord graciously addressed the humble monk: *Tu es filius meus dilectus, in quo mihi bene placui.* After embracing him (*et amplexans eum in brachiis*), he said to his Mother and to the saints: *ecce puer meus electus.*[2]

Thus did the devout prior hold with his Lord mysterious discourse which it is not permitted to man to divulge, but which is manifest in his books. And the *bon cuisinier*, Jan d'Afflighem, asserts that he saw him once raised to such heights of glory that it was not possible for any of his contemporaries to transcend him.

Let us not lay rude hands upon these precious garlands that gather round the biographies of the saints. It may be that psychologists, whose task it is to study exclusively the mechanism of the spiritual life, are right in regarding apparitions, auditory phenomena, etc. as hypnoid states arising from clearly determined causes. Scientifically, supernatural words and visions might be no more than psycho-sensorial hallucinations called forth by "the spontaneous development in consciousness of emotions usually connected with the presence of a being or an object."[3] Of subconscious origin, these hallucinations—in the scientific, the non-popular and pejorative meaning of the word—"differ from hallucinations

---

[1] Pomerius, lib. II. cap. xxv.
[2] *Ibid.*, cap. xxvi.
[3] B. Leroy, *Le Langage*, pp. 199 ss; H. Delacroix, *Études d'histoire et de psychologie du mysticisme*, App. I. p. 440.

of hysterical origin by the fact that they remain concordant with the events of real life."[1] But the explanation of the mechanism in no way changes the intrinsic value of the revelation. This has been well understood and aptly expressed by H. Delacroix when he demonstrates that visions are an exteriorisation of the mystic's own distinctive plans and designs: "Thus does his soul express itself; visions are religious poetry, a stage towards liberation, towards emptiness of mind."[2] In every affective state there is an element which eludes scientific investigation. If this latter could apprehend the mystery in which we are everywhere enveloped, what would remain of the great exaltations of the soul, of prayer, of patriotism, of the sacred pangs that cloud with anguish the brows of the noblest of mankind? Do we not read that

Love is a specific emotive entity, consisting of a more or less permanent variation of the affective and mental state of a subject, on the occasion of the realisation—by the fortuitous exercise of a specialised mental process—of an exclusive and conscious systematisation of his sexual instinct.[3]

Besides, the mystics do not presume on the special favours granted to them, though fully convinced of their reality, any more than Jesus attributed a decisive influence to his miracles or gave them an apologetic value superior to his words and his holy life.[4] These phenomena speak to us of the supremacy of the spiritual life, of an unknown force working within the heart of the believer, they tell of possible union with the infinite, of security and joy.

Ruysbroeck certainly experienced these feelings. Their secret is to be found in the holiness of his life as much as —perhaps more than—in his organism sadly weakened by fasting. Mysticism thus understood, by controlling and directing spiritual forces, rejects religious formalism, the real malady of the spirit. It is a victory, not a defeat. And it remains true, with entire and absolute conviction, in spite

---

[1] De Montmorand, *op. cit.*, p. 135.
[2] *La Religion et la Foi*, p. 272.
[3] G. Danville, *La Psychologie de l'Amour* (Paris, 1919), p. 179.
[4] Sainte Thérèse, *Château*, 6e dem., chap. ix.; Jean de la Croix, *Montée*, lib. II. chaps. viii., xvi.; Saint Ignace.*Acta sanct.*, ad 31 Julii, *Prelimin.*, number 614.

of all mechanistic explanations, that when he raised the cup at the mystic Supper instituted by Jesus, the old prior felt his heart visited and comforted. He felt reassured, strengthened in the darkness of his night. And his deep piety was able to project along his path the mysterious silhouette of that divine Companion who, on the eve of his departure, had promised to leave orphans or comfortless no one of his own.

IV

The sweets of contemplation, however, did not wholly occupy the mind of Ruysbroeck. No sooner was he settled at Groenendael than he took up his pen once more, eager to impart to others somewhat of the spiritual wealth that filled his own soul.

Pomerius relates that the prior wrote only when he felt illumined by divine grace.[1] Then he buried himself in the shadows of the peaceful forest.

It is pleasant to follow our mystic into the heart of some green valley, pulsating with the whirr of thousands of beaten elytra. Emerson's son tells us that his father never had more than one method of working. Every morning he went out into the woods *to listen*. There he would stay for an hour or two, to store up all he had to receive that day. Then he would return home, and transfer to his scrap-book what had been given to him. It was so also with Ruysbroeck. Like a silver mirror exposed to the sun's rays, so did he offer his soul to the illumination of inspiration. He listened to the voice within himself, and things around taught him the same lesson. To him everything was a parable, the transparent symbol of eternal truth. A saxifrage in the anfractuosity of a rock, a tiny insect climbing on to his coarse garment, the golden stamens grouped, like trembling lovers, around the pistil that awaits the moment to open, the mysterious phenomenon of the honeycomb and the great drops of honey falling to the ground with dull thud, the whole

[1] Pomerius, lib. II. cap. xiv.

marvellous and thrilling fairyland of nature appeared before
him as a divine Scripture whose meaning was deciphered by
his own heart. Such deep communion with nature has imparted to every page he wrote a healthy aroma as of
luxuriant undergrowth and ripe strawberries. This sylvan
influence cannot be neglected if we would estimate rightly
the interior life of Ruysbroeck. Far from being the result
of the ramblings of a self-absorbed mind, his books are
the spontaneous outburst of a heart lost in wonder and
poetry and admiration; this it is that, adown the changing
ages, gives them permanent charm.

Let us then listen to what Pomerius tells us of his master,
for penetrating truth can be discerned beneath the naïve
statements of the chronicler. Let us consider Ruysbroeck,
seated on some mossy trunk, and engraving *per clavo* on a
waxen tablet what the Spirit dictated. When evening came,
he returned with the tablet to the monastery, and subsequently developed these brief annotations. Frequently he
would spend whole weeks without writing out his notes,
then, tortured by inspiration, he would resume the interrupted work, "and that with such precision, such a blend
of phrase and idea, that the piecemeal work seemed homogeneous, slowly elaborated in the silence of the cell." [1]

Such appreciation by Pomerius is exaggeratedly lauda-
tory. Gaps in composition are indeed the most pronounced
faults found in most of Ruysbroeck's treatises. The sudden
outbursts of inspiration should themselves be subjected to
the dictates of reason and confined within a very solid mould.
Manifestly such discipline was lacking in our mystic.

Later on, when burdened with years, Ruysbroeck in his
walks took with him a friar whose duty it was to write under
his dictation. The old prior is seated beneath overhanging
foliage. With his right hand he uses a stylus to engrave,
on the tablet lying on his knees, what the Spirit dictates.
Opposite him, seated at a desk, is a youthful dark-haired
monk. Following with his finger the text of a waxen tablet,

[1] Pomerius, lib. II. cap. xiv.

he transcribes on to a sheet of parchment what the old man has just traced.

One day, continues Pomerius, Ruysbroeck, plunged in meditation, forgot the hour for his return. After vainly searching the monastery, the friars began to explore the forest in the dark. One of the monks suddenly noticed a lime-tree enveloped in mysterious light. Making his way towards it, he there found the mystic *in magno fervore divinae dulcedinis sub eadem arbore sedentem.*[1] The miraculous tree became to the monks an object of great veneration. Sanderus sang in verse the glory of the *tilia Rusbrochii.*[2] Even about the year 1500 the religious of Groenendael were well acquainted with it. At that period the prior, Jacques Dynter, had it replaced by another. But when religious strife and war drove the monks from their home (about 1577) the lime-tree began to wither, and did not bloom again until the pious cenobites returned in 1606. In November 1622 the Infanta Isabella caused to be erected beneath its branches a small chapel, with the following inscription:

AETERNO DEO — ET — B. MarIae VIrgInI — LaVre-TANAE — elIsabetha Infans posVIt.[3]

The precious tree seems to have disappeared in the eighteenth century. A Belgian archæologist, however, M. René Stevens, forming his conjectures from an engraving of Lucas Vosterman junior, which appeared in the *Chorographia sacra Brabantiae* of Sanderus, has had the good fortune to find the site of the old chapel of the Infanta on a spot where there happen to be a number of lime-trees. As the lime is not a forest species indigenous to Soignes, and is met with nowhere else in the forest, we may conclude that these are offshoots of the famous tree.[4]

. . . .

[1] Pomerius, lib. I. cap. xv.
[2] *Chorographia sacra Brabantiae*, t. II. p. 29.
  Votum ad Tiliam Rusbrochii,
  . . . Posteritas audi: Tilia est, quae nescia falli,
  Ex jama, judicia relligionis erit . . ., etc.
[3] Wauters, *op. cit.*, t. III. p. 536.
[4] *Annales de la Société d'archéologie de Bruxelles*, t. XXIV. (1910), pp. 27–34.

In this atmosphere of piety and poetry were written *The Seven Cloisters*, *The Mirror* and *The Seven Degrees*.

The book of *The Seven Cloisters* [1] is a treatise on spiritual guidance, addressed to a Clarisse of Brussels, Marguerite de Meerbeke:

> *Lieve suster, boven alle dinc*
> *Si God ghemeint en ghemint.*

After deploring the perversion of the rule, Ruysbroeck deals with the order of the daily occupations of a good nun.

> The rule, alas! is now observed in accordance with the glosses, not with the text. Poverty has become changed into as much opulence, magnificence and comfort as possible. Poverty is indeed extolled in words, but deeds are not in conformity. The spirit of penance and toil has quite languished, for the brothers imagine themselves weak, they desire soothing influences and easy living. Doctrine becomes subtilty, idle questionings and novel discoveries, wherein the honour of God and food for the soul are entirely —or almost—absent. [2]

To keep herself pure, a nun has to create for herself a whole series of cloisters which separate her from the world. Hence the title of the treatise. [3] The work includes a large number of pages deserving of mention: for instance, chapter v., on the nursing of the sick, and chapter xxi., on the evening readings. Ruysbroeck advises the penitent to read three books: the first, which is old, defaced, stained and written in black ink, representing our life of sin; the second, of very white parchment, containing, written in blood, the most innocent life of our Lord Jesus Christ; and finally the third, which is blue and green, with all the characters of fine gold, and representing heavenly life throughout eternity.

The Mirror of Eternal Salvation is also a course of spiritual instruction imparted to a pious soul, perhaps to the Clarisse nun just mentioned. [4] The Brussels MS. Nos. 9320-4, because of its contents, regards it as an *epistola de sacrosancto sacramento altaris*. In effect, a large portion

---

[1] David, t. IV. pp. 63–121: *Dat boec van Seven Sloten*; Surius, pp. 265–82: *De VII Custodiis opusculum longe piissimum.*

[2] Chapter i.

[3] *En hier omme hebbic ghemerct in Sint Claren, die eene beghine was van uwer ordinen, dat si besloten was in VII Sloten.*

[4] And yet the nun to whom Ruysbroeck here addresses himself seems to have just begun her spiritual life: *mer sidi noch novicia* (chapter i.).

of the treatise is devoted to the right attitude and frame of mind to be adopted when approaching the Sacrament. But more than all else the book is an exposition of mystic doctrine. In it Ruysbroeck sums up all his other reflections, dropping details and accessories and retaining essentials. Consequently Van Mierlo does not hesitate to regard *The Mirror* as the author's masterpiece.[1] All the same, this book is far below *The Spiritual Marriage* in architectural construction, and Ruysbroeck is well aware of this, for he says: *En al en bin ic in die materie niet ordelic voertghegaen*, whilst acknowledging that this lack of order is deliberate: "I knew it and did it purposely, whilst waiting for an opportunity to complete what I have omitted."[2]

The Seven Degrees of the Ladder of Love[3] seems also to have been intended for cloistered religious. Certain passages of chapter xii., on the heavenly melodies, may call to mind the *cantersse* Marguerite de Meerbeke; but we have no more precise information. Ruysbroeck borrows the image from the mystic ladder familiar in ascetic literature, from the rule of Saint Benoît, and popularised in the well-known *Scala* of Jean Climaque. Ruysbroeck compares life to a staircase of seven steps, equivalent to the progressive stages which lead to perfection, i.e. the perfectly contemplative life (*een ghewarich scouwende leven*) and a state of not-knowing (*grondeloes niet weten*) which it is difficult to picture to oneself throughout the entangled explanations of our mystic.[4] In the various mystic exercises of the first five degrees Ruysbroeck introduces the celestial hierarchies. But here he abandoned tradition to such an extent that Gérard de Groote hesitated to translate the treatise: *Librum de gradibus teutonicum non optarem publicari nisi quaedam in eo, praecipue de hierarchiis angelorum, essent reformata ; quae aliqualiter ad verba Patrum in latino cum timore reformavi.*[5]

---

[1] Van Mierlo, *Dietsche Warande* . . . (1910), p. 553.   [2] Chapter xxi.
[3] David, t. IV. pp. 1–60: Van VII. *Trappen in den graet der gheesteiker minnen ;* Surius, pp. 282–302: *De Septem gradibus amoris libellus optimus.*
[4] Chapter xiv.   [5] Nolte, *Theol. Quartalschrift* (1870), p. 284.

CHAPTER VIII

THE FOREST MONKS

ANYONE at the present day walking along by the seven beautiful lakes lying hidden in the heart of the *Vallée Verte*, —the surface of the water reflecting the leafy tops of the beech-trees—would seek in vain for the site of the ancient monastery of the canons regular of Saint Augustine. Plunder and fire have left no trace of buildings which, for over three centuries, witnessed the meditations of the forest monks. Nothing could be so desolate as this framework of trees and springs which marks the victorious reconquest that nature has made of the fleeting works of man. The heavy silence of the forest has fallen upon the priestly voices once heard here chanting psalms in the dawn's soft splendour, and again when, in the quiet of evening, the plaints of wood-pigeons and the pulsating throb of innumerable lives were hushed. *Etiam periere ruinae!*

It is just possible that the pilgrim, as he mounts the gentle slopes which rise from the water's edge towards the south-east crest of the vale, may stumble upon a few traces of stone, wholly hidden away beneath grass and fern. These are fragments of the first *enceinte*, ruins of the old red-brick church. Farther on is a vault, fallen into decay. All the same, these débris enable the historian, with the help of old engravings, to fix the site of the famous monastery.

It stood on the slope which now abuts on to the high-road from Mont-Saint-Jean to Malines, and once formed a sort of isosceles triangle, bordered on the north-west by the Vivier which follows the pond of the Patte d'Oie and by the pond of Charles-Quint, south-east by the road and south by the little path of the *Procession* which crosses a grove of resiniferous trees. Standing there, half-way between the Croix-Pay and the Sentier du Curé, it is possible, through a gap in the forest, to see the whole of the ancient domain with the delightful pond of Charles-Quint in the distant background.

It was in such glorious surroundings that the anchorites erected buildings indispensable to life in common. A first view of Groenendael shows that no attention was paid to luxury, to external adornment. In the beginning it was simply a question of sheltering a few poor monks, fifteen at most; and so the most pressing needs were considered first. Sharing out the various duties of carpenter and mason, the monks were not long in surrounding their domain with a wood palisade which protected them from deer and wild boar, as well as from the noisy inroads of the huntsmen. Of wood also were built a humble chapel (*oratorium*) and the monastery properly so called. No doubt this latter, after the fashion of the times, comprised several buildings: the dwelling of the monks, with rooms reserved for a sick-ward, and for a library (*scriptorium*); the *vestiarum*, intended for the arrangement and the repair of clothes; the *cellarium*, which contained the provisions, and where the fruit of the orchard was stored for winter. When Gérard de Groote came to visit the convent, about 1377, the original aspect had scarcely changed at all.

When they arrived at Groenendael [says Thomas à Kempis], Gérard and his companions saw no great luxurious building whatsoever: everywhere marks of that simplicity and humility which were also the characteristics of our heavenly King when he came down to earth.

The sight of this wholly evangelical simplicity made a deep impression on travellers, if we may judge from the letter which Gérard de Groote addressed to Ruysbroeck on his return to Holland: "ardeo adhuc et suspiro vestram praesentiam et de spiritu vestro renovari et inspirari et mihi impertiri." [1]

[1] *Vita Ger. Magn.*, cap. x.

I

Though at the present time we cannot exactly reconstitute the site of the different buildings, we are nevertheless able, thanks to the documents, to obtain a very precise idea of the life of the monks, and of the spirit which prevailed throughout the association. The chief documents are: the Chronicle of the convent of Mont-Sainte-Agnès and that of Thomas à Kempis, the writings of Ruysbroeck and of some of his companions, the letters of Gérard de Groote and the already-mentioned epistle of Pierre de Herenthals, and lastly the rule of Saint Augustine, to which the new monks were subject.

The monastery life being strictly controlled by the Augustinian prescriptions, it is worth while studying this discipline somewhat, and examining the various articles, if we are to obtain a consistent picture of monastic life at Groenendael as a whole.

Scholars are not unanimous as to the origin of the rule of Saint Augustine. It is generally thought that the famous rule was drawn up from a letter addressed in 423 by the bishop of Hippo to nuns who had rebelled against their mother-superior.[1] It might equally well have been taken from the two *Sermones de moribus clericorum* which discuss the same ideas. Nevertheless, the fact that disciplinary prescriptions are, as it were, codified in the letter *ad Moniales* is rather favourable to the first hypothesis. It is the one we adopt.

Saint Augustine had been the one who introduced monastic life into Roman Africa. He had transformed his patrimonial house of Tagaste into a monastery, where he could meditate in the company of Alypius, Evodius and other friends. At Hippo he had founded a community of women, the control of which he had entrusted to his sister. When she died, the sisters rose in revolt against Felicitas, the new superior, and against Rusticus, the almoner. It was on this occasion that Augustine sent them the epistle in question,

---

[1] Epist. CCXI., *ad Moniales* (Migne, *Patr. lat.*, t. XXXIII. col. 960–5).

exhorting them to peace and concord. The tone of the letter is authoritative, almost stern. The great bishop enjoins upon the rebels to conform to a series of prescriptions: *haec sunt quae ut observetis praecipimus in monasterio constitutae.* In his conclusion he specifies that the letter must be read aloud each week, and hints at punishment in cases of delinquency or violation.

Augustine deals minutely with the whole of convent life. One feels that, for him, there are no such things as trifling details: the material and the spiritual are closely inter-blended. And it is just this attention to detail, this *master's eye* everywhere visible, and a profound acquaintance with the human heart which appears from beginning to end of the document, that gave the Augustinian rule so great an influence, and constituted it a model for innumerable religious societies.

Discipline, as conceived by Saint Augustine, is based on the principles of Oriental cenobitism: vow of poverty, vow of obedience, community of possessions, and life in common.

At the outset, Augustine insists on the necessity of perfect union amongst all the sisters. The recruiting of nuns brought to the convent women of different social classes: it is desirable that distinctions be absolutely abolished. To pride oneself on the wealth brought to the community when one enters, or, if one has been disinherited, to rejoice at the prospect of being henceforth sheltered from a precarious existence: these are faults of like gravity. The superior should distribute food and raiment to each sister, not equally, but according to the different needs.

Prayers must be said at the hours appointed, and definite spiritual exercises strictly carried out. At table, attention must be paid to the reading, and, apart from the hours devoted to work or prayer, some book must be read and studied that has been borrowed from the common library.

Without going to the extreme of a debilitating asceticism, great spiritual benefit may be obtained from fasting and from abstinence in eating and drinking: to tame the flesh is to liberate the spirit.

Purity and decency should be evident in deportment, in the manner of arranging the hair, and in dress generally. The nuns may go out, but they should always be three in number. When walking, "if their eyes fall on any one, they ought to be withdrawn immediately."

An entire paragraph is devoted to wardrobe matters: as far as possible, clothes should not become the property of those who wear them. They shall be deposited in the same place always, under the guardianship of a sister specially appointed for the purpose. The sisters shall take care of the garments and shake them regularly, so that they may not become moth-eaten. The clothes shall be washed, though without going to the extreme of too refined a cleanliness: a thing which would entail spiritual defilement.

As regards health, it is bad to make too frequent use of baths. Sisters in good health shall be authorised to take a bath *semel in mense*. One must betake oneself to the bath accompanied by two other nuns, appointed by the superior.

Finally, the relations between the sisters shall be ever inspired by a spirit of gentleness: they shall regard mutual forgiveness as a duty. All must show respect and obedience to the superior.

Such are the main prescriptions of Epistle CCXI. So manifestly did it respond to the needs of convent life that, after the death of Saint Augustine, it became a veritable code which, with certain modifications and adaptations, governed convents and monasteries alike. From the year 426 onwards, the monks of Hadrumetum gave it the authority of law. With certain modifications, we find it in the *Regula ad servos Dei* which Saint Benedict published in his *Codex regularum*.

It was also one of the sources from which Saint Benedict drew inspiration in working out the Benedictine rule, and, about the same period, Saint Césaire of Arles, one of the great regulators of the Church, made use of it in his labours on practical theology.

But it was mainly from the eleventh century that the Augustinian prescriptions were finally set up as convent regulations. In 1067 Gervais, archbishop of Reims, in a charter given for the re-establishment of the abbey Saint-Denys of Reims, stipulated that the canons should conform to the rule of Saint Augustine: *canonicos ibidem ad honorem et laudem Dei constitui Beati Augustini regulam ordinemque profitentes*. From confusion of their rule with the canonical rule of Saint Chrodegang of Metz, arose the institution of canons regular (*canonici regulares*). The canonical rule, set up as a law by order of Louis le Pieux in 816, had indeed been abandoned in the eleventh century. Canons, titularies of seigniorial fiefs, lived in open opposition to all ecclesiastical rule. Such a state of things called for reform, and this was chiefly brought about by Gregory VII., Guillaume de Champeaux, the founder of the School of Saint-Victor, and Saint Norbert. Innocent II., in the council of Latran in 1139, ordered that all canons should submit to the Augustinian rule.

This rule, however, did not follow a single type, as did the other great rules. According to circumstances, it admitted of more or less considerable alleviations. At Saint-Victor, for instance, it was almost as strict as the Benedictine rule: meat was forbidden except for the sick. It was the same in the Ordre des Prémontrés, founded by Saint Norbert in 1120, where the religious inflicted veritable macerations upon themselves. They had to sleep on the hard ground, completely dressed (*caligis calceati*); fasting was obligatory during six months of the year, from the festival of the Sainte-Croix (14th September) until Easter. During this period the sole meal of the religious consisted of two stews or *pulmenta*. Elsewhere, on the other hand, the canons regular could sleep on mattresses, and remove their working clothes for the night. These clothes were strong and warm, including shirt and drawers, as well as pelisse. After matins the religious could return to bed, *recreationis causa*. They devoted the hours of daylight to intellectual tasks or to the practice of their ministry in the vicinity of the monastery (*opus Dei*); but they were forced to devote a few hours per day to manual toil.

II

This information gives us some idea of the life of the new canons at Groenendael. Besides, Ruysbroeck in *The Seven Cloisters* offers us a striking picture of convent life, a reflection of what took place in the heart of the *Vallée Verte*.

First, material life. The resources of the monastery were drawn from regular revenues, such as the money obtained from the sale of chopped wood, and extraordinary receipts from bequests or legacies. At first these bequests were few, though this was compensated by contributions from the novices. It is more than likely that Franco de Coudenberg, a wealthy heir, did not give up all his goods to the poor when he left Brussels, but reserved a portion for the early needs of the association. The dukes of Brabant also, in accordance with custom, certainly allowed the recluses to cut down forest trees and sell them. But it was mainly legacies and contributions that enriched the monastery. Traces of these resources are found throughout the *Nécrologe* of Groenendael. The names of the brothers are almost invariably followed by such mentions as these: *habemus ab eo et per eum circiter C florenos perpetuos; habemus ab eo VII libros Parisienses*, etc.

The dietary of the monks was almost wholly supplied by the produce of garden and orchard. All the monachal rules stipulate that monks must live on the produce of their domain. Old engravings of the convent show us monastery buildings separated by rich orchards, nursery and kitchen gardens parcelled into squares. It is possible that the monks, like their neighbours the Benedictine nuns of Forest, went in for the cultivation of the grape, which proved very successful on the sunlit slopes of the glades. They certainly had a few cows, and flocks of sheep or of goats. In addition, the neighbouring lakes supplied them with fish in abundance.

Manual work was held in great esteem at Groenendael.
"There is no happiness possible without work," Ruysbroeck
was fond of repeating.[1] He attributed like honour to working
tools, the mattock, the trowel, the sickle, as to the sacred
vases, nor did he set himself apart from the common rule.
We hear of him accompanying the brothers to the kitchen
garden, handling the hoe or removing manure.[2] Indeed, the
monks (*patres*) themselves chose, from among the various
manual tasks, those that most especially suited their capacities
or their tastes. The heavy work fell mainly on the lay
brothers or the *fratres conversi*. Employed in menial country
labour, these latter undertook in the monastery the same
kind of work to which they were accustomed in ordinary life.
At a time when the lot of the worker scarcely differed from
that of the serf, entrance upon religious life meant freedom.
Bound down to the vows of chastity and obedience, they
became religious and yet remained workers. This dual condition was apparent even in externals and in dress: instead
of reaching down to the feet, their woollen tunic came only
to the knee; the hood, also, was not so wide. As a rule they
retained the beard intact: for this reason they are designated
in old documents as *barbati* or *conversi laici*.

These humble artisans supplied the monastery with
almost the whole of the necessary handicraft, giving the
association the aspect of a real self-sufficing society. They
were bakers, woodcutters, oxherds, vinedressers, waggoners,
blacksmiths, farm-workers, etc. But they enhanced the dignity
of toil by linking it on to the religious life. Indifferently
educated for the most part, the *fratres conversi* worshipped
God in utter simplicity of heart. Their only obligation was
to know by heart the *Pater*, the *Credo*, the *Miserere mei,
Deus*, and the *Benedicite*. This poverty of spirit, however,
far from checking the spontaneous outbursts of the heart,
favoured that simple piety which is sometimes better

---

[1] *The Four Temptations*, David, t. IV. p. 280: *ende sonder dese werken en
mochten si niet salich syn.* Cf. *The Sparkling Stone*, chapters ix., xi.
[2] Pomerius, lib. II. cap. xx.

informed regarding the final mysteries than the wisdom of the learned. It seemed to these poor *conversi*, whom the monastery had snatched from the wretched world outside and supplied with a haven of peace, that God himself was working by their side, walking close to the plough, appearing to them with renewed glory in the hazy splendour of the dawn when they led out the flocks on to the slopes. It was his face, enveloped in sparks, that shone upon them in the dark cavernous forge.

And on their side, the *conversi* offered up in homage to the Master of life the humblest and most painful tasks, which they never interrupted, except to recite the hours tolled from the monastery bell in the distance. Better than any other could the poor lay brother understand the Gospel text regarding the birds of the air: your heavenly Father feedeth them. In entering the monastery, was he not escaping the brutality of the seignior, the vicissitudes of a precarious existence? Was not peace now assured to him? And so we can understand those sudden joyous impulses which welled up in these simple hearts and sometimes manifested themselves in naïve practices and intemperate words, such as the documents relate.[1]

At Groenendael, the first few years were mainly employed in clearing the soil and making fruitful the land which the duke of Brabant had ceded to the newly-formed association. The assarting of forest-land is extremely laborious. Not only was it necessary to fell gigantic trees, to clear the soil of thorn-bushes, to burn the roots in order to overcome their extraordinary vitality, but also, after this clearing process had been completed, to revivify the soil exhausted by the avidity and greed of age-long forest species. Frequently the soil had to be removed on their backs. The fathers shared with the monks in this laborious task. Nor was it the least instructive of spectacles to see these men, "éminents par leur vie et leur science," masters of arts, important bourgeois or opulent canons, freely devote them-

---

[1] Cf. Pomerius, *op. cit.*, lib. III. cap. xx.

selves to the work of the soil, repair their own raiment or grease their own shoes.

The general control of the work was entrusted to the provost (*praepositus*) appointed by the bishop. This post was first held, as we have seen, by the rich patrician Franco de Coudenberg, who remained in office until his death in 1386. It was the provost's mission to see that the rule was applied, and to treat rigorously any violation of it. As general manager of the community, he attended to the distribution of food and clothes, portioned out daily the various manual tasks, heard complaints and petitions to which he gave a paternal response, seeing to it that there was a general good understanding prevalent.

Immediately below him came the *prior*, whose only duty it was to assist the provost. Except in the case of Ruysbroeck, who had been directly appointed by the bishop of Cambrai, the prior was chosen by the provost after consulting the monks, *per viam scrutinii*.

Another monk undertook the financial administration of the monastery. This was the *cellarius*, or the *refectorarius*, who attended to the preparation of the meals, supervised the fasts, distributed the portions according to the work performed. The *conversi*, who had heavy work outside, had the right every morning to a more plenteous repast, the *mixtum*. The sick, too, profited by the surveillance of the *cellarius*, enjoying a modified regimen. The *pater cellarius* also bought in the needed stores, settled the bills, and was alone privileged to pay the expenses necessitated to keep the monastery in working order.

Subsequently, in addition to these three dignitaries who constituted the original hierarchy, the development of the house necessitated other functionaries (*officiarii*). These were the grand hosteler (*hospitularius*), whose duty it was to welcome travellers or visitors, the father chamberlain (*infirmarius*), the *grand chantre* (*cantor*), the keeper of the wardrobe or the librarian (*armorius, librarius*), the sacristan (*custos sacrarii*), who kept in order the chapel and the various objects of worship, the door-keeper (*portarius*), who, having to open the door to visitors and to receive the poor, had to be chosen from among the monks known for their affability and good temper.

.   .   .   .

Let us now glance at the interior of the monastery, taking for our guide Ruysbroeck, who has left instructions regarding the various occupations that fill up the day.

First of all, the life of a religious should be wholly one of humility, poverty and obedience. "The greatest glory and the highest nobility in the world is the service of God." [1] This service is given in detail in the rule, which must be obeyed absolutely, without seeking such modifications as were desired by many languid monks. After morning prayer, which the monk should say immediately he leaves his bed, the day begins with attendance at mass. The provost then proceeds to the distribution of tasks:

> Take always the humblest and most despised service, whether in kitchen or sick-room. Give order or command to no one who is not appointed to this duty, but always willingly do yourself what is in your power. If you are ordered to perform the humblest service, thank God for it.

Amongst the tasks distributed was that of looking after the sick-room. On this subject Ruysbroeck has written one of his finest pages. [2] He loved and understood the sick. His instructions are still deserving of meditation.

> Serve the sick joyfully, with gentleness and humility and without a murmur. Should they be impatient and hard to please, reflect that you are serving Christ, and show so sweet and loving a countenance that they become ashamed of themselves. . . . The poorer they are, and the fewer their friends, the more eager should you be to serve them. Do not have regard only for the person you serve, but rather see God, for whose sake you serve him. Be very careful not to sadden the patients, to cause them affliction by your deeds, words or attitude. . . . When patients ask for relief, aid must be given them as speedily as possible. But when they ask for that which is neither good nor useful to them . . . act as though you had not heard or understood. Prepare and serve all their food and drink in as cleanly and pleasant a manner as possible, with the object of pleasing them. . . . Make their beds and relieve them as much as you can, according

---

[1] *The Seven Cloisters*, chapter i.   [2] *Ibid.*, chapter v.

to their delicate condition or their greater need. Be so gay and pleasant in your converse with them that each patient is anxious to have you by his side. And do not forget to say comforting words to them as well.[1]

Wherever he be placed, in scullery or sick-room, kitchen or field, the monk should ever rejoice in his task. He should do his work simply and conscientiously, guarding against all pretence.[2] The relations between the religious should always be imbued with a spirit of peace and amiability, free of anything calculated to cause trouble.

Should it happen that someone speaks or acts evilly against you, forgive him immediately in your heart, even though he neither desire nor ask for pardon, and present before him so happy and joyous a countenance that he see cause for self-abasement.[3]

In the refectory,

guard against eating in excess, even though you should feel great hunger, and a great desire to drink or eat. . . . Consider neither your taste, pleasure nor convenience, but rather be content with coarse food and with what others leave.[4] . . . Eat and drink what is given to you. Is it burnt or salted too much, or unpleasant to taste? Reflect that our Lord had gall and vinegar for meat and drink in his greatest sufferings; he held his peace and murmured not.[5]

In the *parloir*, the monk should give proof of the utmost discretion; he should not be affected in dress, neither too careful nor too negligent. He will ask no questions about anything touching the outer world, and will constantly keep his eyes cast down, avoiding more especially the glances of persons of the other sex.[6]

The clothing, in religious orders, is of great importance. It serves not only to protect from cold, but it should also express the spirit of the order. Thus it is entirely symbolic. The religious and his garment form but one, hence the obligation in certain orders, the Cistercians, for instance, to sleep fully dressed. The apparel of the canons regular of Saint Augustine consisted of a broad tunic of white linen symbolising purity (*tunica linea, rochetum, subtile*). This robe or surplice came down to the heels and had wide sleeves. It was shorter for the *conversi* by reason of their occupation,

---

[1] *The Seven Cloisters*, chapter v. [2] *Ibid.*, chapter vii.
[3] *Ibid.*, chapter vii. [4] *Ibid.*, chap. viii.
[5] *Ibid.*, chapter vi. [6] *Ibid.*, chapter ix.

and the sleeves were replaced by wide openings. The tunic of the *conversi* was called *sarracium* or *camisa*. Above the robe the canons wore a full cope of black cloth (*birrus* or *cuculla*), supplied with a hood of the same colour (*caputia*), symbolising death to the world. During the months of summer, from Easter to the middle of September, the monks threw over their shoulders an amice (*almutium*).[1] At first this was a lamb-fleece cape, subsequently reduced to a simple fur, shaped like a mantilla. The lower garments consisted of a second white robe (*tunica superior*), of a rough cloth gown, supplied with sleeves, and reaching the waist (*tunica inferior, interula*), and, for those who wished, of drawers (*femorale*). The foot-gear (*calceamenta, sotularia*) were made of thick black leather, and aimed rather at convenience than at elegance.

In the early days, there was a considerable degree of fancy, even of frivolity and coquetry, in the vestments of the canons. Some adopted red as the colour for the tunic, others violet, the result being that Pope Benedict, in a bull of 1339, had personally to fix the details of the habiliments.

This caused Ruysbroeck to say:

I fear that, as a rule, the religious orders are more anxious and eager to adorn and dress the body externally than the soul internally. This is why I tell you not to concern yourselves at all about the dress you wear. However old or new, coarse or common-looking, content yourselves with what is given to you. If your body is protected against cold and heat, that is sufficient, if you would live in accordance with your rule and remain faithful to God. Be careful, then, not to complain, for, when religious orders were first instituted, the saints always chose the coarsest and commonest cloth, such as they were able to find in the district where they lived, and it was always undyed.[2]

Under such control the monastery rapidly became, for the other religious houses, a model which was all the more admirable from the fact that everywhere else the rule had

---

[1] The etymology of this word is unknown. Jacob Severt (*Chronic. histor. archiep. Lugd.*, p. 432) regards it as derived from *hautement mise*, others refer it to *amicium ab amicine*, the opening of a leathern bottle; and yet others to the German *hooftmutsen*.
[2] *The Seven Cloisters*, chapter xx.

fallen into neglect, and scandalous disorder and licentiousness discredited monastic life in the minds of the people.
"Above all, remain one with the religious of Groenendael,"
writes Gérard de Groote to a friend living near Brussels.
Pierre de Herenthals, who had visited the convent of Groenendael during Ruysbroeck's latter years, communicates as
follows his impressions to Jan de Hollande, a canon regular:

> I have lived for some time in your house, admiring the many and
> wonderful results of the grace of God. . . . I have seen the zeal and solicitude
> of the old for the instruction and sanctification of the novices, the respect
> of the latter for the counsels of the former, the compassion shown to the
> sick, the kind reception accorded to strangers. How promptly and devoutly
> all anticipated one another in serving God! How fervently and obediently
> they united to fulfil the duties of their obligations! One in peace and
> concord, and strengthened by this union, they dreaded neither the ruses
> nor the attacks of their spiritual enemies. . . . Heaven grant that they
> never abandon the rule of life they have embraced and faithfully kept
> up to the present time. . . .[1]

III

Still, the religious of Groenendael were not content merely
to practise the highest Christian virtues and to blend love
of work with contemplation, *in primordiali fervore*. Some of
them, in imitation of their prior, devoted themselves to the
literature of mysticism and acquired a fame to which the
documents render testimony.

We will first mention Guillaume Jordaens, Ruysbroeck's
translator, *vir valde ingeniosus et litteratus*, as Jan Scoonhoven testifies. He was a native of Brussels, where he acquired
all his literary and theological degrees, as we learn from the
list of professed friars of Groenendael, where he is called
magister, clericus sollemnis. He assumed the habit of canon
regular at Groenendael in 1352. He died in 1372, after having
written several works, in addition to the above-mentioned
translations. In the *Nécrologe* of Groenendael we read, *ad diem
IX kl. Decembris: anno Domini MCCCLXXII obiit frater
Wilhelmus Jordani, presbyter. . . . Scripsit enim plura, prae-*

[1] MS. No. 23, Musée archéol. de Namur, fol. 234 ss.; Auger, *Étude* . . ., p. 303.

cipue unum integrum antiphonarium in duobus voluminibus.
He also composed the funeral eulogium on a monk who died
in 1358, Jan de Cureghem: *Planctus super obitu fratris
Johannis de Speculo, alias de Cureghem.* Regarding this
funeral eulogium, the *Nécrologe* says: *hujus vitam virtutibus
plenam frater W. Jordani curioso style neque minus veraci
compendioseque depinxit.*

Jean Stevens, born at Louvain in the early years of the
century, composed a number of pious addresses which he
put in writing under the name of *Exhortationes*, and a
small treatise on mysticism, *Ornamentum Virginum*, also
in manuscript.

In 1377 there came to the monastery a young priest,
without any literary qualification (*magister in artibus*), who,
through his writings, was destined to add largely to the
renown of the establishment. His name was Joannes Theo-
derici de Schoonhovia. He died at Groenendael in 1431,
anno suae professionis LIII°. The *Nécrologe* which mentions
his death, *ad XI Kal. Feb.*, relates the following strange
peculiarity about him: *hic tam fervens et sedulus extitit in
divino officio ut, quamvis multis annis in tantum pateretur
caninum appetitum quod crebro in cella et in choro comedere
cogeretur, tamen vix unquam a choro vel a sacrificio missae
abstineret.*

Jan de Scoonhoven is chiefly known for his polemic with
Gerson, who had accused Ruysbroeck of dabbling in pantheism. His literary work, however, is not confined to this
epistola de unione animae. The *Nécrologe* of Groenendael in
1381 mentions his biography of Ruysbroeck, which was
early lost, for no further mention is made of it. The monk
who drew up the funeral notice of Scoonhoven in 1431 does
not know of it. No trace is found, either, in the large
Brussels MS. No. 15129 which contains the works of Scoonhoven, or in the list of Mastelinus. This list mentions a
tractatus de contemptu mundi, and a *tractatus de passione
Domini, alius tractatus de Ecclesiae Sacramentis.*

Particularly gifted in the art of oratory, Scoonhoven

composed a large number of addresses (*collationes*) and sermons. In 1413, when Groenendael was again united to the chapter of Windesheim, Scoonhoven delivered an important sermon in Latin on the text: *et fiet unum ovile et unus pastor*. Amongst his other speeches, contemporaries praise two sermons in the patois of Brabant, delivered at Windesheim, one on the text: *venite ascendamus ad montem Domini, coemt, laet ons opclimmen*, the other on: *nos autem gloriari oportet, ons behoert te glorieeren*.

.   .   .   .

But of all the brothers who joined Ruysbroeck, not one was more greatly loved or revered than the humble cook of the monastery, Jean de Louvain or d'Afflighem, surnamed *bonus cocus* by reason of his piety and his amiability.

A very touching figure was that of this poor lay brother who, in imitation of Saint Francis, had indeed espoused the lady Poverty. Pomerius, eager to keep alive the glories of the monastery, devoted a whole book to him.[1]

Already attached to Ruysbroeck's person in Brussels, he had followed his master as a *frater conversus* to the monastery of Groenendael, where he made such progress in holiness, says Pomerius, that in his age there was no other man so humble, so devoid of self-consideration and so evidently imbued with divine grace.

Tall and robust, he looked like a lion. His duty was to attend to the material wants of the little congregation, though this did not prevent him from outstripping all the other brothers as regards fasts, vigils and other macerations of the body. He carried out his task with such eagerness for perfection, without ever giving way to an impulse of ill-temper or fatigue, that the brothers had of one accord called him *bonus cocus*. He also carried on the duties of hospitaller, welcoming everyone — *sive nobilis sive ignobilis* — with a smiling geniality as warm as the sun that shone upon the

[1] *De origine monast. Viridis Vallis, liber tertius De Vita frat. Johannis de Leuwis alias dicti de Affliginio, boni coqui Viridis vallis*, pp. 308 ss.

M

Vallée Verte. After conducting the guests into the chapel, he prepared for them a kind of meat-bread (*offa*), and served them himself, *laeta facie, benigno vultu alacrique animo,* being desirous alike to comfort them physically and to gladden them spiritually. This holy man, who was capable of submitting to the greatest of privations, was yet not ignorant of the joys of a well-spread table. And he paid as much attention to the management of his kitchen-range as to the discipline of his soul. Accordingly his kitchen was famous for miles around, and probably more than one knocked at the monastery door for motives less noble than might have been desired.

This human note is not out of place in the biography. It is pleasant to find Pomerius mentioning, in the same rank as his works on mysticism, a *cibum sapidissimum.* The biographer hastens to add that the visitors attached greater importance to the spiritual example given them by Jean de Louvain than to his culinary preparations.[1] In any case, let us be thankful that he did not scorn earthly delights for the other monks, and that he remembered that his Master gladly sat down at the marriage-table of Cana. Let us be even more grateful to him for not forgetting that man does not live by bread alone, and, whilst the pilgrim was recuperating, for conversing with him about the deep realities of the spirit.[2]

As for himself, completely weaned from mundane affairs and from the concerns of the flesh, the only clothes he would wear were of coarse material and practically threadbare.[3] Pomerius dwells on this characteristic with complaisant admiration: even going so far as to break out into lyrical exaltation regarding the sordid *tunica* of the good friar. Soiled with grease and black with soot (*fuliginosa pinguidine*), impregnated with every kind of sauce (*imbibita*), it was a

---

[1] Pomerius, *op. cit.,* lib. III. cap.: v. . . . *plus interdum venire cupiebant ad monasterium Viridis vallis pro spirituali refectione boni coqui, quam pro delectatione sui prandii.*

[2] *Ibid.,* cap. v.

[3] *Ibid.,* cap. vi.

kind of symbol of his detachment from earth and his scorn
of it. The religious made great sport of this tunic, for a certain
sly humour is not inconsistent with holiness. A brother from
the neighbouring convent of Rouge-Cloître, on a visit to
Groenendael, regarded with frank irony the *vestes coqui viles
et sordidas*. Then he jestingly asked: *Frater Johannes, cujus
coloris est tunica tua?* And the biographer adds: *at ille, magis
cultus interius, exterioris coloris omnino nescius, respodit
humiliter se nescire*.[1] There was the same detachment regarding food. The good cook, while fond of making savoury
dishes for his guests, made it a law unto himself never to
touch them. The fragments that remained were sufficient
for him, and we are told that he carried the spirit of abnegation so far as to eat rotten eggs which no one in the refectory
would touch.[2]

The only sign of vanity he ever showed referred to his
lameness, but he concealed this infirmity so well that the
monks did not notice it until his death.[3] Always occupied,
either in his kitchen or at some pious exercise, he scarcely
ever allowed himself time for rest. He regarded time spent
in sleep as time wasted; frequently he lay down to sleep
only after reciting matins.[4] In imitation of the prior, he had
acquired the art of working whilst sunk in contemplation;
his mind was constantly meditating on the Passion; on more
than one occasion, as he mentally associated himself with
the stations of the *via dolorosa*, he was caught up into a
state of ecstasy.[5] Nevertheless, in order that the mystic
might not pride himself on his visions, God sent him great
trials, hellish sufferings, says Pomerius (*septem angustiae
infernales*), which, for our edification, the biographer describes
at considerable length.[6]

His submission to the will of God was an example for
the whole monastery. On one occasion, during a time of
grave epidemic, the good cook, who was one of the victims,
asked that he might receive the Communion. But as he was

[1] Pomerius, *op. cit.*, lib. III. cap. xv.   [2] *Ibid.*, cap. vi.
[3] *Ibid.*, cap. xix.   [4] *Ibid.*, cap. vii.
[5] *Ibid.*, cap. ix.   [6] *Ibid.*, caps. xii., xiii., xiv.

unable to swallow the whole of the host, he began to exclaim: *Domine, ad tuum perpetuum honorem! Domine, ad tuum perpetuum honorem!* To the amazed monks who asked for an explanation, he replied that, if it had been necessary that he were to die in a state of defilement, he accepted this damnation, should such be God's will: *Domine, ad honorem tuum volo etiam damnari.*[1] Such humility met with its reward, for the divine voice said to him: *nunc cognovi quod me diligis. Unde et te, fili carimmime, heredem facio aeternae felicitatis.*[2] Straightway the pious monk became convalescent.

How could joy help finding its abode in so simple a heart? Many a time did it break forth in naïve manifestations, quite apart from things ceremonial.

On St. Martin's day it was the custom to distribute to the children walnuts, apples and medlars, which were subsequently roasted in a pan placed on a bonfire. On the evening of this anniversary, after the cook had just placed a well-filled dish on the monks' table, a feeling of sudden joy came over him, and in his delight he began to sing aloud, in Flemish:

> *Heere sinte Merten, heilich sant,*
> *Goede platte mispelen wassen in u lant,*
> *Kyrie eleyson.*[3]

The provost wished to impose silence, but, raising his eyes, he saw the cook's face as though illumined with celestial radiance. And convinced that the slight breach of discipline was a result of divine grace, he did not rebuke the joyful cause of the disturbance.

This naïveté is found throughout the many writings of Jean de Louvain. Most of them consist of pious ejaculations, very loosely connected. Still, they are not wholly devoid of importance. They reveal the influence of Ruysbroeck, and are also interesting documents from the philological point of view. These works were highly esteemed, and were read

---

[1] Pomerius, *op. cit.*, lib. III. cap. xvi.

[2] *Ibid.*, cap. xvii.

[3] "Seignior Saint Martin, blessed saint, good medlars grow in thy land. Kyrie eleison."

far beyond the limits of the convent. We have already mentioned the appreciation of\ Jean Busch who, in his *Chronicon Windesemense* (i. p. 176), associates the *bonus cocus* with Ruysbroeck, and calls both of them *magna ecclesiae Dei luminaria.* The Groenendael *Nécrologe* speaks as follows of the literary work of our monk, *ad diem 9 februarii:* . . . *perfectionem hujus sancti viri libri sui quos indubie Spiritu Dei plenus ipsemet scripsit atque dictavit, per diversa loca et regiones multiplicati, perspicue dem(onst)rant.* And in the seventeenth century the historian Miraeus confirms this in the following terms: *opera ejus ascetica ibidem Teutonico idiomate exstant manuscripta; digna profecto quae in omnes linguas transfundantur.*[1]

The *bonus cocus* died in 1377. Although seriously ill, he would not leave his kitchen. There he remained, without moving from his chair, for six months; during the latter part of the time he was carried about in a conveyance specially adapted for the sick (*angariatus*). In spite of his robust appearance he felt that death was near. He received extreme unction at the hands of Jan Scoonhoven, and breathed his last three days afterwards, on the 5th of February, the anniversary of Saint Agatha.[2] The brothers buried him in the garden of Groenendael, and inscribed on his tomb the following epitaph:

Reliquiae fratris Joannis de Leeuwis, vulgo Boni Coci, viri a Deo illuminati, et scriptis mysticis clari.

[1] *Fasti Belgici et Burgundici* (Brussels 1622), p. 717.
[2] Pomerius, cap. xxi.

CHAPTER IX

I

MEANWHILE the fame of Ruysbroeck's virtues soon spread far and wide. Learned doctors and nobles, priests and women, children and old men, came in crowds to visit the recluse in his verdant retreat. He endeavoured to offer counsel to all, addressing them, says Pomerius, such fitting words of edification that he might have known beforehand of their coming. And yet it often happened that this man, capable of eliciting sparks from a heart of stone—*ut etiam de silice ignem excutiens corda lapidia*—remained speechless when confronted with high and mighty persons, and, quite undisturbed by their presence, without a blush of shame, stood there and uttered no word, as though he had never experienced the gift of the Spirit. If this interior silence continued, he would say good night, and go away.

An echo of these conversations has reached us through Pomerius, enabling us to judge of the profound good sense of our monk. Here he does not wander away into vague speculations; it may be that he is greater before suffering souls than before wax-tablets. A single word will strengthen and comfort, when this word is inspired by love. One sentence, uttered at the right time, can set working within us invisible levers which determine the whole of our future life. And the reason why the human soul, at certain times, is capable of removing burdens before which the most valiant falter, is because, deep within it, is God himself.

To a woman who was bewailing her poverty, her inability to help the poor, and her lack of inclination for the spiritual

life, he replied, taking care not to dwell upon all these griev-
ances in which the poor creature evidently found pleasure:
"Be assured, beloved daughter, that the best way to serve
God is to give him thanks for all that befalls us, and to
submit humbly to his good will."

Two Parisian students, with the curiosity of youth
(*curiose*), once came to ask him for a phrase which they could
adopt as a rule throughout life. He simply said to them:
"*vos estis tam sancti sicut vultis*: you are as holy as you will
to be." These words scandalised the young men, who, greatly
perturbed, turned away from the old monk and went off
to tell other friars what the prior had said to them. "He made
mock of us," they said again and again. With no little
difficulty, the monks conducted the Parisians back to the
old monk, beseeching him to develop his thought.

Thereupon the prior said:

Is it not true that you are as holy as you will to be? Surely this is the
case. The measure of your sanctity depends on the excellence of your will.
Examine within yourselves the quality of your will, and you will know
the worth of your sanctity. *One is as holy as one is good. Tantum enim
quisque sanctus est quantum afficitur bonitati.*

Wonderful words! They might have been taken, like a
chaplet of gold, from Saint Paul's chapter in praise of Love.
This is the pure Gospel tradition which, in the groves of
Groenendael, claims along with Saint John and the *poverello*
of Assisi its rights over against that false sanctity which
hardens the heart beneath a pitiless cuirass. It is the gospel
of the good life, valiant and helpful, in contradistinction
from academical devotion, so false and barren. And how wise
and prudent the message! It begins by exalting man and
setting him on the path, it leads him on until the time when
he shall understand that, on this arid path which climbs to
the heights, the will is but a reed which pierces the hand,
until the time comes for it to yield to love. Salvation is not
a work of the will, it is a work of love. And this he alone
understands who, like Ruysbroeck, has long prayed at the
foot of the Cross, the pathetic memorial of redeeming love.

We can well understand that such thoughts had power to move and convert souls. Among other conversions, the biographer quotes that of a lady of high rank, the baronne de Marque, who walked barefoot a distance of two leagues to receive instruction from the old saint.[1] Her spiritual master carried her so far along the path of devotion that, renouncing all her wealth, she became a Clarisse at Cologne. Inglebert, her son, contemporary with Pomerius, himself entered as canon regular of Saint Augustine at Groenendael.

II

Still, it was mostly from the banks of the Rhine that eager pilgrims came to the holy prior. See them journeying along the main roads joining the mystic Rhine to opulent Flanders, the perpetual scene either of fair or of battle. They came, says Pomerius, *de Argentina ac Basilea ac aliis Rheni.* Then, when the pilgrims—*doctores ac clerici non mediocres*—had listened to a few words from the inspired saint, they would return, keeping as a precious *viaticum* the message to which they had listened.

At that time the Rhine lands were the centre of an unparalleled spiritual expansion. Monasteries and convents increased rapidly in numbers, keeping alive a mystic fervour which caused the land from Lake Constance to the Netherlands to be called "the path of the popes": *die Pfaffengasse.* Thus we need not wonder at the relations soon established between Ruysbroeck and the German mystics, the *Friends of God,* for instance. We have already seen that Ruysbroeck addressed a copy of *The Spiritual Marriage* (*des bruluft buchelin*) to the Friends of the Oberland in 1350. Unfortunately, our information of Ruysbroeck's relations with the German mystics is taken from a justly suspected book of Rulman Merswin: *De praeveniente gratia et de meritoria gratia.* Father Denifle has thrown light on the story of the

[1] Pomerius, lib. II. cap. xix.

conversion of Tauler as found in the *Meisterbuch* of Rulman Merswin: it is pure fancy.[1] Such information, therefore, as we obtain from Merswin cannot enlighten us to any extent.

On the other hand, Pomerius seems to tell of a visit by Tauler to Ruysbroeck. At all events, this is what tradition, after Surius, gives us to understand, for the first biographer speaks only of a certain *Canclaer, doctor sacrae paginae, ordinis praedicatorum magnae, reputationis et excellentiae.*[2] Surius, who, as we have seen, drew his information solely from Pomerius, does not hesitate to correct Canclaer to *Thaulerus,* and to introduce certain details taken from the legend of Rulman Merswin.[3]

The question is whether Canclaer is the original writing of Pomerius, or whether this name is due to an error in copying. De Vreese claims that the true form of Pomerius is reproduced in MS. No. 966 of the University of Gand, where mention is made of Tauweler. "It is easy to see that the names *Canclaer* and *Tanclaer* originate in a faulty reading of the form *Tauelaer* frequently met with in the Mid-Netherland manuscripts along with *Tauweleer, Tauweler, Tauler.*"[4] This is quite possible; but in that event MS. No. 966 would be the only representative of the original form. The other witnesses, the four known Latin manuscripts of the work of Pomerius, the Latin chroniclers who utilise Pomerius, all read *Canclaer* or *Tanclaer.* Now, in criticism one cannot reject the principle *difficilior lectio potior.* However incom-

---

[1] *Taulers Bekehrung kritisch untersucht; Zeitschrift für deutsches Alterthum* (1880), xii., xiii. A. Jundt, who had upheld the sincerity of Merswin in his *Amis de Dieu au xive siècle* (1879); subsequently approved of the attitude taken by Denifle: *Rulman Merswin et l'Ami de Dieu de l'Oberland : un problème de psychologie religieuse* (1890). The abbé A. Chiquot reconsiders the question in a thesis before the Faculté des Lettres de Paris: *Jean Tauler and the "Meisters Buoch"* (1922). He reaches the conclusion that the Ami de Dieu of the Oberland is but a creation of Rulman Merswin.

[2] Chapter xviii.

[3] Mastelinus speaks of *Conrardus Tanclarius* and of *Taulerus (Necrologium Viridisval.,* p. 30); Petrus Impens, of a *singularis excellentiae et sacrae theologiae professor parisiensis emeritus Mr Conrardus Tanclaer, ordinis praedicatorum (Chronicon Bethleemt,* fol. 25 vo). How is it that Grammaye, who certainly had this information, calls the visitor *Bernardus Tanclaer (Antiquit. Belgiae,* p. 30)? A mystery.

[4] De Vreese, *Biog. nat.,* col. 514.

prehensible this Canclaer, it must be maintained by reason of the very difficulties it raises.

As Impens and Mastelinus give him the surname of *Conrardus*, he has been regarded as a Conrardus de Saxonia, who appears to have lived in Belgium in the second half of the fourteenth century. Impens says also that Conrardus Tanclaer was a famous professor of Paris. Now, his name is found in none of the lists that have been reconstituted. Another hypothesis: is Canclaer derived from the Flemish word *canceleer*, cancellarius, chancellor? But then the mystery would remain insoluble.

If then there is Canclaer—as does not seem doubtful— let us see if what Pomerius says about him can be applied equally to Tauler. Born at Strasbourg in 1290, Tauler was early intended for the ecclesiastical life, and, in 1308, entered the Order of the Dominicans. This quite agrees with what Pomerius says: *ordinis praedicatorum*. Shortly afterwards he betook himself to Paris to study theology in the Collège Saint-Jacques, where Meister Eckhart had taught. Manifestly Pomerius overstates the fact in calling Canclaer-Tauler *doctor sacrae paginae*, for Tauler took no degree whatsoever. All the same, Tauler was early surnamed *Doktor* or *Meister der H. Schrift*. Besides, Ruysbroeck's influence over Tauler is undeniable, particularly in the sermons subsequent to 1350: the book of *The Four Temptations* is wholly reproduced in *Sermo I, in prima Dominica quadr.* Chapters xlv., lxxv., lxxvii. of *The Spiritual Marriage* are included in *Sermo II, in eadem Dominica*. Apart from these important borrowings, the sermons abound in more modest quotations. But though the influence of Ruysbroeck upon Canclaer-Tauler is asserted, other details are less likely. In the first place, it is inexact to say that it was from reverence to Ruysbroeck that Canclaer-Tauler wrote *sub materno idiomate*. The use of the vulgar tongue in preference to Latin was very general at the time. It is also unlikely that Tauler visited Groenendael several times. One passage only in the Sermons appears to refer to the monastery of Groenendael: *ich bin in solichen landen gewesen do die lute also manlich sind und tunt also ware sterke kere und blibent dobi, und bringet das gottes wort do merer wurklicher fruhte in einre iore denne hic in zehen ioren und sach man wunder an diesem wunnechlichen volke und grosse genode.* If it is proved that the relations between Tauler and the Ami de Dieu of Bâle are mostly legendary, this passage can apply only to the quiet retreat of Ruysbroeck.

And so, while the name of Canclaer remains mysterious, we cannot escape the impression that Tauler really is meant. Surius, in correcting Pomerius in this respect, has acted as an historian. He is justified by his special knowledge of the German mystic, whose books he had edited. Absolute textual proof is lacking, but the accuracy of Surius none the less supplies a very strong presumption, one that is still further strengthened by the literary comparisons to which reference has been made. Along with most of the critics, therefore, we maintain that a visit of Tauler to Groenendael actually did take place.[1] As the chronology of Tauler's life is far from being definitely ascertained, it is impossible to assign a certain date for this visit. Possibly the sending of copies of *The Spiritual Marriage* to the Amis de Dieu of Strasbourg is connected with the visit of Tauler. In that case, this visit might be assigned to the year 1350; at any rate it cannot be put much after that date, seeing that the famous German mystic died in 1360.

III

While Ruysbroeck's influence on Tauler was historically far less important than tradition indicates—since Tauler's reputation as a mystic was established long before 1350 [2]—the same cannot be said regarding Gérard de Groote, founder of the associations of the Frères de la Vie Commune.

---

[1] Cf. De Hornstein, *Jean Tauler, sa vie, ses écrits, sa doctrine*, in *Revue Thomiste*, 1918, p. 244.

[2] Denifle says categorically : " Der Einfluss Ruusbroecs, aber, von dem der Biograph des leztern, resp. Surius in der Ausgabe der Werke Ruusbroecs spricht ist nicht nachzuweisen."—*Taulers Bekehrung*, p. 37.

We are aware that Gérard, moved by the objurgations
of his friend Henri Calcar, in the autumn of 1374 renounced
his prebend as canon and bequeathed part of his patrimony
to the Carthusian friars of Arnhem. Released from material
cares, he now retired, in semi-claustration, to the house
where he was born, at Deventer. Shortly afterwards, as
though reproaching himself for retaining even this, he made
a gift of his paternal domain "for the use of the poor who
wish to devote themselves to God."

It seems at that time as though Gérard had had serious
prejudices as regards the monastic life, and these did not
disappear until several years afterwards.

> It is by no means my intention [he writes in a deed of gift dated
> 23rd July, 1379] to found a new order or a new religion, but simply to
> offer hospitality to women seeking a retreat in order that they may worship
> God in humility and penance. These women shall be bound by no vow,
> but shall remain laic and shall call themselves such.[1]

All the same, this semi-retreat could not satisfy Gérard.
He had heard mention of the monastery of Groenendael as
a model of monastic life. Ruysbroeck's books had filled him
with admiration. Accordingly he decided to visit the place,
to judge with his own eyes, and to ask counsel of the aged
prior of Groenendael.

He introduced himself by letter, wherein he gave fervent
expression of his veneration for Ruysbroeck, *cujus scabellum
pedum tam in hac vita quam in future fieri concupisco.*

Accompanied by Jean Sceele, rector of the Latin schools
of Zwolle, and by a certain Gerardus Calopifex, who served
as guide,[2] De Groote set off about the end of 1374, perhaps
the beginning of 1375.

Pomerius has left a detailed account of this visit which
he had from Jean Sceele himself: *praemissa autem veraciter
didici persona tamen interposita, ab ore ejusdem magistri
Johannis.*

When the travellers arrived at Groenendael, it chanced

---

[1] *Epistola Gerardi ad Joh. Cele.*
[2] This third person is mentioned only by Thomas à Kempis (*Vita Gerardi
Magni,* cap. x.).

that, as they were entering the convent enclosure, the very first person they met was the old prior. The latter had never seen Maître Gérard, but, being divinely guided, he greeted him by name, and, welcoming him with the utmost deference, introduced him into the monastery after predicting that some day Maître Gérard would be his disciple.

During this first stay, which was only for a few days, says Pomerius, Maître Gérard was very anxious to become thoroughly imbued with the prior's teachings. He therefore read attentively all Ruysbroeck's books, carefully preserved in the *scriptorium* of the monastery.

All the same, certain expressions did not fail to astonish Maître Gérard. Relying on the prior's friendship, Gérard quite simply remarked to Ruysbroeck: "Father Prior, I admire your boldness in writing on subjects so profound; you thereby attract to yourself enemies who will not fail to decry your doctrine."—"Rest assured, Maître Gérard," answered the prior, "I have never written a word in my books that has not been inspired by the Holy Spirit," or, as a variant states, "I have never written anything except in the presence of the Holy Trinity."

The discussion continued for some time. Doubtless from deference to the old man, Gérard did not persist in his objections. It was not so with the rector, Jean Sceele, who would not yield, and drew upon himself the following retort from the old prior, now touched to the quick: "This truth, now hidden from you, Maître Gérard, you will understand some day, but your companion, Maître Jean, will never understand it in this life." [1]

It was probably about this time that Gérard obtained from Ruysbroeck the authorisation to translate *The Adornment of the Spiritual Marriage* and *The Seven Degrees of the Ladder of Love.* He took away the books with him, to translate them in peace and quiet. He also took away something else from his stay in Groenendael: the conviction that the cenobitic life was the only one suitable for "reforming the interior

---

[1] Pomerius, *op. cit.,* lib. II. cap. ix.

man, created after the image of God." The result was that he shut himself up in a cell of the Carthusian monastery of Monnikhuisen, near Arnhem, where he subjected himself to the strictest macerations. Meanwhile there grew in his mind the idea of founding a religious association, this time subject to a rule. Thinking over this project, the smiling peaceful image of Groenendael presented itself before him.

Being attached by no vow to this Carthusian monastery, Gérard returned several times to Groenendael: *cum autem interpolatis vicibus Magister Gerardus devotum Priorem visitans, semel secum in Viridi Valli manere tempus decrevisset.*[1]

Many doctrinal points were still obscure to him; so, at least, we are given to understand from Pomerius when he says: *ut saltem lumen veritatis caliganti intellectui propalaret.*[2] Perhaps, too, his prejudice against monastic life had not wholly been destroyed. Of all the questions that crowded out one another in the mind of Maître Gérard, one in particular returned again and again: that of the divine wrath. This it was which had decided his conversion. Indeed, Henri Calcar had strongly represented to him all that the afterlife holds in store for one: "Death," he had said to him, "hangs suspended over our heads; we know neither the day nor the hour of its coming; of a sudden, we shall have to give account of the use we have made of our life." [3]

And lo! he finds himself confronted with a man dominated by the feeling of divine love, one in whom the fear of judgment seems to play no part. Such tranquillity of soul appeared so amazing to Maître Gérard that he feared for the salvation of the old prior. Choosing therefore the most awe-inspiring texts of Scripture, he considered it his duty to prove to Ruysbroeck, *industriosis assertionibus*, that he was presuming on divine grace in showing no fear of hell. The humble prior allowed his impetuous friend to continue for some time. Then, after a brief silence:

---

[1] Pomerius, *op. cit.*, lib. II. cap. x. Compare what the *bonus cocus* says: *bi tiden een maent II. of IIJ, of somwile een half jaer.*

[2] *Ibid.*, lib. II. cap. x.

[3] Thomas à Kempis, *Vita Gerardi Magni*, cap. iv.

Maître Gérard, [he said] be assured of this; you will never succeed in terrifying me. I am equally ready to accept everything the Lord sends me, whether in life or in death. There could be nothing more perfect, more salutary, or more sweet to the soul. All my desires and longings have but this object: that the Lord may ever find me ready to do his holy will.[1]

Such complete surrender made the deepest impression upon Gérard. He went all over the monastery, which more and more seemed to him the type of a perfect community. Everywhere he admired the kindly understanding between the brothers, the fidelity with which each kept to the place assigned to him by the provost, the harmonious and effortless union that existed between manual tasks and religious exercises; and, anticipating time by hope, he mentally constructed a monastic house after the model of Groenendael. On leaving the prior, whom he was never to see again, he said to him by way of farewell: "Father, your wisdom and your knowledge are greater than they are reputed to be; you have compelled fame and renown by means of your virtues." [2] Back in Holland, and "ruminant comme un animal pur" over what had fallen from the lips of the holy prior, he hastened to commit to writing an account of these conversations. This was the beginning of the congregation of Windesheim.

Some years later, when lying mortally stricken during an epidemic, the image of Groenendael still haunted his mind as he was dying. To the brothers pressing around his bed he could still say: "Neither the rule of the Carthusians, nor that of the Cistercians, but that of the canons regular of Saint Augustine." Thus, before departing this life, the thought of the great reformer for the last time found repose beneath the peaceful glades of the *V alléeVerte*, as at the gate of heaven itself.

[1] Pomerius, *op. cit.*, lib. II. cap. x.
[2] Thomas à Kempis, *Vita Gerardi Magni*, cap. x.

IV

Meanwhile Ruysbroeck continued writing. Indeed, it was during the very last years of his life that he wrote *The Book of Supreme Truth*,[1] which might be called his intellectual testament. Our prior had discovered that certain expressions in his former books might prove ambiguous, especially those dealing with mystical union. As the Carthusians of Hérinnes were bewildered by the doctrine of divine union which seemed to imply an actual deification of man, Ruysbroeck, in spite of his advanced age, betook himself in person to Hérinnes. He promised the brothers a new treatise which would explain more particularly those passages in *The Kingdom of God's Lovers* over which readers had stumbled.

Ruysbroeck mentions this conversation in the first chapter of *The Book of Supreme Truth*: "Indeed," says he, "no one must be scandalised by my writings, rather must each one be made better thereby." He protests that "no creature can be—or make itself—so holy that it loses its condition as a creature and becomes God." Such is the central thought of the book, wherein mystic union is envisaged under a threefold aspect: union by intermediary (chapters iii. and iv.); union without intermediary, like the union of iron and fire, which, while constituting a single substance, nevertheless remain quite separate (chapters v.–xi.); and, lastly, union so close that, finding no word adequate to express it, Ruysbroeck calls it union *without distinction*. "Here beatitude is so simple and modeless that all essential contemplation vanishes, as well as all inclination and distinction between creatures" (chapter xii.). To this threefold union corresponds a threefold prayer of Christ (chapter xiii.). Ruysbroeck ends by humbly confiding in the judgment which the Church will deliver upon his writings (chapter xiv.).

This treatise is manifestly a work that has taken long to

---

[1] David, t. VI. pp. 241–69: *Dat boec der hoechster waerheit*; Surius, pp. 540–9: *Libellus eximius Samuelis titulo, qui alias de alta contemplatione, alias de unione dilecti cum dilecto dicitur*. In certain manuscripts this book is also called: *liber apologeticus sive retractationis*.

think out and prepare in the silence of the cell. The rigorous plan of its composition excludes the idea that Ruysbroeck, under the urge of inspiration, dictated it to a secretary. Rather is it a well-prepared work, every word of which has been carefully weighed before being committed to writing.

Quite different is the character of *The Book of the Twelve Beguines*. Reading it, we think of what Pomerius tells us regarding the last few years of our prior: *Cum jam gravatus senio viribus inciperet ingravescere . . . assumpsit sibi in socium unum e fratribus monasterii, qui in secum allata tabula arcana scriberet eructanda*.[1]

Into these pages Ruysbroeck seems to have thrown pell-mell all that he has gathered together throughout his long life. An incomparable wealth of language, the flash and radiance of innumerable interblended images which make the book one of continually dazzling splendour, are found side by side with puerilities, long and tedious digressions, unexpected platitudes. One feels that it has all been dictated, without any thought of cohesion and also without the possibility of revision.

And yet this lengthy work is lacking neither in interest nor in importance. Herein can we more particularly judge of Ruysbroeck's theological and scientific attainments.

It is scarcely possible to indicate a logical plan for the book. After a prologue in verse, introducing twelve beguines conversing together of the love of Jesus Christ, the author speaks of the conditions necessary for benefiting by the Eucharist. Then he plunges into what seems to be his real subject: contemplation. Shortly afterwards he gives up verse, in order, as he says, to express himself clearly:

Nu moetic rimen laten bliven,
Sal ic scouwen clare bescriven.

But the good mystic does not keep his promise very well, and it would be impossible to derive a coherent doctrine from what he says of the four acts of contemplation: jubi-

[1] Pomerius, *op. cit.*, lib. II. cap. xiv.

lation, rapture, contemplation strictly so called, the sublime
state of love (chapters ix.–xvi.).

Here he dismisses the beguines who were supposed to be
conversing on these lofty speculations:

Hier gaen de XII. Beghinen ute,

and seems as though he wished to broach a fresh subject:
hier beghint een onderwys, while continuing to speak of contemplation.

Among the unbelieving men who break the unity of the
Church, Ruysbroeck points out four kinds of heretics whom
we have no difficulty in recognising as the Brothers of the
Free Spirit. Then follows a digression on the threefold nature
of God, creation, human nature, and the three paths of the
contemplative life (chapters xvii.–xxix.).

In a third part Ruysbroeck introduces lengthy remarks
on the heavenly bodies and their influence upon the destiny
of men—this subsequently brought upon him the reprobation
of Bossuet.[1] The sign of the Scales leads him to speak of the
balance between divine love and conversion, capable of disturbing the equilibrium in favour of the sinner. This tiresome
digression is fortunately interrupted by some very welcome
chapters on the present corruption of the Church as contrasted with the gospel life of the first centuries after Christ
(chapters xxx.–lxv.). Then he returns to the subjects dealt
with at the end of the second part: the creation, the influence
of the planets, etc. (chapters lxvi.–lxxi.).

Finally the last part, by no means the least beautiful,
is a meditation on the passion of Christ, applied to the seven
canonical hours.

Thus not all must be neglected in this voluminous
work. Here and there are flashes of genius, though of a
genius already fading and which, we feel, is on the point of
flickering out.

Death had already deprived Ruysbroeck of some of his
dearest friends. Guillaume Jordaens, the translator of *The*

---

[1] *Instructions sur les états d'oraison* (édit. de Versailles, 1817), pp. 56 ss.

Spiritual Marriage, had died in 1372; the *bonus cocus* in 1377. Ruysbroeck was conscious of that solitude of the old who feel themselves abandoned one after another by the witnesses of their maturity. Their friends are more numerous on the other side than on this. And then the desire to rejoin them becomes keener.

As though to leave the soul wholly engrossed in the interior vision of the things of God, Ruysbroeck's eyes had gradually become dimmed to the splendour of this perishable world. The aged prior could no longer betake himself to the chapel to partake of the Eucharist. He shared the room of the provost Franco de Coudenberg, old and infirm like himself. And his days were spent in stirring up the ashes of past memories.

Thus going back upon the course of his long life, the old man could more clearly discern the wonderful guiding hand of God. Then his heart would leap with gratitude. A holy fervour filled him, an unquenchable thirst after eternity: *sicut cervus desiderans ad fontes aquarum.* In trembling accents he would now chant the first few lines of Psalm xlii.: *Quando veniam et apparebo ante faciem Dei mei?*

One night—how wonderful is the vitality of that child-heart which never wholly dies in man!—one night his mother appeared before him, announcing that Advent would not pass without God receiving back to himself his old servant. The biographer was perfectly right to mention this. Indeed, is it not a very appealing spectacle—that mother - smile appearing over the death-bed of the old man, as it did over the cradle of the child?

Thus warned, Ruysbroeck prepared for death, *cum tota mentis devotione et alacritate.* And the brothers, as they pressed around his bed, when they saw so joyful a look on his countenance, said: "If it is an act of piety to bewail our brother Jan who is about to die, it is an act of even greater piety to rejoice with one who is about to enjoy eternal life."

As a final act of humility, the old monk was desirous of leaving the provost's room in which he had been nursed up to this stage. He wished to die in the common infirmary. No sooner had he been carried there than fever, complicated with dysentery, laid hold on him. Hastily the monks sent for the dean of the church of Diest, a very dear friend of the prior, *vir artis medicinae expertissimus*. But what can man do when God summons?

The fever lasted two weeks. When the dying man was aware that all his flesh had faded away, he had himself raised in bed, as though to die upright, facing the praying brothers: *coram positis fratribus et orantibus*. Then, after having commended to them his soul, *sanus mente et facie rutilis*, he gently fell back and gave up the ghost, without a spasm of pain.

At the same moment, it is said, Gérard de Groote was informed of his friend's death: the bells of Deventer began to ring as though a divine force had set them moving.[1]

This was in the year of our Lord thirteen hundred and eighty-one, on the second of December, the octave of Saint Catherine. Ruysbroeck was eighty-eight years of age; sixty-four of these had been almost entirely dedicated to the priesthood.

Such was the impression of sanctity left by this man of God, that the brothers who kept vigil over his body saw the dead prior rise from his funeral couch and approach an altar. He was arrayed in his sacerdotal raiment and enveloped in such splendour as no human tongue could express.[2] Thus does the human heart resurrect those it has greatly loved. On the morrow, the brothers—*flentes pariter et gaudentes*—buried their old prior in the church. This they did, says the biographer, with more inner devotion than outer solemnity. They hoped rather to be helped by him than to aid him by their prayers.

Five years afterwards, when the provost Franco de

---

[1] "Cui (G. Magno) etiam Deus obitum amantissimi patris revelavit, ut in compulsatione campanarum multis civibus audientibus manifestavit, ejusque animam una hora purgatam ad caelestem gloriam transisse quibusdam amicis suis secretius indicavit."—Thomas à Kempis, *Vita G. Magni*, cap. x.

[2] Pomerius, *op. cit.*, lib. II. cap. xxxii.

Coudenberg died, Jean Tserclaes, bishop of Cambrai, who had come to conduct the funeral, had the remains of Ruysbroeck, along with those of the provost, transported to the new chapel, which had been consecrated on the last day of the previous October. Thus were the two friends united in death, as they had been in life.

On the tombstone the brothers engraved this inscription:

> HIC JACET TRANSLATVS DEVOTVS PATER
> D. JOANNES DE RVYSEBROECK
> I. PRIOR HVJVS MONASTERII
> QUI OBIIT ANNO DOMINI
> M. C. CCLXXXI
> II DIE DECEMBRIS

What can legend add to the beautiful simplicity of so tranquil a life? It is to be regretted that popular piety, in its desire to honour its heroes, but too often profanes them. Pomerius, usually so prudent, cannot help relating certain miraculous events which mar and disfigure the end of his biography. Does he not tell of a beguine of Malines, suddenly smitten with raging toothache, who was instantly cured on touching the affected tooth with one of Ruysbroeck's? And, when the bishop Tserclaes had the prior's tomb opened, does he not relate that the body and clothes were found perfectly intact, with the exception of the end of the nose—*excepta dumtaxat nasi sui extremitate*—and that a delicious odour immediately issued from the coffin?

We will leave these puerilities, and regard them simply as an expression of the devotion which the masses feel for their benefactors. And, indeed, it was not long before the Church instituted a veritable cult in honour of one whom the people revered as a saint. Once a year the canons of Sainte-Gudule, on the Sunday following the festival of the Trinity, proceeded on foot through the forest of Soignes to Groenendael, to pay homage to the memory of Jan Ruysbroeck, "la fleur odoriférante du monastère."

And yet, in spite of the urgent measures taken by the clergy, the beatification of Ruysbroeck did not take place till long afterwards. In 1624 archbishop Boonen addressed to the Congregation of Rites at Rome all the elements of the informative trial. Interrupted in 1630, this trial was resumed in 1634, and then finally ended by a decree of Urban VIII., who did not regard the justification as adequate.[1] Only in 1885 did the archbishop of Malines, Cardinal Goossens, take the matter in hand again, and in 1909 the Congregation of Rites gave its approval to the institution of particular prayers on behalf of the blessed saint.

But glory of another kind has been reserved for Ruysbroeck: that attributed to him by historians for some years past. We are becoming more and more convinced that the germ of modern thought must be sought much farther back than Cartesianism. Modern philosophy has rehabilitated the hitherto decried mysticism which was elaborated in the monasterial cells of the fourteenth century. Let us too dwell with it in the laborious solitude of Groenendael, to try and find out what we owe intellectually to the humble forest monk whose life has here been traced.

[1] The documents of the trial are preserved in the archbishopric of Malines in two volumes in folio: *Processus auctoritate ordinaria illustrissimi et reverendissimi Jacobi Boonen, anno 1624*, etc. *Acta annis 1626–7 . . . super sanctitate vitae, virtutibus et miraculis Ruysbrochii.*

SECOND PART
PHILOSOPHICAL SOURCES

SECOND PART

PHILOSOPHICAL SOURCES

CHAPTER X

EXPOSITION OF THE DOCTRINE OF RUYSBROECK

SCARCELY any attempt has been made by most of Ruysbroeck's commentators to reconcile his thought with a definite set of doctrines. The utmost they have done has been to analyse the three books of *The Spiritual Marriage*, without seeing that by so doing they were regarding as fixed and immovable the ever-changing and expanding thoughts and ideas of our mystic.

Such work as that of Ruysbroeck is in perpetual flux. To know it well one must have traversed it all over, just as a forester goes about his forest and knows the paths that link together the chief clumps of trees.

If such an effort be made, this work, far from being the fruit of undisciplined contemplation, will stand forth as a strong and definite structure. Ruysbroeck is truly the last of the great speculatives of the Middle Ages. His mysticism is not an end in itself; it is a means of knowledge, in the same way as logic itself.

Like the Gnostics of the third century, like Plotinus, like the elaborators of the great mediæval *Summae*, Ruysbroeck had reflected on the important question of *being*, and on its corollary: How can man, exiled in matter, return to his place of origin? Certainly before solving the problem in his own way he meditated long and caught glimpses of a majestic structure, all of whose parts combine to bear heavenwards the peak of reason, like some cathedral spire.

We will therefore examine this bold edifice as it shows itself to us in its allegorical garb.

I. METHOD

In all research work we should begin, according to Aristotle, by ascertaining the existence of the object of research, and then study the means calculated to enable the mind to apprehend this object.

Ruysbroeck does not long deliberate with himself as to the existence of God. The God *demonstrable to the mind* of the great speculatives becomes the God *perceptible to the heart* of the mystics. God *is*. This fundamental proposition Ruysbroeck admits; at all events, he regards as valid the reasonings of Anselm and Saint Thomas. The five Thomistic paths seem to him to have settled the question.[1]

Not only God *is*, but he is also the one supreme reality whereof the whole created world is but the reflection or the emanation. But what would a God be whom the mind could not grasp, a God set up by reasoning, but who remained separate from the creature by the whole extent of infinity? Besides, says Ruysbroeck, this rational knowledge of God is so limited that it may be compared "to the point of a needle in relation to all that is created, and even less." A pair of compasses can apply only to that which is less than or equal to the utmost distance between its two points.

> The sublime and incomprehensible nature of God transcends all creatures, in heaven and on earth, for all that the creature can grasp is the created, and God is above all that is created. . . . All comprehension is too narrow to enfold him. . . . He therefore who would wish to know what God is and to apply himself to this search would do a thing forbidden; he would go out of his senses.[2]

Though the dialectical path is closed to us, the universal aspiration of beings after their common origin proves the possibility of another mode of knowledge. As hunger is a proof of bread, so the nostalgia for the divine is proof of an apprehensible God. To Ruysbroeck, therefore, it is clear that there is a philosophical science enabling man to raise himself to absolute good.

[1] Cf. Sertillanges, *S. Thomas d'Aquin*, t. I. pp. 142–64.
[2] *The Spiritual Marriage*, book I. chapter xxi.

In determining this science he proceeds by a process of elimination. First of all we are confined within the visible universe. Our senses reveal this world to us, but the revelation crushes us by keeping us within the confines of our prison. Eyes, ears and hands, in their fevered investigation, are able to contact only the prison bars. Again, what confidence can we have in information obtained by the senses? This unstable world, in continual process of change, affords only impressions shifting as itself, "a moving shadow." [1]

But one can *imagine*, one can prolong into the infinite the lines traced in the finite, draw conclusions from what one sees to what one does not see. Still, imagination is too closely knit to sensation; the pictures it creates also carry us off towards unreasonable joys. Being purely subjective, the deductions of imagination can have no reality in God. [2]

Man nevertheless has worked out a *science*; i.e. from the study of the external world he has concluded that there are invariable laws, laws that participate in eternity. Science, then, is an expression of truth, and thus of God. Astronomical numbers, lines and circuits tell us of God, and enable us to contact at least one of his attributes. Will knowledge then show us the path we seek? No, says Ruysbroeck, for however correct the conclusions of science, they apply only to the physical world. And this latter is but a part of the universe; it is, as it were, fitted into the spiritual universe which covers it like a dome. [3] Now the universe, as a spiritual organisation, is solely dependent on spiritual knowledge.

Along each of these three tracks man will fail, for his starting-point is wrong. Fortunately within himself there is a divine element which proceeds from God as the spark proceeds from the fire: the soul. But what is the soul? Buried within us, it is sometimes so ill-treated that it loses even the remembrance of its origin. From the depths of its prison it utters its gentle plaint. What is it? Incapable of defining it, Ruysbroeck piles image upon image; it is a divine exile, a

[1] *The Seven Cloisters*, chapter xi.
[2] *The Mirror*, chapter iii.; *The Twelve Beguines*, chapters xxix., xxx.
[3] *The Seven Degrees*, chapters viii., x.; *The Seven Cloisters*, chapter xvii.

prisoner who sings, a spark, a breath of God, an emanation, the effigy of a divine seal. Whatever it be, it alone can tell us of God, for it is a part of God.[1]

Ruysbroeck's entire work is a chant to the human soul. Distinct from the intellect—on which depend the perceptive faculties: imagination, understanding, deduction—the soul is *one*, and its mission is *one*: to escape from exile and return to God. Thus our essential work is to consider our soul, to possess it "as a kingdom," and, while adapting our freedom to its dictates, to advance towards God.[2]

Ruysbroeck's doctrine is thus nothing else than the story of the drama whose theatre is the universe.

A divine drama, in three acts, which the Gnostics had already attempted to systematise, and whose broad stages had been determined by the Neoplatonists: the soul, born in the divine abode, endowed like its creator with divine attributes; then its decline, its exile within a material universe, and its prolonged nostalgia; finally the groping in the darkness, and, after attempts innumerable, the return to God. The very world itself is carried along in this universal advance, whereof history is but the restless expression.

Now that the principle has been stated, let us see how Ruysbroeck works out his ideas regarding it.

II. The Drama of the Soul

1. The line of human destiny may be represented by a curve. It starts from God, then bends and curves inwards towards the lower world, and afterwards, having completed the circle, rises and returns to God.

§ 1. *God and the Divine Hypostases*

At the starting-point, God, who has not yet realised himself by any creation, is simply *Being*, the principle of all

---

[1] Compare the fine saying: "God is closer to us than we are to ourselves." *The Spiritual Marriage*, book II. chapter iii.

[2] *The Spiritual Marriage*, book I. chapter i.; *The Kingdom*, chapter xxv.; *The Sparkling Stone*, chapter vi.

beings, without attribute. He is "an imageless, desert bareness, which ever corresponds with eternity." [1] From this
being-principle (*overwesen*) proceeds the entire series of
creations. The multiple is a limitation of deity; in its
essence, deity is unity. In naming it the *One* (*de eenheit*), we
express alike its absolute simplicity and the impotence of
philosophy to name God. All the terms employed can be but
approximations: the increate, the unmeasured, the source,
the life, the staff or stay. To define God we must necessarily
apply to him the standards of the created, "intellectual
images conceived of the simple essence of God according to
the created mode." [2]

> God is so sublimely high [says Ruysbroeck] that no created process
> can reach him; he is so simple that in him all multiplicity must cease and
> have its beginning. He is beauty that adorns heaven and earth, wealth
> whence all creatures proceed while remaining essentially connected
> therewith. . . .[3]

And the reason why Ruysbroeck repeats himself in so
many images and analogies is in order clearly to show that
to affirm God is actually to reduce him. To say that God is
good, just, intelligent, is to enclose him within a *created*
conception which is applicable only to created things. God
is not good: he is the principle of Goodness. By giving
attributes to Deity we empoverish it, for it has need of
nothing.

Here we recognise the influence of the two theological
paths of the Pseudo-Dionysius: that which affirms (καταφατικὴ)
and that which denies (ἀποφατικὴ), and the latter is manifestly superior to the former, seeing that it leaves God in
his one and limitless essence, dominating all categories.[4]
Negation is a mode of speech which removes all idea of
limit and of impotence. Indeed, negation affirms, in the
only way possible, the qualities contrary to that which
it denies.

It is futile to enter into the development of method. God
is not eternal, he is above eternity. God is not a being, he is

[1] *The Mirror*, chapter xxiii. [2] *The Kingdom*, chapter xxxiv. [3] *Ibid.*
[4] *The Sparkling Stone*, chapter ix., *in fine*.

above being; neither is God essence, he is superessential, etc. If we go through the same task by setting over against God the categories as Aristotle had established them and as the teachers of philosophy in the thirteenth century had borrowed them from him, we shall arrive at the same result. Essence, quality, quantity, relation, situation, space, time, action and passion—are equally inapplicable to God. This God, unnamed and unnameable, is, in Ruysbroeck's own words: "a simple unity, without any mode, without time or space, without before or after, without desire or possession, without light or darkness. He is a *perpetual now*, the bottomless abyss, the darkness of silence, the desert wilderness," etc.[1]

In reality, the negative path, by setting God above all conceivable limitations, ends in the dissolution of Deity. What is an inconceivable God of whom the least we can say is that he is the negation of our purest conception? God is nothing, without being nothingness. What fear then takes possession of the soul, incapable of reaching that towards which it feels invincibly attracted?

It is here that the rôle of affirmative theology begins. It lends itself to human weakness by restoring the ideas about God which the first process had denied. Wishing to bring God nearer to human thought, it acts like the lens of an astronomical telescope which brings nearer to the observer the distant star that yet remains unchanged. "Who would seek God with intent should make him present to himself." And Ruysbroeck adds the following words which remind one strangely of the monism of the Neoplatonists [2]:

> In whatsoever manner or under whatsoever name one pictures God as master of everything created, one is always right. Whether dealing with one of the divine persons regarded after its nature and its productiveness, or with God regarded as preserver, redeemer, creator, or *qua* authority, beatitude, wisdom, truth, goodness, all this with the infinite character befitting the divine nature, one is right. Though there be many names we thus attribute to God, his lofty nature is a simple and nameless being

[1] *The Spiritual Marriage*, book III. chapter vi.; *The Mirror*, chapter xvii.
[2] *Enneads*, V. 5, 3; 5, 6; 8, 3; 8, 4; 8, 7. Indeed, by insisting on regarding the pagan pantheon as only personified abstraction, Neoplatonism ends in poly-demonism. Cf. Jean Reville, *La Religion à Rome sous les Sévères*, pp. 117, 118.

for every creature; but by reason of his incomprehensible nobility and sublimity, we make use of all these names, being unable to find either a name or a mode of speech that fully expresses him.[1]

Without seeing the consequences that might be deduced from this relativism, Ruysbroeck is now to embark upon the affirmative path.

In the first place the One can be only the Good. It is the central focus whence emanate those rays: the virtues. Thus, by reascending these rays in the opposite direction to their passage, one will come to God. It follows that, in order to know something of the Being whence all flows, its emanations must be studied. God being of the spiritual order, the soul is our widest field of investigation. For "the spirit receives and bears the impress of its eternal image, uninterruptedly, just as an untarnished mirror faithfully retains the image of the object set before it, and gives back a clear impression thereof." [2]

This divine refraction, the source of our knowledge, is systematised by Ruysbroeck in his theory of the Paradigm, which concerns alike his conception of God and his doctrine of creation.

The whole universe is ordered in the likeness of a higher reality. God is the supreme Archetype in whom all things pre-exist ideally.[3] Each sensible being is constituted by virtue of an idea which is imprinted after the fashion of a seal upon wax.[4] But the clearness of this impress depends on the proximity in which beings find themselves to their archetype. Hence the differences in nature, the inequalities of dignity, for the paradigm itself is perfect and cannot be regarded as responsible for the imperfections with which the world is filled. The impress cannot be made clearly except under certain conditions. "Keep thy mind naked and bare, empty of all sense-image; keep thy intellect open, inclined towards eternal life, and thy spirit, like a pure living mirror spread out before God, shall be ready to receive the divine likeness." [5]

[1] The Spiritual Marriage, book I. chapter xv.
[2] Ibid., book II. chapter lvii.   [3] The Mirror, chapter xvii.
[4] The Twelve Beguines, chapter ix.   [5] Ibid., chapter x.

Now, on examining this refraction of the image of God within ourselves, it is seen that the image is not *one*, as might have been expected, coming from the One, but threefold. The divine ray is refracted into three fundamental faculties.[1] These faculties correspond to the three divine hypostases.

In reading Ruysbroeck, it is easy to see how embarrassed he was in explaining the relationship of an impure world to perfect Being, and also the reasons which led him to the solution of the three hypostases. Perhaps he found the Trinitarian doctrine ready at hand. This doctrine, however, far from being an *a priori* to Ruysbroeck, is a logical culmination, just as the theory of the procession of the hypostases in Plotinus is governed by his particular cosmology.[2] Admitting a God, the principle of all being, above movement and action, how has the universe been able to issue from this "eternal repose"? Such is the question that dominates Ruysbroeck's theodicy. Let us try and see how he solves it.

At the outset, what reason has the One to beget? The Neoplatonists explain it by a necessity of his nature.[3] The God of Ruysbroeck also begets by a necessity of nature, as fire emits heat, but also by a determination of freedom. God wills a manifestation of his glory. Ruysbroeck frequently repeats that man is the honour of God, his eternal and immutable exemplar (the πρωτότυπον of the Greeks) exists in God from all eternity. And this virtuality implies a realisation.

The divine essence may be communicated. But as the first effect of divine fecundity should be as perfect as possible, the first manifestation of God will be himself, in *his creative power*, or the Father. Between the Increate and this first hypostasis there is but one degree of difference: it is distinct from him without being separated.[4] The Father will afterwards beget a being wherein he will know himself fully, where-

[1] *The Mirror*, chapter x.
[2] Bréhier, *La Philosophie de Plotin*, in *Revue des Cours et Conférences*, 1922, p. 649.
[3] *Enneads*, V. 1, 6, 7.
[4] *The Spiritual Marriage*, lib. III. chapter v.: "The Father omnipotent, in the deeps of his fecundity, totally comprehends himself."

in not only his own person, but the form of things, will appear to him. This is the Son, or the Word, "begotten as second person in deity. And by this eternal begetting all creatures are born eternally before having been created in time. Thus God has seen and known them within himself, separately, according to the Ideas that are in him." [1]

By the Word, the acting power of God, the world was created. Thus man was born. Is that all? No, for the two hypostases having above them a stage in perfection to cross, in order to return to the cause that begot them, it remains for man also to be secured the means of returning to his source. The Son, therefore, begets an active principle, an energy: the Holy Spirit. Beneath his influence man can return towards him who has begotten him, and become one with him. Thus the circle will be completed: the three hypostases and man, who is the final term of the divine hierarchy, eternally *being converted* towards the One. [2]

As we see, this theodicy is based on the idea of perfection. *Procession* enables us to recognise that every imperfect being is separated, by only one degree, from a being nearer to perfection than itself. Ruysbroeck is thus led to reject all idea of ultimate corruption or evil. Perfection is everywhere, both on the ascending and on the descending arc. Frequently does Ruysbroeck express this idea in the image of the ebb and flow of the tides. "God is a rising and falling sea. He ever extends his flow to those who love him, according to the need and the worth of each, and in his ebb he gathers to himself all who have been overwhelmed." [3] The dual theory of hypostases and procession has enabled Ruysbroeck to do away with the difficulty inherent in every system that insists on deriving the multiple from the one, the imperfect from the perfect. This God, who knows himself, is both creator and creature; what he begets can be none other than himself.

---

[1] *Ibid.* "In that brightness which is the Son, God sees himself, bare, with all that lives in him, for all that he is and has he gives to the Son, with the exception of fatherhood."
[2] *The Book of Supreme Truth,* chapter x.
[3] *The Kingdom,* chapter xxii.; *The Spiritual Marriage,* book II. chapter xli.

O

There is no place where he is not. His energy sustains and guides the worlds in their sure circuit, rises with the sap of the trees, flows in the water of the springs, beats in the arteries of man and beast, sparkles in the crystal, works in human consciousness. Thus does the varied activity of the world appear to Ruysbroeck like some magnificent spectacle. He explains his meaning on this point in his theory of creation which we now proceed to examine.

§ 2. *Creation*

The universe pre-existed ideally in God. The ideal forms, which are the initial causes of creation, Ruysbroeck calls *exemplars* or ideas.[1] This is very similar to the theory of the *germinal reasons* of Stoicism, revived by Neoplatonism.

No wonder we find, in a mystic like Ruysbroeck, a metaphysical introduction of this nature. The whole of the Middle Ages was shaken by the problem which had divided Plato and Aristotle: that of universal ideas. Hence, in the schools, we have the quarrel between the realists and the nominalists, and Abélard's doctrine of conciliation: conceptualism. Assuredly Ruysbroeck did not remain alien to these jousts. He made his own that one of these conceptions which regarded the first reasons of creation as being in God.

In this theory the Son, or the Word, corresponds to the Intelligence of Plotinus. In him God knows himself, and perceives, projected into the universal life, not only the intellectual and moral essences, like goodness, beauty, virtue, etc., but also physical beings. Fire, air, trees, stones exist in idea. And it is the Word, on whom devolves the rôle of a veritable Demiurge, that secures for the idea its sensible or visible translation.[2]

The exemplar, then, of a being or a thing is in God a perfection, and, by the law of procession, this being and this

---

[1] *The Spiritual Marriage*, book III. chapter v.
[2] *The Sparkling Stone*, chapter ix. Note, however, that Ruysbroeck sometimes attributes creation to the third hypostasis, as in this passage: "The Holy Spirit is the finger of God that created all nature, the heaven, earth and all beings" (*The Kingdom*, chapter xxxv.).

thing, however far removed they may be from their exemplar in the scale of creations, inevitably tend to return to their primitive perfection. Ruysbroeck himself says:

> We have a living life which is eternal in God, before all created being. It is *according to* this life that God created us, not from this life nor from his own substance. . . . God is a living exemplar of all that he has done. . . . And all that he sees, in distinct knowledge by the mirror of his wisdom, in images, orders, forms, reasons—all this is truth and life. . . . All of us have, above our created being, an eternal life in God as in our living cause, who made and created us from nothing.[1]

It follows that man does not constitute a reality in itself any more than do things. He is a *theophany*. This is what Ruysbroeck means when he speaks of creation *ex nihilo*, creation being properly a vision of God: "By this eternal begetting," he says, "all creatures are born eternally before having been created in time. God has seen and contemplated them within himself, separately, according to the ideas that are in him, and as other than himself." [2]

On the third hypostasis devolves the rôle of ordainer of the world. The Holy Spirit keeps alive and upholds what has been created. Above all else, he is energy. He *actively* envelops and permeates all things, stirs up spiritual energies, pours himself forth like fertilising water into all creatures. It is also he who effects the return of creation to God: "Hence comes a Love which is called the Holy Spirit, a link between Father and Son and between Son and Father, and beings are wholly enveloped in and permeated with this Love which causes them to return to the unity whence the Father begets eternally." [3]

This theory responds to a dual question: How can God, who in essence is *eternal rest*, work externally? And how can an imperfect creation derive from Perfection? There remains a third: the question of the multiple, which Parmenides had purely and simply suppressed, but which insistently asserted itself upon Plotinus and his followers.

To solve it, Ruysbroeck introduces, along with *eternal*

---

[1] *The Mirror*, chapter xvii.   [2] *The Spiritual Marriage*, book III. chapter v.
[3] *The Kingdom*, chapter xxv.

creation, a *perpetual creation in time*. This—although the expression is found nowhere in the writings ·of our mystic —is the Neoplatonist theory of emanations. Fire is created, but the heat it radiates is not a creation, it is an emanation. A grain of amber is a creation, but the odorous particles released therefrom are emanations.[1] Emanation, strictly speaking, is the projection without of the virtues which constitute the essence of created things. Manifestly, the farther the emanations remove from their source, the feebler they become. Their virtue diminishes in direct ratio to the distance traversed, and finally becomes so diluted as to be no longer perceptible. Thus, emanations from the divine hypostases, striking with gradually diminishing energy, can beget only multiple and different beings. We have really to deal with a veritable degradation of energy: this explains the inequalities, differences of worth and quality, right throughout the world of sense, which only the diminished reflections of the original ray any longer reach. This is what Ruysbroeck means when he says: "this fecundity of the divine persons . . . ever works in a living *differentiation*."[2] On the lowest rung of the ladder of beings there still subsists, however tiny it be, an emanation from the generating hypostasis. This it is which, by successive conversions of inferior to superior, ensures the return to God. Return to God, then, is nothing else than the reduction of the many to the one.

.   .   .   .

Let us now see at work these living reasons, these first causes from which all things are derived. Ruysbroeck here sketches a magnificent picture in which the universe appears as a threefold structure. In reality there are three worlds: a divine world corresponding to the essence of Deity; a spiritual world; a material world. This tripartite universe (*macrocosm*) is completely reflected in man (*microcosm*).

First, there is the higher heaven, the *Empyrean*, "which

---

[1] *The Book of Supreme Truth*, chapter x.
[2] *The Twelve Beguines*, chapter xiv.

is pure and simple clearness, enclosing and enveloping all the heavens, as well as every corporeal and material creature, as with a sphere. . . ."

It has for its adornments God himself and the saints. The Empyrean, pure and simple clearness, corresponds to the superessence of God.

The second heaven is called Crystalline, by reason of its clearness. Its summit is the *primum mobile*, "because it is the starting-point and the beginning of all the movements of heaven and of the elements. It corresponds to the spiritual nature of man."

Lastly, below the Crystalline heaven, we have the firmament. "By reason of its movement . . . all creatures move, live and grow, and it has received, for its adornment and light, the splendour and clearness of planets and stars. . . ." Indeed, it is on the influence of the planets that depend the life and growth of all creatures, in a mode peculiar to each. To the firmament correspond in man the higher forces (*overste crachten*), which are in immediate correlation with the movements of the planets. "God created the planets," says Ruysbroeck, "to serve men in two ways: the movement and influence of the heavens have to do with begetting, with life and growth . . . and secondly, the sky was created because of its beauty and its clearness."[1] To the seven planets correspond the seven gifts of the spirit.

Finally, in the centre of the firmament is the earth, made up of the four elements: earth or clay, water, air and fire, which correspond to the four lower forces of man (*natuerlike* or *nederste crachten*).

Enveloping the cosmic world, and dominating it, is the spiritual creation. This latter comprises angels and men. "The wherefore of the creation of angels and men lies in the infinite goodness of God and his munificence which have inclined him to reveal to reasonable creatures his own beatitude and his sovereign riches."[2]

The angels are divided into three hierarchical orders, all

[1] *The Kingdom,* chapter xxxvii. [2] *The Spiritual Marriage,* book I. chapter ii.

placed above man to help and direct him in the three lives: the mystic life, the interior life, the active life. With the mystic life is related the superior hierarchy, Thrones, Cherubim and Seraphim. The Principalities, Powers and Dominions help man to live a perfect interior life. The members of the inferior hierarchy, Angels, Archangels and Virtues, sustain man in active life. The angels were created before man, and endowed with free-will. Those who used this free-will to find delight in themselves turned aside from God, and fell into the accursed darkness where they are to remain eternally.

Man was created to take the place of the fallen angels. He is the end and the crown of all creation. Not only is he the living and eternal mirror of God, he also reproduces in his nature the three stages of the universe. His soul, *in its simple bareness*, is the reflection of the One seated in the Empyrean. His spiritual nature corresponds to the *primum mobile* and reflects the Father. His physical nature, in its higher powers, corresponds to the firmament, whose planets maintain physical life on earth. Finally, his corporeal person is formed of the four elements which make up the earth. The earth is permeated by a living energy which is none other than the Holy Spirit, and this energy works in man to ensure his return to the One.

In this ensemble the soul constitutes itself a creation apart, gifted with the three properties corresponding to the three persons of the Trinity.

It is like an eternal and living mirror of God, continually and uninterruptedly receiving the eternal begetting of the Son. . . . Hence it comes about that the substance of our soul possesses three properties which form but one in nature. The first property of the soul is an essential imageless bareness: through this we resemble and are one with the Father and his divine nature. The second property may be called the higher reason of the soul: it is a mirror-like clearness wherein we receive the Son of God, eternal truth. By reason of this clearness we are like him. The third property we call the spark of the soul: it is an intimate and natural tendency of the soul towards its source, and it is there that we receive the Holy Spirit.[1]

Such is the broad-based structure wherein Ruysbroeck wishes to find a setting for the divine drama of the soul.

[1] *The Mirror*, chapter viii.

In his details this image is manifestly very far from our own conception, though none the less on that account do we regard it as a mighty attempt to solve the problem of destiny.

By closely linking religious life with a representation of the universe, by establishing with almost geometrical precision the manifold interplay of concordances and analogies, Ruysbroeck shut out all mechanical ideas and introduced life and intelligence into every province of the Cosmos. At the same time he eliminated fatality: God communicating himself to everything by a series of processes, there is in each part of the universe an element superior to corruption and death. Such a world is eternal, and whatever the changing conditions of being, there is only one issue: that which sheds light upon Deity.

But is not this limitless animism so like pantheism as to be mistaken for it? The divine emanations produce the cosmic forces; the latter slough off into spiritual activities. Nothing, then, is outside of the dynamic current which eternally issues from Deity; this current permeates the stone as well as man, the star as well as the animal. The only difference is one of degree. We are confronted with a veritable fractioning of Deity, and Ruysbroeck evades the extreme consequences of pantheism only by the final reabsorption of all things into unity.

Besides, this vitalism is not without a certain grandeur. Ruysbroeck traverses the universe as if it were a sanctuary. His emotions are all of a religious order. He is never tired of admiring the beauty of the world and delights in describing the starry heavens, the leafy forests, the rippling streams, the minerals; he piles image upon image, unable to pour into the narrow mould of verbal expression his state of exuberant and wild enthusiasm. "God," he says, "has made nothing finer or nobler, in heaven or on earth, than the order and the diversity that reign amongst all creatures." [1] Such is

[1] *The Kingdom,* chapter xxxix.; *The Seven Cloisters,* chapter xvii.; *The Seven Degrees,* chapter v.

the theme running through the whole work of our mystic, a theme he succeeded in enriching, by means of his powerful verbal gifts, with amazingly varied means of expression.

§ 3. *Man*

We have seen that man, placed between the world of spirit and the world of sense, participates in both. In him the image of the Trinity is perfectly reflected. In the Son he has been created, known and elected from all eternity.

(i.) Apart, however, from this eternal creation, there is, as in the cosmic order, a creation in time. This it is that fashions individual temperaments. It borrows, as its agent, the intelligent forces that are in the stars and so determines the life of sense (*sinlike leven*). Thus there are seven temperaments (*wisen van complexien*) as there are seven planets.

This determinism is corrected by the spiritual action of the planets, to which action the seven gifts of the spirit correspond. This dual action has its origin in God: the one is exercised upon our lower and the other upon our higher nature. Man, however, by a determination of will, can escape both from planetary action and from the influence of the Holy Spirit. "Over our free-will neither thing nor person has power, neither the heavenly bodies, nor creatures, nor anything other than God alone and ourselves." [1]

The corporeal nature, formed of the four elements, cannot wholly perish, in this sense that its elements return to the great reservoir from which they were taken. Man has therefore no right to despise his body, to hand it over to inferior lusts and desires. Is not this body the marvellously wrought casket intended for that incomparable jewel: the soul? The physical nature, then, constitutes the substructure upon which must be built the human personality. And the latter, exclusively spiritual in its nature, is similar to—whilst all the time less than—God.

The human personality is animated by a single life, which appears under a dual aspect: soul and spirit.

[1] *The Kingdom*, chapter iv.; *The Twelve Beguines*, chapter xxxi.

(ii.) The soul (*siel*) is not a creation, strictly speaking; one may say that it was created from nothing, for it is a reflection of the image of God. In it a distinction must be made between powers and properties.

The lower powers (*nederste crachten*) "are governed and ordered by the virtues which adorn the moral life of man." These are: the irascible power (*tornighe cracht*), which has to dominate everything opposed to morality, with prudence as its representative virtue; the concupiscible power (*begheerlike cracht*), with its virtue, temperance, whose duty it is to restrain all material or carnal excess; the reason (*redelicheit*), adorned with justice, which regulates, orders and directs all things; and finally, freedom of will (*vriheit des willen*), which finds its exercise in moral force and gives man the courage to dominate the vicissitudes of life.

These lower powers regulate the moral life; the higher powers (*overste crachten*) dominate the intellectual life. First, we have memory (*verhavene gedachte* or *memorie*), not to be confused with the faculty of recollection.[1] This is thought directed towards God dwelling in the human soul. Afterwards we have intelligence (*verstennisse*), or thought turned towards God as the cause and creator of the universe. Lastly, will (*wille*).

Independently of these powers, the soul is endowed with three properties (*eyghenscape*) which are none other than projections into the soul of the three hypostases. The first is an essential imageless bareness (*onghebeelde weselike bloetheit*), "whereby we resemble and are united to the Father and his divine nature." The second property may be called the superior reason of the soul (*overste redene*), wherein the Son is reflected. The third property is the spark of the soul (*vonke der sielen*), "the intimate and natural tendency of the soul towards its source; it is there that we receive the Holy Spirit and become like him."[2]

By uniting together, the powers and the properties of the

---

[1] Cf. St. Thomas, *Summa*, I.^{a}, quaest. LXXIX., art. 6.
[2] *The Mirror*, chapter viii.

soul constitute a higher state which is called the spirit (*gheest*), and in which alone union with God is realised.

(iii.) Thus the spirit is another name for the soul, made capable of unity (*enicheit*). This unity may come about in threefold form: First, there is the unity of the lower powers and of the five senses in the heart, the principle of corporeal life. Then, strictly speaking, it is called soul (*anima*), for it is the mover of the body which it animates. The second unity is reasonable and spiritual. This is the unity of the higher powers, regarded from the standpoint of their activity. It is adorned and possessed supernaturally by the three theological virtues. The third unity is the unity of the higher forces in the spirit, above all sensibility.

> Every creature in its essence, its life and preservation, depends wholly on this unity: to separate from God, in this respect, would be for it to plunge into nothingness. . . . This unity is essential in us by nature, whether we be righteous or sinners. But it can make us neither holy nor happy without our co-operation. It is the unity from which we came as created beings, whilst remaining there in our essence, and we return to it by way of charity. . . . This is a natural kingdom of God, and the term of all the processes of the soul.[1]

2. Such was man, in his eternal essence. Within the bosom of the blessed light, he was in God. The gifts and forces just mentioned existed in him but virtually; for, united to God, he had no reason for setting his powers to work. The latter were to function only in order to realise a new unity (*moghelike enicheit*) in case the original unity should be broken.

Here we come to the second act of the divine drama: the fall or decline of the soul.

§ 1. *The Fall*

We are made aware of the loss of our pristine nobility by a sense of uneasiness. Here below we dream of realisations which remain unfulfilled. We conceive of beauty and perfection, but our passions prevent us from attaining thereto. We feel confined in every way, and the discrepancy between

---

[1] *The Spiritual Marriage*, book II. chapter ii.

our mutilated lives and our desire for expansion is the source of endless suffering. Our homeland is elsewhere and, until we return to it, what we call happiness will be no more than the shadow of happiness. And so there has been a catastrophe between our sojourn in our divine homeland and our existence on earth.

What has been the nature of this catastrophe? There is not a philosopher of old who has not attempted to picture it. Plato's myths tell us of the journeyings of the soul above the celestial vault, and its fall to earth, with broken wings (πτερορρυήσασα), because it can no longer remain in the heavens. Plotinus shows us the soul fascinated by its image reflected in the bodies from below, and, in longing desire, springing forward towards this image and falling into the world of sense.[1] With variations in detail, the Gnostics describe the soul as floundering in matter. Now, as in the myth of Sophia, wholly imbued with Biblicism, the soul renders itself guilty of the charge of inquisitiveness in wishing to discover the secret of Deity; then again, as in Valentinus, it is robbed, by the framers of the Cosmos, of the divine element surreptitiously introduced into its constitution by God. The Pseudo-Dionysius translates in a Christian form the Neoplatonist conception as he received it from Proclus. The element common to all these conceptions is the longing for the divine which tortures the human soul here below, and gives inimitable emphasis to the inspirations of Plotinus.[2]

It is the same with Ruysbroeck: man, lost in a world of darkness ruled by suffering and corruption, may be compared to an exile. " Knowledge of ourselves teaches us whence we come, where we are, and whither we are going. We come from God, and we are in exile; it is because our potency of affection ever tends towards God that we are aware of this state of exile." [3]

It happens that man falls into a kind of languor and impatient desire to be set free from the prison of his body. Then tears often gush forth and

---

[1] *Enneads*, IV. 3, 12; 3, 17. [2] *Ibid.*, I. i. 6.
[3] *The Kingdom*, chapter xviii.

burning desires are born. Then, carrying his gaze back to this earth, the poor man sees in what an exile he is imprisoned, without the possibility of escape. And he sheds tears of impatience and of yearning for home.[1]

Ruysbroeck looks upon the Fall as the consequence of a spontaneous initiative on the part of the soul, the result of a choice made possible and obligatory by the gift of *freedom of will*. Man can choose: herein lies his greatness. He is forced to choose: herein lies his servitude. He has chosen ill-fortune: herein lies his guilt. But what were the terms in question? On the one hand the soul could choose to remain in unity. On the other hand it could separate from the universal soul and live an individual life. Here Ruysbroeck is clearly influenced by the Plotinian conception.[2] He invests it, however, with images found in the Biblical account of the Fall. God had conferred upon Adam all the supernatural gifts: immortality, immunity from suffering, and integrity, whereby the good will retained mastery over the inferior powers of the soul. These privileges Adam transmitted to all who, his offspring, should participate in human nature. He had only a single gift of his own: the gift of knowledge which he was unable to hand down to his descendants.

> Then came a cheat, the hellish foe who, filled with jealousy, deceived the woman, and the two of them deceived the man in whom was the whole of human nature. Thus did the foe, by his false counsels, ravish this nature, the spouse of God. And she was exiled to a foreign land, became poor and wretched, captive and oppressed beneath the yoke of her enemies. . . .[3]

This miserable condition was transmitted, and became the lot of all mankind: "Human nature fell by the sin of the first man, and the nature that was free became a dungeon and an exile, a blind alley in which all who are born go astray, for they are the children of disobedience."[4]

This state of separation is called sin. It is the soul's consent to separation from the original unity. This acquiescence constitutes the whole of man's guilt. As set forth, this doctrine is not free from a certain Pelagianism. It amounts to the statement that there is no evil; evil is but separation

---

[1] *The Spiritual Marriage*, book I. chapter xxiii.   [2] *Enneads*, IV. 8, 3.
[3] *The Spiritual Marriage*, book I., prologue.   [4] *The Kingdom*, chapter ii.

from good. Again, the soul in its fall retained all the possibilities of regaining the lost blessedness: "the nobility and freedom of its will; it knows what is called dying and living, what good and evil are. It loves good and hates evil; and so it returns to God and obtains his compassion." [1]

Nevertheless all this involves a contradiction. Indeed, we no longer see the necessity of a redemption, the work of an agent external to man. Now, redemption by Christ holds an important place in the return of the soul to God. The contradiction is more formal than fundamental. For if, indeed, the return of man to God is the personal work of man, this return is possible only in a purified nature. The rôle of Christ consists in liberating the human soul, in permitting the expression of the potentialities slumbering therein. In this sense Ruysbroeck may say that man, after the Fall, lost nothing substantial that God had created in him, and the rôle of Christ remains primordial, being the very condition of the return to God. We will now examine this rôle which is to make possible the third act of the divine drama of the soul.

§ 2. The Work of Christ

Man is the exclusive framer of his destiny: this is one of the ideas upon which Ruysbroeck most insists. No force whatsoever can exercise constraint upon him, neither God, nor devil, nor heavenly body. The conclusion has therefore been drawn that redemption held but a secondary place in Ruysbroeck's system.[2] This is not the case. For while, in various forms, Ruysbroeck repeats his well-known formula: *vous êtes saints comme vous le voulez*, a close study of our mystic proves that, in his mind, the will is exercised towards God only under the influence of grace. Left in its natural state the soul can but hate evil and desire grace, without being able to sanctify itself. Grace, i.e. this liberating influence, is the work of Christ. It annihilates the consequences

---

[1] *The Twelve Beguines*, chapter xxxiv.
[2] Altmeyer, *Les Précurseurs de la Réforme*, t. I. p. 114.

of the Fall, but it does not realise union, i.e. a return to original purity.

As regards the personality of Christ, Ruysbroeck sometimes clearly departs from traditional teaching. Humanity as understood by the Word is a complete humanity, made up of human flesh and a rational soul. Both natures, divine and human, exist in Jesus without confusion or division, each nature retaining its properties and acting in accordance with them. Jesus, *qua* historical person, was not born of the Father by nature: he acquired divine filiation only through his union with the Word. This doctrine recalls to mind the heresy of Theodosius of Mopsuestia and of Nestorius as to the two natures: between them no mingling or combination whatsoever (κρᾶσις, σύγχυσις). Christ is διπλοῦς τῇ φύσει.[1] Now what does Ruysbroeck say?

His humiliations have not caused him to decline and fall, for he still remains what he was whilst assuming what he was not. He remains God in becoming man, in order that man may become God.[2] He has put on our humanity, as a king does the raiment of his familiars and his servants; so that we with him have assumed the same garment, which is human nature. But at the same time . . . he gave to his soul and body, born of the all-pure Virgin Mary, the royal robe of divine personality.[3]

The Son of God [Ruysbroeck says again] has a soul created from nothing, i.e. *emanated*; also a body formed of the pure blood of the Virgin Mary. Soul and body are so much his and so well united that he is at once Son of God and Son of Mary, God and man in a single person. And as soul and body form but one man, so the Son of God and the Son of Mary are but one and the same living Christ, God and Lord of heaven and earth; for his holy soul is animated or inspirited by the wisdom of God. Still, it is not God, nor is it of divine nature, for God does not become creature. But the two natures remaining distinct are united in a single divine person: our dear Lord Jesus.[4]

Ruysbroeck thus comes to see in Christ not God's own son but his adoptive son; i.e. he establishes duality of persons. By his divine nature and as Word, Christ is natural son of

[1] See L. Fendt, *Die Christologie des Nestorius* (Kempten, 1910).

[2] This declaration recalls almost literally the phrase of Saint Augustine: "Homo propter nos factus, qui nos homines fecit; et assumens hominem Deus ut homines faceret deos." *Sermo* CCCXLIV.

[3] *The Mirror*, chapter viii. Cf. *The Spiritual Marriage*, book I. chapters ii., iii.; *The Kingdom*, chapter ii.

[4] *The Mirror*, chapter xix.

God; this he is *proprietate atque substantia*; but by his human nature he is son of God *non natura sed gratia atque electione*. "The Holy Spirit dwelt in his soul and in his human nature with all his gifts; he it is that made him rich and generous, lavish of himself towards all." [1] This characteristic passage is clearly adoptionist, and others that express heterodox conceptions might be quoted. Passages might also be found to contradict them and bring Ruysbroeck back to the traditional point of view:

> The humanity of Our Lord has indeed no substance of itself, for it is not its own personality as in all other men; but the Son of God is its hypostasis and its form (*hare onderstant ende hare forme*). Thus it is uniform with God (*eenformich*) and the hypostatic union confers on it wisdom and power, above everything that is inferior to God. [2]

And so it is not possible to give a coherent account of the Christology of our author. Shall we find greater cohesion in his soteriology?

At the outset Ruysbroeck admits that Christ voluntarily assumed the condition of humanity. [3] But at the same time, Christ, on coming down to earth, obeys a necessity of nature, implied in the theory of emanations. [4] More frequently he is the delegate, the proxy of God moved to pity by the wretched condition of mankind: "When God judged that the time had come, moved with pity at the suffering of his beloved, he sent his only Son to the kingdom of earth, into a richly-adorned palace and a glorious temple, by which I mean the body of the Virgin Mary." [5]

He is the channel whereby the goodness of God can reach down to us.

The work of Christ is interpreted in different ways. The divergencies, however, affect only the details. At bottom we have to deal with a liberation of human nature, subjected to evil. "Christ has worked and fought like a valiant champion against our enemy; he has broken down the prison and won

---

[1] *Ibid.*, chapter xx.   [2] *Ibid.*
[3] *The Seven Cloisters*, chapter i.
[4] *The Book of Supreme Truth*, chapter x.
[5] *The Spiritual Marriage*, book I., prologue.

the victory, by his own death destroying our death. His blood has redeemed us." [1]

Ruysbroeck did not state who should benefit by the ransom paid: now it is the devil, now it is God. In other places the idea of a ransom disappears, and the death of the Saviour is no more than the victory won in the fight for which man was the stakes. To profit by the merits that this death won, it is necessary to adhere personally to this work of love alone, "to put on a new life . . . renounce the devil and his service, and believe in Christ.[2] The sinner must meet God in contrition and a free return to him, with the firm intention henceforth of serving him always and never sinning again." [3]

Those who do not decide upon this free return place themselves outside of divine pity. Frequently will the opportunity to repent be offered to them. If they finally reject this opportunity, they will condemn themselves to hell. Among the six categories of evil men Ruysbroeck distinguishes two for whom there is no remission: the first is that of those Christians who have despised the death of Christ and his sacraments; the second comprises infidels, pagans or Jews, who are unable to benefit by the death of Christ.[4]

This doctrine of perdition for a portion of mankind evidently seems to contradict the ensemble of Ruysbroeck's system. We have seen, indeed, that the human race is indivisible. On the other hand, evil cannot be eternal, for it does not exist substantially. Ruysbroeck solves the question in his eschatology. The wicked will not be annihilated, but "by means of fire, God will renew their elements in clearness and will make them subtle, giving them a more beautiful form than they had before. For these elements have been sullied by sin and must be purified by fire." [5]

To return to the work of Christ. A thrill passes through the frame of man as he contemplates the Saviour. On that

[1] *The Spiritual Marriage*, book I., prologue; *The Seven Cloisters*, chapter xxi.
[2] *The Kingdom*, chapter ii.
[3] *The Spiritual Marriage*, book I. chapter xxv.
[4] *Ibid.*, book I. chapter x.; *The Kingdom*, chapters vii.–xii.
[5] *The Kingdom*, chapter xxxvii.

divine countenance he has recognised the reflection of his origin. He becomes exalted at the recollection. His life now seems to him dull and despicable. He turns aside therefrom in conversion, fortifies his will by the practice of the sacra- ments. And now a force unknown works within him. "Man is so severely stricken that he becomes attentive, continues in dread, and considers within himself."[1] He is ready to undertake the long journey.

3. Here really begins the third act of the divine drama: the return to unity. "The pilgrim takes his staff and sings, as he smiles upon his homeland."

§ 1. *The Three Paths*

Everything tends inevitably to return to its origin. The physical world is a vast parable illustrating this law: dew evaporates and condenses into rain; the tree draws from the juices of the earth the sap circulating through its foliage, and when the leaves fall they become soil once more; the corporeal nature of man is of mineral origin and, on the dissolution of the body, its elements return to the crucible from which they have been drawn. Now, the laws that govern the material world are those that control the spiritual: man's eternal destiny is to aspire after God.

The whole of religion then consists in recognising God as our first origin and our final end, in returning to him in a way conformable with his will. It is perfectly represented by a ring, an unbroken circle without either starting-point or finishing-point.[2]

But this search after God is subject to definite rules, ignorance or neglect of which would lead to perversions of the faith, such as the Quietist heresies and the sect of the Free Spirit. Apart from the sacraments, which visibly express

---

[1] *The Spiritual Marriage*, book I. chapter i.
[2] *The Sparkling Stone* is also entitled *dat hantvingherlijn*, the ring, symbol of the return of the soul to unity. Surius dropped this second title.

the spiritual laws of our religious progress, the mystical life is prefigured in us by the *three unities*, where it is seen how the nature within us can unite with the supernatural: the inferior corporeal unity, which expresses itself in the practice of external works; the spiritual unity, which is shown in the theological virtues and the imitation of Jesus Christ; the sublime unity, which causes us to find rest in God above all intention.

To this threefold unity corresponds a threefold path, which will progressively lead us to the desired union. Now the mystic life will be represented by a ladder; then again by the forest tree: the tree grows both in height and in depth; through its foliage it assimilates the virtue of the air, through its roots it extracts the juices of the earth. Its trunk and limbs strengthen and expand in concentric circles, while the extreme branches, ever more slender, blend with the sky. Nevertheless, no one will say that the tree has become sky; or the sky tree. Likewise, through the mystic life, man unites with God, without becoming God or without God becoming man.

Ruysbroeck deals with this vast subject in all his books, though with variations corresponding to the progressive precision of his thought. And so, under the risk of giving an imperfect sketch of his ideas, we must take into account the successive improvements and adornments of his thought, and regard the later treatises as the basis of our exposition. It is for this reason that we choose *The Seven Degrees* as our starting-point. Therein we find the original form of Ruysbroeck's thought, as showing itself in *The Spiritual Marriage*, along with fresh developments.

On the road which man has to traverse in attaining to perfection Ruysbroeck distinguishes seven stages: (i.) the identification of our will with the divine will; (ii.) voluntary poverty; (iii.) purity of soul and chastity of body; (iv.) the intimate consciousness of our own baseness; (v.) delight in God alone; (vi.) a clear intuition into purity of thought; (vii.) not-knowing in limitless repose.

These divisions enter into the threefold scheme drawn

up by the Pseudo-Dionysius: κάθαρσις, φωτισμὸς, τελείωσις, or μυστικη ἕνωσις. It is the scheme adopted by Ruysbroeck in *The Spiritual Marriage*, where he speaks of the three lives: the active or beginning life (*beghinnende, werkende leven*); the interior life (*ynnighe, verhavene, begheerlike leven*); the contemplative life (*godscouwende, overweselike leven*).

§ 2. *The Active Life*

In this category are "the virtuous men of good-will who, masters of themselves, are incessantly dying to sin."[1] The beginning of this life is marked by a *moral act*, conversion, essentially a work of the will though rendered easy by an interior predisposition whose agent is the Holy Spirit. We are here dealing with *predisposing grace*, upon which Ruysbroeck dwells at length.

This grace is offered to all, but is not implanted in all. It finds exercise either in tests and trials or in examples, sermons, religious meditation. Hence is born a natural affliction for sin and a natural good-will, perfect contrition and purification of conscience. These processes do not yet constitute more than the preliminaries of the active life. Conversion is but a starting-point, for sin, although blotted out, leaves behind something impure which allures to other faults: "The holy life is warfare which can be maintained only by fighting."[2] This fighting is called self-discipline or self-mastery: "Keep possession of yourselves and never let go your own soul."[3]

In this struggle we must consider our relations with ourselves, with our neighbour and with God, relations expressed by the three virtues: charity, justice and humility. "Of themselves alone, these virtues bear the whole weight of the edifice,"[4] and correspond to the three persons of the divine unity.

[1] *The Mirror*, chapter i.
[2] *The Seven Degrees*, chapter iv.; *The Mirror*, chapter ii.
[3] *The Mirror*, chapter ii.; *The Seven Cloisters*, chapter xi.
[4] *The Spiritual Marriage*, book I. chapter xi.

The whole moral philosophy of Ruysbroeck is based on regarding the powers of the soul as conformable with the divine hypostases. The active life consists above all in combating the effects of sin—dimness of intellect, weakness of will, the three Johannine concupiscences—by the opposite virtues. He makes the study of these virtues an opportunity for drawing vivid psychological representations; he is more intent on describing the good that *ought to be* than the evil that is. We cannot stop to analyse all the virtues that form part of Ruysbroeck's system, but simply note the order in which they should follow one another in the soul struggling for self-conquest.

Obedience, humility and resignation of will correspond to the first gift of the Holy Spirit, the gift of fear, and constitute the first step on the spiritual ladder. The next step, corresponding to the gift of piety, introduces man to the practice of gentleness, compassion and liberality. Lastly, the practice of zeal, sobriety and purity raises man to the third and last step in the active life, where he places himself under the influence of the third gift of the Spirit: the gift of science or of true self-knowledge. Thus will man rule his own soul as a kingdom.

Although the active life is not yet, strictly speaking, the mystic life, it enables man to meet God, to have a foretaste of the longed-for union, " for every virtuous act presupposes a meeting with God." [1] This is what Ruysbroeck calls the mediate union.

This is what I say concerning the first state of union: all good people are united to God by an intermediary. This intermediary consists of divine grace and the sacraments, the theological virtues, and a virtuous life in conformity with God's commandments. All this implies death to sin and the world, to all the disorderly appetites of nature.[2]

As we see, the mystical life is far from being regarded by him as a dreamland into which material necessities and moral struggles disappear beneath the light of interior illumination. Other mystics may lose foothold, take no

[1] *The Spiritual Marriage*, book I. chapter xxv.
[2] *The Book of Supreme Truth*, chapters i., iii.

account of human weakness; our philosopher retains close contact with life. Nowhere does Ruysbroeck set forth the spiritual life as an easy path. He dwells on the eclipse of inspiration, on sudden darkness, on dull, depressing days.

When you least expect it, God will hide and withdraw his hand; between himself and you he will place darkness through which you will be able to see nothing. Then will you complain, crying and moaning like a pauper. . . . Though God has disappeared from your sight, you are not hidden from him.[1]

Ruysbroeck is fond of picturing life as a garden which it is incumbent upon man to cultivate. God willed that, along with the delectable fruits of virtue, there should also grow the flower of joy, made for the delight both of eye and of heart. He points to this joy as existing not in glorious adventures and great riches, but in the humblest departments of daily life. Not a single day but brings its offering of beauty. How lovingly he sheds new lustre upon little duties and occupations, "the knowledge and supernatural wisdom" of seeing God beneath the most modest and uncouth aspect! Long before Luther he repeats that one can serve God in scullery, kitchen or sick-room, as well as in the sanctuary! "Go to your work," he advises some monks, "and if you are so busy that you can neither listen to mass nor receive the Sacrament, be not displeased thereat, for God prefers obedience before sacrifice."[2]

No one has insisted more strongly than Ruysbroeck on the great dignity of work, which he recommends one to undertake most conscientiously. And religious life, so greatly menaced by the spirit of routine, is work. "When you read, whether in chant or in prayer, understand what you say; attend to the meaning of the words and to the ideas they express."[3] Do not force inspiration, nor cultivate the ambition to climb the summits at a bound: stage by stage proceed along the road that is to bring you to God. They are mad who think they can arrive more speedily by rushing

[1] *The Mirror*, chapter ii.   [2] *The Seven Cloisters*, chapter v.
[3] *The Mirror*, chapter ii.

along at full speed. Life is an art that must be learned in detail; nothing is so trifling or unimportant as not to affect the condition of the soul. And so our excellent prior refuses to split up mankind into two orders of sanctity—the lower sanctity of the lay people and the higher sanctity of the monks: *"We make profession to God in the order of true sanctity, whatever raiment we wear or in whatever state we may be."* [1]

This is a new expression of life, but the words are eternally true. Religion is more than morality; still, it cannot be based upon anything less than morality. The "good life" or the "active life" is the mother earth in which faith is rooted. This latter, like a tree, fades away and dies unless it be supplied with sap by the living juices slowly elaborated in the depths of human consciousness. Is it not worth while, even in these days, to learn this lesson and ponder deeply over it?

In *The Sparkling Stone* Ruysbroeck describes—by personifying them—the various stages of the spiritual life. From Saint Bernard he borrows the image of the hirelings, of the faithful servants, of the friends and sons of God. [2] The hireling represents man before his conversion, serving God from fear or from personal interest. The faithful servant is attached to God; he knows and serves him, but he has not yet entered into a state of intimacy with him; this privilege is reserved for secret friends. With these we enter the second sphere of the spiritual life: the interior life.

§ 3. *The Interior Life*

There are to be found souls who, going beyond the mere practice of virtues, discover within themselves and recognise a life that is truly living, wherein are united the created and the uncreated, God and the creature. [3]

But this life is greatly threatened by various dangers which Ruysbroeck compares to diseases, and it is profitable to take warning from them.

[1] *The Seven Cloisters*, chapter xiii.
[2] St. Bernard, *On the Love of God*, chapter xii.; *Sermones de diversis*, sermo iii.
[3] *The Mirror*, chapter xvii.

At the autumnal equinox . . . the temperature lowers. At this period those who are not careful run the risk of incurring harmful humours, which load the stomach and cause maladies and indispositions of various kinds. . . . In the same way, when those who, being of good will, have tasted somewhat of God, afterwards decline and fall away from God and truth, they begin to languish. . . . Some would gladly welcome divine consolation if it could be obtained without effort . . . they regard as indispensable all that they can supply to their body in the way of comfort or ease. When man thus condescends to nature and indiscreetly pursues the satisfaction of his own body, then this satisfaction corresponds to the harmful humours . . . his heart is disturbed thereby and he loses all appetite and taste for good food, i.e. for all the virtues.[1]

There is also a spiritual analogy to dropsy.

Such is the greed for earthly possessions, so that, the more one receives, the more one desires; for water accumulates, and the body—i.e. the appetites and desires—becomes enormous without any diminution of thirst.[2]

Finally there is a third evil, consisting of four kinds of fever: multiplicity of affections, inconstancy, spiritual blindness and habitual negligence.

Let man then put on armour as does a knight before entering upon this difficult path. Here too his best help will be a strong will, without which divine grace is unable to work. And none enters the interior life unless entreated by grace.

Indeed, the grace of God within the soul may be compared to a candle in a lighthouse or glass globe, for it illumines and penetrates with its rays the crystal, i.e. the just man. But it reveals itself only on condition that he, the just man, be attentive to perceive it.[3]

This true vigil must then precede the consecration of the knight of the interior life. Only afterwards, from being a faithful servant, will he be promoted to the rank of a secret friend.

During this lonely vigil he must first strip himself of all representations apart from God. He must possess nothing ardently, nor bind himself to anyone by natural inclination, for all attachments and affections that do not tend solely to the honour of God burden the heart of man.[4] Then, too,

[1] *The Spiritual Marriage*, book I. chapter xxx.
[2] *Ibid.*, book I. chapter xxxi.
[3] *Ibid.*, book II. chapter iv.
[4] *The Sparkling Stone*, chapter ii.

he must be born to that interior freedom which consists "in being able to raise one's thoughts to God without images or shackles in all inner exercises: thanksgiving, praise, worship, devout prayers and intimate affections." In brief, he must feel truly united to God in spirit, having free access to him and in all things considering nothing but divine honour.

When these conditions are satisfied he truly enters into the interior life. There he enjoys the full radiance of Christ, the eternal sun.

> The sun shining upon the high-lands,[1] in the centre, over against the mountains, gives birth to an early summer which produces much good fruit and potent wine, and fills the earth with joy. Whereas in the low-lands, no doubt the sun's rays also shine forth, but the country is colder and the warmth less great. Good fruit may grow there in considerable quantity, but wine is rare.[2]

.   .   .   .

(i.) To express how the Christ-illumination gradually enters the soul, first in its inferior and then in its superior powers, and finally in its very essence, Ruysbroeck pursues his analogy with the sun, in its conjunction with the various signs of the Zodiac.

(a) The sun rises in the east and in a moment floods the world with warmth and light. Thus do we feel the interior impulsion of the divine spirit illuminating the inferior part of man, i.e. his heart. The warmth of this glow and radiance produces unity of heart or inner peace, calm, the consciousness of divine love, the devotion whereby "there blossoms in body and soul honour and reverence before God and before all men," gratitude, accompanied by a sense of our impotence to apprehend fully the divine goodness and bounty, and of the tardiness of our growth in grace. The interior fire and ardour of the Holy Spirit works within us like the flame which "by its power raises water to boiling-point: that is the utmost it can do. Then the water is set

---

[1] *Overlant*, the Brabantine tableland, in opposition to the *nederlant*, the Netherlands.
[2] *The Spiritual Marriage*, book II. chapter viii.

moving, and descends again to the bottom of the vessel, when
it is driven up afresh by the same powerful action of the fire";
or, again, like the sun's heat, "which attracts the moisture
of the earth through the roots and trunk of the tree right up
to the branches, thus bringing into birth leaves, flowers
and fruit."

(b) When the sun rises high in the heavens and enters the sign of the
Twins, in the middle of May, it has twofold power. . . . If at the same
time the planets that govern nature appear in the order required by the
season, the sun sheds his beams over the earth and draws the moisture
into the air. Hence dew and rain, the growth and increase of fruit.

Likewise, under the influence of the Spirit, there is shed
abroad "a gentle rain of new interior comforts and a heavenly
dew of divine sweetness." This is that inner joy, that spiritual
transport, which expresses itself in various ecstatic manifestations. It is "the May of the interior life," when the
things to be dreaded are the dim mists and the hoar-frost of
pride, the "desire to find repose in interior consolation."
Let man then imitate the prudent bee: it wanders from
flower to flower without resting on any one of them; "it
gathers honey and wax, i.e. that which is sweet and that which
will give brightness, and then it returns to the unit, the
swarm, in order that its labour may bear fruit."

(c) When the sun reaches its highest point in the sky
it enters the sign of the Crab. It is then, at the point of
return, that the sun is hottest; it draws away the moisture
of the earth, which now becomes dry, and fruits become ripe.
Likewise Christ, at the highest stage of our affections, attracts
to and concentrates upon himself all our powers. The heart
then expands with joy and desire, "the fruit of the virtues
ripens." This languor and impatience for love increase still
more, for the sun enters the sign of the Lion; this is the
season of storms and soothing rain, reminiscent of transports
and visions, of tears of ecstasy: "sometimes God arouses
in the mind a swift flash, something like lightning in the sky.
It is a brief stream of light, of dazzling clearness. In an
instant the mind is raised superior to itself; but immediately

the light is no longer, and man returns to himself." These effects, the prudent Ruysbroeck is careful to add, may come from Satan as well as from God, "and so one can trust in them only in so far as they agree with truth and the Holy Scriptures, no more." Here is the greatest peril of this canicular state: similarly,

during great heat there sometimes falls a certain honey-dew, falsely sweet, that taints and even contaminates the fruit; this happens in particular at noon when the sun is shining in all his brightness; and we see great drops that can scarcely be distinguished from rain.

The other danger is debility of the body through excess of rapture. Let man then be prudent and take example from the ant, "which does not pursue various paths, but goes straight along the same way, and after the requisite lapse of time becomes capable of flying."

(d) Lastly, the sun, in its decline, enters the sign of the Virgin, "which is so called because then the season, like a virgin, produces no fruit." The crops are gathered into barns, and in this autumn "man resembles one who has unlearnt everything, who has lost his knowledge, and the fruit of his pains." This destitute state gives birth to the dread of falling, to semi-mistrust. Let man then have confidence in God, glad that he can suffer somewhat in his honour. Meanwhile the sun has entered the sign of the Scales. Days and nights are of equal duration. Similarly, we have Christ confronted with forsaken man: "Whether he give this man sweetness or bitterness, dark or light, to restore the balance: all things are the same to him, with the exception of sin, which should be wholly banned."

Such is the first stage of the interior life, that which realises the unity of the lower or corporeal powers of the soul. The following stage should lead to unity of the higher powers, those of the *spirit*.

(ii.) In this new state, divine grace is installed in man as its abode, like a living spring. This spring divides into three streams which fertilise each of the three higher powers of the soul.

First there is *simplicity* (*pure eenvoldicheit*), which raises the spirit above all cares or preoccupations, above all instability of thought. Then there is *spiritual illumination* (*gheestelike claerheit*), which enlightens the intellect and enables it to contemplate God in his perfection and his incomprehensible nature, and to rise to the mystery of the Trinity. The third stream is that of *inspired ardour* (*inghegheeste hitte*), which enflames the will and enriches the soul with great possessions.

The man aflame with this ardour feels compelled to respond to these renewed tokens of divine love. However sweet be the solitary delight in his spiritual possessions, he must come out of himself. He therefore betakes himself to God and all the saints: "he traverses all choirs, all hierarchies, all glorified beings; he considers how God dwells in each according to his nobility." Then he turns to the sinners, and presents them before God with pitying, generous heart. His eyes again fall upon the souls in purgatory, having regard to their misery and to their hopes. Lastly, returning to himself, he unites with all men of good will, experiencing the union and harmony which love creates between them, and coming as a mediator and peace-bringer.

(iii.) But divine grace must penetrate even farther into the depths, and touch the very essence of the soul. The preceding stage was compared to the flow of a living spring; here the analogy bears rather upon the very vein from which the spring gushes to the surface, " for in this domain none other works than God alone in his freely-given goodness." Light ineffable, above all imagination, and in whose presence we are by nature blind, for "all intelligences with their created light are like the eyes of the bat before the brightness of the sun." Once the soul has apprehended this supernatural light, it acquires an unappeasable hunger, a devouring greed (*mengherael*, *bulimia*, insatiable appetite). In this hunger and thirst after love,

this man is continually abandoning all action, spending and annihilating himself in love; for his hunger and thirst is after God. . . . He lives and yet dies, and in dying lives again. . . . He bears great labour of love, for he has caught a glimpse of his rest. He is a pilgrim, and he now perceives his homeland. He is a combatant in love for victory, and he sees the shining of his crown.

In this impetuous condition the spirit of God strives with the spirit of man (*minnenstrijt*), each wishing to possess his beloved,

and the mutual contact incessantly renewed raises up a fresh tempest of love. The fire of love leaps forth like sparks of molten metal or the flaming lights of heaven. The flash descends right into the powers of the sense-world, and all that lives in man tends to reach up to union, where the love contact arises.

Thus do the deeps of life enable the soul to realise a closer union than that by an intermediary: this is *immediate* union, with which is linked the prayer of Christ: "that the love wherewith thou hast loved me may be *in* them, and I *in* them" (John xvii. 26).

To define this union, Ruysbroeck proceeds by way of comparison:

You know how the air is bathed in the light and heat of the sun, and how iron is so permeated with fire that it forms one with it, burning and illuminating like fire itself. . . . Nevertheless each element retains its own distinctive nature; fire does not become iron any more than iron becomes fire. But the union takes place without intermediary since iron is interiorly in fire and fire in iron, as air is in sunlight and sunlight in air.

Similarly in immediate union,

intellect, raised aloft and stripped of all imagination, is permeated with eternal brightness as the air is permeated with the sun; *will*, raised aloft and unadorned, is transformed and imbued with unfathomable love, as iron is permeated throughout by fire. *Memory*, raised aloft and unadorned, feels itself caught up in an unfathomable absence of all mental imagery. And so beyond reason, the image created is united in threefold fashion to its eternal type . . . but the creature does not become God.

§ 4. *The Contemplative Life*

In the contemplative life, union without distinction or difference is consummated. In it is realised the prayer of Christ: "that they may be *one*, even as we, the Father and I, are one" (John xvii. 22).

Few men can attain thereto [says Ruysbroeck], both because of their own unfitness and by reason of the mystery of the illumination in which contemplation takes place. . . . No one could succeed by profundity of learning or any kind of perspicacity, nor by any religious exercise; but he whom God would unite with his spirit and himself enlighten is alone capable of this contemplation, and none other.

This privileged individual is called the mystical or hidden son of God. The *secret friends* cannot rise to these mystical heights, for even in union they ever retain a certain distinctive spirit of their own.

They remain ignorant of and unattracted by the simple transition to plainness and absence of mode, so that the highest interior life is always an impediment of reasons and modes. . . . Resolved to live always in the service of God and to please him eternally, they are not yet willing to die in God and live a uniform life with God.

The hidden sons, on the other hand, to whom applies the saying of Saint Paul: " ye are dead, and your life is hid with Christ in God " (Col. iii. 3), have immolated themselves. This is a second spiritual death, the first being death to sin in order to be born to a virtuous life.

In our progress towards God, by the practice of the virtues, God dwells in us, but in the death of ourselves and of all things, it is we who dwell in him.

Transcending reason, we should enter into God by faith, and then remain there, simple and unadorned. . . . Then, in our spirit, released from all activity, we receive the incomprehensible brightness . . . which is nothing else than endless vision and contemplation. In this simple glance we are with God one single life, one single spirit; and this is what I call a contemplative life.

But how is this to be explained? For it supersedes all reason and understanding, and is above all creation. Only those know it who have experienced it. Only by analogy can one speak of immersion in God: "it is like rivers that incessantly pour themselves into the sea, for that is their own place" (*haer eighen stat*).

What are the conditions for attaining to this blessed state?

Ruysbroeck is very obscure in dealing with these delicate points. The six conditions mentioned in *The Sparkling Stone* [1] evidently refer to a state of simplification and interior void, as realised by mystics of all ages, both yogis of India

---

[1] Chapter xiii. See also chapter iii., where these conditions are reduced to three.

and shamans of Australia, as well as by Plotinus,[1] who, says Porphyry, entered into a state of ecstasy four times whilst he was living with him.[2] It is the abolition of all thought, all feeling, the absolute fixity of the mind upon itself, the suppression of all individual life.[3] In this utter passivity man no longer exists. It is no longer man who lives in God, it is God who lives in man. And so Ruysbroeck says that in this state God reflects himself, imprints himself as an eternal seal. In mystic union the Trinity finds its perfect expression in its threefold character: repose, flow and ebb.

> For in us the Father gives himself in the Son and the Son in the Father, in eternal delight and loving embrace, and this is hourly repeated in the bonds of love. Just as indeed the Father ever contemplates anew all things in the begetting of his Son, so all things are loved anew by Father and Son in the emanation of the Holy Spirit.[4]

Nevertheless, although ecstasy transcends time, it is possible to discern therein three successive states. At the beginning it is a *knowing*.

> From the Father's face emanates a simple light, which illumines this soul, raised above senses, above images, above reason and without reason, in the supreme purity of the spirit. In this light, which is called the *coruscation* of God, God perceives himself simply, not according to distinctions or the mode of persons, but in the privation of his natures. . . .

The act of knowing is followed by an act of *love*: "from the face of divine charity descends a swift light, like a flash, into this open heart." And the Spirit of the Lord speaks: "I am thine and thou art mine; I dwell in thee and thou livest in me." This feeling of grace is followed by an outburst of grateful fervour on the part of the soul: "this man does not indeed know what has happened to him nor how he can continue to live, a state called *jubilation* . . . i.e. heartfelt love, an ardent flame accompanied by devotion, gratitude and an everlasting reverence of God." In the heat of jubi-

---

[1] *Enneads*, VI., book IX. chapter xi.

[2] *Life of Plotinus*, chapter xxiii.

[3] The Pseudo-Dionysius has noted the threefold character of mystical experience: passivity, obscurity, renunciation. Cf. Hugo Koch, *Pseudo-Dionysius Areopagita in s. Beziehungen zum Neuplatonismus u. Mysterienwesen* (1900), pp. 135 ss.

[4] *The Spiritual Marriage*, book III. chapter vi.

lation, Ruysbroeck does not lose sight of the practical tendency of his doctrine. Even ecstasy must culminate in action . . . moral action.

> For this reason [he says] I offer a rough comparison to such as have never climbed this summit. Take a mirror curved like a basin, put in it dry and inflammable straws, and hold the mirror so as to catch the sun's rays. These dry straws, by reason of the heat of the sun and the concavity of the mirror, will rapidly catch fire. So within thyself, if thou hast an open heart, devoutly lifted up to God, the light of his pity, illumining this open soul, consumes all thy shortcomings in the fire of divine love.[1]

This practical tendency of Ruysbroeck's mysticism is certainly the best of correctives; it anticipates the consequences which the Quietists of his time were inevitably bound to draw from a doctrine in which, verbally at least, all distinction between God and man disappeared. We know that Ruysbroeck was aware of this danger, from the explanations he subsequently gave and the corrections he made in doubtful passages of his writings—such expressions as the following: "we shall be melted and liquefied, engulfed and immersed throughout eternity in divine glory," or "spirits melt and become annihilated from delight in the essence of God, the superessence of all essence. There they escape from themselves and lose themselves in bottomless non-knowledge," or again, "the spirit expands so widely to apprehend the Bridegroom when he appears, that it is transformed into the very immensity it knows," remind one unmistakably of the most audacious assertions of the votaries of the Free Spirit. We also find that Ruysbroeck, at the end of his life, gives repeated warnings and remarks of the following nature: "Pay attention, I did not say that. . . . I again say that no creature can be or become so holy as to lose his state as a creature and become God. I do not wish anyone to misunderstand my words . . ." etc.; "The spirit of man does not become God by any means, but it is deiform."

Besides, it is not improbable that the thought of Ruysbroeck passed through two phases: that of *The Spiritual Marriage*, largely imbued with the spirit of pantheism, at

[1] *The Twelve Beguines*, chapter x.

all events in expression, and that corresponding to the publication of *The Sparkling Stone* and the other corrective
treatises, in which practical tendencies were stronger than
speculation. *The Spiritual Marriage* was written in Brussels,
in the course of Ruysbroeck's active ministry, and in all
probability about the year 1335. The author had not yet
seen the disastrous results about to be wrought on the
people by the pantheists of the Free Spirit.

Since that time it may be said that this sect always
occupied his mind. Not one of his treatises but combats it,
directly or indirectly. Certainly it was from reflecting on
the quietism of the heretics that he assigned the place of
honour to the *practical* value of the mystic life. This latter
should not be its own aim and object. If we think so,

we are mistaken [he says at the end of *The Sparkling Stone*], for,
in order to attain to God, we must have a heart that is free, a conscience at peace, a frank unveiled countenance devoid of artifice. Then
only can we ascend from virtue to virtue, contemplate and enjoy God,
and, as I have told you, become one with him.

Elsewhere he places in the same category those who engage
and lose themselves in works of every kind and those who keep
aloof from practical life in order to find rest in contemplation:
"those who, rejecting action, abandon themselves to interior
idleness, are unable to understand these things."

Again, there is a law of the spiritual world which forbids
man to isolate himself in a state of contemplation. This is
the law of *aspir* and of *expir*. In the contemplative life God
aspires us to himself: when God draws us within we must be
wholly his. But afterwards

the Spirit of God *expires* us without, for the practice of love and good
works . . . just as we breathe out the air within our bodies and breathe
in new air, and therein consists our mortal life in nature. To enter, therefore,
into inactive enjoyment, and then go out to practise good works, and
remain ever united with the Spirit of God, is what I mean.

Work, the moral life, is man's very element. It is there
that God looks for him, it is there that he brings him back,
so that, in the mystic cycle, the practice of the virtues is
both the starting- and the arrival-point. It is important to

note this essential aspect of the doctrine of Ruysbroeck. In this he is different from most mystics; if it were possible to make a *rapprochement*, the only name with which he could be compared would be that of Bernard de Clairvaux, from whom he assuredly received inspiration.[1]

Besides, supposing an impossibility, if the spiritual creature, as regards action, were reduced to a nonentity, becoming as devoid of activity as if it were not, it would deserve nothing. It would be neither more holy nor more happy than a stone or a piece of wood.

And so, to enjoy and act constitutes the beatitude of Christ and of all the saints; it also constitutes the life of all just men. . . . Such logic will never disappear.

This practical life, which Ruysbroeck distinguishes from active life, the first step in mystic development, he calls the *common life (ghemeene leven)*.[2] The active life, inspired by grace, is essentially the work of the human will. The common life, on the other hand, depends on God alone.

The man who, from these heights, is brought back to the world by God, bears with him a wealth of virtues. He seeks not his own good, but the honour of him who sends him. And so he is upright and true in all things. He is in possession of a rich and liberal property which, grounded in the wealth of God himself, should ever be distributed to all who need it, for its abundance flows from the living spring of the Holy Spirit that is inexhaustible. This man is a living and spontaneous instrument used by God for the doing of his will. . . . This is the common life, in which one is equally ready to contemplate and to act by engaging in both with like perfection.

In another place Ruysbroeck says of this *common life*:

Although living wholly in God and wholly in ourselves, we have yet but one single life. True, we feel in it both contradiction and duality, for poverty and wealth, hunger and satiety, activity and idleness are mutually opposed to each other. Nevertheless, it is here that we attain to our highest nobility.

Thus it is in action that the mystic life reaches its culminating point. And, while on the borderland of pantheism, it is this which prevents Ruysbroeck from wholly espousing the depersonalisation and the dissolution of the *I*. On the other hand, he means to be always and everywhere a faithful

[1] St. Bernard, *In Cantica*, sermo xxxiii. (Migne, *Patr. lat.*, t. CXXXLIII.).
[2] Cf. Auger, *Sur une doctrine spéciale des mystiques du XIVᵉ siècle en Belgique: Ruysbroech et la Vie commune*, in *Compte rendu du troisième congrès scientifique international des catholiques. Section des sciences religieuses*, pp. 297–304.

and obedient son of the Church. His passionate mysticism is moulded after the model supplied to him by the Church and the Christian doctrine. The mystical system cannot therefore be separated from Ruysbroeck's special ecclesiology: the two support and explain each other.

III. The Church and the Sacraments

Ruysbroeck's love for his Church did not prevent him from being very clear-sighted regarding the state of decline into which the institution had lapsed. We do not intend to reconsider the pitiable scene. True sons always love a mother, however wrinkled her brow or soiled her garb. Thus did Ruysbroeck love his fallen Church: tenderly for her great past, mournfully for her degraded present, and hopefully for the future. He was not thinking of a mystical Zion, an ideal Church, but of an earthly foundation, divinely instituted and invested with power as enduring as the world itself.

The holy Church that cannot err instructs us by its teachings and its practice that have been in vogue ever since the first days of Christianity. . . . This Church is called apostolic, for the high prince Saint Peter and the other apostles founded and established it upon the rock Jesus Christ. . . . An order and a power give to them, and to their successors, the means of carrying out their functions to the last day. They will ordain bishops and priests in the name of the Lord, and in his name will give them the power they have received from God to exercise priestly functions throughout the world. The holy Church thus has its foundation in Christ, and Christ lives in it . . . and it shall remain, unchanged, in possession of its ministry to the last day.[1]

As an instrument of the Holy Spirit, its judgment has all the force of law. Ruysbroeck, both for himself and for his writings, is the first to submit thereto in terms which permit of no restriction. At the end of his life he writes: "For all that I understand or feel, and for all that I have written, I submit to the judgment of the saints and of holy Church. For I wish to live and die in the Christian faith, and, by God's grace, I desire to be a living member of holy Church."[2]

[1] *The Mirror*, chapter vii.   [2] *The Book of Supreme Truth*, chapter xiv.

The commandments of the Church are the commandments of God himself. Those who imagine they can dispense with them are froward and perverse, "for they think they have found and hold the why and wherefore of all the sacred scriptures . . . nevertheless they have lost God and all the ways that might lead to him, possessing no more devout fervour or holy practices than a dead beast." These men, who trust in their own strength to approach God and scorn the intermediary of the sacraments, Ruysbroeck compares to the eagle, "an impure bird." He is impure because he trusts to the power of his wings alone to rise ever higher, and has no pity for birds feebler than himself. Such are the votaries of the Free Spirit,

who regard themselves as free and united to God without any intermediary, raised superior to all the practices of holy Church. . . . Detached from everything, they imagine they thus possess that for which the exercises and offices of holy Church are instituted and established.

And so Ruysbroeck demands perfect obedience to the Church.

None are therefore disobedient to God, none set themselves in opposition to him, except those who transgress his commandments, for everything that is prescribed or forbidden by God in the Scriptures, the teachings of the Church, or the dictates of conscience, must be done or left undone under penalty of disobedience and of the loss of divine grace.

In no man can the spirit of God either will, counsel or work things opposed to the teaching of the Church. Consequently obedience to the Church is one of the three qualities which make a man just and upright.

The sacraments are the channels of the love of God, the visible form of invisible grace.[1] It is through them that Christ draws near to man.

There is also another mode of approach for Christ, our bridegroom, which is daily brought about by increase of grace and new gifts. This is when man, with humble heart, partakes of a sacrament without placing any obstacle to its efficacy. Indeed, he thus acquires new gifts and additional graces, both by reason of his humility and on account of the mysterious working of Christ in the sacraments.

[1] Hugues de Saint-Victor says: *Sacramentum est visibilis forma invisibilis gratiae in eo collatae.*

The sacrament thus acts *ex opere operato*; its virtue is not diminished by the state of sin on the part of the priest. The latter, "though he be in a state of mortal sin and condemned to hell, cannot profane or defile the sacrament."

The sacraments are connected with the Incarnation of Christ; it is through them that Christ remakes man. The efficacy, however, of the sacrament is utterly inoperative unless there be in the worshipper an impulse of will and heart towards Christ, and also sincere repentance. "Then will the priest rejoice and administer to that man the holy sacrament, whatever season of the year it be."

Ruysbroeck bore a special love for the sacrament of the Communion. To it he devoted the greater portion of his book *The Mirror of Eternal Salvation* (chapters iv. to xvii.), in an attempt to explain the virtue of the sacrament and to state in what manner one may fittingly partake of it.

In its external aspect, the Communion first of all represents the Jewish Passover, abolished by Christ, and then restored by him. It is the testament of the Saviour,

and this testament is none other than himself, God and man, present in all his gifts.

In saying: This is my body, he changed the substance of the bread into the substance of his body, not in such fashion that the bread was reduced to nothing, but that, ceasing to be bread, it became the body of our Lord. . . . At the moment of consecration, the entire Host is no more than one simple substance of the body of our Lord . . . and though it be scattered to the ends of the earth, the sacrament is one, and the living body of our Lord remains in its undivided unity. . . . It is the same with the wine.[1]

Thus does Christ, in this sacrament, offer and promise us his divinity to enjoy eternally. "Can one then wonder that they are in a state of rejoicing who taste and experience such things? He died through love in order that we may live, and he lives in us in order that we may remain living in him throughout eternity."

Those excluded from the sacrament are "first of all the heathen, Jews, and all infidels. Then come those evil Christians

[1] This is the doctrine of *Transubstantiation*, as exalted into a dogma in 1215. Cf. St. Thomas, *Summa*, III.ᵃ, quaest. lxxiii. art. 2; quaest. lxxv., arts. 2–4.

who blaspheme and despise Christ, who do not esteem his august sacrament, or do not believe that he is there in flesh and blood." And Ruysbroeck concludes in characteristic words expressive of his vigorous moral teaching: "They shall not be buried alongside of Christians. For so long as man persists in his evil will and feels no contrition for his sins, there is neither pope nor priest living who can absolve him: if he dies, he is damned." [1]

[1] *The Mirror*, chapter xvi.

CHAPTER XI

Now indeed we have reached the very heart of our subject.

The foregoing pages have been an attempt to point out exactly all those historical influences which, operating from the outside, have entered as constituent elements into the formation of Ruysbroeck's mind. Persuaded that man is largely determined by his environment, we have deemed it necessary to describe the historical ground whereon his personality grew and developed. Evidently the first inspiration of Ruysbroeck's thought is to be found in the turbulent soul of his time. He has bent low over it, listened to its plaints, divined its needs, and attempted to supply it with the food for which it asked.

We think we have defined and fixed the progress of this thought with tolerable exactness. Beneath the pressure of circumstances—corruption of the Church, individual disorganisation and social upheavals—it sprang into being almost spontaneously, attaining at the very outset, in *The Kingdom of God's Lovers* and *The Adornment of the Spiritual Marriage*, the level at which it was to remain, without perceptible variation. Before taking his religious vows Ruysbroeck had already thought out the main lines of his system. This system we can now look upon as a mysticism based on speculation and tending to action.

The second stage of Ruysbroeck's thought coincides with his acceptance of the rule of the Augustinian canons. From this moment, without reconsidering the speculative premises, his mind expands and develops, broadens like an estuary, and culminates in a conception of the *common life* which claims to harmonise contemplation and action.

These two great intellectual stages, then, are intimately linked up with the very career of our author. In determining the undoubted facts of this career, in following chronologically the expression of this thought wherein events are vividly mirrored, in fitting, as it were, the facts of intellectual life into the framework of material life, we have simply allowed ourselves to be instructed, without, of ourselves, obtruding anything upon history.

And now we are led, by the progress of our task itself, to deny *in toto* the idealised portrait which most biographers have viewed with complacency. We are not dealing with an illuminate, detached from things terrestrial, solely taught and controlled by the unrestrained inspirations of an ecstatic nature. Ruysbroeck is a man, a combatant, a reformer whose mind is engrossed with realities above all else. And though in all his aspirations attached to his age, though absolutely linked thereto in pitying devotion, he is also quite as much dependent on it for his mental processes and intellectual methods.

When we release Ruysbroeck's thought from its allegorical garb, and translate it, so to speak, we cannot deny a strangely perceptible scholastic influence. There is revealed a solid theological mould in the exposition and presentation of the various parts, in the choice of arguments and even of actual terms. So fixed and definite a conception of the world cannot be improvised. And however great the element of personal inspiration, we cannot understand Ruysbroeck apart from the masters who shaped him.

We must now attempt to determine these masters.

And so the object of our inquiry is the following: to set up and determine the filiation of ideas whose ensemble constitutes what is called the *thought* of the author. We must ask ourselves what was their source, influenced by what reading or circumstances they took root.

This, in the case of Ruysbroeck, is an altogether new work, one doubtless that cannot claim to receive a clear and final solution, for, though of thrilling interest, the search after the generation of ideas is the most arduous and the least favoured of a critic's tasks. It is therefore fitting, at the outset, to diminish all risks of error, and, with this object, to set up an absolute rule and allow the various texts to speak quite impartially. There can be no history where research is fitted in to preconceived theories and the elements of information artificially grouped with a view to support a theory established from the first. By submitting strictly to this stern discipline, we hope to be able to shed new light upon the strange phenomenon of speculative mysticism in the fourteenth century.

To attain this object as nearly as possible, what will be the method to follow? There can be but one: the comparison and analysis of texts. By utilising the ordinary practices employed in the history of philosophy and proceeding to a series of demarcations and eliminations, it may be possible to distinguish the various philosophical currents interblended in the work of Ruysbroeck. We shall be able to determine what comes from his contemporaries and what is obtained from his predecessors, to isolate the original contribution of the author from his origins, strictly so called. And thus maybe we shall be carried back, retrogressively, far beyond the period within which is embodied the literary activity of our mystic.

I

Even a slight acquaintance with the end of the Middle Ages enables us at once to recognise that Ruysbroeck made his own many of the ideas in vogue during the fourteenth century. Still, the mere fact of having definite knowledge of his inspirers does not make Ruysbroeck of any great help to us. Is this from discretion regarding whatever affects him somewhat intimately? Or is it in order to conform with the habits of a period which, ignorant of our literary scruples, took what it wanted from any source? However it be, the fact remains that Ruysbroeck is almost completely silent regarding his origins.

We say *almost* completely, for here and there he quotes some of his masters: Saint Ambrose, Saint Augustine, Saint Gregory, Saint Anselm, and more frequently Saint Bernard, whose influence over him was predominant. Still, however precious these indications, they are too infrequent and precarious to make it possible to set up the exact spiritual links between these writers and Ruysbroeck.

Reduced then to our own resources, we must first outline briefly the intellectual development of the period.

This development is wholly confined to the problem of the relations between reason and faith and to the attitude assumed more especially by the masters of the University of Paris, where the philosophy of Aristotle, recently introduced by the Arabs, found enthusiastic adherents and no less fervent opponents.

The great philosophical problem has always been *to think* the world. Now, up to the thirteenth century, what had been the position of Western thinkers regarding the phenomena of nature? A dogmatic position, one resulting from an intellectual *a priori* tending to make the explanation of the world conformable with the data of revelation. This position is maintained in its entirety by Scotus Erigena, who conceives of the world solely from the religious angle. But the Neoplatonist inspiration of Scotus Erigena was destined to carry him beyond the confines of the Christian dogma. The true master of the Middle Ages, previous to Scholasticism, is Peter Lombard, the "maître des sentences," whose instruction, solemnly consecrated in 1215 in the Lateran council, dominates the schools, and only wanes before the growing influence of Thomas Aquinas, at the dawn of the fourteenth century.

The University of Paris had been constituted, in 1200, under the auspices of Philippe-Auguste and Pope Innocent III., by uniting into one body the three groups of masters and pupils, which, on this side of the Petit-Pont, formed real faculties though they did not bear the name. The new university, founded under the inspiration of the Pope for uniting all the masters and students, was thus in reality the citadel of religion (*arx catholicae fidei*), where the faculty of theology had for its daughters and subordinates the faculties of arts and of law. The popes scrupulously watched at the doors of the new institution to prevent the profane sciences and philosophical systems of the pagans from entering the sanctuary.

Meanwhile, within the university, the masters, as well as the students, did not fail to be tormented in soul by the intellectual unrest. All felt more or less the sense of a gap in the representation of the world as set forth in the teaching. This gap consisted of the absence of any logical bond which would have co-ordinated the incongruous elements of this teaching. To debate endlessly on some particular point may sharpen the dialectical sense, but the mind above all else called for a coherent system furnishing a rational explanation of the universe. The fragments of Aristotle then studied, along with Augustinism wholly imbued with Platonism, prevented any kind of reconciliation.

It is at this time of disturbance that the university became acquainted, through the translation made by the College of Toledo, with the physics and metaphysics of Aristotle. The misrepresentations of this Peripateticism, travestied by Avicenna and Averroës, did not prevent teachers of philosophy from finding in the philosophy of the Stagirite the very thing lacking in the official teaching, i.e. a *systematisation*. This philosophy, if one may say so, exactly fitted into the yawning gap. " For the first time, and simultaneously, the men of the Middle Ages found themselves confronted with an explanation of the phenomena of nature as a whole." [1]

Such was the repercussion of this influx of Hellenic thought that two opposing currents manifested themselves within the university itself.

Following on the ecclesiastical authority which, in 1210, 1215 and 1231, forbade, under penalty of excommunication,

[1] E. Gilson, *La Philosophie au moyen âge*, t. I. p. 122.

the study of Aristotle's writings, came such famous masters as Guillaume d'Auxerre, Philippe de Grève, Guillaume d'Auvergne and, at a later date and with certain reservations, Saint Bonaventura. These remained Augustinians, resolutely upholding against Aristotle the Platonic theory of ideas which the doctor of Hippo had introduced into Christianity and the hierarchical plurality of forms. Other masters, no less illustrious, Boëtius of Dacia, and above all Siger of Brabant and his followers, commonly designated as Latin Averroïsts, while maintaining the priority of the Catholic faith over the doctrine of Aristotle, enthusiastically welcomed, as the expression of truth *in toto*, the Peripateticism as interpreted by Averroës. Certain of Siger's disciples went so far beyond their master that their philosophy degenerated into an amorphous pantheism, denying Providence, creation, immortality.

Victory could not belong to either of these extreme positions. Was there not a *via media* between the two? Clearly Aristotle's physics was absolutely coherent and manifestly answered all the questions framed by the mind regarding the constitution of the universe. On the other hand, Augustinism offered a system of metaphysics which the Christian faith could not abjure without committing suicide. It appeared to synthetic minds like Albertus Magnus and Thomas Aquinas that the two parties, far from excluding, complemented each other, and that the Aristotelian universe might serve as a groundwork for the imposing metaphysical structure in which Plato and Augustine had collaborated.

The strange thing was that this philosophical dispute, considerably magnified in scope, was not long in overstepping the limits of the schools and penetrating into the monasteries. The Franciscans, along with Bonaventura, whilst deviating, as regards Aristotle, from the irreducible hostility of the dispute, nevertheless remained the faithful apologists of Augustinism. The Dominicans, on the other hand, offered wide hospitality to the philosophy of Aristotle, and undertook the big task of introducing Peripateticism into Christianity and blending them into a single system of the most authoritative cohesiveness.

To Albertus Magnus falls the honour of conceiving and laying the first foundations of this vast work, one that has not even yet spent its force; but it was Thomas Aquinas who really built up the system, and, with truly sublime intellectual suppleness, succeeded in permeating with the philosophies of Greece and the East the ideas in vogue even at the present time.[1]

The parallel study of the Alberto-Thomist philosophy and of the speculative mysticism of the fourteenth century no longer permits us to uphold the generally accredited opposition between the Scholasticism of the thirteenth century and the mystical schools of the following century.

The merit of being the first to glimpse the relations between the Thomist Scholasticism and speculative mysticism falls to Denifle, in a series of articles on Meister Eckhart that appeared in the *Archiv für Literatur und Kirchengeschichte des Mittelalters*.[2] The thesis was so stoutly upheld and so well supported by texts that such a thinker as Harnack was won over to it, designating as *epochemachend* the works of Denifle on this subject.[3] The thesis, justified in the case of Meister Eckhart, is also justified in that of Ruysbroeck, though with greater reserve, for Ruysbroeck by no means drew exclusively on the springs of Aristotelian Scholasticism. And though following Thomas Aquinas in a great number of points, in others he does not fail to prefer the Augustinian Bonaventura.

In Ruysbroeck, on the one hand, we have the effort of thought, the undertaking of a metaphysical structure. For knowledge precedes love. On the other hand, we have an impetus of the spirit, following on the speculative work, an

---

[1] E. Gilson very justly calls Thomas Aquinas the first of modern philosophers, "because he is the first Occidental whose thought was enslaved neither to a dogma nor to a system." *Études*, preface, p. v.

[2] See especially t. II. pp. 416 ss., the article entitled: *Meister Eckharts lateinische Schriften und die Grundanschauung seiner Lehre* (1885).

[3] *Dogmengeschichte*, t. III. pp. 394 ss.

interior development which attempts to outstrip the limits imposed on human knowledge.

We have seen how Ruysbroeck establishes the legitimacy of a method embracing religion and philosophy alike. In effect, for him as for Saint Thomas, the distinction does not exist. Both paths have their end in God, so that philosophy and religion are names that apply alike to the same study. This is the point of view of Scotus Erigena. Whether speculation precedes mysticism, or the effort of the spirit that attempts to lose itself in God precedes reasoning, the only difference is in the point of outlook. And we find very similar thinkers pronouncing in favour now of the one, now of the other point of view. The common thought is that which has been expressed by Saint Anselm in the following terms: *non tento, Domine, penetrare altitudinem tuam, quia nullatenus comparo illi intellectum meum; sed desidero aliquatenus intelligere veritatem tuam quam credit et amat cor meum.*[1]

To attribute to Scholasticism the impossible presumption of reaching God by speculation alone, is to misunderstand the repeated declarations of the greatest Scholastics. No one experienced the limitations imposed by language as did Saint Thomas Aquinas: *impossibile est quod per definitiones horum nominum definiatur id quod est in Deo.*[2]

Scholasticism contented itself with placing God at the summit of being, with applying to him not definitions but analogies, and, once the demarcation has been clearly traced, with establishing itself within the field of what is humanly intelligible. As in the case of the mystics, the effort of the Scholastics culminates in a *theology of feeling.* After that, whether the former give a wider development to personal piety and the latter mainly deal with speculation, signifies but a difference in degree.[3] By carrying this proposition even to extremes, we should come to admit that mysticism is treading a path on which the Scholastics are setting up an insurmountable barrier. As has been said,

---

[1] *Proslogium*, lib. I. cap. i.   [2] *Compendium theol.*, cap. x.
[3] Harnack, *Dogmengeschichte*, t. III. p. 314.

mysticism admits of no mystery whatsoever. God himself becomes intelligible, and with him all things. Adopting this attitude, mysticism evidently approaches nearer to modern philosophy than does Scholasticism.[1] Still, however far mysticism claims to go, its starting-point is always speculation.[2]

This is what we have now to show in the special instance of Ruysbroeck. We shall try to discover what ideas connect his system with the teaching of the great Scholastics of the thirteenth century.

II

§ 1. Ruysbroeck and minds similar to his are connected first of all with Scholasticism through the position they take up in the famous controversy on the nature of *universals*.

We know what was the object of this dispute, which stirred three centuries to such an extent that John of Salisbury could speak of "this question upon which the world in travail has grown old, to which it devoted more time than the Cæsars spent in conquering and governing the world empire, for which more móney was spent than Crœsus with all his wealth ever possessed."

The question is set forth in the preliminary epistle of the *Isagogics* of Porphyry. Its three terms may be summed up in this single proposition: have genera and species a real existence or do they exist only in the mind? We know that theologians were divided into three categories: the *nominalists* (Roscelin), maintaining that genera are but simple abstractions of the mind, clad in verbal form, *flatus vocis*; the *realists* (Anselm, Guillaume de Champeaux), affirming on the contrary that genera are the only realities that exist, that the universal essence subsists eternally in the divine ideas, and,

---

[1] H. Delacroix, *Essai sur le mysticisme spéculatif en Allemagne au XIVᵉ siècle*, pp. 13–16.

[2] Harnack says: *die Mystik ist die Voraussetzung der Scholastik* (*Dogmengeschichte*, t. III. p. 303).

as type, in human intelligence also; and lastly, an intermediate party represented by Abélard: *conceptualists*.
According to this theory individuals constitute the essence
of beings, and genera are not mere words, since they are in
the mind, which is a very real form of existence.

It is outside of our purpose to relate the varied fortunes
of this joust. Still, it must be mentioned because of the part
played in this affair by Bernard de Clairvaux and Hugues de
Saint-Victor in bringing mysticism into the lists against
Abélard. Although at the end of the thirteenth and the
beginning of the fourteenth century the quarrel had lost
almost all its bitterness, both sides still confronted each other.
Thus, in the days of Ruysbroeck, Durand de Saint-Pourçain
and Guillaume d'Occam resurrected nominalism, and it is to
their action, combined with that of the Latin Averroïsts,
that must be attributed the gradual decline of the Thomist
school, the last representative of which, Capreolus de Rodez
(1380–1444), vainly endeavoured to restore its authority in
his monumental *Liber defensionum theologiae divi doctoris
Thomae*.[1]

After the classification just mentioned, we may divine
which side the speculative mystics chose. They are all
realists, though of a moderate type. It could not be otherwise,
for the theory of exemplarism is in a way but the development of the formula *universalia ante res*. Besides, they found
the theory clearly formulated by Albertus Magnus. The
latter, evading the meaning that Plato had given to his
ideas as subsisting in themselves, showed them eternally
formed in God and serving as a model for all created things.[2]

§ 2. The influence of Albertus Magnus, however, from
the purely philosophical point of view, on Ruysbroeck and
the speculative mystics, was very limited. Far more powerful

---

[1] De Wulf, *Hist. de la philosophie médiévale*, pp. 434 ss.

[2] *Sum. theol.* (édit. Jammy), I. tr. 15, p. 335: *Dicendum quod omnia dicuntur
esse in Deo per rationes exemplares et ideales, quibus facta sunt omnia, et quibus
sunt in arte divina et sapientia.*

In Sent. I. dist. 29, p. 329: *Universale comparatur ad particulare quod est sub
ipso, addens ei aliquid quod non est ipsum, quo efficitur particulare.*

was the influence of his cosmology; in this domain Albertus was indeed a master, an initiator. He studied almost all the sciences known in his day, and some of his personal observations, especially in botany, earned for him such enthusiastic testimony as that of Alexander von Humboldt. Urged by the Dominicans to collect in a book of natural science the results of his experiments, Albertus wrote no fewer than eighteen treatises on the subject. And we may gauge the progress effected by this sagacious observer if we compare his learning with the puerilities that abound in the writings of the Middle Ages.[1]

Undoubtedly it was on this prolific source that Ruysbroeck drew for all that part of his work which may be called scientific. We have mentioned the rôle played by nature in the system of our mystic. He was not satisfied, like Saint Bernard, to obtain instruction from the beeches, he passionately investigated the most varied phenomena of the universe, attempting, behind the forms and developments of the material world, to lay hold upon analogies that could be applied to the spiritual world. It would be possible to obtain from Ruysbroeck's work a singularly consistent picture of the stage of development of the various sciences during the fourteenth century. Ruysbroeck interests himself in everything: mineralogy, botony, zoology, astronomy, though everywhere scrupulously following the lead of Albertus Magnus. He is acquainted with grafting, floral fertilisation, meteorological phenomena, the tides, the habits of ants and bees; he speaks of experiments in physics, he mentions by name a great number of forest species and flowers. But his dependent attitude is most pronounced in cosmology. He follows absolutely Albertus Magnus and Saint Thomas, whose labours were principally directed to restoring—by adapting it—the cosmology of Aristotle. Basing itself on the geocentric system of Ptolemy, the Scholasticism of the thirteenth century set up an astronomical system framed

---

[1] Cf. V. Langlois, *La connaissance de la nature et du monde au moyen âge* (Paris, 1911).

upon three concentric spheres: the sphere of the planets, that of the fixed stars, and lastly the sphere designated as *primum mobile*. The revolution of these spheres round the earth accounted for the diurnal motion from east to west.

The *sublunary* bodies, i.e. terrestrial substances, are not dependent, like the heavenly bodies, on intelligent motor forces, but on the influence of these heavenly bodies. The planets direct the rectilineal motion of the four elements that enter into the composition of sublunary bodies: fire and air, endowed with an ascending motion as regards the earth; earth and water, on the other hand, tending towards the centre. The astral universe is not subject to change, whereas the terrestrial elements become transformed, and, permeating each other, determine those incessant modifications of which the earth is the theatre. Identical modifications take place in the human body, wherein the humours (choler, or yellow bile, phlegm, blood, and black bile, or melancholy) correspond to the four elements and determine the four temperaments.[1]

Hence for Ruysbroeck—as for Saint Thomas, Albertus Magnus and Duns Scotus—the correlation between the life of the universe and the moral life. Man is a part of the world; in his material organism he is subject to it, and in proportion as this material organism reacts upon the life of the spirit does it participate in the vicissitudes of the Cosmos, and conversely. Thus it is that fevers, occasioned by marshy emanations, disturb the imagination, modify our thoughts and make languid the will, though these are spiritual faculties. Nevertheless, and even though the temperament be determined by some particular planet, man can evade this domination by his will. Human freedom remains unimpaired. Thus the angry man, determined by a planetary sign, can nevertheless restrain the impulses to which his temperament inclines him; the impure man can subjugate his carnal

[1] See principally *The Kingdom*, chapters iv. and xxvii.; *The Spiritual Marriage*, book II. chapter l. Cf. St. Thomas, *Summa*, I.ᵃ quaest. xci. art. 1; I.ᵃ quaest. xciii. art. 6. Cf. A. Dufourcq, *Les Origines de la science moderne*, in *Revue des Deux Mondes* (15 July, 1913), pp. 349 ss.

desires. Thus, too, will and freedom are opportunities given to man by God so that he may evade his determinism and make himself secure in the spiritual life, in which there is no fatalism.

Astrology has in these modern times fallen into such oblivion that it is difficult to understand how important to Ruysbroeck and the Scholastics was the influence of the heavenly bodies. Nor must we forget that astronomy preceded metaphysics, nor the close relationship between Scholastic speculation and Aristotelian physics. It is well known that the Stagirite attributed to astral substance a perfection superior to that of terrestrial substance. In the rotation of the celestial bodies he saw the action of astral souls, intelligent and divine forms, immutable determinations of the soul of nature, thus removing the astronomical world from the laws of deterioration. Plotinus himself, whose influence upon the Scholasticism of the thirteenth century is no less manifest than that of Aristotle, though he considerably minimises the rôle of the heavenly bodies in human destiny, yet devotes the whole of the third book of his second Ennead to planetary influences. And Proclus, his disciple, regards them as divine animals endowed with a universal soul, whereas individuals possess only a particular soul. Is it to be wondered that the great Scholastics, drawing upon the dual spring of Aristotelianism and Neoplatonism, recognise intelligent motor forces connected with the spheres on which they imprint their mechanical motion? Besides, in virtue of the law: *omnis motus ab immobili procedit*, Thomas Aquinas relates to the heavenly bodies the incessant mutability of things terrestrial, these bodies being the most immovable of all, for they are subject only to a single local motion. Hence we can understand the importance acquired by astrology, and we cannot blame an age which knew nothing of the telescope for drawing conclusions from principles vouched for by the greatest minds of antiquity. By adopting this Scholastic cosmology as he found it, Ruysbroeck did nothing more than prove himself the product of his times.

§ 3. The theory of creation, as expounded by Ruysbroeck, depends alike on Scholasticism and on the Neoplatonism of Scotus Erigena. Moreover, the two schools have in common, apart from modifications of detail, the theory of exemplarism of the *rationes aeternae*, which upholds the entire system.[1] Creation is nothing else than the mode according to which being emanates from its universal cause, which, from the fact of the emanation, becomes efficient cause: *id a quo aliquid fit.* Thus we are enabled to speak, in expressing the state of an object or being before its creation, of non-being or of nothingness. Thomas Aquinas points to three reasons for proving that creation is the result, not of a necessity inherent in divine nature, but of an act of free-will. Ruysbroeck accepted this conception, while all the time maintaining the Neoplatonist idea of a creation of necessity: as fire necessarily radiates heat, God radiates life; but, while pressed by his very munificence and wealth to manifest himself, the creation of man and of angels is the act of his free-willing. "We are no longer emanations from God according to nature or from necessity, but in the freedom of his willing."[2]

We also find in Ruysbroeck the theory of ideas as Saint Thomas expounds it to explain how the many comes from the one, the imperfect from the perfect. As an architect cannot build a house unless he mentally possesses *in idea* each of the parts of the house, so creation could not be unless all things had previously had their being *in idea* in the thought of God. The inequality of created things is explained by the distance from which the idea is projected. As God is unable to express perfectly his resemblance upon a single being, he has been compelled to scatter this perfection over the entire multiplicity of beings. Thus has come about a veritable hierarchy, each stage of which is a little nearer to perfection.

God, the efficient cause of creation, is also its final cause.

---

[1] Rohner, *Das Schöpfungsproblem bei Moses Maimonides, Albertus Magnus und Thomas von Aquin*, Münster (*Beitr. z. Geschichte der Philos. des Mittelalters*, 1913, Bd. xi. 5).

[2] *The Mirror*, chapter xvii.

All beings tend towards him in never-ceasing progress. Hence that finality of nature which Albertus Magnus, in especial, has developed so magnificently; hence too that fullness of life everywhere distributed, that *virtus activa* which makes of matter a perpetual becoming: *corruptio unius est generatio alterius*.

In a word, man, the object and the centre of creation, is the microcosm. He reproduces not only the universe which is again found in him with its constitutive laws, but he also reflects divinity in its essential unity. Of himself he does not constitute an entity, but he is a compound of two elements, body and soul, which separately would have no distinctive existence of their own. Nevertheless, the soul, of itself alone, constitutes a *forma substantialis*; it is only that, and not a compound of matter and form, as Bonaventura claims.

Still, the soul of man is distinguished from the sentient soul of animals, which has being and subsistence only in its union with matter. Indeed, its essential property is its intellectuality. Clearly the intellectual functioning of the soul takes place without the direct participation of the body and its organs, and it extends to realities absolutely separate from matter: namely, the eternal and the divine. None the less, of itself alone it can form neither the essence of man nor his person; for, if the manifestations of life all derive from the soul, they cannot really exist without an essential participation of matter or of body. Again, the human soul can have perception and sense-desire only with the co-operation of the body to which it gives activity.

So far Ruysbroeck faithfully follows Saint Thomas Aquinas. Now, however, on one question he leaves him and follows Scotus Erigena. The latter admitted that man bore the tripartite impress of the divine hypostases. The Alberto-Thomist philosophy, on the other hand, recognises in the soul no trace whatsoever of a trinity of persons. Knowledge of the trinity is one we can acquire only by way of revelation. The path of observation can lead us only to comprehend in God the unity of essence. Saint Thomas is categorical on this point: *per rationem naturalem cognosci possunt de Deo ea quae pertinent ad unitatem essentiae, non ea quae pertinent ad distinctionem personarum. Qui autem probare nititur trinitatem personarum naturali ratione fidei derogat.* Now on this point Ruysbroeck is not less categorical in deviating from his Scholastic predecessors. As we shall see later, he prefers to adopt the Neoplatonist theory as he found it in the Pseudo-Dionysius and in Scotus Erigena. Immediately afterwards, however, he again takes up the psychology of Scholasticism.

Few philosophies advanced so far in the study of the soul and its powers as did Scholasticism. In consequence, Ruysbroeck found ready prepared the elements for his mystical structure. Nothing could be more instructive than to set out in parallel columns the doctrine of the *Summa* of Thomas Aquinas and those chapters from *The Spiritual Marriage, The Kingdom* and *The Tabernacle* that deal with the subject. The identity is carried to the point of verbal literalism. To pursue this parallel into details would be fastidious. Nevertheless, if we are to establish the dependence—still greatly disputed—of Ruysbroeck on Scholasticism, it is necessary to note the points in common.

From the outset Ruysbroeck adopts the Thomist distinction between the soul—properly so called—and mind, or intellect. In reality the two blend; they are one and the same substance. Their prerogatives, however, are different. In this one single substance of the human soul there is plurality and distinction of faculties. And it is precisely the multiplicity of the faculties of the human soul that gives it its place in the hierarchy of creatures. This place is a secondary one, for perfection bears a direct relation to simplification. The angels, for instance, are at a higher stage than the human soul by reason of their greater simplicity and of the fewer processes to which they are subjected. But the soul, *anima separata*, that part of the one substance which will manifest after resurrection, has for its main process the reduction to unity. It is a principle of simplification, and hence an instrument of perfectionism. Thus it constitutes an *active* power.

The intellect (*gheest*), on the other hand, is a *passive* power, i.e. in the meaning which Saint Thomas gives to this term, one that is capable of receiving, of being enriched by, the action of agents external to itself. These two powers, *intellectus agens*, *intellectus possibilis*, unite and collaborate to complete the work of knowledge. The majority of spiritual processes do not thus constitute particular powers: memory, the deductive mind (*ratio, redelicheit*), conscience (*synteresis, vonke der sielen*) are, so to speak, both in Ruysbroeck and in Saint Thomas, various forms of spiritual working.

The soul, regarded as a whole, thus seems to be gifted with two orders of capacity: it is capable of knowing, though, being gifted with inclination, it is still capable of desiring and willing.

We will examine these two capacities in succession.

Saint Thomas—and after him Ruysbroeck—begins with the Aristotelian study of the five faculties. Leaving on one side the faculties of nutrition and locomotion, which are apart from our subject, although they also have to do with knowledge, we shall consider only the faculties of sensation, the intellectual faculties and the appetitive or inclinatory faculties.

The sentient power of the soul constitutes the first stage of knowledge. This is, however, a very degraded form, seeing that it affects the soul only through the medium of the senses. Sensations received from without are interpreted by the soul, so that to the five outer sentient powers with which we are all acquainted there correspond five inner sentient powers.

At the outset we have at the bottom of the scale the inner general sense which receives perceptions supplied externally, without being able to analyse them. These perceptions are received separately by the general sense; it is incapable of associating them when they are different in nature. For instance, this sense may perceive the colour of a rose, but it cannot, *at the same time*, perceive its perfume, these perceptions being different in nature. Afterwards these perceptions must be registered in such a way that the soul can experience them even when the object from which they emanate is absent: this is the rôle of the *phantasia*, which reproduces and preserves the images of absent objects. This *phantasia* is distinct from imagination, which Alexandre de Halès regarded as one of the sentient inner powers. Here we have one of those points in which we see at once Ruysbroeck's dependence upon Saint Thomas. Along with the latter, he regards imagination as one of the intellectual powers, and the reasons he invokes for this are none other than those of Saint Thomas: imagination is a power which combines the various sense-representations to make a new whole of them; it thus enters upon a genuine intellectual process. Saint Thomas then replaces imagination by what he calls the *particular reason*. And this third power, when developed, gives way to a fourth: the *vis aestimativa*, which judges of the utility or the harmfulness of things with reference to our needs. The estimative power, however, of itself functions only in the presence of objects. Therefore a fifth power must intervene which will retain the judgments pronounced separately by the *vis aestimativa*: memory or reminiscence.

We see that the inner sentient processes already border upon the real intellectual domain. It is here that knowledge is completed: *nil in intellectu quin prius fuerit in sensu*. Thus the intellect acts as a reader, in accordance with the etymology of the phrase: *intus legere*.

Saint Thomas carried to its slightest details his theory of knowledge, a very abstruse one. Ruysbroeck, whose aim is practical above all else, did not concern himself with details, but reduced the theory to its main elements. He thus sums up the life of the spirit as thought (*memorie, gedachte*), intelligence (*verstennisse*) and will (*wille*).

Intelligence, as understood by Ruysbroeck, is nothing else than the *intellectus agens* of Saint Thomas. Indeed, chapter v. of *The Kingdom of God's Lovers* alludes in a few lines to the passive intellect,[1] though in reality, to Ruysbroeck, all the processes of the mind are actions of prehension, combination and interpretation.

Clearly the human mind could not apprehend objects without being inclined towards them by interior illumination that comes from supreme truth. Here we recognise the idea of eternal essences, so dear to Saint Augustine. Saint Thomas introduces certain improvements in the Augustinian theory. He does not think that by reason of his imperfection man can perceive the eternal essences; but, by divine grace, the human intellect holds in germ all knowledge. These germs thus constitute the first indications of our intelligence.[2] It is upon these first indications that the distinctive work of the intellect must be expended. This work consists in setting the intelligence free from the notions transmitted to us by our senses. For instance, touch or sight gives us the perception of a mineral, of something indeterminate. It is the intellect that is to disentangle from this perception the ideas relative to the nature of this stone. It will discern whether the latter is a fragment of antimony, an emerald, or a splinter of sandstone. To work out this dissociation, which is also necessary for learning the nature of spiritual realities, memory— Ruysbroeck more frequently says *thought*—will intervene in the first place. This intellectual memory is different from sense memory, which applies only to sensations: the intellectual memory applies exclusively to the intelligible. It is the mental retention of a previous process, effected once for all, and to which all like situations are applicable.

But the data supplied by memory are, so to speak, in their rough state. After receiving them they must be comprehended, and this is the rôle of the understanding or of discursive knowledge (*verstennisse*). And this understanding bears at the same time upon substances that are naturally inferior or superior to the human intellect. *Ratio* is then the

---

[1] "The intellect quite naturally ceases to act and takes its rest," etc.
[2] *De Veritate*, xi. 1, ad Resp.: *Primae conceptiones intellectus, quae statim lumine intellectus agentis cognoscuntur per species a sensibilibus abstractas.*

capacity to descend by deduction from general to particular ideas, or to ascend by induction from the particular to the general.

Nevertheless, if knowledge were limited to the comprehension of objects with which we are connected by the natural operations of life, a great part of reality would evade our ken. And so the mind possesses a third capacity: *intellectual will*. This latter inclines man towards the objects which intelligence offers him as a boon in general or as a means of obtaining this boon: *bonum conveniens*, which, in its highest expansion, constitutes beatitude.

The intellectual will acts in the same way as the appetitive powers we have now to consider, and it is the relation between the two that determines spiritual ill-fortune or good-fortune. The intellectual will does not flow towards goodness by a necessity of nature. If it dominates the appetitive powers, the will will turn towards the good; if, on the other hand, it allows itself to be dominated and controlled by the sense-appetite, disorder and sin will have control in the will, for sin exists, says Saint Thomas, when the appetite freely inclines in the direction of disorder. In this case the faculty of intellectual discrimination is perverted; indeed, a passion may picture before us as good some object which really is evil.

The *willing* of the soul, which should bring it to complete knowledge, is thus closely connected with the appetitive powers. Here too the parallel between Ruysbroeck and Saint Thomas is absolute. The sense appetite (*sensualitas*) may be divided into two distinct powers: the concupiscible appetite (*appetitus concupiscibilis, begeerlike cracht*), which desires and wins the good perceived as true, and the irascible appetite (*appetitus irascibilis, tornighe cracht*), which struggles against the difficulties in the way of obtaining this good. In themselves these phases are neutral, i.e. neither good nor bad; their quality depends on reason, which controls them. *Passiones ex seipsis non habent rationem boni vel mali ; bonum enim vel malum hominis est secundum rationem.*

Here comes in the question of free-will. At once we must admit a constraint coming from nature: for instance, the desire for happiness in general, or rather the exclusiveness of a means for attaining the freely-determined end. But when the choice is left between several means, there remains an extensive domain over which the intellectual will can play with freedom of choice. It follows that the *liberum arbitrium* of Saint Thomas, like the *vriheit des willen* of Ruysbroeck, does not constitute a particular faculty along with the intellectual will, but simply a manifestation of this will working in a particular domain.

Apart then from his corporeal organism, destined to decay, man consists of two superimposed organisms. The first consists of the faculties of the soul, governed by the will, which is all-powerful, seeing that it can prevent the action of grace. The supernatural organism, or spirit, formed of the three higher powers of the soul, is alone qualified to produce divine acts: it is the theatre for the exercise of grace, which therein begets the virtues and introduces the gifts of the Holy Spirit. In order that grace may be efficacious, it should be founded on the power of obedience which God himself has bestowed on the soul.

Grace confers on the soul the so-called *infused* virtues: faith, hope and charity; they are called infused in order to distinguish them from the *acquired* virtues, which simply introduce man, by prolonged repetition of the same virtuous acts, into the natural order.

The gifts of the Holy Spirit are virtues or higher perfections. Saint Thomas and Ruysbroeck adopt the classification of Gregory the Great in determining these gifts and distinguishing them hierarchically.

We have seen that, in the case both of Saint Thomas and of Ruysbroeck, intelligence constitutes the first and the highest faculty of man. Moreover, the final end of man, *qua* spiritual creature, is the complete possession of sovereign good, i.e. beatitude. Spiritual possession, however, is not obtained by the will, but by perfect knowledge or *vision*. We can well understand how interested Scholasticism was in this question of the beatific vision. Is it possible for the human intelligence, in this world, to attain to this contemplation? Here Scholasticism found itself caught between the Aristotelian theory of intelligence and the Scriptural doctrine. As we are aware, the apostle Paul compares the knowledge we may have of God to the reflection of a mirror; in heaven alone spirit will behold face to face (*visio faciei*) (1 Cor. xiii. 12). It is this latter doctrine that is adopted by Saint Thomas, and it is on this point also that Ruysbroeck parts company with the "Angelic Doctor"—in the third book of *The Spiritual Marriage*, at all events. In chapters i. and ii. of this book Ruysbroeck gives us to understand that the believer, even in this life, can attain to the "face-to-face vision," an opinion which Pope John XXII. would seem to have shared.[1] In the state of indecision in which theologians found themselves, Benedict XII. was anxious to decide the matter, and formally defined the dogma in the bull *Benedictus Deus* (1336): *Homines pios plene purgatos vel justos ex hac vita decedentes statim consequi beatitudinem et visione Dei beatifica perfrui.* This bull enables us, as mentioned above, to declare that *The Spiritual Marriage* was written previous to 1336, and to set up a direct connection between this book and *The Sparkling Stone*, which evidently appeared as a corrective. The sentence at the end of chapter ix.: "our eternal life then involves distinct knowledge," is an echo of the papal bull, as well as the whole development that follows in chapters x. and xi.:

There is a great difference between the brightness of the saints and even the highest we can attain in this life. For though the shadow of God lighten the desert within, on the lofty mountains of the promised land there are no shadows at all. True, it is the same brightness . . . but the saints are in a state of translucidity and glory that enables them to receive the light without an intermediary; whereas we are still in the condition of dense mortality, and this constitutes an intermediary which makes a shade so capable of veiling our intelligence that it is impossible for us to know God and things celestial with the same brightness as do the saints.

[1] St. Thomas formally condemned as heretical such an opinion (*Suppl.*, quaest. lx. art. 2).

In this passage Ruysbroeck clearly returns to the Thomist doctrine.

The relation is continued regarding other doctrinal issues. The Fall has not affected man in his natural organism. The sin of Adam, however, has deprived the creature of supernatural gifts. The work of Christ consisted in restoring to man his spiritual nature. To bring this about Christ espoused human nature.

We might continue this parallel which shows the influence exercised by the "Angelic Doctor" upon Ruysbroeck's thought. Far from being a reaction against Scholasticism, Ruysbroeck's speculative mysticism is rooted in the Thomist philosophy. His dependence occasionally goes as far as verbal identity. We even find in Saint Thomas the gradation of the spiritual life as pictured by Ruysbroeck: the division of the three lives, active, intimate, contemplative, themselves subdivided into degrees or stages. But here Thomas Aquinas himself depends on prior representations, such as are to be found, amongst others, in Saint Gregory and Richard de Saint-Victor, who themselves came largely under the influence of Dionysian literature.

§ 4. All the same, Ruysbroeck did not become exclusively enslaved to the thought of Thomas Aquinas. He came under the inspiration of another great Scholastic, one who had supported Augustinism against the Peripateticism of Saint Thomas: Saint Bonaventura.

The Franciscan master is evidently more akin spiritually to Ruysbroeck than is Saint Thomas. Both of them, from the mildness of their disposition, are more inclined towards practical mysticism than towards speculation.

That for which our mystic is most indebted to the Parisian doctor is the representation of the spiritual life according to the *Itinerarium mentis ad Deum* and the *Vitis mystica*. *The Seven Degrees* is clearly an adaptation of the *Itinerarium*; chapter xvi. of *The Seven Cloisters* is likewise but a summary of chapter vii. of the *Itinerarium*, on the repose of the spirit in rapture. But what must chiefly be considered here is not so much analogy of detail as general inspiration. The entire work of Ruysbroeck appears before us as the development of the philosophy of Bonaventura as summed up in his *Itinerarium*. The human soul is a traveller journeying to God, and on the journey man is kept to the right path by innumerable signs. No one ever chanted the beauty of the physical world as did Bonaventura. He it is who said that the footsteps of God were imprinted on the dust along the wayside.[1] Blind and deaf is he who neither sees nor understands the message proclaimed by the universe. "The splendour of things shouts to us of God."[2] All things here below are signs: *spectacula nobis ad contuendum Deum, preposita et signa divinitus data*. But these signs are still, in the universe of sense, but *umbrae, resonantiae*, or *picturae*. To apprehend the image of God himself, it must be sought in the soul, whereon it is graven. This is the second stage of the journey, in which we contemplate God in the natural faculties of the soul, *per speculum et in aenigmate*. But the natural soul, plunged wholly in the things of sense, is powerless to find within itself the image of God. Consequently this soul must be restored by divine grace: a new stage of the spiritual life. And this stage itself comprises several degrees, for it is now necessary to apprehend God no longer in his image, but in his unity, in his *being, per se* and *a se*. From this point a new degree will raise us to the contemplation of *sovereign good*, or of the Trinity. It finally remains for us to rise above the world of sense, and above ourselves: this is rapture, or ecstasy, a veritable death of our personality "which leaves behind it all the processes of the mind."[3]

This ascending progress, thus briefly summed up, supplied Ruysbroeck with the very framework into which he is to fit his theory of the mystic life; that too, not for any particular treatise, but for the whole of his work.

But, the objection will be urged, is not this representation

---

[1] This image is found in Albertus Magnus: *Vestigium .   . proprie est impressio pedis in pulvere vel via molli (Summa*, I. 3, 15).

[2] *Itinerarium*, chapter I. 15.   [3] *Ibid.*, chapter VII. 4.

prior to Bonaventura? Do we not already find it in the Pseudo-Dionysius and in Scotus Erigena? Doubtless we do. But we have proof, from analogies of detail, of the direct utilisation of Bonaventura by Ruysbroeck. The latter says of the man who practises humility that "all his enemies flee before him as does the serpent before the vine in bloom." [1] Now this image is found word for word and with the same application in Bonaventura.[2] We find it nowhere else, and it is well known that mystics use the same forms of speech. On the subject of the gifts of the Holy Spirit, whenever Ruysbroeck breaks away from the *Summa* of Saint Thomas, it is to follow Bonaventura.[3]

Much thought has been given to the meaning to be attributed to the expression: *spark of the soul* (*vonke der sielen*), which appears so frequently in Ruysbroeck's works.[4] This expression refers to that property of the soul which Saint Thomas calls *synteresis*. To him *synteresis* or *scintilla* is at one time the apex of man's intelligent nature,[5] at another the natural impulse of the mind towards the good to be done.[6] Bonaventura classifies the properties of the soul into three categories: *sensus et imaginatio; ratio et intellectus; intelligentia et synteresis.*[7] Thus we are dealing with a particular property of the soul. And we find a confirmation of this meaning which is special to Bonaventura in chapter i. of the *Itinerarium*: "our soul possesses six powers: senses, imagination, reason, intellect, *apex mentis* and *synderesis scintilla*." [8] Now this special meaning is also found in Ruysbroeck,[9] and he can have come across it only in Bonaventura.

[1] *The Seven Degrees*, chapter ix.
[2] *Vitis mystica*, chapter xlv. (*Opera*, t. VIII. p. 222).
[3] Cf. *The Kingdom of God's Lovers*, chapters xv., xviii., xxv., and Bonaventura, *Collationes de septem donis Spiritus Sancti* (*Opera*, t. V. pp. 455–503).
[4] *The Kingdom*, chapter xxv.; *The Spiritual Marriage*, I. chapter i.; *The Mirror*, chapter viii. Meister Eckhart uses the same expression: *Funken der Seele.*
[5] *In Sentent.*, II. dist. 39, quaest. iii. art. i.
[6] *Summa*, I.ᵃ quaest. lxxix. art. 12; *De verit.*, quaest. xvii. art. 2.
[7] *Comment. in Sent.*, II. dist. 39, quaest. ii. art. 2.
[8] F. Palhories, in *Saint Bonaventure* (1913, Paris), translates *apex mentis* by *intuition*, and *synderesis* by *éclair de la conscience* (p. 298).
[9] *The Kingdom*, chapter xxv.

§ 5. The result of this first comparison is that we can no longer isolate Ruysbroeck from the great Scholastic trend of thought. He did not, however, borrow much from it, and we cannot say of the Brabantine mystic what Denifle and Harnack say of Meister Eckhart: *ganz von Thomas abhängig . . . auch sonst dass er das Beste ihm verdankt.*[1] From the rich stores offered him by the imposing synthesis of Albertus Magnus and Saint Thomas, Ruysbroeck made his choice, only taking from it those elements which seemed to him likely to serve as a substructure for his own system.

And so Ruysbroeck plunges deep into the Scholastic tradition. The trend of his mind was not towards mere speculation, consequently there was no need for him to go over the groundwork so splendidly exploited by his famous predecessors, a work which, after all, considering the object he had in view, could but be of a preparatory nature.

Does this imply that, in the mystical and moral part of his work, he gave free play to his originality? No doubt this latter had full opportunity for expansion. But here too Ruysbroeck has chosen masters, finding them in the moderate Scholastic schools—with mystical tendencies—of the twelfth century: the schools of Saint Bernard and of the Victorines.

But before studying these new influences we should ask the question: How are we to explain the influence exercised over Ruysbroeck by Albertus, the "great magician" of Cologne, and by Thomas Aquinas?

The influence of the former is indubitable. And, seeing that Saint Thomas held a considerable number of the ideas of Albertus, it is difficult to say, in many respects, on which of the two Scholastics Ruysbroeck drew most. The influence of Albertus had already been suspected by Böhringer, but this learned Church historian did not proceed to verify his intuition.

This latter would appear to be confirmed, first by a comparison of the two systems, and secondly by the philosophical ground they covered. The two principal intellectual centres

[1] Harnack, *Dogmengeschichte*, t. III. p. 394, note.

of the fourteenth century are Paris and Cologne. The Flemish scholars, however, preferred Cologne, which was connected with the *Nederlant* by a highway passing through Liége. This road was continually being traversed by students, and books travelled no less than human beings. Now, at this period, the influence of Albertus Magnus was predominant at Cologne. Even prior to his death (1280) his teaching had supplanted that of Peter Lombard, which hitherto had prevailed throughout the schools. It was also in Cologne that there had grown up around Meister Eckhart the new mystical school, with which Ruysbroeck was undoubtedly brought into contact. The fact that we find, combined in one and the same doctrine, the revived Aristotelianism of Albertus Magnus and the Christianised Neoplatonism of Meister Eckhart, supports this theory. And we should regard it as proved if the texts provided any certainty on the matter. Unfortunately textual proof is lacking. A manuscript of 1657, described by Engelhardt, asserts that Ruysbroeck made the journey to Cologne, where he probably became acquainted with Eckhart, but in all likelihood this annotation is but a personal deduction of the copyist, who was perhaps struck by the resemblances between the works of the German mystic and the doctrine of Ruysbroeck. It would therefore be prudent to regard the journey to Cologne as possible, and nothing more. This hypothetical though not improbable journey should at all events be dated prior to 1327, which was the year when Eckhart died. However it be, the combined influence of Albertinism and of Eckhart's mysticism is revealed in the earliest works of Ruysbroeck, shortly after 1335.

If we connect too closely Ruysbroeck with Scotus Erigena, we misinterpret the meaning of the revolution effected by the famous Dominican of Cologne. He was the first to bring the outer world within the domain of theology as a reality subject to investigation. This innovation we find in Ruysbroeck as one of the main buttresses of his system. Evidently Ruysbroeck no longer looks upon the world as does Joannes

Scotus: a mirror wherein the divine beauty appears reflected, a symbolical writing to be interpreted by the spirit. The divine mark on this world, in the opinion of Albertus and his pupils, is at most a *vestigium*, a footprint on the sand, according to the well-known image. Now, what does this footprint tell us about the pilgrim? Nothing, except the fact that he has passed that way. Hence, if the divine footprint can adequately shape religious conviction, the science of the world remains complete and entire. The universe is a sealed book whose seals must be broken, whose pages must be read. And so the true theologian will be as fond of experiment as of speculation. Albertus was an experimenter above everything. Mineralogist, alchemist, botanist, physicist: he collected together a prodigious number of observations which he related to the philosophy of Aristotle, though they were quite independent of the Stagirite. Now, this scientific basis is regarded by the speculative mystics of the fourteenth century as firmly established. It entered wholly into their work, and the reason why the rôle of the outer world therein is somewhat small, is because it was actually the intention of mystics to pass beyond the faint *vestigium* imprinted on this perishable earth.

> The first path [says Ruysbroeck] is therefore exterior and sensible; it consists of the four elements and the three heavens to which God has given suitable adornment. For him this constitutes a kingdom, though wholly exterior, one that offers but a faint and distant resemblance to his beauty.[1]

Thus did mystics meet on their way two successive barriers: the confines of the outer world and the limits of speculation. What wonder that, on arriving at these two terms equally impenetrable to reason, they had recourse to a new mode of investigation, strictly that of *mystical research*?

It is unnecessary to dwell longer on the influence of Saint Thomas. The special works of the historians of Thomism prove the extent of his influence and the fame he won during his lifetime. There is no instance of a scholar's apotheosis so general

---

[1] *The Kingdom*, chapter iv.

as that which fell to the man who, from the outset, was called: "le grand bœuf muet de Sicile." The very struggles that his doctrine called forth in the Augustinians made no impression on this fame. In vain did Étienne Tempier, chancellor of the University of Paris, in 1337, include in his condemnation of Averroïsm a score of Thomist propositions: the doctrine responded to the intellectual aspirations of the time but too manifestly to suffer from this condemnation and from the violent opposition of the Franciscans. From the fourteenth century onwards the authority of Saint Thomas almost exclusively dominates theological teaching, and the *Summa* replaces the *Sentences* of Peter Lombard. No wonder, then, at the powerful influence of this great master on Ruysbroeck.

In our opinion, then, the links are clearly established which connect speculative mysticism with the Scholasticism of the thirteenth century. But for the latter, the former would be non-existent. Scholasticism supplies mysticism both with a philosophical tradition and with a dogmatic conception. Such a foundation, however, is not sufficient for the mystics: it serves them merely as a springboard from which to take a greater leap forward.

III

The predominant rôle accorded by Scholasticism to reason could not be accepted by all: this is why there are several currents circulating within the heart of Scholasticism itself.[1] And the intellectualistic current never absorbed the mystical current, that "philosophy of the heart" whose brief and refreshing stream flows beneath icy formulae. And so it would be historically false to separate Saint Bernard from the Scholastic movement of the thirteenth century. The founder of Clairvaux belongs to Scholasticism through the

[1] De Wulf has clearly proved that Scholasticism cannot be regarded as a homogeneous philosophy but rather as a group of systems. *Introd. à la philosophie néo-scol.* (Louvain–Paris, 1904), p. 57.

position he took up in the quarrel on the nature of universals and his famous struggles against Abélard and Gilbert de la Porrée. And yet this same Saint Bernard is the first to dethrone reason, or at least to assign to it a subordinate part.

The identity established by the Scholastics between philosophy and religion as paths of investigation doubtless expressed a fine confidence in the powers of human thought. The starting-point, however, being wrong, could but lead to an impasse. And so Scholasticism knows nothing—or scarcely anything—of the joy that illumines the writings of the mystics. It represents the melancholy of a clouded sky, not the full clearness of the mountain-tops. Its work has justly been compared to the toil of Sisyphus, forever rolling uphill a huge stone which forever falls back again. *Quaesivit coelo lucem, ingemitque reperta.*

Saint Bernard is the first representative of this intellectual scepticism. He looks upon philosophy as consisting in "knowing Jesus Christ and him crucified." Not that he denies the utility of dialectic; but he thinks he can succeed more surely by the practice of virtue and the intuitions of faith. He carries to its extreme consequences the famous proposition of Anselm's *Proslogium*: *neque enim quaero intelligere ut credam, sed credo ut intelligam.* He says: *nil autem malumus scire quam quae fide jam scimus. Nil supererit ad beatitudinem, cum quae jam certa sunt nobis fide, erunt aeque et nuda.*[1] To him truth is the fruit of a great duty, nobly accepted. And therefore he abandons all restraint when he has to refute the intellectualistic method which Abélard defined as follows: *dubitando ad inquisitionem; inquirendo ad veritatem.* The point of view defended by Saint Bernard at the Council of Sens in 1140 is actually that of speculative mysticism. By subordinating to practical life both the soarings of the spirit and the flights of contemplation, Saint Bernard keeps himself free alike from the pride of the one and the errors of the other.[2]

---

[1] *De considerat.*, lib. V. chapter iii.

[2] *Quis enim, non dico continue, sed vel aliquandiu, dum in hoc corpore manet, lumine contemplationis fruatur? at quoties corruit a contemplativa, toties in activam se recipit (In Cantic., sermo lviii.).*

No wonder Ruysbroeck fell under the charm of this extraordinary moulder of men. The description of the monastery of Groenendael recalls the beginnings of the abbey of Clairvaux, and the two men offer striking analogies in character and in outlook. Both regarded as of like importance contemplation and manual toil, absolute submission and the fullest liberty, greatness and humility. Both fought strongly against depraved morals, and the degeneracy of the evangelical ideal in the bosom of the Church. Besides, Saint Bernard on several occasions visited Belgium, where, in 1146, his presence caused unparalleled enthusiasm; if we are to give credit to the chroniclers, his journey was a veritable succession of miracles.[1] But the influence of Saint Bernard upon Ruysbroeck was not simply that of a model of a good life. We find it very marked in all the writings of the Brabantine mystic.

First we have the Scriptures restored to a place of honour. Not the Scriptures distorted by commentaries or allegories, but the living Scripture, an inexhaustible fountain, adapted to the needs of practical life. "The reason why I know the Psalms so well," said Bernard, "is because I have pondered long over them." His writings, like those of Ruysbroeck, are interspersed with Scripture texts in which he recognises three meanings: historical, moral and mystical.

Why should it be otherwise with the Scriptures than with the things we use every day? Does not water, to cite but one instance, perform various duties for our bodies? Similarly a Bible phrase, which offers different meanings, according to the varying needs of the soul, cannot be inappropriate.[2]

Bernard frequented another school also, one with which Ruysbroeck was very familiar: nature. "What I' know of the divine sciences and of holy Scripture," he was wont to say, "I learned in woods and fields, by prayer and meditation. I have had no other masters than the beeches and the oaks." To his pupil Henry Murbach, the future archbishop of York, the abbé of Clairvaux wrote: "Listen to a man of experience: thou wilt learn more in the woods than from

---

[1] Vacandard, *Vie de Saint Bernard*, t. II. p. 300.   [2] *In Cantic.*, sermo li.

books. Trees and stones will teach thee more than thou canst acquire from the mouth of a magister."

The real thought of Saint Bernard is summed up wholly in the necessity for man to know himself, to practise self-discipline in order to rise from *consideration* to *contemplation*. The aim of the believer is to regain possession of his lost homeland (*repatriare*), to find again the image of God which sin has obliterated in his soul. For this work Ruysbroeck points out three paths or degrees, one leading to another without our being allowed to dispense with any of them. First *consideratio dispensativa*, which is nothing else than morality in action; then *consideratio aestimativa*, which sets reflection working; and lastly *consideratio speculativa*, which leads the soul to the confines of contemplation.

Of God it is possible to have threefold knowledge: opinion (*opinio*), faith (*fides*), and knowledge (*intellectus*). True revelation, however, above all intellectual processes, can be received by the pure heart alone. Of itself intellectual knowledge cannot be condemned, but it leads to pride and melancholy. The only beneficent science is knowledge of our own heart. Besides, science can teach us nothing about God. Is it possible to define him? All we can say of him is: *He is.* He is, according to the four dimensions capable of being conceived by the human mind: *length, height, breadth, depth.* To this fourfold conception Bernard devoted one of his finest treatises: *De diligendo Deo.* Ruysbroeck certainly had access to this treatise. From it he borrowed his hierarchy of the virtues which is given with greater detail in another treatise of Bernard: *De gradibus humilitatis et superbiae.* The one supreme virtue is humility; man rises to the heights of contemplation the farther he removes from pride. The love of God thus presents four stages: man first loves himself; this *amor carnalis* is natural and instinctive, and so not culpable, so long as it does not degenerate into exclusive preoccupation. This love, extending to our fellow-beings in need, becomes social. "Then man, feeling his inadequacy, begins to seek God in faith and to love him as his necessary helper. At this second stage he loves God not yet for God's sake, but for himself on account of the benefits he receives." Subsequently he rises to the love of God, so that God's will may be done. Here it is the intrinsic goodness of God that is the motive for loving, though still without excluding his beneficence towards us.

> A prolonged sojourn is made in the third stage, and I do not know if any man in this life has ever arrived fully at the fourth, in which a man no longer loves himself except for God's sake. If there are any who have experienced this, let them tell of it. For my part, I confess, it seems to me impossible. Without any doubt, this will take place when the good and faithful servant has entered into the joy of his Lord. . . . But even though in ecstasy the believer were to taste this sweetness, love for his wretched fellow-mortals would tear him down from those heights.[1]

Ruysbroeck, in *The Sparkling Stone*, also distinguishes believers as servants (*servi*), hirelings (*mercenarii*), and sons (*filii*). The first are attached to God by fear; the second serve God in the hope of reward; the sons alone love him for himself, and honour him as the Father who supplies all things.

Regarding the *comings* of Christ into the human soul, Ruysbroeck is manifestly inspired by Saint Bernard, whose method of exposition he follows: "for this threefold coming, three things must be considered: the cause and the wherefore, the interior mode, and the exterior work." [2]

Still, though contemplation—mystic union—constitutes the summit of the spiritual life, Saint Bernard and Ruysbroeck are too realistic to look upon this summit as an end in itself. Besides, rapture is an intermittent phenomenon, of short duration: *cum autem divinius aliquid raptim et velut in velocitate corusci luminis interluxerit menti spiritu excedenti.* Ruysbroeck frequently described this phenomenon in his work, but in chapter viii. of *The Book of Supreme Truth* he expressly quotes Saint Bernard as his inspirer. This chapter

---

[1] *De dilig. Deo*, cap. viii., x., **xv.** Cf. Ruysbroeck, *The Spiritual Marriage*, book I. chapters xiv., xxxv.; book II. chapters v., vi., viii.; *The Sparkling Stone*, chapters vi., vii., viii.; *The Seven Degrees*, chapters vi., vii., viii.

[2] *The Spiritual Marriage*, book I. chapter ii. Cf. S. Bernard, *Sermo in fer. iv. hebd. sanctae*: "*in hac igitur passione . . . tria specialiter convenit intueri: opus, modum, causam. Nam in opera quidem patientia, in modo humilitas, in causa charitas commendatur.*" These are the very three virtues which Ruysbroeck studies in the following chapters—iii., iv., v.

is an almost identical reproduction of chapter v. of *De Consideratione.*

As a tiny drop of water falling into a large quantity of wine seems to become diluted and disappear while assuming the taste and colour of the wine; as a piece of reddened incandescent iron becomes like the fire and seems to lose its original form; as the sunlit air seems transformed into that same luminous solar clarity, to such a degree that it no longer seems illumined, but itself the very essence of light; so all human affection in the saints must coalesce and become molten in order that it may flow wholly into the will of God. How indeed would God be everything in all things if there remained in man something of man? No doubt the substance will remain, though under another form, another power, another glory (*non est idem profecto consubstantiale et consentibile*).[1]

True, these images are actually to be found in the Pseudo-Dionysius and in Scotus Erigena, but from the mere mention of the name of Saint Bernard there can be no doubt but that Ruysbroeck drew his inspiration from him, though all the time acquainted with the other two.

You know how the air is bathed in the light and warmth of the sun, and how iron is so permeated by fire that beneath its action it does the work of fire itself, like it, giving heat and light. Similarly the air, if it were endowed with reason, might say: I give light and illumination to the whole world. Nevertheless each element retains its own distinctive nature; fire does not become iron, any more than iron becomes fire. But union takes place without intermediary, since iron is interiorly in fire and fire in iron, as the air is in the light of the sun and *vice versa*. . . . If material things can thus unite without intermediary, *a fortiori* God can unite with his beloved. . . . Neither does the creature become God nor God become the creature, as I have said regarding iron and fire . . . and this, according to Saint Bernard, it is " to be one with God."[2]

Elsewhere Bernard pictures this union as the consummation of mystic nuptials. And although this is a frequent image in writers of the Middle Ages, we may yet wonder if Ruysbroeck is not here still dependent on the abbé of Clairvaux, who, we must not forget, is the author he most frequently mentions by his name. The three books of *The Spiritual Marriage* are scarcely anything else than a magnificent amplification of this theme, summarised by Saint Bernard in the following words:

When the soul is completely purified it becomes nubile, and enters upon a spiritual marriage with the Word. . . . When, therefore, you see a

[1] Cf. *De dilig. Deo*, x. 28.
[2] *The Book of Supreme Truth*, chapter viii. Cf. *The Seven Cloisters*, chapter xvii.; *The Twelve Beguines*, chapter cxxx.

soul, having left all, unite with the Word with all its might, subject itself to the Word, conceive of the Word what it has to bring forth (*de Verbo concipere quod pariat Verbo*) . . . know that this soul is the spouse of the Word (*conjugem Verboque maritatam*) and that it has entered upon a spiritual marriage with the Word.[1]

What inclines us to think that Ruysbroeck is here directly under the inspiration of Saint Bernard is similarity of expression. In contradistinction to what one might think, Germanic speculative mysticism did not create a vocabulary of its own: it had but to draw upon the ample store of ideas and images in Romanic mysticism. Two centuries prior to Ruysbroeck, Saint Bernard had used, with reference to contemplation, such expressions as *to lose oneself in God, to glide away into God: diffluere, effluere, dimanare.* We find many instances in the *De diligendo Deo* of Saint Bernard:

> *Te enim quodammodo* PERDERE *tanquam quis non sis, et omnino* NON SENTIRE TE IPSUM, *et a te ipso* EXINARIRI *et pene* ANNULLARI, *coelestis est conversationis.*[2]
> *Quasi enim ebrius, miro quodam modo* OBLITUS *sui et a se penitus velut* DEFICIENS *totus perget in Deum et deinceps* ADHAERENS *ei unus spiritus erit.*[3]

All these expressions pass unchanged into the vocabulary of Eckhart, Tauler, Suso and Ruysbroeck.

This state of spiritual *adhesion*, in which the uncreated and the created unite, Ruysbroeck calls a *living life* (*levende leven*).[4] Now, this is an expression peculiar to Saint Bernard: *ibi vere vivitur ubi vivida vita est et vitalis.*[5]

The influence of Saint Bernard cannot be disputed.

IV

As with Saint Bernard, the school of Saint-Victor holds a position intermediate between the great Scholastics and the speculative mystics. The Victorines expected to find ground for conciliation in the Platonist idealism as expounded by Saint Augustine. It was in this spirit that Guillaume de

---

[1] *In Cantic.*, sermo lxxxv. 12.   [2] *De dilig. Deo*, cap. x.
[3] *Ibid.*, cap. x. 15, 28.   [4] *The Mirror*, chapter xvii.
[5] Sermo xvii.; *De modo bene vivendi : sermo de brevitate vitae.* Migne, *Patr. lat.*, t. CLXXXIII. col. 250; t. CLXXXIV. col. 1301.

Champeaux, tired of Scholastic disputes, withdrew in 1108 to the outskirts of Paris, into a small priory, of which to-day there remain but a few arcades in the court of the house— n° 20 rue Cuvier. This priory was a dependence of the abbey of Saint-Victor in Marseilles; its inmates were governed by the rule of Saint Augustine.

In reality it was born of the state of *malaise* almost always occasioned by abuse of the speculative method.

It is fitting [said John of Cornwall] to refrain from the distinctions peculiar to logic, when dealing with articles of faith . . . or at all events, if the syllogism prove too boisterous, let it be turned out of doors. . . . The waters of Siloam flow silently along, and neither hammer nor axe was heard in the building of the temple of God.

§ 1. The Parisian abbey exercised enormous influence not only on mysticism, to which it applied the Scholastic methods, but on culture in general.

The splendour and renown of the school date from Hugues, a Fleming from the neighbourhood of Ypres. Born at the end of the eleventh century, Hugues arrived in 1128 at Saint-Victor, where his reputation gained for him the surname of *lingua Augustini*. In spite of his sarcastic remarks against the *cupiditas scientiae*, in spite also of his declarations as to the insurmountable limits of reason,[1] Hugues was a Scholastic in the full meaning of the term. Far from despising human knowledge, he urged upon his pupils to absorb as much information on all things as they possibly could, regarding *cogitatio* as the first step by which one ascends to God; in this respect he is a genuine Aristotelian. The universe has its duplicate in miniature within ourselves, and there is no true knowledge without comparison of these two revelations.[2] But interrogation of the universe also results in our experiencing how exceedingly vain and unprofitable are all things, save the love of God. On this point we are acquainted with the dialogue, of undoubted literary beauty, between

---

[1] "Deus ab initio sic cognitionem suam im homine temperavit ut sicut nunquam quid esset poterat ab homine comprehendi." *De Sacram*, I. 3, i.

[2] "Sic respondent quae foris sunt iis quae intus videntur ad veritatem comprobendam." *De Sacram*, I. 3, 10.

the soul and the reason: "What seest thou, Indaletius?"[1] And so *cogitatio* must be succeeded by *meditatio*, whereby man comes into contact with the interior God, and by *contemplatio*, a supernatural process leading to the union of the created and the uncreated.

The influence of Hugues de Saint-Victor on Ruysbroeck is evident. From him the Brabantine mystic borrowed in particular an entire page on the pre-existence of things:

> All things have received life and existence from the wisdom of God; therefore it is right to say that they were life in the place from which they drew life. . . . It was the exemplar of God, and the whole world was made after the image of this exemplar: this is the archetypal world in whose likeness the world of sense was made. We must not indeed say that in divine intelligence there are ideas which are below the Creator and above the creature; in God there is nothing that is not God. There cannot be diversity of property where nothing is except Being. In God, to be and to live is one and the same thing: this is why he is a pure essence, without parts and without property.[2]

Another proof of this influence lies in the analogy offered between Ruysbroeck's *Spiritual Tabernacle* and the two allegorical treatises of Hugues de Saint-Victor: *De arca Noe morali* and *De arca Noe mystica*; Ruysbroeck utilised the former at all events of these treatises, parallel with a work by Richard de Saint-Victor on the same subject: *Benjamin major*.

§ 2. Whereas Hugues was the true inspirer of the school, Richard was its systematic theologian. As the spiritual son of Peter Lombard, Richard brings into his teaching the same orderly and systematic spirit that characterises the *Liber Sententiarum* of his master. A far less prolific writer than Hugues, Richard, who became prior of the famous abbey in 1162, condensed his system mainly into two books, the latter of which alone interests us: *De Trinitate* and *Benjamin major, de gratia contemplationis libri quinque*.[3] This latter work begins with the ideas of Hugues on the three ways that lead

---

[1] *De Vanitate mundi*, lib. I. (Migne, *Patr. lat.*, t. CLXXVI. col. 705–10).

[2] *Adnotationes elucidatoriae in Ev. Joan*, cap. ii. Cf. Ruysbroeck, *The Mirror*, chapter xvii.: *thus we possess a higher life*, etc., commentary on St. John's Gospel, chapter i. verses 3 and 4.

[3] Migne, *Patr. lat.*, t. CXCVI. col. 63 ss. The life of Richard, who was of Scottish descent, is not at all well known.

to God: *cogitatio, meditatio, contemplatio*. Each of these stages, however, comprises a number of degrees, subdivided in their turn. In Ruysbroeck we find the entire division dealing with the third stage of contemplation.[1] The first degree consists in admiration of the material world (ii. 1–6). This is followed by an intellectual process which consists in deducing, from contemplation of the universe, religious teachings on the wisdom of the marvellous Ordainer of the world (ii. 7–11). From the material world man passes to the spiritual universe, of which the former is but the reflection (ii. 12–111). At the fourth degree, man rises to the contemplation of spiritual beings and angelic creatures (iii.). After this, man is qualified to receive instruction by grace as to the real meaning of the Scriptures wherein is revealed the essential nature of God (iv. 2–5). Finally, at the sixth degree, man understands the mystery of the Trinity, which the reason alone would refuse to admit (iv. 6, etc.). Richard allegorically correlates these six degrees with the ark of Israel. The degrees are successively symbolised by the construction of the ark, the gilding (*deauratio*), the crown (*corona*), the mercy-seat, with the two cherubim on right and left, shading it with their wings (I. chapter xi.).

This brief summary affords no adequate idea of the refined symbolism of our Victorine. It is extremely difficult in these modern times to understand this excessive allegorism, so highly esteemed in the Middle Ages. Nevertheless, the Victorines were indebted to it for a good share of their popularity. Besides, this method, clearly encouraged by the Church, is as old as mysticism itself—which found therein a means of expressing the inexpressible.[2]

Students, who frequented the famous Parisian abbey in large numbers, took home with them all this variegated symbolism. It was probably through some such means that Ruysbroeck learned of the allegory of the spiritual tabernacle which he developed into a volume. But though he borrowed

---

[1] *The Seven Degrees*, chapters viii., ix. and xiv.

[2] Clement of Alexandria speaks of the μυστικὴ ἑρμηνεία (*Paid.*, II. cap. viii.). Hugues de Saint-Victor says: *sensus mysticus, i.e. allegoricus.*

his subject from Hugues and Richard, he dealt with it quite differently. It is really a personal work, perhaps the one in which it is possible fully to apprehend the very special psychology of our mystic.

.   .   .   .

If we wished, however, to explain Ruysbroeck's doctrine by Scholasticism alone, to include it in the official orthodox doctrine, we should be forced to curtail it.

Indeed, Scholasticism starts with a presupposition: it is the harmony between the data of reason and revelation, the latter all the time remaining inferior to reason. Truth thus comes into the soul only by an outer channel; Ruysbroeck's starting-point is quite different: he presents the soul simultaneously with Deity. Hence the problem of Being, which lies at the very heart of Ruysbroeck's doctrine, offers itself as an incessant development: the soul becomes the theatre of a real genesis wherein Deity, representing the first stage of the divine life, is about to beget the Trinity, and the soul to follow out its deification. As we see, such a conception does not harmonise with Scholasticism, which maintains above all else the distinction between the *being* of creatures and the *being* of the Creator.

Scholasticism is a philosophy of reason. Ruysbroeck's doctrine is a philosophy of the conscience. Ruysbroeck drew largely upon the Scholastic treasury because he found in it the scheme of a tradition ready at hand. But into this scheme he is to bring a very different doctrine, one that will owe its origin not to the Stagirite, but to Neoplatonism.

This is what we now have to demonstrate.

CHAPTER XII

I

W<small>E</small> have attempted to characterise the relations between Ruysbroeck and Scholasticism, thus rectifying the current opinion which looks upon the speculative mysticism of the fourteenth century as a sporadic phenomenon, without any very consistent link with the past, as well as isolated in contemporary mentality. We are confronted with a doctrine that is perfectly coherent, with a genuine philosophy, if we are to interpret philosophy as being an explanation of the world.

Only those who neglect the sole existing basis of operations . . . the comparison of texts . . . still regard mysticism as a dense mass of undergrowth over-running an untilled soil. The critical editions of texts, that have rapidly increased in numbers during the past thirty years, will no longer allow us to depreciate to such an extent the intellectual value of a doctrine whose sturdy framework, in spite of being concealed beneath a special terminology, is none the less quite easy to apprehend.

On the other hand, it would be equally erroneous to side with Denifle and Harnack and to regard speculative mysticism as a sentimental excrescence of Scholasticism. We think we have demonstrated that the influence of Scholasticism, however important, affects but a small part of the doctrine of Ruysbroeck. If one may say so, it supplies this doctrine with the stamp of time, by transmitting to it a contingent of scientific ideas, of Scholastic images, and of principles that can readily be isolated. This contact between Ruysbroeck and Scholasticism is precisely that which exists between a man and his age. It is henceforth evident that Ruysbroeck assimilated the general instruction of his times; he had other masters than the Holy Spirit beneath the shade of the sacred lime-tree.

But let there be no mistake: Scholasticism is far from being a homogeneous system, lasting several centuries without the slightest modification. As has been well said: "regarded as a whole, the philosophical work of the Middle Ages may be compared to a mosaic of systems; no doctrinal unity can be discovered in its productions."[1] And if there is one common characteristic in these many systems, it is to be found in the acknowledged supremacy of theology. This it is that constitutes the summit of the pyramid into which all other disciplines enter, like huge blocks. This is what is expressed by the celebrated fresco of Taddeo Gaddi in Florence: in the centre of the composition Saint Thomas is holding on his knees a copy of the Scriptures, open at the passage: *propter hoc optavi et datus est sensus et invocavi et venit in me spiritus sapientiae et praeposui illam regibus et sedibus* (*Sap.* vii. 7). Around the "Angelic Doctor," like humble vassals, are grouped the symbolical figures of the cardinal virtues, of the seven liberal arts, of civil law and of canon law.

Such is the view it is most fitting to entertain regarding Scholasticism: not confusion, but rather a hierarchical arrangement of knowledge. Hence, if there is no doctrinal unity, neither can there be a single master. Scholasticism is an eclecticism wherein are combined the most varied influences, the most important of which is not Aristotelianism, as is generally imagined.

When the first Scholastic structures were instituted, what was known of the Stagirite? Scarcely anything: a few extracts incorporated in the *Compendium dialecticum* of Cassiodorus and the translation of the *Categories* by Boëtius. Is Aristotle, represented as a deacon by the side of Saint Thomas in the paintings of Gozzoli and Orcagna, better

[1] De Wulf, *Introduction à la philosophie néo-scolastique*, pp. 55, 95, etc.

known in the thirteenth and fourteenth centuries? In the early years of the thirteenth century the Jews bring from Toledo in Spain, where there lived a number of translators, the work of Aristotle. But is this really and truly the philosopher of Stagira? A twice-distorted Aristotle, translated from Greek into Arabic, from Arabic into Latin, watered down and mitigated by the Platonist or the pantheistic commentaries of Avicenna and Averroës, inlaid with cabalistic extracts. How can a distinction be made between the original and the work of the commentators? Gregory IX., who was extremely cautious, was in no wise deceived; scenting the germs of pantheism hidden beneath the pseudo-Stagirite, he twice refused the work. Saint Thomas, charged with the task of expurgating this Aristotle, makes a choice of everything capable of harmonising with the orthodox teaching,[1] in such fashion that he brings together in his work elements that are authentically Peripatetic and those that are indubitably Neoplatonic.

In addition, these latter had already found their place in theological speculation. Up to the thirteenth century Scholasticism was almost exclusively nourished on Neoplatonism, chiefly through the writings of the Pseudo-Dionysius, translated into Latin by Scotus Erigena. The extraordinary fortune, too, of these writings was maintained even after the enthroning of Aristotle as *precursor Christi in rebus naturalibus*. Dionysian literature is commented on in nearly all the schools; the abbey of Saint-Victor, in particular, is almost exclusively wedded to the diffusion of the mystical ideas of the Areopagite, and Saint Thomas himself, like his master Albertus Magnus, is almost as much indebted to the Pseudo-Dionysius as to Aristotle.[2]

Apart from this there circulated, under the name of Aristotle, purely Neoplatonist writings such as a *Theologia Aristotelis*, taken from Plotinus, and a *Liber de Causis*, from

[1] Picavet, *Esquisse* . . ., p. 210.
[2] It may truly be affirmed that, if we had lost the works of the Pseudo-Dionysius, we should recover them all in these of the "Angelic Doctor." Guignebert, *Le Christianisme médiéval et moderne*, p. 74.

the works of Proclus. Under the pontificate of Boniface VIII. the apostolic library possessed a summary of academician philosophy by Proclus,[1] and this clearly indicates the spring upon which Christian thought drew. As a matter of fact, Scholasticism is largely based on Neoplatonism, for the Aristotle of the Middle Ages is still a Neoplatonist. The genuine Aristotle, with his dualism of principles, his eternity of the world, his far-away God so completely disinterested in human beings, would not have found it easy to recognise himself in his image as perpetuated by the Scholastics. The dissimilarity was clearly visible at the Renaissance, when the humanists brought out the first critical edition of the Greek text. The Church then perceived that, in incorporating Pseudo-Aristotelianism, it had given refuge to its most dangerous enemy, the very one from which had proceeded the more or less pantheistic developments which the Inquisition had not completely succeeded in quelling.

The result was that Ruysbroeck and the whole of the speculative mystic school, by adopting the traditional scheme of Scholasticism, found themselves already in contact with Neoplatonism.

All the same, the contact was but indirect and wholly external. We are now about to see how Ruysbroeck is going to introduce purely Neoplatonist elements into these ready-made schemes borrowed from Scholasticism.

II

What, then, is this philosophy whose potent vitality supplied nourishment for ten centuries of speculation? It has even been possible to say that the development of Christian theology could not be understood apart from Neoplatonism.[2] How is this extraordinary influence to be explained?

Above all, in our opinion, by the identity of circumstances

---

[1] Ehrle, *Historia bibliothecae pontificum romanorum*, t. I. p. 121.

[2] Rudolf Eucken, *Die Lebensanschauungen der grossen Denker* (Berlin–Leipzig, 1921), p. 107. Eucken calls Alexandria *die Geburtstatte der christlichen Theologie*.

and aspirations which regards the Middle Ages not as an arbitrarily isolated period, but as the actual extension of the third century. The third century is the beginning of a period of spiritual awakening directly connecting Græco-Latin antiquity with modern times. And if philosophy voices the aspirations and needs which periodically manifest themselves in the human mind, with all kinds of modifications, it is worth while examining in some detail a century which left so profound a mark upon succeeding ages. Besides, Plotinus, that figure of towering genius, could not fully be understood were we not previously acquainted with the outer circumstances which largely determine the thought of a man.

This was a dull and sombre period. Marcus Aurelius had left behind him a world resigned, one from which joy had fled. A few years suffice to generalise the feeling of pessimism expressed both by pagan and by Christian authors. "The world is old and corrupt; dissolution is at hand," says Saint Cyprian,[1] his plaintive moan echoing the lamentations of Dion and Censorinus.

This general sense of depression coincides with political vicissitudes. The emperors who succeeded Septimus Severus fell one after another beneath the dagger of the assassin; Decius was slain in battle against the Goths; after the assassination of Aurelian, civil war broke out, disorganising the army itself. It was with difficulty that the energetic Diocletian succeeded in restoring discipline for a time, before ceding the Western empire to Constantius Chlorus and to Galerius, and retiring to his garden at Salona.

During the whole of the century Rome is like a simmering cauldron. The distinctively national element, however, is gradually diminishing. It is not only wars and banishments that are exhausting the old stock of the race; it is also the voluntary restriction of births. One would say that the people refuse to live any longer. There now came about a disturbance of equilibrium which was destined to have a most serious

---

[1] *Ad Demetr* 3.

T

influence upon the material and moral life of the West: there came a moment when the foreign superseded the national element. In Rome the slave-system blended together the most diverse races, from the Orientals to the Germanic peoples, who were predominant in the army; the result being that the already expiring Græco-Latin civilisation was maintained, so to speak, by foreigners.[1]

And yet this world, already in its decline, still sends out flashes of light. Whilst Longinus, Philostratus and Ulpian seem almost to revive the splendour of the past, the new spirit powerfully manifests itself in the Latins—Tertullian, Cyprian, Minucius Felix, Lactantius; and in the Greeks— Clement of Alexandria, Origen and Methodius.

In spite of these great names retrogression is practically general in art and literature. Apart from law there is but one province of intellectual activity that really appeals to men, and that is religious philosophy.

What was the cause of this almost exclusive orientation of the human mind? It is difficult to relate it to one cause alone. It may, however, be stated that the age, after finding its amusement in the jesting impieties of a Lucian, has become painfully aware of a state of spiritual barrenness. We see various philosophical and religious currents of thought begin to appear. While some of them attempt to awake the slumbering gods, others search within themselves, dimly conscious that true divinity lies hid deep within the human heart itself. Others again rise to the idea of the universal; all these deities, this people of semi-gods and heroes who had come to blend with the national gods of Egypt and Syria, Phrygia and Palestine, caused one to reflect that, behind these multiform manifestations, there was in reality but one and the same divine principle.[2] The most amazing superstitions thus found protection beneath a benevolent tolerance, in which scepticism and true religious aspiration were equally combined.

[1] Inge, *The Philosophy of Plotinus*, vol. I. p. 31.
[2] Cf. Jean Reville, *La Religion à Rome sous les Sévères*, pp. 41 ss.

All the same, no philosophy worthy of the name was discovered capable of expressing clearly these needs of the soul. The last representatives of Stoicism and Epicureanism preached distorted systems wherein phantasy ran riot. It is indeed the funeral oration of these two great schools that Plotinus pronounces when he writes:

> There are men who imagine that the things of sense are the first and the last. . . . They regard suffering as an evil and pleasure as a boon; they think the one must be avoided and the other sought. This constitutes the wisdom of those among them who pride themselves on being reasonable, like those ponderous birds which, having increased their weight by taking too much from the earth, are unable to fly aloft, though they have received wings from nature. . . . There are others that rise above terrestrial objects, because their soul, endowed with a superior nature, detaches itself from worldly delights in order to seek something higher; but, incapable of contemplating the intelligible and not knowing where to alight after having left this earth, they come to regard virtue as inherent in those actions and common occupations the narrow sphere of which they had at first attempted to transcend.[1]

There are many Neopythagoreans who had found at the court of Julia Domna a sort of princely academy; an account of the philosophy of this academy Philostratus presents in the highly idealised portrait he has left of Apollonius of Tyana; though, as a matter of fact, this reform rapidly degenerated into petty details of ritual.

There is also Pythagorean Platonism — one of whose representatives, Numenius, inspired Plotinus — with which must probably be connected the Hermetic writings, edited and prepared at different periods. But neither can this vast eclecticism lay claim to the title of philosophy.

As for Gnosticism, which Plotinus discusses, judging it by a few genuine thinkers, " the last survivors of a time that was no more," [2] it was scarcely more than a theurgical occultism, where the rôle of the Christ, in the Coptic documents, for instance, is that of a singularly material *thaumaturgus.*

Plotinus does not speak of the Christians, but he certainly was acquainted with them apart from this degenerate

---

[1] *Enneads*, V. iv. 1.
[2] De Faye, *Gnostiques et gnosticisme* (Paris, 1913), p. 469.

Gnosticism; it may have been owing to his intervention that Gallienus revoked his father's rigorous edict and took under his protection the bishops of Egypt.[1]

At all events, it is certain that Plotinus, with his synthetic turn of mind, caught a glimpse in the new religion, as well as in the degeneracy of the expiring schools, of the universally experienced need of redemption, of a saving contact between creature and Creator.

The *mystery religions* especially, so widely spread along the shores of the Mediterranean, had thrown light on the decline of the human soul. This soul was sullied not by nature, but by the addition of an impure element similar to the slime that might soil a golden gem. The essential aim of religion thus appeared as a practice tending to release the soul from this impure element, i.e. to save it; in other words, to restore its identity with the divine principle: ἡ κρύψις ἡ μυστικὴ σεμνοποιεῖ τὸ Θεῖον.[2] Hence the purificatory and initiatory practices which guaranteed access to immortality. Similarly, in Gnosticism, where unity of doctrine no longer exists, the mutilated sects, which rapidly increased in the third century, have yet all one common character: initiation into expiatory mysteries or rites. Behind a complicated cosmology, sometimes even behind unclean practices, this represents the drama of the soul that has gone astray in matter and seeks to return to God. But this God is so far away that he is inaccessible to human efforts alone. Consequently Gnosticism —or rather *the* Gnosticisms—multiplies its intermediaries, and though Christ, in the system, plays a primordial part, it scarcely differs from that of the Archontics and the Æons as understood by those great theorists of Gnosticism, Basilides and Valentinus; this it is that controls the redemptive processes, disposes of the seals of salvation, gives life to the sacred formulae.

On the other hand, Pythagorean Platonism, along with Amelius, relegated the supreme God to an unapproachable

---

[1] Eusebius, *Hist. eccl.*, vii. 13, 23. C. Schmidt, *Plotins Stellung zum Gnosticismus und kirchlichen Christentum (Texte und Untersuch,* Leipzig, 1901), pp. 12–13.

[2] Reitzenstein, *Die hellenistische Mysterienreligionen*, pp. 110 ss.

distance. This inaccessible God is even called an idle king, βασιλεὺς ἀργός. The whole of the divine activity falls upon the second God, or Demiurgus, who, endowed with a dual nature (διττός), governs both the spiritual and the material world. The soul, fashioned after the likeness of this Demiurgus, is also dual: there is the rational soul, which is none other than the Good, and the irrational soul, Evil, or matter. Salvation is thus effected in the predominance of Good over Evil, in the union of the rational soul with the spiritual nature of the Demiurgus.

If we free these beliefs from external modalities, what do we find at the bottom of them all? A grievous pessimism: man feels himself wretched, he sees the instability of his ephemeral state in a hostile world, and he suffers. All the schools culminate in the most decisive dualism: on the one hand, infinitely far away from mankind, an impassive God, the source of all good; on the other hand, the world, the domain of matter and evil. And man finds this irreducible dualism deep within his soul, in his barren strivings after perfection. Where is the old Hellenic ideal of beauty and joy? It has given way to Oriental pessimism.[1]

This it is with which Plotinus is confronted. In the name of Greek philosophy he aims at reinstating human destiny, restoring faith and hope to man, and thus supplying a rational and optimistic conception of the universe. He wishes to pour out a goblet of delight before the thirsty soul, to show the beauty of the Cosmos to eyes that no longer saw, to teach man the way of happiness in glad obedience to the majestic order that controls the progress of the universe. To the man overwhelmed by his loneliness he will say: God is not far from thee.

We are not separate from Being, we are in it.[2]
Seek God with assurance, he is not far away, and you will attain to him; the intermediaries are not numerous. All that is necessary is to take from the soul, which is divine, the part which is most divine.[3]

---

[1] E. Bréhier, *Le Sage antique*, in *Du sage antique au citoyen moderne*, by Bouglé, Bréhier, Delacroix, Parodi (Paris, 1921), p. 45.
[2] *Enneads*, VI. xx. v. 4.　　　　　　　　[3] *Ibid.*, V. i. 3.

The world, so depreciated by the philosophic and religious pessimism of the time,

reveals the greatness of intelligible nature. If the world has a continuous, clear and manifold existence, all-pervading and shining with marvellous wisdom, how can we help acknowledging that it is a beautiful shining statue of the intelligible gods? . . . He who complains of the nature of the world, therefore, knows not what he does nor how audacious he is. Instead of blaming, we must gently submit to the laws of the universe, we must ourselves rise to first principles.[1]

Here we find outlined that assuredly new conception of a moral order superimposed on the cosmic order and included in the same reality. To this conception Plotinus devoted his most noteworthy treatise: On the Beautiful (*Enneads*, I. book VI.). Thus evil appears to him as a negation, a privation, "in brief, we must not imagine that evil is anything else than what is less complete as regards wisdom, less good, following all the time a decreasing gradation." [2]

Plotinus, then, regards salvation as conformity with the moral order by purification. A wholly interior purification, which may also be called a simplification in the sense that the soul should disburden itself of corporeal passions and adopt interior attitudes that conform with the intelligible world which has been glimpsed. And so Plotinus is to contrast new men with degenerate Stoics and Epicureans, with joyless Gnostics. These new men,

endowed with piercing vision, cast a penetrating glance upon the brightness of the intelligible world to which they rise, winging their flight above the clouds and darkness of this material plane. Then, disdaining things terrestrial, they remain in their heights and dwell in their real home, filled with the unspeakable joy of the man who, after long journeyings, has finally returned to his rightful home.[3]

As we see, in all this Plotinus is eager to respond to the general religious aspirations of his times. He is the product of his age in every fibre of his being, and, however powerful and original his genius, it cannot be denied that the circumstances in which he lived—both political and spiritual—exercised a visible influence on the trend and character of his philosophy. Doubtless genius is characterised by its

---

[1] *Enneads*, II. ix. 13.   [2] *Ibid.*, II. ix. 13.   [3] *Ibid.*, V. ix. 1.

power to react against inevitable nature and the influence of environment; still, it cannot altogether dominate these outer influences. The most independent genius belongs to a clearly circumscribed ensemble; it can attain to its end only *in* this ensemble and *through* the environment of which it is but a fragment.

And so Plotinus shares with the whole of his epoch the religious unrest that characterises it. On the other hand, he is repelled by the solutions of the schools which lay claim to a spiritual hegemony; he is also quite as much opposed to the dramatic conception of the universe elaborated by the Gnostics as to the degenerate survivals of the Neohellenic schools. For the great problem brooding over the soul of his age, the soul's restoration to its original state, Plotinus sees but one solution—obedience to the divine Order.

On this basis Plotinus built up one of the finest doctrines that antiquity has bequeathed to us. It owes its marvellous vitality principally to a psychological analysis so definite and precise that, in certain respects, it has never been surpassed.[1] It is not simply a religious initiation destined to develop the unknown powers of the human soul; it is also a genuine moral discipline, summed up in that declaration of the *Enneads* which might be inscribed on the pediment of the edifice: "To obtain a vision of Beauty and of Deity, each man should begin by making himself beautiful and divine."[2] This is optimism, and that of the purest; an optimism that is bountifully nourished by life itself, and quite different from the declarations of a Stoicism which finds a wholly intellectual joy in contemplation of the Cosmos. It is the echo of Plato's voice, not of the voice of Epictetus.

But Plotinus is still quite other than a Greek; a study of the origins of his thought reveals far more remote influences. Manifestly it was not Hellenism that led him to that scorn of the body which constitutes one of the stages of the religious

---

[1] Picavet, *Esquisse*, p. ix. J. Simon had already said that Plotinism is "the most audacious attempt ever made by human genius to fathom the mysteries of the nature of God" (*Histoire de l'École d'Alexandrie*, I. p. 65).

[2] *Enneads*, I. vi. 9.

discipline he recommends. Nor is the idea that ecstasy brings us to the heart of knowledge more surely than all other means of knowledge, a Greek idea. It is more particularly the theory of intelligence as universal being that has specially attracted those who write on the history of philosophy.

Now, it is these very elements that mediæval Christianity revived, though in slightly different form. Regarding their origin, such writers as Ritter, Christian Lassen, Deussen E. Bréhier do not hesitate; they regard the identification of universal being with the self, to the suppression of all intermediary, as a strictly Hindu conception. The existence, indeed, of a stream of Hindu philosophy in Rome during the third century cannot be denied; this it was that, at the court of Julia Domna, the beautiful Syrian, gave birth to the romance of Apollonius of Tyana by Philostratus: the hero of Philostratus crossed India, and, on the banks of the Ganges, "discovered a wisdom superior to that of the Egyptians."

Moreover, Plotinus himself not improbably came into direct contact with these speculations. Indeed, Porphyry relates that Plotinus, "desirous of studying the philosophy taught among the Persians and that prevalent among the Hindus," joined the army which Gordian had raised against the Persians. Gordian was slain and his army scattered; our philosopher even found it difficult to escape to Antioch. In any case, Alexandria, where Plotinus lived up to the age of forty, was the great commercial harbour on the route to India. It was assuredly the best centre of information about everything dealing with the mysterious empire of the Brahmans. There can be no doubt but that Plotinus, when in this city, made inquiries regarding the things of India.

However it be, by presenting the theory of identification as the keystone for his system, Plotinus distinguishes himself from all the philosophies of his age: even the philosophical relationship so frequently set up between himself and Philo the Jew appears to be justified only in secondary matters. The more Plotinus puts trust in human might, the more

Philo despises it: ὅτι ἄτρεπτον τὸ θεῖον. The God of Plotinus is an ever-present God, ἀεὶ πάρεστιν; the God of Philo is only determinable by the intermediary of the creative Logos and of at least five other *logoi*, or powers. To Plotinus the pathway between man and God is free; Philo shares the ideas on salvation widely prevalent in his time throughout all religious circles regarding the necessity of mediatorial agents.

The philosophical position, then, which Plotinus held at Rome, in the middle of the third century, is an entirely independent one. The teaching of his masters becomes so refined by his mystical temperament that quite a new aspect is given to it. Plotinism, instead of being a syncretistic eclecticism, is the original creation of a powerful mind.

If we intend to designate Neoplatonism as a syncretism, we can apply this term only to the later Neoplatonism, that of Iamblichus and Porphyry. And perhaps it is because the doctrine of the philosopher of Lycopolis supplied quite a new response to the aspirations of the time that he asserted himself with extraordinary authority, and that he regained this authority afterwards whenever the circumstances or the needs happened to be identical with those of the third century.

Now this is what took place from the fifth century onwards: the dislocation of the Western empire, followed by the preponderance of the barbaric element over the Latins, while supplying the Western world with a new spirit, makes but little change in the general mentality, and, in certain respects, even intensifies the symptoms of degeneracy that mark the third century.

It is still religious unrest that prevails. Saint Augustine, in spite of having worked out, largely upon the principles of Plato, a mighty system which is to constitute the framework of all theological thought, up to and including the Reformation, in spite also of having attempted to check the extreme mobility of speculation with the dike of the principle of authority in matters of faith, was unable to stifle that spiritual disquiet working in the soul of the people.

No sooner is the famous bishop of Hippo dead, than there seems to be an attempt to dry up the great fertilising streams which placed the new world in contact with the Græco-Latin past. First we have the condemnation of Origen by Justinian in 543 [1]; then the barbarian invasion of a mentality that has nothing Christian about it except the outer polish spread over a pagan superstition; then the reconciliation to this state of things by the Church which, dissolute and debauched, never dreams of teaching the ignorant hordes that came to it, but baptises them, though well aware of the inferior elements which it thus protects with its authority. Thought—if there is such a thing during these troublous times—consists solely in setting up the orthodox belief, as it issued from the Council of Nicæa, against Arianism, with which the descendants of the Goths, formerly evangelised by Ulfila, were all more or less infected. Thus, hastily and *grosso modo*, there is realised an outer unity, but, beneath this thin surface, what we find is a new form of religious syncretism.

What a difference between the syncretism of the third century and that of the sixth and seventh! In Rome, despite the torrent of superstitions, there was a vein of intense religious feeling, "a nobility and purity of sentiments which it would be puerile to disregard." [2] In the Christian West of the sixth and seventh centuries, syncretism is scarcely more than a blend of Germanic and autochthonous superstitions [3] beneath which we vainly seek a genuinely religious aspiration.

That which is everywhere dominant is ritual materialism, practices that are nothing else than a new form of theurgy. An entire pantheon of demi-gods, in whom alone the people —incapable of rising higher—believe, is organised under the guise of devotion to relics. The ancient gods are still worshipped, though by other names, and so we find the cult of trees and springs, sorcery, sacrificial practices and the

---

[1] The struggle against Origenism is studied in all its details by F. Diekamp, *Die origenistischen Streitigkeiten in sechsten Jahrhundert* (Münster, 1899).

[2] Jean Reville, *La Religion à Rome sous les Sévères*, pp. 159-67.

[3] Ch. Guignebert, *Le Christianisme médiéval et moderne*, p. 19.

entire pagan mythology permeating the Church in Christian garb. In vain does Gregory the Great multiply ordinances and condemnations. He dies, rejected and despairing, though his noble qualities save the honour of Christianity, once again menaced by its own victory. The reason why Christianity did not then perish, stifled beneath pagan parasitism, is because a few learned and pious monks, dwelling under the shade of an Italian mountain, strictly bound to stern rules, and, in accordance with the apostolic vow, bent upon combining knowledge with holiness of living, became guardians of the treasure-stores of classic antiquity, and of the Gospel ideal.

It was then that, with the aid of such lofty-minded civilians as Charlemagne and Alfred the Great, an attempt was made to remedy the widespread degradation of faith and thought. We have the creation of courts of justice, the rehabilitation of theology, moral reparation, unity of control both in the civil and in the religious domain under the form of a genuine theocracy. In the intellectual reorganisation, however, aimed at by Charlemagne, it is Neoplatonism that is to come to the fore. *And finally we have Scotus Erigena,* who brings with him into theology that lofty Plotinian idealism which henceforth is to feed the whole of the Middle Ages and supply modern thought with some of its strongest and most substantial elements.

III

It is not our object to study in detail the philosophy of Plotinus. Still, with the doctrine of Ruysbroeck in mind, we must try to discover what are the Neoplatonist elements which found their way into the system of our author, and along what channels.

It is clear that Ruysbroeck was not himself acquainted with the writings of Plotinus, and that contact with Scholasticism could not have supplied him with that imposing contingent of Neoplatonist ideas which characterise the system of our mystic. We will take these ideas one by one and endeavour to find out along what lines they reached him.

From the philosophical point of view, the two main trends of thought in the Middle Ages start from Saint Augustine and from Scotus Erigena.

The rôle of Saint Augustine in Christian thought is unparalleled. He it was largely who brought into the Christian patrimony the treasures of antiquity and supplied those solid frames into which the speculations of the doctors of the Church were subsequently fitted. He was also the inspirer of mysticism, as well as of Scholasticism. A powerful Church organiser, he none the less helped to elaborate the piety of a Luther, thus providing the Reformation with a vein which Scholastic disputes could not exhaust. He inspires Jansenism in the seventeenth century; and for the future his rôle seems as though it must equal, if not surpass, that now played by Thomism, more correctly called Neothomism.

The influence of Saint Augustine over Ruysbroeck is evident. His name frequently recurs in the writings of our mystic, though he is sparing in mentions of this kind. This was the first influence to bring Ruysbroeck into contact with Neoplatonism.

§ 1. The question of the Neoplatonism of Saint Augustine is one of those that have been most fruitfully discussed by scholars. If we are to believe Saint Augustine himself— books VI. and VII. of the *Confessions*—he was converted to *Catholicism* in 386, and retired a few days after that event to the villa of Cassiciacum to prepare himself for baptism by prayer and penance. Now, it was at Cassiciacum that he wrote the four following dialogues: *Contra Academicos, De Beata Vita, De Ordine* and *Soliloquiorum libri duo*. And these dialogues are not the expression of the faith of a neophyte, but of an almost full-fledged Neoplatonist. A comparison of the text of the *Confessions*—belonging to the latter years of the century, 387-400—with the text of the *Dialogues*, shows that in the former Augustine anticipated the real evolution which was to lead him to Catholicism. He was scarcely a complete Catholic before the year 400, and if conversion took place in 386, it was one from Manichæism or from academic doubt to Neoplatonism.

If this theory is correct—and we think it is [1]—we see how important for the future of Christian thought was so prolonged an impregnation of the mind of the great teacher by the Neoplatonist philosophy. Neoplatonism entered as a constituent element into Augustinian dogmatics, for a man does not utterly divest himself of his former ideas unless some violent crisis disturbs the very depths of his being. Now, this crisis did not come about after the garden scene: having found peace in Neoplatonism, Augustine gently and naturally passed into Catholicism. Nor did he ever forget the masters who had filled with beatitude the calm retreat of Cassiciacum; he pays them homage in terms which proclaim his indebtedness to them. He calls Plotinus, Porphyry, Iamblichus and Apuleius *famous Platonists*. He delights in acknowledging their perspicacity and ingeniosity.[2] They are *his chosen philosophers*, and, while criticising them, Augustine considers that they are *learned men, rightly superior in glory and renown to other philosophers*. These testimonies, purposely culled from the *De Civitate Dei*, are subsequent to the conversion of Augustine to Catholicism, consequently they are of even more convincing force than the homage paid to Plotinus in the third book of the dialogue *Contra Academicos* (cap. xviii.); early enthusiasm is toned down and the heart inclined towards another doctrine, but the mind

---

[1] Up to the present it has had but few opponents: F. Worter, *Die Geistesentwicklung des hl. Aur. Augustins bis zu seiner Taufe* (Paderborn, 1892), pp. 64 ss.; J. Martin, *St. Augustin* (*Les Grands Philosophes*) (Paris, 1901), pp. 43 ss.; W. Montgomery, *St. Augustine, Aspects of his Life and Thought*, pp. 33 ss.; Ch. Boyer, *Christianisme et Néo-platonisme dans la formation de St. Augustin* (Paris, 1920), pp. 192 ss.

[2] "Plotini schola Romae floruit, habuitque condiscipulos multos acutissimos et solertissimos viros" (*Epist.* cxviii.).

has not forgotten the consolation found in the lofty speculations of Plotinus, of whom Augustine had said:

> The message of Plato, the purest and most luminous in all philosophy,
> has at last scattered the darkness of error and now shines forth mainly in
> Plotinus, a Platonist so like his master that one would think they lived
> together, or rather—since so long a period of time separates them—
> that Plato is born again in Plotinus.

Saint Ambrose, whose teaching in Milan Augustine
followed from the autumn of 384 to that of 386, does not
seem to have played, in the conversion of the future bishop
of Hippo, the important part attributed to him by Possidius.[1]
Possibly he saved him from Manichæism, but he could
not make the young rhetor profess Catholicism; he himself,
in addition, by the allegorical method of interpretation of
the Scriptures which he applied in the manner of Philo,
strengthened still further the Platonist sympathies in his
pupil. Subsequently he even congratulated him on reading
the translation of Victorinus, "because all the reasonings of
the Platonists tend to raise the mind to a knowledge of God
and of his Word."

At this very time the drama being enacted in the soul of
Augustine turned upon the problem of evil. The anguish
caused by this problem had already driven him to Manichæism, the dualistic solution of which suddenly appeared
ultra-simple. Then we are faced with the desolation of one
who, after leaving the spiritual refuge which hitherto had
sheltered him, finds himself on the open road, without
having discovered the new shelter. This state of desolation is
fully expressed in a line of the *Confessions : et quaerebam unde
malum et non erat exitus !*[2]

The problem of evil, it must not be forgotten, dominates
and explains the entire theology of Saint Augustine: the
theories of the Creation, of the Word, of original sin, of
freedom and of grace, are immediately correlated with it.
But where does Saint Augustine find the elements of this

[1] "Et factum est divina praestante opitulatione, ut per illum talem ac tantum
antistitem Ambrosium, et doctrinam salutarem Ecclesiae catholicae et divina
perciperet Sacramenta." *Vita S. Augustini*, in Migne, *Patr. lat.*, t. XXXII. col. 35.
[2] Migne, *Patr. lat.*, t. XXXII. col. 739.

imposing system which constitutes the solution of the problem of evil? We claim—and on this point we cannot challenge the ground of Saint Augustine's testimony [1]—that he finds them in Neoplatonism; consequently the Middle Ages, in adopting the Augustinian conceptions, adopts Neoplatonism.

Let us now see how far this influence is exercised. The fact that it became less and less, according to M. Grandgeorge,[2] does not prevent a certain number of the main elements of Neoplatonism from having become constituent elements in the theological thought of the great Doctor of the West. M. Grandgeorge reduces these ideas to two: the doctrine of the absolute simplicity of God and the conception of evil regarded as a non-reality. On the question of the Creation, M. Grandgeorge considers that the independence of Saint Augustine remains entire and indisputable. We cannot be so categorical.

First there is the idea of the Deity.

The system of Plotinus is summed up in the book on the Beautiful (*Enneads*, I. vi.), which, as Porphyry tells us, was the first he wrote. Plotinus undertakes to reply to the question: What must one do to succeed in contemplating that ineffable Beauty which, like the Deity in the mysteries, remains hidden from us deep in a sanctuary, and does not show itself without, so as not to be perceived by the profane? Let him who has the power to do so advance and enter this sanctuary, closing his eyes to the sight of things terrestrial. Now, there is identity between the good and the beautiful. Accordingly it is rightly said that goodness and beauty consists in the soul making itself like unto God, because he is the principle of Beauty . . . or rather, being is Beauty, non-being is ugliness. . . . Without genuine virtue God is but a

---

[1] "Procurasti mihi . . . quosdam Platonicorum libros ex graeca lingua in latinam versos." *Confess.*, lib. VII. cap. ix. 13; Migne, t. XXXII. col. 740. "Commemoravi legisse me quosdam libros Platonicorum, quos Victorinus quondam rhetor urbis Romae, quem christianum defunctum esse audieram, in latinam linguam transtulisset." *Confess.*, lib. VIII. cap. ii. 3; Migne, t. XXXII. col. 750.

[2] *St. Augustin et le Néo-platonisme*, pp. 152-3.

word.[1] But in this initiation, on the one hand, God must remain absolute perfection; on the other hand, there must be identity of nature between God and man: τῇ Θειοτέρᾳ φύσει συγγενὴς ἡ ψυχὴ καὶ τῇ ἀϊδίῳ.[2]

Saint Augustine does not say anything different. His treatise *De beata vita* is wholly given up to proving that happiness is nothing else than the possession of God by beauty and truth. *Make thyself beautiful*, Plotinus repeats again and again. And Saint Augustine echoes the saying in the words: "when the soul is composed and orderly, when it has made itself harmonious and beautiful, it will dare to contemplate God, the source whence flows all truth and the Father of truth."[3]

Such a discipline indicates that Deity, capable of being attained only by a special contact (νοερῶς ἐφαψάσθαι, says Plotinus), is superior to all determination and all thought. This is why it can be called only the One (τὸ ἕν), Being (τὸ ὄν), the Limitless (τὸ ἄπειρον); to come nearest, therefore, to an adequate notion of Deity, it is fitting to proceed in negative fashion and ask ourselves not what God is, but what he is not.

This utter simplicity of God is again one of those ideas on which Saint Augustine is glad to dwell. In *Sermo* CXVII. he gives us one of those wonderfully striking phrases in which he excels: *Si enim comprehendis Deum, non est Deus*. And so, Deity, in its essence, both in the case of Plotinus and in that of Augustine, is inapprehensible, incomprehensible, inexpressible. It eludes thought (ἐπέκεινα νοήσεως): *non possit penuria sermonis humani quavis oratione vel modice comprehendi*.[4]

Still, how is man to come in contact with the Unknowable?

We know that Plotinus, in answering this question, sets up a rational and necessary bond between all the forms of being. The one being perfect, acquiring nothing, having neither need nor desire, *superabounds*, so to speak, and this superabundance produces a different nature of being.[5] As

---

[1] *Enneads*, I. vi. 6; I. vi. 9; II. ix. 15; V. v. 10.
[2] *Ibid*., IV. vii. 10.
[3] *De ordine*, lib. II. cap. xix. No. 51; Migne, t. XXXII. col. 1019.
[4] *De Civit*., lib. IX. cap. xvi.   [5] *Ibid*., V. i. 6.

fire radiates heat, and snow cold; as every organic being, immediately on attaining to its full development, produces its like; so the Perfect, which is also the Eternal, produces from the superabundance of his perfection that which, like himself, is eternal and good. Thus it is that the One produces Intelligence (Νοῦς). "Intelligence is the word and the act of the One . . . when that which begets is supremely perfect, that which is begotten should be so closely united with it that it is separate only in respect of being distinct therefrom." [1]

As M. Bréhier has shown,[2] the notion of Intelligence, in Plotinus, is far from being homogeneous: now it corresponds to Platonist ideas, then again it constitutes a world apart, the κόσμος νοητός; and finally it images a stage of the spiritual life. Here we have to consider it only as a *cause*, for it is in this aspect that Saint Augustine has adopted it when he gives it the name of *intelligible truth*, synonymous with the *Word*.

Regarded as *cause*, Intelligence, says Plotinus, contains the ideas, images or paradigms of all that exists. In it is found, first of all, the idea of the world in its ensemble or universal archetype; then come general ideas, such as that of man *per se*; and lastly particular ideas, for instance, the idea of a flower, a mountain, etc.[3] Now this rôle played by the Intelligence of Plotinus is the same that Saint Augustine attributes to the Word: *In Verbo Patris sunt omnia quae creantur etiam antequam creentur, et quidquid in illo est vita est et vita utique creatrix.*[4] And again: *Antequam fierent res, apud Deum erant eomodo quo sempiterne atque incommutabiliter vivunt et vita sunt, facta autem eo modo, quo unaquaeque creatura in genere suo est.*[5]

An important difference must here be noted, however, between the second Plotinian hypostasis and the Word of Augustine. *Intelligence*, being immovable, cannot be placed in direct relation with the world of sense. As the One super-

---

[1] *Enneads*, V. i. 6.
[2] *La philosophie de Plotin*, in *Revue des Cours* (1922), pp. 157 ss.
[3] *Enneads*, V. i. 6, 7; VI. vii. 2.
[4] *De Gen. ad lit.*, II. 6, 12.   [5] *Ibid.*, V. 15, 33.

abounds into Intelligence, so Intelligence superabounds into the third hypostasis, the Soul of the world (ἡ ψυχὴ τοῦ κόσμου) or universal soul (ἡ ψυχὴ ὅλη). This latter is in reality the begetting power. The *Soul* is acquainted with the paradigms contained in Intelligence and derives therefrom its own processes. It *organises* matter according to the order which it has contemplated in Intelligence; thus it is strictly ἡ γεννητικὴ ψυχή. From this procreative soul which organises the world in its ensemble there afterwards emanate particular souls, each of which, according to its degree of perfection, organises a portion of matter. Creation thus pursues an order of progressive degradation.[1]

The Word, the second hypostasis in Augustine's system, is superior to the Intelligence of Plotinus in that its creative power acts direct upon the world of sense; it becomes subject to movement by an incomprehensible mystery.[2]

Still, the Word, thus determined, goes through the same processes as those attributed by Plotinus to the Soul. See once more on this point book II. of the treatise *De libero arbitrio*, where Saint Augustine gives a lengthy explanation of the cohesion of the created world, the manifestation of the original unity through the agency of the Word or of creative Truth.

The interversion of rôles between the second and the third hypostasis naturally leads Augustine to attribute to the third hypostasis, the Holy Spirit, an altogether special activity, relating not to the descending movement which proceeds from the One to man, as with Plotinus, but to the ascending movement which leads man to God. The rôle of the Holy Spirit is exclusively religious, so to speak: it consists in remitting sins and thus allowing of purification.

With this reservation, Saint Augustine is at one with Plotinus in his theory of the return to God: ἐπιστροφή.

Man is the reflection of the divine Triad, Plotinus had said; this is a theme that Augustine developed with a wealth of language which the Scholastics could not surpass.

---

[1] *Enneads*, V. i. 2; III. v. 6; IV. viii. 6.
[2] *De Trinit.*, XV. vii. 12; XV. 14, 23.

Books IX. to XV. of *De Trinitate* consist almost entirely of analogies which Saint Augustine sets up between the Trinity and the created world. The human soul thus reflects the Trinity in its three faculties: *mens, notitia, amor,* or again, in memory, intelligence, will. And so we are dealing with a moral discipline which Plotinus calls ἕνωσις and Saint Augustine *purification.*

> Retire within and examine thyself [says Plotinus]. If still thou dost not find beauty there, do like the artist who strikes away and removes, refines and purifies. . . . Remove from thy soul all that is superfluous, correct everything that is not upright, purify and illumine what is obscure, and cease not to perfect thy statue until Virtue shine in thine eyes. . . . When thou no longer encounterest in thyself any obstacle which prevents thee from being *one,* when nothing alien any longer debases the simplicity of thine inmost essence . . . then look attentively, for only through the eye which then opens within thee canst thou perceive supreme Beauty.[1]

This discipline is a simplification of the inmost being by a process of progressive divesting, ἅπλωσις. To seek God outside of this simplification is to court deception: we shall find the reflection of God, not God himself: ἀλλὰ σὺ μὴ δι' ἑτέρων αὐτὸ ὅρα· εἰ δὲ μὴ ἴχνος ἂν ἴδοις, οὐκ αὐτό.[2]

Now listen to Saint Augustine: "The multitude of things from which we must flee is not that of men, but the host of everything the senses reach."[3] The obstacle existing between man and God is the mass of sense-images: *et abduxit cogitationem a consuetudine, subtrahens se contra dicentibus turbis phantasmatum.*[4] The soul should therefore proceed to its adornment by stripping itself bare: "when it has made itself harmonious and beautiful, it will dare to contemplate God, the spring from which flows all truth."[5] That is the interior God which the *oculus animae* alone is able to behold. He alone beholds him who becomes ever more like him: *Si ergo Deo quanto similior, tanto fit quisque propinquior, nulla est ab illo alia longinquitas quam ejus dissimilitudo.*[6] This is the doctrine of Plotinus himself; the borrowing is all the more probable seeing that the preceding passage is but a trans-

---

[1] *Enneads,* I. vi. 9.
[2] *Ibid.,* V. v. 10.
[3] *De ordine,* I. ii. 3.
[4] *Confess.,* lib. . VII. cap. xvii. 23.
[5] *De ordine,* II. xix. 51.
[6] *De Civit.,* lib. IX. 17.

lation of the *Enneads*: *Fugiendum est igitur ad charissimam patriam et ibi pater et ibi omnia.*[1]

Frequently Augustine describes the union of the soul with God in Neoplatonist terms.

> God is the source of beatitude, the end of our desires. Attaching ourselves, then, to him, or rather, re-attaching ourselves instead of detaching ourselves from him to our misfortune, we tend towards him in love, in order to find rest in him and—by possessing perfection—to possess beatitude. The one sovereign good, indeed, is nothing else than union with God; it is by apprehending him, so to speak, in a spiritual embrace,[2] that the soul becomes fruitful in true virtues.[3]

A few lines farther on Saint Augustine recognises how much in this conception is due to Plotinus: "This vision of God, indeed, is that of a Beauty so perfect, so deserving of love, that Plotinus does not hesitate to declare that, lacking it, though abounding in other blessings, one is necessarily unhappy." [4]

Saint Augustine is also a Neoplatonist in his conception of evil regarded as a deprivation: *Nihil aliud est malum quam corruptio vel modi, vel speciei, vel ordinis naturalis. . . . Non est malum nisi minui bono.*[5] If evil were a substance, it would not be evil, for all substance—the reflection of God—is good. Goodness and being coincide; evil is the deprivation of a good thing.[6]

In conclusion, we find the influence of Neoplatonism on Saint Augustine: first, in the doctrine of a God absolutely simple in his essence and unknowable; second, in the doctrine of the Word, the second divine hypostasis charged with creation; third, in the doctrine of exemplarism or divine ideas; fourth, in the doctrine of the dual stream which proceeds from God to man and from man to God; fifth, in the conception of evil envisaged as a *minutio boni.*

[1] *Enneads*, V. ix. 1.
[2] Plotinus says: "It suffices to attain thereto by a sort of intellectual contact (νοερῶς ἐφαψάσθαι)." *Enneads*, V. iii. 17.
[3] *De Civit.*, lib. X. cap. xiv.
[4] *Ibid.*, lib. X. cap. xvi. Cf. *Enneads*, I. vi. 7.
[5] *De natura boni*, iv. 17.
[6] *Confess.*, VII. xii. 18. Cf. *De Civit.*, lib. XI. 22; *Soliloq.*, I. i. 2; *Enneads*, II. ix. 13.

§ 2. Now these doctrinal points are also to be found in Ruysbroeck. Clearly it is not possible to say always exactly whether these ideas of Ruysbroeck come direct from Saint Augustine or from thinkers who appropriated them subsequently, such as Scotus Erigena, Saint Bernard, the Victorines, or the Scholastics. All the same, the pronounced influence of the ideas that originated in Scotus Erigena, so different from the Augustinian theology, makes it possible to attribute the Neoplatonist ideas—which are not to be found in Scotus Erigena, though we discover them in Augustine— to the direct or indirect influence of the great bishop of Hippo.

What we first find in Ruysbroeck of Neoplatonist Augustinianism is the conception of the One-God, whose essence is absolute simplicity and of whom one can say more truly what he is not than what he is, for he is above all positive definition. This God would consequently be unknowable did not man possess within himself an element of divine origin, a spark of God: the soul. As each thing tends to return to its source, the soul turns naturally towards God. In this simple unity, which is the essential form of God, is found the Archetype of all things. God, determining himself by emanation, radiation or effigy,[1] the Ideas that are in God will manifest themselves in decreasing order, so that created things will be less and less perfect the greater the distance separating them from their Archetype. On the other hand, as divine Unity is manifested in the form of three hypostases, this trinity will also be reflected in the created world: thus the soul will be endowed with three—among other—faculties that will each enable it to rise to the divine hypostasis with which it corresponds.

As the One is perfection, if man would return thereto, would apprehend and contemplate God, he should endeavour to attain perfection. The separation from God, in which man finds himself naturally, is not evil; evil indeed possesses no

---

[1] The image of the seal, which Augustine passed on to mediæval philosophy, after borrowing it from Plotinus, is also found in the Gnostics (τύπος, ἐκμαγεῖον, σφραγίς). We also find in Valentinus the conception of degradation by separation. Clement of Alexandria, IV. *Strom.*, chapter xiii. 89, 90.

reality *per se*, since it is in the nature of God to manifest himself in differentiation of potency. What we call evil is only a lower degree of being. But sin—which is quite different from evil—is the voluntary acceptance of this lower state wherein man delights. The idea of the Fall, which Ruysbroeck here introduces, but slightly modifies this conception. The Fall is the result of the choice made by Adam between unity with God and life in the world of sense. He who obtains his enjoyment solely from the world of sense confirms for himself the sin of Adam; and if he continues in this state, he goes of his own free-will—not by God's decree, for God cannot determine ill-fortune—to final downfall and ruin. He effects his own annihilation.

These irreducible sinners, however, are few. Most men have a feeling of their divine origin, and this feeling is kept alive by the Holy Spirit. Thus comes into being a higher life, the first stage on the return path. This higher life is the gradual recovery of the mastery of the mind over the senses, a stripping off, a simplification. In proportion as man breaks away from his senses, in like proportion is he enriched with the gifts of the Holy Spirit. When his liberation is completed he may unite with—though not yet behold—God; he may unite with the Son, the second hypostasis. There still remains for him to unite with Deity in its essential oneness; this constitutes vision or ecstasy, which can doubtless come about in some instances even in this life, though it is really complete only in saints whom death has robbed of their physical body.

Although the theory of ecstasy came to Augustine largely from Plotinus, in the case of Ruysbroeck it includes developments which are mainly derived, as we shall see, from the Pseudo-Dionysius and from Scotus Erigena.

This is the second Neoplatonist current which we must now study with reference to Ruysbroeck.

IV

Apart from the Plotinian elements which Saint Augustine transmitted to Christian theology, a parallel Neoplatonist vein nurtures mediæval philosophy. This vein is connected by the Pseudo-Dionysius not with Plotinus, but with Proclus, who is thus really the father of mediæval mysticism.

§ 1. Proclus is the final and glorious light of Greek philosophy.

He taught at the school of Athens which the Antonines had founded to secure the regular transmission of the same principles down the ages ; the masters of this veritable *university* were for this reason called διάδοχοι. None of them was better qualified than Proclus to effect this vast philosophical synthesis. His great learning made him as well acquainted with foreign mythologies as with the national pantheon. He was at the same time a philosopher, an astronomer and a geometrician. All this knowledge, however, he regarded from the religious point of view; he wished to be, as he expressed it, the universal hierophant, τοῦ ὅλου κόσμου ἱεροφάντης. Thus gifted, Proclus worked for the systematisation of Neoplatonism; because of his rare powers of co-ordination he came to be called the Saint Thomas of Alexandrian mysticism.

Porphyry had already attempted this synthesis in his *Sentences*, though without setting up the logical bond which united to one another the various parts of the Plotinian system. Proclus, on the other hand, in his treatise Στοιχείωσις θεολογική, by applying the geometrical method to the expounding of theological ideas, succeeded in constructing an imposing edifice of harmoniously combined parts which enabled Neoplatonism to survive the closing of the school of Athens.

The principle of Proclus is as follows: the object of life being sovereign good, the true philosopher should rise from the things of sense to ideas; he has yet to reach the intelligible and distinct causes of ideas. Granted the principle, what will be the method? First of all Proclus modifies the Plotinian conception of the One, a negative conception, seeing that, in order to attain the One, it was necessary, as it were, to empty creation of its positive content. To the mind of Proclus, the One, posited alone, in absolute immobility, does not appear to explain the many. To explain the many, and also the various phenomena of the world and of thought, Plotinus had shown the One as emanating from a first hypostasis, Intelligence, and this, Proclus thinks, creates an impassable gulf between God and Intelligence.

To evade the *vacuity* of such a conception Proclus first identifies the One with the Good, which is a positive reality; now, as the character of the Good is to share itself out, the One is capable, through its identification with the Good, of producing the many. Here, in the distinction made by Plotinus between the One and Intelligence, Proclus inserts an analogy of the Pythagorean theory of numbers: his triadic theory, expounded in the *Platonician Theology*, by virtue óf which both the spiritual and the material worlds are subject to the law of triplicity. Being is thus divided into three moments: ὕπαρξις, πρόοδος, ἐπιστροφή. These moments take place in the *infinite*, the *finite* and the *mixed*. All emanations, which afterwards succeed one another degressively, contain each in their turn three terms, and each of these terms constitutes a new triad, itself also capable of manifesting in the threefold aspect of the infinite, the finite and the mixed. Thus we have in succession, starting with the One, the triad of being, or the *Father*, comprising the intelligible unities; the triad of intelligible life and of eternity, the *Mother*; and lastly, the third, corresponding to the Intelligence of Plotinus, τριὰς νοερά.[1]

Then come the triads that relate to the Soul, each also comprising three terms: the demiurgic triad set in

---

[1] Hegel, who was greatly inspired by the system of Proclus, approves of him for placing intelligence last. Lindsay, *Le Système de Proclus*, in *Revue de Métaphysique et de Morale* (1921), p. 505.

charge of creation, the conservative triad, the vivifying or zoögonic triad.

Lastly, the triad of the anagogic powers has for its aim to restore all things to Unity by a threefold movement. The world of sense also possesses powers of its own: angels, daimons, genii, heroes, who serve as intermediaries between the higher world and the world of sense.

Such, in brief, is the conception of Proclus. We have dwelt upon it because it is to be adopted by the Pseudo-Dionysius, and, through him, to pass into Christian mysticism along with the conception of the return to Unity, which differs but little from that of Plotinus.

> All that comes forth from several causes returns by an equal number of intermediaries. The return takes place for the same causes as the going forth . . . one must return first to the intermediary, then to that which is immediately superior to the intermediary.[1]

This retrogression comes about in all domains. In that of knowledge the soul surmounts in succession the entire series of intellectual processes: opinion, reasoning, analysis, synthesis, science, comprehension, enthusiasm. Finally it reaches the last, ecstatic knowledge:

> There is a mode of knowing that is above intelligence, a divine madness. The like alone knows the like; sense, the sensible; intelligence, intelligence; the one, that which is one. Let but the intelligent soul transcend intelligence, and it forgets itself and the rest. Adherent to unity, it therein peacefully dwells, closed to all knowledge, mute and silent . . . this, my friend, is the divine working of the soul: he who is capable of it is set free from the bonds of authority; he is sheltered, not only from exterior but also from interior impulses: he is made God.[2]

This passage is characteristic; we find in it not only the germ of the *deificatio* of Meister Eckhart and of Ruysbroeck, but even the principle which the Brethren of the Free Spirit alleged in justification of their spiritual anarchy and their various excesses.

§ 2. In 529 the school of Athens was closed by an edict

---

[1] *Instit. théolog.*, chapter xxxviii.

[2] The original text of this passage is lost; we find only a Latin translation of the Middle Ages, collected by V. Cousin: *Procli philosophi platonici opera inedita, Prima pars : de Providentia et Fato et eo quod in nobis*, pp. 171-2.

of Justinian. The last of its masters, Damascius, Isidore of Gaza, Olympiodorus, Simplicius, driven from their posts, were compelled to seek refuge with Khosru, the king-philosopher. The spirit of the school, however, could not be destroyed. It simply assumed a Christian garb, and afterwards spread, with amazing vitality, first in the Eastern Church through the instrumentality of John of Damascus and Jean Philopon, and then into the Western Church, which Saint Augustine had already brought in contact with Neoplatonism.

Indeed, a few years after the closing of the school of Athens, there appeared a series of writings which, though seemingly Christian, are none the less clearly Platonist in essence.[1] These writings were issued under the name of Dionysius, a member of the Athenian Areopagus who, according to Acts xvii. 34, had been converted by Saint Paul.

From the outset there began a controversy—one that is not even yet ended—as to the personality of the author. The first attribution of these writings to the Areopagite was made at the Conference of Constantinople in 533, by the Monophysites of Severus, who were disinclined to find the doctrine of the new books suspected by the orthodox.

As a matter of fact, the author really is named Dionysius, though nowhere appearing as the Areopagite. Furthermore, Christianity shows itself in his writings only as a kind of veneer. The terminology is Christian; but the subject-matter is not.[2] This contrast can be explained by the historical circumstances. It is a noteworthy fact that these mysterious writings appear just at the moment when the school of Athens was closed. Their doctrine is that of Proclus but thinly veiled; Proclus and his treatise *De malorum subsistentia* are quoted. When the author ventures upon the domain of

---

[1] *On the Celestial Hierarchy ; On the Ecclesiastical Hierarchy ; On the Divine Names ; On Mystical Theology,* along with ten *Letters,* to which subsequently were unduly added three apocryphal epistles—to Apollophanes, to Timothy and to Titus—which now exist only in Latin.

[2] "Der Anschluss an Proklus erklärt uns auch die befremdende Erscheinung dass D. . . . gar nichts spezifisch Christliches ins Feld führt." H. Koch, *Pseudo-Dionysius Areopagita in seinen Beziehungen zum Neuplatonismus und Mysterienwesen* (Mainz, 1900), p. 91.

Christian dogmatics, he refers to his Θεολογικαὶ ὑποτυπώσεις, a treatise which he alone mentions and no trace of which has been found anywhere, so that we may here suspect some artifice intended to throw one off the scent—a blind.

Besides, it is well known how readily the eclecticism of the Neoplatonists assimilated all doctrines. Would it be any wonder that, to outlive the decree of Justinian, the teaching of the school of Athens outwardly submitted to its enemies in order to save its real existence which was menaced? As already stated, the masters of the condemned school were received at the court of Khosru, king of Persia. Perhaps it is amongst them that we must seek the elusive author of these sensational books. This at least is a hypothesis strangely favoured by comparing the doctrine of the Pseudo-Dionysius with the teaching of the most recent masters, especially Damascius, who merely repeated Proclus.[1] Not to go beyond what is permissible in the field of conjecture, we will confine ourselves to regarding the Pseudo-Dionysius as a disciple of Proclus.

Besides, the case of these books is no isolated one; indeed, there appeared in the fifth century a complete Neoplatonist literature which attempted to rescue from the ruins everything that it could induce Christianity to accept. There is the dialogue of Æneas of Gaza, *Theophrastus, or the immortality of souls and the resurrection of bodies,* and the dialogue of Zacharias, *Ammonius, or the construction of the world.* To this literature may very probably be attributed the works with which the name of Dionysius the Areopagite is connected.

The interest, however, in the writings of the Pseudo-Dionysius is due to the fact that this mysterious literature was the channel along which passed almost the whole of Neoplatonism in Christian speculation and mysticism, that

---

[1] Baumgarten-Crusius (*De Dionysio Areopagita,* Jena 1836), J. Stiglmayr (*Das Aufkommen der pseudodionysischen Schiften,* Feldkirch, 1895), and Hugo Koch have quite clearly shown that the ideas of the Pseudo-Dionysius and the imagery with which he clothes them mostly originate in the religions of the mysteries and in Proclus: sun, chalice, mirror, house, food, intoxication, sleep, etc. For details and parallels see Koch, *op. cit.,* pp. 198 ss.

Saint Thomas revered the Pseudo-Dionysius almost as much as he revered Aristotle, and that from the time of Scotus Erigena all the schools, particularly that of Saint-Victor, devoted themselves to the study of these writings.

The wide diffusion of these treatises during the Middle Ages leaves us in no doubt that Ruysbroeck had read them. This presumption is confirmed, as we shall see, by the striking analogy of ideas and terminology.

From the Pseudo-Dionysius Ruysbroeck adopted the idea that mystical knowledge is a science with definite and precise rules, one which holy men alone can acquire. This knowledge is obtained by realising a state of mental vacuity,

by means of a union superior to intelligence, when intelligence, withdrawing from all beings and again left to itself, unites with the splendours that shine above it, and, inundated with brightness on all sides, obtains illumination from the unfathomable deeps of wisdom.[1]

This knowledge, then, implies a privation, a stripping off, a veritable mutilation of the natural man; it is in this sense that we must interpret the declaration of our author: οὐ μόνον μαθών, ἀλλὰ καὶ παθὼν τὰ θεῖα; the things of God are learnt not by study alone, but also by suffering.[2]

Mystic science, with its prolonged discipline, is exacted by the very nature of God: inapprehensible, incomprehensible and inexpressible. The Neoplatonist theodicy of Dionysius is also found in Ruysbroeck, without any important modification. God is the being above all, the One without a predicate.

God is called one, because in the excellence of his absolutely indivisible singularity he comprehends all things, and, without departing from unity, is the creator of multiplicity. . . . And this unity, the principle of beings, is not part of a whole, but rather, prior to all universality and multitude, itself has determined all multitude and universality.[3]

God being the Absolute, "the essence above all essence, the One above being," [4] is superior to all our conceptions. We can form an idea of him only by approximation. This

[1] *De div. nom.*, chapter vii. 3.   [2] *Ibid.*, chapter ii. 9.
[3] *Ibid.*, chapter xiii. 2.   [4] *Ibid.*, chapter i. 1.

approximation is realised in two ways: the negative or *apophatic*, and the affirmative or *cataphatic*, a conception based on a text from Plato's *Timæus*, borrowed by Plotinus, but carried to its ultimate developments in the Pseudo-Dionysius. As we have seen, it is also the method utilised by Ruysbroeck.

But how can this God, one, absolute and indeterminate, be related to the Christian trinity? To escape the difficulty our author proceeds in the same way as Proclus, by identifying the One with Goodness (τἀγαθόν), which cannot exist without radiating. Thus we are not dealing with the Plotinian hypostases, although Dionysius uses the term: ὑποστάσεις; in Plotinus the hypostases depend on one another in descending order. The trinitarian notion would seem to have been introduced almost forcibly into the conception of Unity; it certainly appears adventitious.[1]

These hypostases [says the Pseudo-Dionysius] dwell one within the other, so that there is the strictest unity along with the most real distinction. Thus, in a room lit by several torches, the various lights combine and are all in all, though without blending or losing their own individual existence, united though distinct and distinct in unity (ἀμιγῶς).[2]

In this God, the supreme Archetype, the paradigms of all things exist in the threefold aspect implied by trinity.

Creation is thus the result of a radiation, and this explains the progressive descent of the manifestations of life, for the ray becomes feebler the farther it travels from its centre.

Here too Ruysbroeck strictly follows the unknown mystic: he too places trinity at the centre of the One, and thus causes to proceed from the One the threefold impress which characterises creatures, from the most perfect being to the confines of matter.

This dynamism of Deity is expressed by the Pseudo-Dionysius in a form peculiar to himself,[3] and which we shall

---

[1] Delacroix, *Le mysticisme spéculatif* . . ., p. 247.
[2] *De div. nom.*, chapter ii. 4.
[3] The germ of this is already to be found in Proclus, who likes to speak of a chain connecting the various universes: θεῶν σειρά. *Com. in Tim.*, 65; *in Parm.* 5.

also find in Ruysbroeck: it is his conception of the *hierarchy*, in close connection with his theory of the return to God. To fill up the gap which separates God from creation and enable the latter to return to its source, Dionysius interposes two orders of hierarchically-arranged powers. The one constitutes a stream from above downwards: this is the celestial hierarchy, composed of three triads forming together nine choirs of angels. The other is a reverse stream from below upwards: this is the ecclesiastical hierarchy, corresponding to the purely spiritual celestial hierarchy and consisting of three degrees, represented by three sacraments, three priestly orders, three orders of believers.[1]

To ascend to God, man must pass the three degrees of purification (κάθαρσις), illumination (φωτισμός), and perfection (τελείωσις).[2]

Granted the degradation of divine virtue, evil can have no real existence, for it is simply the absence of good. This is purely a Neoplatonist conception.[3] Strictly speaking, in Dionysius there is no theory of sin, no redemption by Christ. On these questions the author refers to his Θεολογικαὶ ὑποτυπώσεις, whose existence is very problematical. Nevertheless, evil is punishable when it manifests man's opposition to the stream which carries him towards the good. In spite of its Christian colouring, the work of the Pseudo-Dionysius regards redemption only as the goal of the man who unites himself with God. Here, then, is a gap which Ruysbroeck has filled, as we have seen, with the traditional elements supplied to him by Scholasticism.

---

[1] Purification, illumination, perfection — baptism, eucharist, ordination— liturgies, priests, hierarchs—catechumens, initiates, therapeuts. *De coel. hier.*, chapters v., vi.

[2] *De coel. hier.*, chapter vii. This division is generally regarded as peculiarly that of the Pseudo-Dionysius. Its principle is to be found in Plato, who inspired in turn Philo and Plotinus. Iamblichus speaks of the degrees of virtue: ἀγνεία, ψυχῆς-κατάρτυσις εἰς θεαν-ἕνωσις (*De myst.*, chapter x. 5). Proclus also: ἐπιστήμη-ἐλλαμψις-ἕνωσις (*In Alcib.*, chapter iii. 103). By way of the Pseudo-Dionysius this division has passed into Scholasticism and into Christian mysticism: *via purgativa—illuminativa—unitiva*.

[3] The theory of evil in Dionysius (*De div. nom.*, chapter iv. 18–33) is but the so-to-speak literal reproduction of the treatise of Proclus, *De malorum subsistentia*. Cf. H. Koch on *Philologus* (1895), pp. 438 ss.

The supreme object of the spiritual life is θέωσις or μυστική
ἕνωσις. Those who attain to this height (οἱ θεοειδεῖς νόες)
have entered, by cessation of all intellectual process, into intimate union
with the ineffable light.[1]
Then, set free from the worlds of sense and of intellect, the soul enters
into the mysterious obscurity of a holy ignorance, and, renouncing every
scientific datum, loses itself in him who can be neither seen nor apprehended; wholly given up to this sovereign object, without belonging either
to itself or to others; united to the Unknown by the noblest part of
itself, and because of its renunciation of science; finally, obtaining from
this absolute ignorance a knowledge to which the understanding could
never attain.[2] Then the soul comes to know a special joy: *fruition* or the
touch divine.[3]

It is unnecessary to demonstrate the similarity between
the doctrine of Ruysbroeck and that of the Pseudo-Dionysius; the latter supplies Christian mysticism with all its elements, and, besides, transmits to it an ample supply of
images which we shall find in all who have come to draw
upon this bounteous spring. For instance, the image of the
torches whose individual flames nevertheless constitute
but one undivided brightness, that of iron and fire whose
elements interpenetrate, that of air and light, etc. No single
influence is more clearly marked. Ruysbroeck is the genuine
disciple of the Pseudo-Dionysius and, through him, the
inheritor of the Neoplatonism systematised by Proclus, just
as through Saint Augustine he was the inheritor of Plotinian
Neoplatonism.

All the same, in Ruysbroeck there is an unconcealed
tendency towards pantheism. We should not dare to say
that he remains, like his master, on the brink of pantheism.
It may be that he refrained from crossing the limits permitted; still, it must be acknowledged that, as regards
expression at least, he gave just grounds for suspicion.
Gerson was labouring under no delusion when he called
attention to such a phrase as the following: "Man sees himself as engulfed in unity, by the close consciousness of his
union, and as though plunged in the living being of God, by

[1] *De div. nom.*, chapter i. 5.
[2] *De myst. theol.*, chapter i. 3; *De div. nom.*, chapter i. 2.
[3] *De eccl. hier.*, chapter i.; *De div. nom.*, chapter vii.

death to all things. And there he feels that he lives one and the same life with God." [1]

By affording ground for these accusations, was Ruysbroeck simply following the natural trend of his thought? Was he developing of himself the premises he had found in his masters, the Pseudo-Dionysius or the Victorines? Or was his pantheism rather the result of a new influence brought to bear upon him? This is the question we now have to examine.

V

At the outset there is evidently at the very centre of Ruysbroeck's doctrine, in his theory of the return to God, a virtual pantheism, to release himself from which he need but drop its Scholastic elements. It is not in vain that God is shown to be in everything, so much so that he is nowhere, that he is nothing. [2] Nor is it with impunity that the interpenetration of divinity and humanity is assigned as the supreme end for human destiny. Scholasticism, which also contained equally dangerous premises, had evaded pantheistic conclusions only by counterbalancing the Neoplatonism it had adopted with an imposing element of Aristotelianism. It thus brought about an exact equilibrium between rationalism and mysticism; but the precise balance was so nicely effected that but little was needed to turn the scales in favour of Neoplatonism. This was clearly seen in the case of Meister Eckhart.

We must acknowledge that there existed some external influence whose effect Ruysbroeck did not gauge exactly, or which, more probably, was exercised upon him without his knowledge. This influence we attribute to the doctrine of Scotus Erigena, popularised by the Beghards and the Free Spirit associations and systematised by Meister Eckhart of Hochheim.

---

[1] *The Sparkling Stone,* chapter iii.
[2] The true formula of pantheism is found in Scotus Erigena, from whom it passed into all the mystics directly or indirectly inspired by him: *erit enim Deus omnia in omnibus, quando nihil erit nisi solus Deus (De div. nat.,* v. 8).

§ 1. Ruysbroeck, needless to say, was not directly acquainted with the doctrine of Scotus Erigena. For three centuries the Church had bitterly opposed Erigena's philosophy, which it rightly regarded as the origin and fomenter of spiritual anarchy and of popular pantheism. In 1225 Honorius III. fulminates against a book entitled *Periphysis*, mentioned to him by the bishop of Paris, and which is none other than the *De Divisione Naturae*.[1] After this epoch the condemned book would seem to have disappeared; at all events it is no longer read either in convents or in schools. Its doctrine, however, had already passed into popular thought, by means of Amaury and David de Dinant; after which it continued its course apart from the Church, though not without being seriously debased and giving rise to interpretations which could not have been foreseen by the one who had elaborated it.

And so it is worth while considering briefly the man and the work destined to play so important a part in the history of ideas.

Of all the masters whom Charlemagne and Charles the Bald had summoned from Italy and England to reconstitute Scholastic knowledge, Scotus Erigena was really the only one who appeared as a philosopher. He was also a Hellenist, capable of placing himself in contact with the soul of antiquity and thus borrowing from the great traditions, of which only fragments remained, the very elements wherewith his personal genius was imbued. Now what will he choose out of all this wealth of the past? Neoplatonism and the Alexandrian philosophy.

Summoned by Hincmar to defend orthodoxy against the Saxon monk Gottschalc, who upheld the theory of predestination,[2] Scotus Erigena draws his main arguments from

---

[1] "Nuper . . . est quidam liber qui perifisis titulatur, inventus, totus scatens vermibus heretice pravitatis." Denifle and Chatelain, *Chartular*, I. i. pp. 106-7.

[2] "He who would be saved," said Gottschalc, "and labours in ardent faith and with good works to obtain eternal life with the aid of God's grace, loses his time and trouble, if God has not predestined him to life." *Letter to Count Héberard*, in Migne, *Patr. lat.*, t. CXII. col. 1554.

x

the Neoplatonist theory of the non-reality of evil. "How can God predestine a man to sin and evil seeing that sin and evil do not exist? Simple negations of being, how can they be the results of the will of God? The sole cause of sin is the defective will of man; his sole chastisement is remorse." Manifestly the Church had made a bad choice of its advocate; justly alarmed, it hastened to condemn the *De Praedestinatione* at the Councils of Valence and Langres, in 855 and 859. After this, and in spite of opposition, Scotus Erigena kept to his original source of inspiration. More than this, he was eager to secure for his age the benefits of this lofty idealism, and so translated and commented on the writings of the Pseudo-Dionysius, thus directly linking up the Middle Ages with the noblest products of the thought of antiquity. It is impossible to say what would have been the trend of mediæval thought but for this famous translation; assuredly it would have been quite different. The mention of it here is the creation of the first link of the philosophic development which, by way of speculative mysticism, takes us right to the Substance of Spinoza, the Indifference of Schelling, the Idea of Hegel; all these being names whereby the human thought has attempted to express the inexpressible God.

Thus brought in contact with Oriental emanationism which permeates the writings of the Pseudo-Dionysius, Scotus Erigena was forced to follow up the logical consequences of his thought. During the latter years of his stay at the court of Charles the Bald, about 870, he brought together the various elements of his doctrine into a powerful system, the originality of which consisted in introducing the best of Oriental thought into the Christian dogma.

This was no longer, as with Dionysius, a forced marriage, an arbitrary juxtaposition, but a genuine fusion. And while Scotus Erigena was effecting a harmonious balance between two worlds, two thoughts so different in many respects, with singular intuition into spiritual life he was also reconciling the rights of reason with those of the heart. While, in stating the equation: *recta philosophia vera religio, conversimque vera religio recta philosophia*, Erigena is the father of Scholasticism, he is equally deserving to be called the father of speculative mysticism, because he set up within creation a vast circuit with a God, inapprehensible to the reason, both as its beginning and as its end.[1]

From this imposing construction we will disentangle those elements which were adopted by the Amalricians and, through them, constituted the doctrinal basis of the heresies, pantheistic in tendency, which, as we have seen, were prevalent in the Middle Ages.

Let us recognise, above all, that, while the Church condemned Scotus Erigena, he was the first to be astonished at such action. No one was ever more convinced that he was faithfully interpreting traditional doctrine.[2] But when form has to be given to this interpretation, by a singular turn of mind our author always chooses, out of two expressions, the one which seems the farther removed from doctrinal orthodoxy. Hence all his troubles and the ulterior deviations to which his system gave rise.

The conception of God does not differ from that of the Pseudo-Dionysius, the God One and absolute, indeterminate, so far removed from our standards that he cannot even be aware of what he is. We may then say that, judged by human conceptions, he is a Nothingness, and, for that reason, the man who, in a negative approach, removes all determination from his conception of God, will come nearest to him. This is the well-founded superiority of negative theology.

To explain the world, then, the thinker cannot take his starting-point from God, who, by definition, is inaccessible. He must begin with his own mental ideas. Thus he assumes that the created world is a projection of God, according to the images that exist in him as the eternal Archetype. And so the world is a representation of God, a theophany in the

---

[1] "Et sibi ipsi infinitus et incomprehensibilis. Nescit se quid ipse est; Deus itaque nescit se quid est, quia non est quid; incomprehensibilis quippe in aliquo et sibi et omni intellectui." *De div. nat.*, ii. 28.

[2] Saint-René Taillandier, *Scot Érigène*, p. 238; E. Gilson, *La philosophie au moyen âge*, t. I. p. 25.

third degree. In the beginning there is God *per se*, the principle of all things, immutable and absolute: *natura creans sed non creata*. Finally the manifestation of the eternal ideas constitutes the third degree of being; this is the world of sense, *natura creata et non creans*. The world thus issues direct from God; it is God, simply separated from the first Principle by differentiation of degree. God is immediately in the world, and this latter is co-eternal with God: *proïnde non duo a se ipsis distantia debemus intelligere Deum et creaturam, sed unum et id ipsum*.[1] There is identity of substance between Creator and creature.

This conception implied a genuine depersonalisation of the members of the Christian Trinity. Thus, to Scotus Erigena, the Word or divine Logos (*natura creans sed non creata*) is less a person in the Christian sense, a hypostasis in the Neoplatonist sense, than an intellectual representation. This may not be what Scotus Erigena says in so many words, but his conception is really grounded on a consideration of the Word as a pure metaphysical entity, *habitus substantiae Dei*.[2]

It is generally considered that the culminating point of the doctrine of Scotus Erigena is his anthropology. It would be more true to regard his conception of the Word as the axis of his whole philosophy. For while there is to be found in the Word the cause of all the theophanies, including man, which constitute the ensemble of the *natura creata et non creans*, it is also the Word that determines the return movement of creation towards God, a movement culminating in a fourth state of being, *natura non creata et non creans*, i.e. in a veritable deification of man and of the world.

To justify this return, Scotus Erigena utilises the doctrine of the Fall. Man in his origin was the purest theophany of deity, bearing in the trinity of his fundamental faculties, *intellectus, ratio, sensus*, the impress of the divine Trinity. He lost his divine dignity, however, in the Fall, while remaining capable of continually receiving within himself the

---

[1] *De div. nat.*, chapter iii. 17.
[2] Delacroix, *Le mysticisme spéculatif* . . ., p. 24. Cf. Buchwald, *Der Logosbegriff des Joh. Scotus Erigena* (Leipzig, 1884).

influx of the divine energy. It is his destiny to return ᴛᴏ God, but he is incapable of doing this himself; hence the necessity of a redemption, wrought through the Word. This deification is progressive; its principal stages can take place only after the dissolution of the body in death. Still, man is able in this world — *virtute contemplationis* — to unite with God by a series of mystical processes. God being within himself, he has to penetrate to this extreme essence of his personality wherein Deity lies hidden. Visible nature, too, will share in this final return which to it is nothing else than the supreme expression of the divine dynamism working within it.

Such, briefly outlined, is the undoubtedly grandiose conception of Scotus Erigena. In its broad aspects we can the better see what a dangerous declivity it offered to minds of every kind. The conception of this God in a state of perpetual becoming was bound to strike the imagination of philosophers, just as the deification of man, propounded to religious souls as an immediately realisable end, could not help raising their spiritual aspirations. On the other hand, however, in an economy thus conceived wherein man is represented as moved by an irreducible force towards God, what became of the Church and the sacraments, of the very conception of Christian redemption? And what consequences were the people to draw from a doctrine which, apparently at least, deified man and denied that there was any substantial reality in evil?

We have seen that these two orders of conclusions, so widely contrasted, became actualised in the thirteenth century. Theorists like David de Dinant and Amaury de Bêne lay hold upon the ideas expressed by Scotus Erigena, as did the sectarians of Swabia or the libertines whose immoralities threw discredit on the associations of Beghards or the Brothers of the Free Spirit.

As we note in several parts of Ruysbroeck's work a strange similarity of thought and expression to the doctrine of Scotus Erigena, we may ask ourselves whether, in opposing Bloemardinne and the heretical Beghards, he may not have unwittingly come under the influence of their ideas.

There is nothing improbable in the hypothesis, and we find that it was first made by Gerson. Ruysbroeck, says the chancellor of Paris, was wrong in asserting

that the contemplative soul beholds God in a brightness which constitutes the divine essence, that the soul itself is this divine brightness, that it ceases to be in the existence it has had in its own kind; that it is changed, transformed, absorbed into divine being, and flows into the ideal being it had from all eternity within the divine essence; that it is so utterly lost in the ocean of divine splendours that no creature can find it again, somewhat like a drop of wine thrown into a large amount of water; that the ideal being it has in God is the cause of its existence in time . . . *in speaking thus the author was not a conscious (pertinax) heretic, but probably, unknown to himself, came under the influence of the doctrine of the Beghards to whom he himself was opposed.*[1]

In this connection we do not hesitate to recognise the perspicacity of the chancellor of Paris. As regards the substance-matter we must believe Ruysbroeck himself, for he lets slip no opportunity of defending himself against the charge of pantheism. Still, the expression he has given to his doctrine inevitably lends itself to grave misunderstandings. If we reflect that Ruysbroeck attempts to put in writing the most elusive moments of the contemplative life, the inexpressible intuitions of the mind raised far above all tangible reality, then we understand that he may not have been able to find adequate translation for his interior experiences. You cannot coin a language for that which transcends words. Rather had he, in the Dionysian translation among others, a ready-made vocabulary, the one utilised by the Brothers of the Free Spirit to express their illuminations. What wonder that orthodox doctor and heretics met at that boundary of language where words are nothing more than approximations? The hypothesis is all the more probable seeing that Ruysbroeck, aiming at rectifying the disastrous opinions of the sectarians on the contemplative life of union with God, borrows, in order to combat them, the very weapons of his adversaries; he wishes to demonstrate that, behind identical terms, another reality must appear.

§ 2. Still, may there not have been a more definite in-

[1] *Gersonii Opera*, edit. Dupin (Antwerp, 1706), t. I. p. 62.

fluence which would have brought Ruysbroeck in contact
with the philosophy that had its origin in Scotus Erigena?
In studying the doctrine of our mystic, we cannot help
recognising in it striking analogies with that of Meister
Eckhart. Tradition tells of a visit Ruysbroeck made to
Cologne, where he became profoundly influenced by the
teaching of Albertus Magnus and Meister Eckhart. There is
nothing improbable in such a journey, though it is not
necessary for the purpose of recognising the influence of the
master of Hochheim upon our author. The sermons of Meister
Eckhart were known in the Netherlands from the beginning
of the fourteenth century; there is even a contemporary
manuscript containing a translation of them into the Brabant
dialect. Besides, Eckhart's condemnation took place in 1329.
At that time, in all probability, Ruysbroeck's ideas were
already defined and may have comprised elements originating
in the famous mystic. Van Mierlo rightly remarks that the
same Latin expressions are habitually translated in identical
fashion by Eckhart and by Ruysbroeck, although such translation was not absolutely obligatory.[1] Ruysbroeck had no need
subsequently to retract these borrowings, for he had firmly
incorporated them into his own system; blending with his own
personal conceptions, they had lost their subversive character.
   Indeed, Ruysbroeck's main concern is to include his
mystical theories within the scheme of orthodox tradition.
Such concern is almost non-existent in Meister Eckhart,
and though claiming to begin with Church doctrine, he
manifests a certain degree of scorn for the vulgar conceptions
upheld by traditional theologians, *die wol gelert seynd, und
grosz pfaffen wöllen sein, das sy sich also schier lassen genügen.*
Thus his aim is to complete the traditional teaching, and the
origin of the elements he utilises concerns him but little. There
is nothing of this kind in Ruysbroeck. He candidly borrows
from Meister Eckhart what agrees with his own conceptions,
without suspecting that he is thus investing with the authority
of the Church what the Church had frequently condemned.

[1] *Dietsche Warande*, p. 438. For instance: *vonke, ongeest, grond*, etc.

The general trend of Meister Eckhart's system is found in his *Sermons.*[1] It is in this imposing collection that we shall now seek the ideas found in Ruysbroeck's works.

Needless to say such an investigation can be no more than approximate. Nowhere, indeed, does Ruysbroeck mention Meister Eckhart. To limit, therefore, all risk of error, we will confine ourselves to the only elements for which there exists a dual analogy: that of subject-matter and that of terminology. The analogy of subject-matter alone would be inadequate, for as Eckhart's ideas were widely promulgated among the Beghards and the Brothers of the Free Spirit, some of them may have come to Ruysbroeck along this channel. The analogy of expression, too, considered alone, would be quite as indecisive, for the terms used by Meister Eckhart are largely to be found in the other German mystics—Kraft von Boyberg, Tauler, Suso—and sometimes in a different sense.

The entire system of Eckhart is but the development of his notion of *being*, which is the only reality. God is *he who is*, and outside of him there is nothing, i.e. reversing the terms of the proposition, nothing is outside of God. This state of *being* superior to all determination is one that Eckhart expresses by calling God: *ein überswesende wesen : Got ist ein wesen ? ez ist nicht war : er ist ein überswesende wesen und ein überswesende nichtheit.*[2] We can neither express him thus by a name nor imagine him under any form. He permeates all things, but is above all things: *Er hat aller creaturen wesen in im, er ist ein wesen das alle wesen in im hat. . . . Dasz er ist in allen creaturen, daz ist er doch dar uber.*[3]

---

[1] We shall use the classic edition of Franz Pfeiffer (vol. II. of *Deutsche Mystiker des vierzehnten Jahrhunderts*, Leipzig, 1857), which, in spite of the works of P. Denifle on Eckhart's Latin sermons, is still the basis of all the critical studies dealing with the thought of the great mystic. For parallels in Ruysbroeck, we shall refer to the edition of J.-B. David.

[2] Pfeiffer, p. 319. Ruysbroeck also says: *Het overwesen Gods, de onghebeelde bloetheit* (*The Twelve Beguines*, p. 36; *The Mirror*, p. 206).

[3] Pfeiffer, p. 268. Ruysbroeck: *Die onbegripelike hoghe nature Gods, die onthoeghet allen creaturen . . . want God is boven allen creaturen, ende buten ende binnen allen creaturen, ende alle ghescapen begrijp is te inghe hem te begripene* (*The Spiritual Marriage*, p. 37).

But this amorphous God is potentially fruitful. He could not remain in the state of "unnatured" nature (*ungenaturte natuur*), of a silent wilderness wrapt in deep slumber.[1] Now if begetting is the work of a thought, deity must begin by thinking itself. Thus Eckhart sets forth that the first manifestation of Deity is Intelligence: *Der herr ist ein lebende, wesende, ystige vernünftigkeit, die sich selber verstet . . . sein wesen ist sein bekennen . . . seine substancie und sein natur und sein wesen ist sein beckennen.*[2] The act whereby God knows himself is therefore an act of begetting. In thinking itself Deity begets the Word: *Der fürwurf des verstentnisses ist daz ewige Wort. . . . Der vatter sicht aff sich selber mit einer einfaltigen bekantnusz, und sicht in die einfaltige lauterkeit seins wesens, da sicht er gebildet alle creaturen, da spricht er sich selber; das wort ist ein klar bekantnusz, und das ist der sun.*[3] This begetting of the Son is an eternal begetting, i.e. God eternally differentiates himself from himself: *Das ewige verstentnisse des vater erbildet er sein bild sin selbes, sinen sun. . . . Sein würcken ist seinen sun geberen, den gebirt er allzeyt.*[4] In its turn, the association of Father and Son begets the Holy Spirit, for they cannot refrain from begetting, so great is the delight and enjoyment they experience in creating. The Holy Spirit is thus nothing else than the joy of Deity made manifest. *Er gebirt einen sun und gebirt in alzemale nüwe und frische, und hat so grozen lust an dem wercke, daz er anders nicht entut danne daz er daz wercke wircket und den*

---

[1] Pfeiffer, pp. 242, 266. Ruysbroeck uses the same figures to express this first stage of deity: *abys der onghenaemtheit, die donkere stille, die grondelose zee, die wilde woestine* (*The Twelve Beguines*, p. 79; *The Spiritual Marriage*, p. 107).

[2] Pfeiffer, pp. 336–7. Ruysbroeck: *Nadien dat die almachtige Vader, in den gronde sine vruchtbaerheit hem selven volcomelike begrepen hevet* (*The Spiritual Marriage*, p. 187).

[3] Pfeiffer, p. 337. Ruysbroeck: *Al dat levet in den Vader, onvertoent in enicheit, dat levet inden Sone ute ghevloten inder openbaerheit. . . . Soe ist die Sone, dat ewighe Woert des Vaders, ute ghegaen, een ander persoen inder Godheit* (*The Spiritual Marriage*, pp. 187–8).

[4] Pfeiffer, p. 378. Ruysbroeck: *Want daer is altoes nuwe ghebaren in nuwe bekennen, nuwe behaghen ende nuwe untgheesten* (*The Sparkling Stone*, p. 258).

heiligen geist in ime und alle dinc. The essence of the Spirit is Goodness or Love; in it God loves all creatures: *Güete ist der heilige geist; güete daz ist da got uz smilzet und gemeinet sich allen creaturen.*[1]

Here we find Scotus Erigena's idea of Deity in becoming, with its final stages: absolute Being, *natura quae creat et non creatur;* the Word, *natura quae creatur et creat;* the universe, *natura quae creatur et non creat.* At this point Eckhart and Ruysbroeck part company with Scotus Erigena, who regarded the fourth and last stage of deity as the return of the body-liberated spirit to the divine reasons: *natura quae nec creatur nec creat.* Eckhart and Ruysbroeck reflect rather on the Holy Spirit: *ende dese gheest en baert noch en wert gheboren, maer hi moet ewelike uutvloyen.*[2]

The divine Being is thus regarded in dual aspect: in its essence and before all differentiation of persons, Deity is motionless; its characteristic is rest: *Gotlich nature ist ruowe.*[3] Through activity of persons Deity becomes active; it becomes self-determined as God.[4]

This God in becoming, from whom the whole created world originates, inspires Meister Eckhart with a kind of metaphysical intoxication which was communicated to Ruysbroeck. A perpetual torrent of life gushes forth from Deity and spreads to every degree of being: *in disem ewigen uzflusse, da alliu dinc uzgeflossen sint ane sich selber da waren*

---

[1] Pfeiffer, p. 124. Ruysbroeck calls the Holy Spirit, with reference to the two other persons of the Trinity, their mutual love: *Hare beyder minne, die een met hem beyden is inder selver naturen. Ende si beveet ende doregheet, werckelijc ende gebrukelic, den Vader ende den Sone, ende al dat in hem beyden levet, met alsoe groter rijcheit ende vrouden, dat hieraf alle creaturen ewelike swighen moeten ; want dat onbegripelike wonder dat in deser minnen leghet, dat onthoeghet ewelike allen creaturen verstane* (*The Spiritual Marriage*, p. 191).

[2] Ruysbroeck, *The Spiritual Marriage*, p. 109; Eckhart, édit. Pfeiffer, pp. 92, 206, 479.

[3] Pfeiffer, pp. 152, 214; Ruysbroeck, *The Twelve Beguines*, p. 84.

[4] Pfeiffer, p. 181. Eckhart clearly specifies the distinction between motionless deity and God: *Got der würcket, die gotheyt nit, sy hat auch nit zu würkend, in ir ist auch kein werck. Gott und gotheyt hat unterscheyd an würcken und an nit würcken.* This distinction is far less clear in Ruysbroeck, who contents himself with showing the divine essence to be motionless: *Van naturen ende van wesene ewelic stille, ende onbeweghelic* (*The Twelve Beguines*, pp. 82-3; *The Spiritual Marriage*, pp. 187-90).

si in im.[1] Relinquishing the expression of the eternal cycle of things coming from and returning to God, our two mystics call creative activity a *perpetual now*: *Got schöpfet die welt und alliu dinc in einem gegenwürtigen Nu.*[2] Along with this eternal creation, however, which maintains perpetual youth in the universe, there has been creation in time. This creation is a voluntary act of God, on which he has resolved in love. Therefore Eckhart regards this creation as being in time, with relation to the Holy Spirit, who is goodness (*guete*): *er ist ein werkmeister und ein würker des werdens in der ewikeit und in der zeit.*[3] Consequently, as God in his beginning is Nothing, one may say that things were created from nothing: *die Dinge sint geschaffen aus nichts.*[4] Evidently Eckhart here attempts to retain the dogma of creation *ex nihilo*, without however succeeding in fully concealing his true thought, which is to regard creation as a manifestation not of the divine *ideas*, but of divine *Being* itself. On this point Ruysbroeck amended his thought in the direction of the Christian dogma and thus avoided the pantheism into which Eckhart inevitably falls in identifying the world with God. And so Ruysbroeck attributes far greater importance to the theory of *ideas* and comes nearer to the Pseudo-Dionysius than to Scotus Erigena, whom Meister Eckhart here follows.

The Flemish mystic takes the same precautions when dealing with the return of creation into God. Indeed, he considers only the union of the soul which, at the crown of the mystical life, dissolves in God. Along the lines of his eschatology, he accepts the dissolution of material things and the destruction of unrepentant sinners.

[1] Pfeiffer, p. 582. Ruysbroeck also speaks of the *ewich uutvlieten, overmits die gheboert des Soens in ere anderheit met onderscede na ewigher redenen* (*The Spiritual Marriage*, p. 188).
[2] Pfeiffer, p. 266. Ruysbroeck: *God bescouwet hem selven ende allen dinc in enen ewighen Nu* (*The Spiritual Marriage*, p. 187).
[3] Pfeiffer, p. 497. Ruysbroeck: *Omne dat hi sine . . . goede toenen woude, so hevet hi ghescapen* (*The Kingdom of God's Lovers*, p. 127).
[4] Quoted by Preger, *Niedners Zeitschrift für hist. Theol.*, 1864, p. 175; Delacroix, *Mystic. spéculatif*, p. 185. Ruysbroeck: *Mit sinen vrien wille, overmits sine ewighe wijsheit, soe heeft hi alle dinc ghescapen van nieute* (*The Twelve Beguines*, p. 78).

Still, in spite of these amendments, he clearly shows that he is influenced by Meister Eckhart.

The common starting-ground for both speculatives lies in the conception of the soul. Eckhart regards the soul as another form of God; Ruysbroeck sees in it simply a fragment of Deity. Still, this difference does not prevent him from adopting the series of processes which Meister Eckhart attributes to the soul progressing towards the first form of Deity: indeterminate Unity. Like all things, the soul is carried along by the incessant stream which emanates from Deity, but the fact that it is imprisoned in a body implies a discipline which will enable it to disengage itself and so to enter into contact with God. This discipline is of a dual nature. First it is a relinquishing (*geläzenheit*): man must renounce himself, his inclinations and joys, things created. Then it is a simplification, an abstraction (*abschiedenheit*): the soul creates unity within itself, it becomes motionless, wholly intent upon one and the same object, God; and in this repose it finally perceives simple and motionless Being wherein it melts away: man becomes God. It is unnecessary to supply texts in proof of this; almost the entire work of Ruysbroeck would have to be quoted to demonstrate his agreement with Meister Eckhart. Besides, the latter himself relies upon prior conceptions, by which Ruysbroeck may also have been directly influenced.

As regards the psychology which maintains the entire theory of mystic union, both Eckhart and Ruysbroeck adopted it, just as it was, from Scholasticism. But as Ruysbroeck translates the Latin terms in the same way as does Meister Eckhart, whereas he might have chosen from among several synonyms, here also we must recognise his dependence upon the German mystic.[1] Even the conception of evil re-

---

[1] The powers of the soul (*Kraften, Krachten*) are of two kinds: the natural powers (*natürliche, natüerlike, nederste krachten*) relate to the world; these are the irascible power (*zürnerin, tornighe kracht*), the concupiscible power (*begerunge, begeerlike kracht*), reason (*redelicheit, redelicheit*), freedom of will, which Eckhart does not mention (*vriheit des willens*). The higher powers (*oberste kraft, overste krachten*) concern God and eternity; these are memory (*memoria, memorie*), intellect

garded as a lower degree of being is found expressed in almost identical terms by Eckhart and by Ruysbroeck, although the latter holds a definite theory as to sin, in accord with the Church dogma: *alles das gebrechlich ist, das ist abfahl von wesen*.[1] And does not Ruysbroeck, when he magnificently extols the priority of charitable duty over religious enjoyment, supply a wider interpretation to the words of Meister Eckhart: to give food to one who is hungry is better than to abandon oneself to barren contemplation?[2]

. . . .

So we see that there can be no doubt as to the influence of Meister Eckhart upon Ruysbroeck; he forms a new link between our mystic and Neoplatonism.

Is this equivalent to asserting that there is no originality in the system we have been studying, that the mind of Ruysbroeck slavishly subjected itself to the letter of inspirational doctrine? The few brief hints throughout this work testify to the creative efforts which mark out our author. Besides, how are we to explain the independent position taken by Ruysbroeck and his school in the fourteenth century amid the most diversified systems, or the influence subsequently exercised by speculative mysticism? Life alone propagates life. Consequently, what we now have to do is to gather together the results obtained, arrive at a comprehensive judgment, and so justify the task we have undertaken: that of restoring a thinker, so long disregarded, to his rightful place in the history of philosophy.

(*verstentnisse, verstennisse*), will (*wille*). Cf. Pfeiffer, pp. 170, 171, 319, 366, 383; Ruysbroeck, *The Spiritual Marriage*, pp. 56, etc.; *The Kingdom of God's Lovers*, pp. 139–42; *The Mirror*, pp. 167–8.

[1] Pfeiffer, p. 376. Ruysbroeck: *Ende hier om alsulc ghebrec en maect ons niet onghehoirsam* (*The Sparkling Stone*, p. 216).

[2] *Wie wol das inner leben das best an im selber sey, doch ist etwan das unzer besser, so das not ist, an leiplicher hilff, als dem hungerigen besser ist essen geben, denn die weyl sich über an innerlicher schauwung. Darumb an rechter not ist besser über die werck des usseren menschen zu der erbermde mir oder dem nechsten, denn sich setzen in ein inner mussigkeit des innern menschen an bekennen und begerung* (Pfeiffer, p. 295).

CHAPTER XIII

LIKE the soul, the mind has its own secret. The originality of a thinker does not consist only in the value of the materials that enter into his thought, but also in the particular laws whereby he organises these materials to make them his own. To content oneself with dissociating and isolating the constituent elements of a system is to remain outside the thought of a man.

Now the very development of thought is combination, following on analysis. The quality and intensity of this personal effort alone enables one to form an all-round judgment upon a thinker and his doctrine.

I

At the outset we will remark that this state of combination obeys the law of development, which is the law of life itself. The doctrine of such a man as Ruysbroeck is singularly illumined when we are able to perceive beneath the ever-shifting pattern of his thought the solid framework of his life. Ruysbroeck is not a being inspired, in the usual sense of the term which completely does away with the element of logic. Neither is he a sort of solitary genius, elaborating apart from his age a system devoid of any relation to this earth of ours. No sooner had life itself placed the pen in his hand than the evolution of his thought followed closely the progress of events. Hence those successive modifications, those backward movements, those enthusiastic outbursts, followed by renewed checks and restraints.

Let us take, for instance, the central doctrine of Ruysbroeck's system: mystic union. This is shown, in its main outlines, in the first book of our prior: *The Kingdom of God's Lovers*. Opposed to the libertine theories of the Brothers of the Free Spirit, it presents itself as a discipline, with definite rules. Shortly afterwards, however, as though carried away by his own enthusiasm, Ruysbroeck oversteps the very rules he himself prescribed, and in *The Adornment of the Spiritual Marriage* the workings of his mind no longer seem to be under any constraint whatsoever: Deity offers itself to man as an apprehensible reality. Indeed, Ruysbroeck has here departed from concrete facts; he has risen to the absolute, into a domain where his early theories on the sacraments and Church authority appear as stages that have been superseded. In this he is manifestly expressing a personal experience, possible for him because he possessed within himself the necessary counterpoise. But he quickly perceives the danger of such a generalisation for those devoid of the counterpoise of a previous doctrine. And so he makes rectifications and explanations; in a series of treatises he returns to the indispensable union of the practical and the contemplative life. There are evident traces of a prolonged focussing of his position. Indeed, he comes to a firm conclusion only after the inflammatory polemics roused by his early writings have calmed down: *The Book of Supreme Truth* and *The Twelve Beguines*, instinct with the calm serenity of the evening of his days, bring together, as in a last will and testament, the experiences of a whole lifetime.

This is the first element to be considered in judging the work of our mystic. Accordingly we have deemed it necessary to afford history every opportunity of speaking. In such an age of social and religious effervescence as the fourteenth century, the doctrine of Ruysbroeck aims at satisfying the needs of human souls as they manifest themselves. His thought finds explanation in the strictly circumscribed times during which he lived. And so it may fittingly be judged, not from the standpoint of the sixteenth century—as do Protestant writers who mainly regard Ruysbroeck as a precursor of the Reformation—nor from that of the thirteenth century—as do those Catholic apologists who consider the times of Saint Thomas as the golden age of Christianity, —but rather from the standpoint of the religious situation of the period.

The other elements that combine to make up the very specialised form of thought called speculative mysticism are of an intellectual order.

These are the two great streams of Scholasticism and Neoplatonism. How have these combined and interpenetrated? In the answer to this question lies the great interest of the study of philosophical origins.

Although Scholasticism undoubtedly contains a mystic —even a pantheistic—element, it yet mainly represents a dialectical construction. To establish this construction Scholasticism appeals to very diverse elements: it may be asserted that there is no great system in antiquity that has not found refuge in this imposing edifice: Aristotle and Plotinus, Plato and Saint Augustine, Arabic and Jewish philosophers, have all contributed to it. The genius of Saint Thomas welded firmly together these heterogeneous materials. But the main character of Scholasticism lies in a presupposition: religion—by which term the Christian religion is meant—is a direct revelation handed down to the Church. By utilising the data of Scholasticism, Ruysbroeck found a shelter for his own thought, a solid framework that had all the guarantee of ecclesiastical authority. He found that he was protected against himself.

Indeed, Ruysbroeck is nothing less than an intellectualist. Even when he pays the widest tribute to Scholasticism he does not succeed in abjuring its spiritual nature. He is keenly aware that God is not within the reach of metaphysics. Then, for the purpose of apprehending this great *Unknown*, Neoplatonism presents itself. And now we witness the enthralling interplay of a mind that attempts to reconcile within itself tradition, represented by Scholasticism, and spiritual initiative, represented by the mysticism born of Neoplatonism.

This reconciliation Ruysbroeck finds in a series of extremely delicate and precise adaptations, clearly testifying to his own originality. He does not wholly bow to either of the two systems.

It may be permissible to connect Ruysbroeck with the great stream of Neoplatonist thought. We have pointed out the striking resemblances which unite them to each other. The main lines of the structure appear somewhat similar: there is the unnamed God manifesting himself in creation to effect self-determination; the powerful dynamism circulating even in the most distant parts of the universe; the intense yearning for the divine working in the whole of creation; and finally, the return of all things to their original source, the beatitude obtained by repose in motionless Deity.

Closer examination, however, shows that the differences are not less great than the resemblances. In what does the Neoplatonist speculation culminate? In a conception of God that is absolutely different from the Christian conception. The God of Christian theology draws near to man just as much as man draws near to God. The two dimensions, human wretchedness and divine compassion, finally meet in Jesus Christ, a mediator who partakes alike of divinity and of humanity. The God of Neoplatonism, on the other hand, seems to recoil every time that man tries to reach him. This fleeing God thus loses every characteristic, every attribute. Consequently redemption has no longer any meaning. If salvation is nothing more than the reintegration of the creature into the great divine All, then the redeemer abandons the rôle he has voluntarily assumed. The consequence again is that life is clearly sacrificed to metaphysics. The social worth of such a religion is practically nil. This is distinctly seen when the Brothers of the Free Spirit and the Beghards undertook to popularise these principles, which were assuredly the offspring of vigorous thinking but were incapable of stimulating the courage to live.

This is what Ruysbroeck clearly saw. Charmed undoubtedly by the lofty idealism of Neoplatonism, he borrows from it his general conception of things. He disentangles from the system everything that, in his opinion, can be reconciled with dogmatic orthodoxy, fitting into the ready-prepared framework offered by Neoplatonism the data of Christian theology. He upholds the Plotinian procession, the return of the soul to its source, though he associates them with the dogma of the Trinity and with the Redemption. He retains divine determinism which secures the soul in its progressive deification, but he introduces into the work of sanctification the prescriptions of the Church and the sacra-ments. And so he does not say—as does Meister Eckhart, who was less bound by tradition—that man is necessary to God, but rather that God is necessary to man. The point of view is absolutely different, and, as a result, the meaning of life is not the same. Neoplatonism shows beatitude in a genuine depersonalisation; Ruysbroeck assigns a duty to man and subordinates knowledge to action, in accordance with the words of the Johannine Christ: If any man will do God's will, he shall know of the doctrine.

In this state of combination, does orthodoxy remain intact? As a matter of fact, the orthodox tradition is found complete in our author. It is in his cosmology, in his pessi-mistic views of human nature, in the rôle of the sacraments and the Church, even in the very glance he casts beyond death. But all this is presented as a veil. We need but raise it to discover the inner mind, the personal religion of Ruys-broeck. We admire the ease with which he has succeeded in harmonising together notions apparently irreducible: the en-closed universe of Ptolemy and the splendidly graded world— ever in process of construction—of the Neoplatonists; the Scholastic conception of life regarded as an ensemble of rational phenomena and the mystical conception of cosmic and human destinies; a definite faith and the triumphant ascension of the soul towards its principle, far beyond terres-trial distinctions; and lastly death, with its incorruptible tribunal, of whose sentence there can be no revision what-soever, and the incessant outflow of divine energy, extending

to every stage of being and invincibly impelling the world in the direction of universal redemption.

Ruysbroeck's entire originality lies in this masterly re-conciliation. The conceptions he harbours in his mind do not act like corrosive acid which eats away the vessel into which it is poured. Nor do they remain side by side, without interpenetration. Ruysbroeck is not satisfied with borrow-ing materials: he assimilates them and makes them mentally his own to such a degree that, blending with his inmost thoughts, they lose even the tokens of their alien origin.

Will the objection be raised that this combining process is inadequate if it is our object to prove Ruysbroeck's originality? But in that event we should have also to claim that the architect gives no proof of personality when arranging the stones at his disposal in accordance with his mentally conceived plan. Similarly a long philosophical tradition supplies materials; any attempt to build up a new system can only be inspired by some aspect of Aristotelianism, Platonism or Neoplatonism.[1] The genius of the thinker, however, has free scope to arrange, in accordance with an end which he has glimpsed, these gathered elements, to form, mould and combine them in such a way that the final out-come is in very truth a new creation.

Man being unable, as has been said, "to elude his own facial angle," submitting to the past without which he would not be, originality consists less in *innovating* than in giving a new meaning or aspect to existing material. This is proved by the fact that, in so many different systems, that which constituted *a novelty* at the time it appeared has not always been the most durable part of these systems. In this connection it is worth while remembering Pascal's words:

Let it not be affirmed that I have said nothing new: the arrangement of matter is new; when one plays tennis, both players use the same ball, but one places it better than the other. I should like just as much to be told that I have used old words. As if the same thoughts did not form another frame or body of speech with a different arrangement, just as the same words form other thoughts when differently arranged.[2]

[1] H. Bergson, *La Philosophie (Coll. la Science française)* (Paris, 1915), p. 8.
[2] *Pensées*, édit. Havet, art. vii. 9; t. I. p. 99.

Now in the case of Ruysbroeck this different arrangement reveals a degree of perspicacity, a sense of the actual, to which receding time gives singular value. From out of the vast wealth of Scholasticism he divined what were those doctrines that would rapidly become a dead weight, that would speedily prove incapable of supplying nourishment for human souls. Into the gaps which he thus found, after removing from Scholasticism its fleeting theories, he planted sturdy living elements taken from other philosophical streams, and so reconstituted a spiritual tradition capable of holding its own against the judgment of the future.

We will give but one instance of this, since in the immediately preceding chapters we have closely studied these methods of combination.

We have seen that Ruysbroeck, with singular boldness, takes up his position in the very centre of the mind, in order to establish its independent reality. In this he openly broke away from Scholasticism. What, indeed, did Saint Thomas say? He looked upon man as a compound, the result of so close an alliance between soul and body that these two elements could have no substantial separate existence. The soul could be genuinely soul only through its association with the body; and as it is the seat of intellectuality, there could take place no intellectual process apart from corporeal participation. Now, foreshadowing in this respect the modern theories of the independence of thought, Ruysbroeck, when he appeals on this point to Neoplatonism, is not afraid of establishing the personality as entirely resident in the soul, and of attributing to this latter an existence of its own, wholly detached from all material support. And as a consequence he sets up a *direct* mode of knowledge, an *intuition* (from the Latin *intueri*) which we shall find in the Cartesian doctrine of radical distinction, a doctrine which has become one of the main pillars of modern philosophy.

Another proof of Ruysbroeck's originality may be seen in his metaphors. There is room for an entirely new and very instructive work on the deeper meaning of mystic terminology.

There is more here than a study in art or in literature: the analysis of a process whose supremacy over all other means of philosophic expression has been acknowledged by such modern schools as attribute the utmost importance to the spiritual life.[1]

If our intelligence, in its long past, has accumulated, as regards one and the same original perception, different concepts that frequently contradict one another and have been distorted along the ages by a sort of utilitarian twist, then manifestly the terms that aim at expressing this perception answer but very imperfectly to the reality from which they originate. The word, such as it comes to our lips nowadays, is thus, if one may so express it, sheer indolence; it exempts us from going over again, in the inverse direction, the whole series of stages which an idea has traversed, from the day when it sprang spontaneously fresh from life itself down to the present moment, when we limit it to an accustomed vocable. This is equivalent to saying that terms are inadequate to immediate reality, and consequently the image or metaphor which, in various aspects, evokes the reality and gives a hint or suggestion of it in its vernal originality, is in very truth "l'instrument de choix pour la pensée philosophique." Terms cannot reach down to the essence of things; the image, by forcing the mind to come out of its mechanical routine, has at all events a chance of approaching this essence.

This method, which the moderns—such as Bergson, that master of metaphor—have so admirably developed, has been that of the mystics. Incapable of pouring into the narrow mould of words the sensations experienced in the course of their investigations into the realm of the spirit, they have only succeeded in expressing the reflection of their contemplations in images as varied as possible. Metaphor is thus a sort of golden key to their system, and we should run the risk of extracting nothing from mystic thought, did

[1] E. Le Roy, *Une philosophie nouvelle* (Paris, 1913), pp. 47 ss.; H. Bergson, *Introduction à la Métaphysique*, in *Revue de Métaphysique et de Morale* (January 1903).

we neglect this work of interpretation. It is the skilled embroidery made up of the very threads that constitute the fabric itself.

And so it comes about that the whole of Ruysbroeck's work is one great allegory. Here his originality is unparalleled. He is not content to draw upon the common reservoir of images which the mystics had at their disposal. He creates for himself, with endless patience and labour, metaphors which stamp him as a master both of language and of thought. To grasp the system of our mystic when he is attempting to express reality, it would be necessary to take these metaphors one by one, to compare and study them closely, to tone down the discrepancies they may show, and thus, by steady concentration, to call forth the intuition behind their motley wrappings. An impossible task. The utmost that can be done is to bring them deliberately into an exposition of the doctrine, and, with this object, to travel as far as possible along the paths they suggest. It would be real mutilation to disentangle too thoroughly the system from its allegorical clothing: the image adheres to it as does the skin to the flesh.

. . . . . .

The originality of Ruysbroeck, we have said, has largely consisted in the combination he has been able to effect between different philosophical elements — some coming from Scholastic Aristotelianism and the rest from Neoplatonism—and in permeating Christianity with this combination. By doing this he has truly been *the man of the hour*, another way of being original. In blending such different materials into one homogeneous doctrine he was obeying a necessity of history, and was reproducing in his own person a phenomenon that had taken place ten centuries previously, though on a far greater scale.

Then, Christianity was seen not simply to take the place of the ancient civilisation, as is generally imagined, but to become imbued with the resources which that civilisation

offered it, whilst retaining its own distinctive character.
Consequently the new organism built up on the ruins of
the ancient world had the singular good fortune of bringing
together the religious inspiration of the Gospel and the soul
of mysticism which Neoplatonism and the universalistic
syncretism of the third century had awakened. We may say
that this combination protected the new institution against
materialism; it protected it alike against invading ritualism
and the intellectualism of the scribes by safeguarding the
independence of religious feeling. Right on to the sixteenth
century, when the two elements became dissociated and
resumed their own proper character, it was this combination
that allowed the vista upon the infinite to be maintained.
And it makes its appearance every time this issue threatens
to become obstructed.

No wonder, then, that we find the Christian mystics
adopting this compromise. In the fourteenth century, beneath
the urge of misery and of social aspirations, the world is
carried along by a great impulse, as it were, towards God,
towards a God it is possible to grasp and possess with all the
intensity of human grief. To this universal aspiration the
fallen Church could offer no issue. And in the intellectual
domain, Scholasticism also, degenerating into mere logomachy, was incapable of supplying the minds of men with
the nourishment for which they asked. What could Aristotle
do, in these times of inanition, with his fierce intellectualism,
with his efficient cause, his final cause, his motionless God
who knows nothing of things beneath him, his lesser virtues?
Neoplatonism, on the other hand, with its religious *morale*,
its God who increases in greatness according as man rises,
its perfect Being such as we should like to be ourselves and
to whom one is united by resembling him, was quite calculated to raise man superior to himself, to release him from
his slavery.

But here lay the danger of which indeed the fourteenth
century offered the most pitiable instances. When man was
placed on the incline of mystical piety, was not this exposing

him to fall away either into moral anarchy or into barren quietism, perhaps into both at once ? Ruysbroeck anticipated these formidable possibilities by introducing a fourth element into his system: a practical *morale*. The agent of mystical union is not intelligence, but will; it is not speculation, but sanctification.

Perhaps Ruysbroeck had previously found the germ of this realism in the Neoplatonists, in Saint Augustine, in Saint Bernard, etc. But by resolutely directing mysticism towards action—*common life*, as he says—he was able to keep free of that excessive intellectualism which invariably exhausts life itself. There are few instances among philosophers of a like determination not to lose his footing, to keep in touch with the earth and with everyday life. And so his mysticism may equally be called a *morale*, a simple valiant *morale* which exempts men from none of the stages that lead to perfection. It believes that work is a sacred law, that to be a man is a hard and noble task, that evil is not a fatality to be passively borne, but an enemy to be fought. It does not resignedly think that sin is eternal; it allows that sin indeed exists in human nature by virtue of a grievous heritage, but it straightway declares, in ringing accents, that mankind is not a motionless reality, that it makes itself a little more, day by day, that it is in process of becoming, and that our highest expectations are yet no more than a faint symbol of what we shall eventually realise. There will never be an end of loving, hoping, serving; for the loftiest contemplation, by endowing us with new virtues, urges us on to ever fresh activities.

The image, assuredly an original one, suggested by this rule of life is not the mystic ladder whose top is lost in the boundless heavens, but rather the gushing fountain which springs aloft, spreads around in wheatsheaf jets and falls back into the basin, whence it will again be propelled upwards in identical rhythmic motion.

We see what a practical application Ruysbroeck was able to make of the Neoplatonist theory of the two movements, upwards and downwards. We also see how great was the stimulus he gave to piety and to life in general. Here, too, this supremacy of action brings Ruysbroeck nearer to our modern tendencies, which reject all intellectualistic orthodoxy and attach chief importance to an experimental proof that precedes the explanation. In postulating the perfect adequation of knowledge and being Ruysbroeck reverses the terms of the dogmatic aphorism: *what one is worth depends on what one believes.* He says: *what one believes depends on what one is worth.* And so once again his doctrine, in spite of being manifestly inadequate, is still a very modern one.

Tantum homo habet de scientia quantum operatur. Man really knows only in so far as he acts. Offspring of a mechanical age, we have mostly to relearn, along with Saint Francis, Ruysbroeck, the masters of French thought, Descartes and Pascal, that he alone will know who has set himself free by rough bodily toil, that knowledge is subordinate to purification, and that existence—we mean the whole of existence which is not imprisoned in the finite—is not " an immediate datum which is inevitable, but a problem which must be solved . . . a distant object to which we must attain."[1]

II

If Ruysbroeck's voice had not possessed an altogether new accent, if his doctrine had contained nothing original, it would be impossible to understand the extraordinary influence of our author.

Truly great men are not so much innovators as intelligent interpreters of their times, healers of souls capable, in periods of wavering, of keeping a firm check on spiritual libertinism and moral anarchy, and of instilling renewed faith, mental sanity and human dignity. It is because Ruysbroeck lent his soul, like a huge conch, to the myriad voices of a distracted age, and thrilled with every fibre of his being before

[1] J. Chevalier, *Descartes* (Paris, 1921), p. 344.

all the storms that distressed men's minds, that he roused such prolonged reverberations. The men of his age, and those who came after them, recognised themselves when they read this wonderful interpreter of their own wretchedness. But they also found a remedy in a call to true living and a beneficent spiritual discipline. Thus did Ruysbroeck and the school born of his thought contribute, more than others, to a spiritual quickening. Down to the sixteenth century, which stirred up new disciplines against the same weaknesses, practical mysticism—the documents are explicit in this matter—was one of the great reorganisers of thought and ethics. And in this work the influence of Ruysbroeck could not be over-estimated.

From the fourteenth century, indeed, there is no intellectual centre which was not permeated with his doctrine. In 1360 Ruysbroeck could truly say that his thought had travelled as far as the Alps.[1] In effecting this propagation, unprecedented at the time, the Latin translation of Jordaens was an inestimable instrument, as was the version of Gérard de Groote, not so literary as, though perhaps even more painstaking than, the other. There were other contemporary translations, but their authors have remained anonymous; no trace has ever been found of the translation of *The Spiritual Marriage* made by Thomas à Kempis, though strong testimony was given as to its existence down to the seventeenth century.

It was in the sixteenth and seventeenth centuries more particularly that the renown of Ruysbroeck became really widespread: a fact which would seem to prove that the attacks of Gerson, repeated by Bossuet at the end of the *grand siècle*, had not the scope or importance one might be tempted to attribute to them. This age witnessed an imposing growth of translations. In Italy, in the year 1538, there appeared Latin translations of *The Seven Degrees* and of *The Sparkling Stone*, by an unknown author, dedicated to Nicolas Bargilesius, a priest of Bologna. In 1552 there appeared in

---

[1] *Prologue* of Frère Gérard, in *Bijdragen*, p. 14.

Germany the first edition of the famous translation by Surius, republished in 1608, 1609 and 1692, long extracts from which Louis de Blois included in his religious anthologies. Latin, however, in spite of being so widely known, was an obstacle to the introduction of Ruysbroeck's thought into popular circles. The first translation of our mystic into the vulgar tongue was an Italian translation, edited in Venice in 1565 *per M. Mambrino da Fabriano.* At the beginning of the following century appeared a French translation of *The Spiritual Marriage,* republished in Toulouse in 1619.[1] Lastly, mention must be made of two German translations in 1621 and 1701, and a complete translation of the treatises of the prior of Groenendael into Spanish in 1696. There were also important fragments of Ruysbroeck's work which the writers of a vast number of treatises, in accordance with the spirit of the times, incorporated into their own works without mentioning their origin.

Such abundant testimony shows that Ruysbroeck, up to and including the seventeenth century, was one of the most popular guides in spiritual living.

This authority, especially in the seventeenth century, is largely based on the analogy then found to exist between the religious situation and that we have described in the fourteenth century. On a smaller though equally disturbed stage, Groenendael had played a part but slightly different from that of Port-Royal and the Congrégation de l'Oratoire.[2] This parallelism, striking enough when we study the environment, becomes singularly suggestive when we find such defenders of the spiritual order as Descartes and Malebranche draw in their turn upon the spring of Neoplatonism which Ruysbroeck and his school had found so useful. As a matter of fact, in the combination which mystical

---

[1] The following is the exact title of this translation: *L'Ornement des Nopose spiritvelles. Composé par le divin docteur et très excellent contemplateur Jeaan Rusbroche. Traduict en François per vn Religieux Chartreux de Paris. Auec la vie de l'autheur à la fin du liure,* 1606. *A Tolose, Par la Vefue de J. Colomiés et R. Colomiés, imprimeurs ordinaires du Roy. Avec privilège de sa Majesté.*

[2] Cf. F. Strowski, *Histoire du sentiment religieux en France au xviie siècle; Pascal et son temps,* t. I. pp. 126 ss.

thinkers had elaborated, piety had never been sacrificed to speculation, perfect equilibrium had been maintained between tradition and the foreign elements.

This also explains why the line followed by Ruysbroeck's influence is so different from the direction taken by the speculation of Meister Eckhart, though its philosophical origin is the same.
Whereas the philosophy of Eckhart strips itself more and more of its Christian elements and stirs up the revived pantheism of Jacob Boehme and Schelling, of Hegel and Feuerbach, the mysticism of Ruysbroeck, starting from the same premises, determines a stream of thought infinitely warmer and more religious. With this stream must be connected the institution of the *Frères de la Vie commune*, destined to give birth to the finest book ever written by human hand, *The Imitation of Jesus Christ*, and to the spiritual reform movement with which the congregation of Windesheim is associated.[1] It is this stream of thought also that revives the languishing spirituality of the Franciscan order, through the writings of Henri Herphius, author of a *Miroir de la perfection*, almost a textual reproduction of *The Spiritual Marriage*. In all probability it also inspired the mysterious *Theologia Germanica*, thus preparing the ground for the Reformation.

There can be no doubt regarding the *Frères de la Vie commune*. We have spoken of the deep impression made upon Gérard de Groote by his visits to Groenendael. When in 1382, a year after Ruysbroeck's death, Raynaud Minnenbosch, or Munenbode, founded the monastery of the Saint Sauveur at Eemstein, Gérard de Groote obtained permission from Raynaud that the friars should follow the rule of Saint Augustine, after initiation by a professed priest of Groenendael, Godefroid Wevel. The same year Gérard decided to

---

[1] In his *Chronicon Bethleemticum,* Impens calls Ruysbroeck *vena unde processit fons et inchoatio reformationis novae canonicorum regularium in his terris* (cap. i.).

establish as a religious order the young scholars with whom
he was living. *Ad hunc ordinem regularium instituendum,*
says Thomas à Kempis, *praecipue inductus fuit propter
singularem reverentiam et amorem venerabilis domni Johannis
Rusebroec . . . et aliorum ibidem religiose conversantium
probatissimorum fratrum in ordine regulari : quos · dudum
personaliter in Brabantia visitaverat, a quibus magnam aedi-
ficationis formam ob multam ipsorum humilitatem et simplicis
habitus deferentiam traxit et annotavit.*[1] Death prevented
Gérard from realising his project, but the brothers who had
heard him repeat his desire on his deathbed undertook to
carry out his last wishes. Thus, in 1386, was founded the
famous monastery of Windesheim, which was destined to
have so profound an influence on the reformation of the
morals of the clergy by the diffusion of the *moderna devotio.*[2]

In the Netherlands, Ruysbroeck's doctrines were spread
abroad by the mystics of the association: Henric Mande,
born in 1360, surnamed *the Ruysbroeck of the North,* who in
his numerous works confines himself to reproducing the
mysticism of our prior,[3] and Gerlach Peters, born in 1378.

Windesheim's main claim to glory, however, lies principally in having sown the seed of the Renaissance by em-
phasising the importance of culture allied to godliness. "It is
impossible to find anywhere a more serious cause of distortion than in the neglect on the part of our contemporaries to
add on to the study of literature and science, above all else,
the practice of virtue and honesty of living." These words
of Jean Standonck express the whole work of the masters
and pupils of the school. Amongst those of Deventer must be
mentioned Nicolas de Cues, Longolius, the friend of Melanch-
thon, and above all, Erasmus. Amongst those of Zwolle, Jean
Wessel, surnamed Gansefort, the master of Reuchlin, to whom
Luther rendered grateful testimony. In the world of education

[1] *Vita Gerardi Magni,* cap. xv.
[2] Ruysbroeck's influence made itself also felt in France, especially in the
monastery of Château-Landon, which was reformed after the model of Groenendael. Sanderus, *Chor. Sacr. Brab.,* t. II. p. 30.
[3] See Busch, *Chron. Widnes.,* pp. 450 ss.

it is fitting to mention the names of Rodolphe Agricola, the chief promoter of the study of Greek, of Jean Standonck, rector of the University of Paris in 1485, of Ludwig Dringenberg, rector of the Latin schools of Schlestadt in which were educated most of the creators of the German Renaissance, and lastly of Jean Sturm, head of the University of Strasbourg.

We would seem to be very far from Ruysbroeck. Literary concerns have no place at all, so to speak, in the mind of our lowly prior; he little suspected the incomparable springs of intellectual culture of which the rich treasure-house of the works of antiquity consisted. And yet religious humanism proceeds from the same inspiration and answers the same end as does the work of Ruysbroeck. It is a vast pity for the degenerate, uncultured and wretched Church that finds expression in Ruysbroeck and stimulates the reformers of Windesheim. For corruption advances side by side with ignorance. Ruysbroeck, of a practical turn of mind, assails the former; the *Frères de la Vie commune*, the latter. However different our forest-monk from the learned humanists of Deventer, Zwolle or Liége, none the less is he directly related to them, seeing that it was he who directed Gérard de Groote in his work of reform and that Windesheim was the embodiment of Gérard's inspiration.

Now that this link has been forged, can we regard Ruysbroeck as a precursor of the Reformation of the sixteenth century?

There is too close a connection between human events for it to be possible to find at will more or less likely arguments in favour of this theory. One may doubtless bring forward the influence upon Luther of Jean Wessel, of whom the great reformer said: "If I had read his writings sooner, my enemies might believe that Luther has drawn solely upon Wessel's works, so united is his mind with my own." [1] But while Wessel teaches justification in terms that

[1] In *Opera*, édit. Walch, t. XIV. p. 220.

remind one of the doctrine of Luther,[1] his exposition, strongly imbued with Neoplatonism, is purely intellectual and does not go down into those depths of consciousness wherein the Saxon monk so long struggled. Again, it is possible to notice a certain similarity between Luther and another *frère de la Vie commune*, Johann Pupper de Goch, the author of *De libertate christiana*, a treatise in which attempts have been made to discover the central dogma of the Reformation,[2] without seeing that, in reality, Goch regarded justification as depending on merit. And so these instances do not seem adequate; at most they prove that the atmosphere in which the Reformation developed emanated largely from Windesheim.

Still, there is the famous *Theologia Deutsch*, the mystical work of the anonymous Frankfürt writer. It is undoubtedly possible to see the influence of Ruysbroeck in this treatise which Luther edited, at first partially in 1516 and afterwards as a whole in 1518, after adding an enthusiastic preface. In his introduction Luther says that the doctrine of the anonymous author "recalls that of the enlightened doctor Johannes Tauler." But Tauler had been influenced by the hermit of Groenendael, and we think we have succeeded in proving that the mysterious Canclaer who came to visit Ruysbroeck in his hermitage and Tauler were one and the same individual. In addition, the doctrine of the *Theologia Germanica* is at least as reminiscent of the doctrine of Ruysbroeck as of that of Tauler. There is the same mysticism based on speculation, the same doctrine of the substantial unity of God and the world incessantly renewed by divine dynamism, the return of creation into the bosom of the Creator. As in Ruysbroeck, however, metaphysics is wholly subordinated to morality. The general tendency of the book is practical, above all else.

We are acquainted with Luther's testimony to the *Theologia Germanica*: "I fear not to place this book alongside of the Bible and the works of Saint Augustine, for, more than

---

[1] See the texts in Döllinger, *La Réforme et son développement intérieur*, trad. Perrot, t. III. p. 4.

[2] Ullmann, *Reformatoren vor der Reformation* (Gotha, 1886), 2 t. I. p. 92.

any other book, it has taught me what God, Christ and man are." And yet the reformer, whose mentality was so different from Neoplatonist speculation, was far from assimilating the entire doctrine of the anonymous writing. If he received inspiration thereby, he had previously purged it of its pantheistic elements. And if we find it in him, it is exclusively in his practical piety which looks upon happiness as harmony between the human and the divine will. Thus it is somewhat exaggerated to regard Luther as a disciple of the Frankfürt writer. The *Commentary on the Psalms*, which has been declared to be an application of the ideas of the *Theologia Germanica* to the sacred texts, can be traced back mainly to Saint Augustine. Luther's doctrine is essentially his own; it is the spontaneous outcome of his conscience and his heartrending meditations. From 1512 to 1515 he may have nourished his emotions on the fervent godliness that runs through the *Theologia Germanica*; in any case his mind remained untainted by the pantheistic leaven which, a few years later, Calvin denounced as the "hidden venom" of German mysticism.[1]

The necessity of a Church reform so strongly advocated by Ruysbroeck is an anxious task which he shares with the great founders of monastic orders, with Gregory VII., and with many a heterodox sect of the Middle Ages; it is insufficient to procure for him the title of pre-Reformer. Since the Gospel of Jesus of Nazareth—Spirit made for freedom—became incarnate in an institution, the best of men have never sided with the deviations to which it has been subjected. This Protestant stream traverses the whole of the Middle Ages, whether exercised within the Church or acting outside of traditional lines and occasionally, in strangely distorted form, superseding the Christian truth. Will it be alleged that it paves the way for the Reformation because Luther and Calvin also rose against the decline of the Church and the corruption of the clergy? Among the Reformers there was something more: a doctrine and a conception of Christian

---

[1] *Lettres de Jean Calvin*, édit. Bonnet, t. II. p. 259.

life which show how far removed they are from the piety
of the Middle Ages, and more particularly from the
speculative mystics.

III

To obtain a right estimate of the speculative mystics they
must be seen in the historical conditions that gave them
birth. In particular they ought to be studied in their true
philosophical alignment. Then only is their doctrine found
to possess its full emphasis, its sturdy originality so unjustly
disregarded.

We are still too much disposed to look upon mysticism
as religious morbidity, manifesting as sentimental trickery
and extravagance, and far removed from all genuine thinking.
We do not deny that such vacuity of mind is but too frequently
found in mystics. Still, should we ever have dreamed of raising
Ruysbroeck from the dust in which he lay if we had had to
pursue such vapourings?

But if, on the contrary, mysticism is essentially the effort
of the mind to grasp the infinite; if, more than all else, it is
sincerity, intuition, interior freedom reacting against all
formalism; if it outstrips the domain of extent and establishes
itself at the heart of thought; if finally, in alliance with
speculation, it is a continuation of Neoplatonism, and like
this latter attempts to supply a philosophy of the intelligible,
then it has a place of its own in the history of ideas.

In our opinion this place has not been rightly fixed. From
the studies on the Middle Ages that are now being made, we
are justified in hoping that greater honour will be accorded
to the speculative mystics than they have yet received from
historians of philosophy, for they already appear before us,
no longer as passive inheritors in whose hands a great tradition has been made of none effect, but as initiators, precursors of the present age.

The specialised works of Pierre Duhem have already
shown that the principles which modern science invokes go

back farther than the days of Newton, Galileo and Copernicus. These works have stripped the Renaissance of its usurped pride and restored to the Middle Ages the honour of having given wings to experimental science. It would thus appear, in the light of the best authenticated texts, that the main features of our present knowledge of the world must be sought for within the University of Paris in the fourteenth century. Buridan de Béthune, Albert de Saxe, Grégoire de Rimini, Nicole Oresme, bishop of Lisieux, Jean de Bassols and others are the true initiators of modern times.[1]

And now the history of philosophy, in attempting to discover the source whence flow the methods of thought that make up the modern mind, also passes beyond the *grand siècle* and the Renaissance, and tends to restore speculative mysticism.

It is to this, indeed, that we can rightly trace the modern doctrines that set up the supremacy of mind and regard intuition and the inner life as legitimate means of investigation for attaining to immediate knowledge. And it is with Thomism, even more than with Descartes, that we must connect the second stream of modern thought: that which comprises the philosophies of pure reason.[2] Now we have seen to what extent the doctrine of Ruysbroeck is imbued with Scholasticism. The result is that the two streams which cross our contemporary philosophy meet once more, blended though clearly discernible, in that strange intellectual phenomenon which goes under the name of speculative mysticism.

Descartes, generally looked upon as the father of modern philosophy, is himself an heir, an inheritor of genius doubtless,

[1] Cf. A. Dufourcq, *Le Christianisme et l'organisation féodale* (Paris, 1911); id., *Les origines de la science moderne d'après les découvertes récentes*, in *Revue des Deux Mondes* (15 July, 1913), pp. 349 ss.

P. Duhem, *Études sur Léonard de Vinci* (Paris, I. 1906; II. 1909); *L'évolution de la mécanique* (1903); *Les origines de la statique* (1905); *Le système du monde, histoire des doctrines cosmologiques de Platon à Copernic*, etc.

[2] Apart from Picavel, see E. Gilson, *La doctrine cartésienne de la liberté et la théologie* (Paris, 1913); *Index scolastico-cartésien* (1913); *Le thomisme, introduction au système de S. Thomas d'Aquin* (1920); *Études de philosophie médiévale* (1920), pp. 1–124.

one who in many ways was able to give ultimate form to the material provided by tradition, though finally a transmitter, an arranger as much as, and even more than, an innovator. We shall certainly grieve impenitent Cartesians by dealing thus with the great methodologist who, like some towering peak, seemed to divide the world of thought into two slopes: one of shade, the other of light.

Still, we do not think we have done anything to disparage his incomparable glory, and, to shelter from the indignation of his enthusiastic disciples, we can but take refuge behind his own words: "I am by no means," he says, "of the nature of those who desire that their opinions should appear new; on the contrary, I adapt my own opinions to those of others, in so far as truth allows me to do so." [1]

What are these "opinions," and who are these "others"? Once this point is settled, we shall see that the genius of Descartes was employed not so much in assuming a personal initiative as in grouping together and revivifying, by a new method, the elements he found in the mystical and Neo-platonist tradition of the Middle Ages.

What indeed is it that Descartes seeks? The story of the famous night of the 10th of November 1619, when Descartes saw flash before him the rudiments of his method, informs us.[2] This is absolute certainty, in conformity with the essence of things and with the immediate vision which the soul, *qua* exclusive agent of the mental processes, can obtain thereof. Thus Descartes purposes to set up his fixed centre in the transcendental region of first principles. And so, even at the very start, our philosopher meets with mystics who also take up their stand in the infinite or the perfect. To reach this central position, however, there is much to be done. From periphery to centre stretch several concentric circles which must be crossed one after another.

In the first place, the mind, meditating upon itself,

---

[1] *Lettre du 2 mai*, 1644 (*Œuvres*, édit. Adam et Tannery, Paris, 1897–1910, t. IV. p. 113).
[2] Adrien Baillet, *Vie de Monsieur Des-Cartes* (Paris, 1691), t. I. p. 84.

recognises that it has no power of itself to see direct. It apprehends the world only through a medium or a reflection. It finds itself "darkened and blinded, as it were, by the images of sense-objects." Its experience is that the thoughts which come to it are not immediately impressed by reality, but consist of alien intruders. As a rule we think with the opinions of others; the mechanism of thought has taken the place of original thought, which, in its pure form, is reached by the contemplation of reality itself. Thus it is indispensable to free oneself from the second-hand or dubious opinions, the false reasons and prejudices with which, as its heritage, the mind finds itself burdened. As Descartes says, we must "lay aside those old and ordinary opinions to which their long and familiar acquaintance with me give the right to occupy my mind against my will." [1]

In like manner we must supersede the testimony of the senses, which are evidently deceptive, seeing that the data they supply are either illusory—such as the pain a man feels in a limb that has been amputated—or erroneous, since distance, for instance, modifies, to our eyes, the height of a tree or the form of a house.

Reason itself, that instrument of discursive processes, cannot be considered perfectly pure; two mathematicians, for instance, may deduce different solutions from the same data. As regards all the things that appeal to the mind, if we make an experiment of this kind, in the last analysis the subjective reality will always be found to be elusive, and, in Pascal's words, it will be seen that "the final stage of reason is the recognition that there is an infinity of things which transcend reason." [2]

Such is the *doute méthodique* whereby Descartes provisionally calls in question the ideas supplied by reason, sense testimony and opinion. Here there is neither scepticism nor deliberate negation, but a discipline of which the mystics had already made use and which, in its negative form, is

---

[1] *Méditation Ire* (*Œuvres*, édit. Adam-Tannery, t. XX. p. 17).
[2] *Pensées*, édit. Havet, art. xiii. 1; t. I. p. 192.

essentially positive, seeing that it aims "at flinging back the shifting earth and the sand in order to find the rock or the clay . . . at seeing if after that there should not remain something altogether indubitable." [1]

When the thinker has thus made *tabula rasa*, does he find himself confronted with absolute nonentity? No, for he discovers within himself *innate ideas* which he has received from no one, which reason has not worked out, which are universal and self-imposed on the understanding. Among these ideas is the inborn knowledge that men possess of God. Consequently the sincere man is compelled to recognise that he is connected with a Reality that transcends him in all directions, the intelligent cause and origin of all things. Now innatism or exemplarism constitutes the very centre of the doctrine of the speculative mystics, who had obtained it from Saint Augustine and from Neoplatonism. By establishing it in their own system they had openly broken with Saint Thomas, who had been strongly opposed to this doctrine. [2]

The existence of God, then, as principle, is for Descartes the first and the fundamental certainty. There is another closely connected with it. Descartes, as we have just seen, before reconstructing on new bases, destroyed everything by the aid of methodic doubt. But by what instrument did he effect this process? By thought. Consequently the fact of thinking could not take place apart from a really independent personality whose existence is actually manifested by intellectual processes.

Such is the meaning of the famous *cogito ergo sum*. "Whilst I thus willed to think that all was false, I, who was thinking it, was necessarily obliged to be something." [3] Now in the vast desert which Descartes has just created by his provisional doubt, this "something" cannot be other

---

[1] *Discours de la méthode pour bien conduire sa raison* (*Œuvres*, t. VI. pp. 29, 31). Cf. Ruysbroeck, *The Spiritual Marriage*, book I. chapters xxx., xxxi.; book II. chapter xxxii.; *The Sparkling Stone*, chapter ii.

[2] "Intellectus quo anima intelligit, non habet aliquas species naturaliter inditas." *Summa*, I.ᵃ quaest. lxxxiv. art. 3.

[3] *Discours de la méthode* (*Œuvres*, t. VI. p. 32).

than a reality absolutely independent of external things, as detached from the body as from the limitations implied by ordinary reasoning. Alongside of God, thought — distinct from reason — thus appears as a second and indubitable reality, as the very principle of life. And this second and indubitable reality at the same time supplies us with indubitable information as to the nature of God: God is Thought, Mind, for the more cannot come from the less. Human thought is a flame lighted from the great torch of Deity.

Descartes found this doctrine, in the amazing development he gave to it, only in Neoplatonist mysticism, where it had already assumed a strangely consistent form, especially in the works of Meister Eckhart and of Ruysbroeck.[1]

The corollary of the proposition is naturally that soul, the seat of thought, dependent on the infinite, is wholly distinct from body, dependent on space. Body indeed is not necessary—whereas thought is adequate and necessary—for man's being. This is the doctrine of the root distinction between soul and body, a doctrine that has had so great an influence upon modern philosophy. First, thought exists; then, matter is given in addition, and strictly the material world could exist only as a mental picturing.[2]

Not, however, that the body is quite unprovided with all means of knowledge; there is a very special intelligence, an animal knowledge, evidence of which may occasionally agree with the information supplied by the soul. In addition, the perceptions of the soul may be influenced by the corporeal perceptions. But it is the soul alone that *thinks* and *wills*. We also find this theory dealt with at length by our mystics. Three centuries before Descartes, they posited the soul as a substance, a complete being, really distinct from—and capable of existing without—the body. They too regarded the body as a kind of particular intellection, an inferior

---

[1] Cf. *The Spiritual Marriage*, book II. chapter ii.; *The Kingdom*, chapter v.; *The Mirror*, chapter viii.; *The Twelve Beguines*, chapters xxxi., xxxii.
    On the sources of the Cartesian doctrine, see L. Blanchet, *Les antécédents historiques du "Je pense, donc je suis"* (Paris, 1920), pp. 25 ss.
[2] H. Bergson, *La Philosophie*, p. 6.

representative of the mental processes. Thus, like Descartes, they distinguished between two kinds of memory: the one, which retains the traces of material things and is nothing else than the faculty of recalling; the other, the higher memory or recognition, directed towards God and the eternal realities.[1] Like Descartes also, they gave special emphasis to the will among the mental powers, thus ushering in the modern philosophies of free-will.

The link between Descartes and mysticism, however, is found above all in their common theory of knowledge considered as a *vision*. To know is to see. Vision or intuition precedes deduction: the whole of knowledge is reducible to these two successive processes.

The term *intuition* may give rise to confusion. It is generally regarded as a presentiment, the faint glimpse of a truth that passes rapidly before the mind. Descartes takes the word strictly in its etymological sense: the clear, direct immediate vision of truths which, to be grasped, do not need the intermediary of reasoning. It is thought planting itself at the heart of reality and contemplating it, with every image stripped away.

Intuitive knowledge [explains Descartes] is an illumination of the mind whereby it sees in the light of God the things it pleases him to lay bare before it by direct impression of divine enlightenment upon our understanding, which in this is not regarded as an agent, but only as receiving the rays of Deity.[2]

Might we not think we were here listening to the speculative mystics when they speak of contemplation in nakedness of images? Their conception, whole and undistorted, has passed into Descartes. In the voice of the geometrician-philosopher we hear, amazed, the echo of Ruysbroeck's voice singing of interior freedom, of the power to

rise to God without images or shackles by every interior practice. Superseding reason, we ought to enter into God with faith, and remain there

[1] Cf. Ruysbroeck, *The Kingdom*, chapter v.; Descartes, *Lettre au P. Mesland*, 2 mai, 1644 (*Œuvres*, t. IV. p. 114); J. Chevalier, *Descartes*, pp. 233, 245.
[2] *Lettre au marquis de Newcastle*, 1648 (*Œuvres*, t. V. p. 136); quoted by Chevalier, *op. cit.*, p. 172.

simply, stripped and free of images. Then, in our mind, released from all
activity, we receive that incomprehensible brightness . . . which is nothing
else than boundless contemplation.[1]

Though to this conception Descartes added developments
revealing his great originality, though he adapted it to his
geometrical conception of the world, though he widened
its province by his personal theories on analysis and synthesis
in elaborating a complete philosophy of the intelligible, it
is none the less true that the Neoplatonists and the speculative mystics had entered before himself into the world of
spirit and described—as far as language could depict—
uncontrovertible experiences.

It is really unjust to regard these experiences as valid
only through the *Méditations métaphysiques* of Descartes,
and yet to discredit them in mystics by attributing them to
some morbid illumination or other. An equitable estimate
of the doctrines will assuredly correct this judgment; even
now a study of the origins of Cartesian thought has clearly
determined the relation that exists between Descartes and
the mystical tradition.

Who indeed are those "others" whose participation in
the formulation of his doctrine Descartes has acknowledged,
unless they be the Christian heirs of Neoplatonism? We must
not forget that Scholasticism, with which Descartes was
thoroughly acquainted, was quite as much permeated with
Neoplatonism as with Aristotelianism.[2] And we must remember that, long before the seventeenth century, the authority
of Saint Thomas was not so universally recognised as it is
supposed to be, and that the Jesuits, for the purpose of
refuting him, did not fear to appeal to Neoplatonism, as
filtered through Saint Augustine. Thus, at the famous
Collège de la Flèche, where Descartes studied philosophy
in 1609, the teaching of Suarez, infinitely nearer to Neo-

---

[1] *The Sparkling Stone*, chapters ii., ix.
[2] The only two books that Descartes took with him to Holland were the
Bible and the *Summa* of Saint Thomas Aquinas. *Lettre de 25 décembre*, 1639
(*Œuvres*, t. II. p. 630).

platonism than to Aristotelianism, had in effect supplanted
that of Saint Thomas.[1] But it was chiefly the foundation of
the Congrégation de l'Oratoire by the Cardinal de Bérulle
that, under the auspices of Saint Augustine, secured the predominance of Neoplatonism in the thought of the seventeenth century. The undissembled aim of this foundation
is well known. Frivolity, scepticism and corruption, under
the general name of libertinage, gravely menaced the Christian
tradition. A languid religious sentiment degenerated into
barren sentimentality or was content to be a shallow optimistic *prudhomie*, regarding everything as for the best in
the best of all worlds. In fact, decked out in the spoils of
Stoicism, cynically denying or scornfully disinterested,
libertinage was nothing else than atheism. Then, under the
inspiration of the Cardinal de Bérulle, there came into being
a new school, happy to find in Neoplatonism, with its doctrines of immediate vision and exemplarism, decisive arguments for confounding sceptical libertines. Was it indeed
possible to deny a God vouched for by irrefutable intellectual
experience, a God who was in man, as innate idea, just as
the spark is in the flint?

Descartes, like the Oratorians, has but one object: to
confute atheism. He desires but one thing: to prove God
and make him apprehensible to the human mind. And so
we find that he keeps in close touch with the Oratorians.
He chooses Bérulle in person as spiritual director; he greatly
appreciates the book of the school systematist, Gibieuf,
author of a treatise on the freedom of God and of the creature.[2]
He joins with Jean de Silhon, who in the *Deux Vérités* had
brought together a veritable Neoplatonist arsenal against
atheists, and also with Mersenne, another Neoplatonist who
subsequently became his correspondent and philosophical
confidant.

Such were the men of whom Descartes saw a great deal

---

[1] E. Gilson, *Études de philosophie médiévale*, pp. 166, etc. On Suarez, see
Lechner, *Die Erkenntnislehre des Suarez*, in *Philos. Jahrbuch*, bd. xxv. pp. 125–50.
[2] *Lettre à Marsenne, octobre*, 1631 (*Œuvres*, t. I. p. 220).

between 1626 and 1628, a period when he was combining and assimilating material for thought. Fully equipped, in this latter year he betook himself to Holland, there to find the solitude necessary for the compiling of his great work. There also he was to meet with the Neoplatonist tradition which the speculative mystics had inherited. At Deventer in particular he must have encountered the influence of Ruysbroeck and the *Vie Commune* movement, the tradition of which had been kept alive. What wonder, then, that the *Méditations métaphysiques*, as we have seen, were inspired by those lofty mystical speculations which had supplied spiritual nourishment to the whole of the Middle Ages? Or that these speculations, adopted at the same time by the Augustinians of the Oratoire, Thomassin, Du Hamel, Ambrosius Victor and particularly Malebranche, supplied through them some of the principles on which our modern philosophy is based?

IV

As a rule biographers are blamed for unduly exaggerating the importance of their hero, for seeing the world only through him. A man of second- or third-rate importance thus finds himself, as the result of a blind exclusive affection, raised to the level of a master or a saint.

We will not ruin our historical perspective by such puerile complaisance. The place held by Ruysbroeck in the history of ideas is sufficiently honourable for us to feel no obligation to regard him as the ancestor of modern philosophy. On the other hand, however, historical justice and a true estimate of intellectual values will not allow us to leave our thinker in the shade to which historians, ever since the eighteenth century, have relegated him. We wish for him:

Ni cet excès d'honneur ni cette indignité,

but only a little of the gratitude due to the dead.

In this restitution of esteem we are not thinking of Ruysbroeck alone, but of the whole of speculative mysticism as it appeared in the fourteenth century. To show that it is not so distant from us as one is pleased to imagine, we should like, in these few closing remarks, to unravel the characteristic features of the doctrine, to compare them with the general trend of contemporary thought, and so to prove that in many respects this thought has indeed advanced along the lines of mystical speculation.

The first thing that strikes one in the doctrines of the past thirty years is a justified depreciation of positive science, hitherto regarded as a full and complete explanation of the phenomena of life. Whether we reflect on the mechanistic psychology of Taine and Stuart Mill, or read again the passionate pages of Renan on the future of science, we see what intellectual pride stirred the men of the generation preceding our own. Science appeared to them as alone capable of producing a philosophy co-extensive with life; nothing existed which could not immediately be verified, weighed or numbered. Before such pride, mystery vanished like the mists of the morn, and metaphysics, like religion, went to join the ancient idolatries in the hypogea of the past.

It soon appeared, however, that science, notwithstanding its claims, really affected only a part of life, the surface-film which masks and conceals the deep realities. The penetration line of science snapped just where its vision and its instruments could go no farther. Beyond lay mystery, a vast region that grew in extent the more one thought one had encroached upon it.

"We are decidedly tired of hearing 'Reason' invoked in solemn and tender accents, as though merely to write the revered name with a big capital R provided a magical solution for all problems." This phrase of Le Roy well expresses the mental state of the psychological school which succeeded scientific rationalism. Not that this school—inaugurated nearly a century previously by Maine de Biran—denied the legitimacy of science as a means of knowledge. But it could not admit that science should be the one and only mode of knowledge. Hence the anti-intellectualistic stream which still carries us along, and, like the glowing fires of the dawn on some inviolate mountain-top, throws a dazzling brilliancy on to the summits of life itself. In various modes, though combining in one uniform direction, such thinkers as Ravaisson, Lachelier, Boutroux, Bergson and Le Roy have regarded the human mind as capable of aiming at the heart and centre of things, of attaining the absolute, and, in fugitive flashes at least, of glimpsing that one eternal essence from which the universe originates in all its amazing complexity.

This position, as we see, is that of the speculative mystics. But the analogy does not stop at the origin; it continues into the various developments of the doctrine. Modern thinkers, indeed, on unifying the results of interior observation and the data supplied by clinical psychology, were led to supersede the intellect, to reduce its operations to the rôle of a mere interpreter, and finally to establish the existence of a mental substance extending beyond the brain in all directions. This substance, the Mind, gives us indications regarding itself which are passed on like waves. The delicate antennæ of the brain perceive and interpret them, perfectly or imperfectly according as the receiver is in good or bad condition. But in any case the intelligence, by which term we mean the cerebral activity, can supply nothing original; it is but a camera obscura in which the universe is reflected, a sensitive plate registering an impression.

This being so, how are we to come in direct contact with this generating Mind? Here contemporary psychologists of the school of Bergson introduce a doctrine of the intelligible, which, as we have already seen, bears a remarkable relation to the views of the mystics.

Kant, who also had endeavoured to attain to pure reason, really came to a halt before a static conception of intelligence. His pure reason is motionless intelligence, localised on one particular subject which, so to speak, has modelled and moulded it after its own nature, and which, instead of receiving indications from a generating- station external to itself, itself projects ideas outside of itself. It is easy to see what this idealism is capable of achieving: are the universe, God, the soul—offshoots of reason—anything more than illusions? This deceptive philosophy could produce nothing but a monstrous pride which, in no slight degree, has contributed to drive humanity downhill to catastrophe.

Modern French philosophy, on the contrary, starts with *actual* intelligence. It says that "idea is an arrest of thought,"[1] and that original information on reality must be sought beyond the successive forms which the primitive perception of reality has mentally assumed. This is a return to the standpoint of pure contemplation which, as we have seen, Ruysbroeck and other mystics regarded as knowledge superior to intelligence. Beyond symbol, terminology, acquired ideas, the usual forms of analytical and discursive thought, and the other representations which mystics call "images," the mind comes truly *to see* things in their essential reality. It breaks the intellectual crust under which—like water under ice—flows life in its primal limpidity.

The method, then, of attaining to intuition is a disburdening, a purification, a throwing off. It is the ἅπλωσις of Plotinus, the κάθαρσις of the Pseudo-Dionysius, the elimination of images (*phantasma*) of Saint Augustine and Ruysbroeck, the provisional doubt of Descartes, i.e. detachment from the outer world which vitiates our perceptions of its impress. This work of purification, when accomplished, can alone give us virginal freshness of vision, the direct sensation of reality.[2] It places us at the heart of things; in mystic parlance, it stablishes us in God. This is the return to the immediate.

Now, what is the revelation here given to us? That fundamentally the universe is movement and life. We must henceforth abandon the static idea of a finished edifice. Creation goes on endlessly, by virtue of an initial movement

---

[1] H. Bergson, *Mind Energy*, p. 4.

[2] See H. Bergson, *Time and Free Will*, p. 132 and conclusion; *Matter and Memory*, Preface and p. 118; *Laughter : An Essay on the Meaning of the Comic*, pp. 150–61; and especially *Introduction à la métaphysique*, in *Revue de Métaphysique et de Morale*, janvier, 1903.

which, with infinite profusion, indefatigably engenders
new forms and manifests itself on this globe of ours by
the evolution of species and the constitution of human
personalities.[1]

This powerful dynamism also had been glimpsed by the
mystics. Doubtless they conceived of it under the aspect
of a circuit starting from God and returning to God, first
dragging creation along in a descending movement and then
urging it onward with vigorous impetus up the ascending
arc. Evolutionist philosophy, with biology as its teacher,
does not look upon things quite so simply. According to it,
the development of life has not taken place along one uniform
line; it has encountered obstacles and has split up; retrogression has set in; some of the very currents which it has
set going have stopped and become motionless. All the same,
some faint suggestion of this conception of the living universe
is found clearly defined in the works of our mystics, as is also
the consequence that springs therefrom: man forming an
integral part of this vast scheme of things whose first reason
and whose end are in God. "Like eddies of dust raised by the
wind as it passes, the living turn upon themselves, borne up
by the great blast of life." [2]

It follows from this that modern philosophy is not far
from reinstating the idea of survival. After establishing the
independence of mind and matter, after showing that we
are completely laved in a mind-atmosphere which is the
primal source of all our perceptions, that the brain interprets
only what passes through the consciousness, it can but
thereby deduce for the personality the conclusion that it
is immortal,

for the only reason one can have for believing in the extinction of consciousness at death is that we see the body become disorganised, that this
is a fact of experience and the reason loses its force if the independence of
almost the whole of consciousness with regard to the body has been shown
to be also a fact of experience.[3]

[1] H. Bergson, *Creative Evolution*, chapter ii.
[2] *Ibid.*, p. 134; pp. 285–6.
[3] H. Bergson, *Mind-Energy*, p. 59.

Let us listen reverently to these solemn accents which thrill the inmost fibres of the soul and are so manifestly attuned to the mystic song of triumph on the threshold of the infinite.

Not to leave our task unfinished, we must also remember the practical value of modern philosophy. With deliberate purpose it tends towards life from all directions. In its attempt ever to bring thought within the scope of will and of action, not only does it widen the province of the lofty teachings of Maine de Biran, the great initiator of the philosophies of the soul, but it also finds itself once again in accord with the profound thought of Ruysbroeck. To him and to modern philosophy alike, the masterpiece of the mind is a great and noble human life, a life carved out in matter as a statue is in stone.

If the universe is traversed by a dual stream of force —one part descending to constitute materiality, the other part ascending in the direction of spirit—the upright man deliberately steps into the latter. Evil is fall and retrogression, both in the moral and in the cosmic order of things. Good is the ascent towards the light. Consequently "the men of moral grandeur . . . are revealers of metaphysical truth. Although they are the culminating point of evolution, yet they are nearest the source and they enable us to perceive the impulsion which comes from the deep." [1] Similarly, as we have seen, it is in good deeds that the doctrine of Ruysbroeck culminates. Reaching the peak of contemplation, like Moses that of the burning mountain, he again comes down to the plains, having discovered that God summons men not to inaction, but to the daily task; that in goodness there dwells a might invincible, and that the final interpretation of life is to be found in the word "effort." [2]

. . . .

When we began this book, mankind was staggering, stunned and exhausted, to its feet after such carnage as

[1] *Ibid.*, p. 25. [2] *The Seven Degrees*, chapter xiv.

the world had never before witnessed. The lurid glare of the vast conflagration, stretching from the Vosges to the sea, had revealed to us the meaning and significance of the unspeakable catastrophe which almost destroyed the whole of our Latin heritage. The voice of the cannon howled and shrieked—a fitting expression of those doctrines of force indicative of our scientific and philosophical materialism. An exclusively mechanical civilisation, one that excludes the spirit, removes God with a stroke of the pen, replaces metaphysics with physics and regards as illusions the sublime realities of the spirit, has brought itself to the very edge of the abyss. This is but too evident.

On the other hand, a certain mode of living—which it is heartrending to find so prevalent nowadays—cannot but lead to ruin also. Subjection to the needs of the body, enjoyment set up as an idol, contempt for disinterested work, and above all, that ignoble materialism of money which corrupts all relations between human beings: these are so many departures from that *divine Order* wherein Plotinus saw salvation. Notwithstanding the long and precious spiritual tradition behind us, we seem to have lost recollection of that divine order, or at all events to have become incapable of examining it fully.

This saving economy for which a Jesus of Nazareth sacrificed himself—a vision which all down the ages has raised up a countless procession of apostles and martyrs— is, in a word, *the supremacy of the Spirit.*

There is a higher life whereby man is related to his source and origin—the channel which brings strength to his arms and love into his heart. This life, however, is not offered us along with the other. No school, no church has a monopoly of it. It is learned as the result of prolonged and laborious effort; it calls for stern sacrifices. But without it our surest impetus turns aside or stops altogether, our thought grasps but the semblance of things, our love and tenderness expire with those we lay in the tomb.

Much is said nowadays of a full and integral life, of the

cult of personality. The spiritual life alone is capable of drawing from us the riches buried in the human soul; it alone pledges our complete development, and that through a single human example, whether as hero, thinker or saint, manifesting human dignity and worth raised to its highest point.

Such is the ultimate significance of Ruysbroeck's doctrine, set in its true alignment. Whatever differences may seem to exist between this doctrine and our own mode of thought, the springs that nourished it and upon which we still draw are the same. For if we are to live *humanly*, we can no more dispense with the noble inspirations of Græco-Latin antiquity than with the Gospel itself. Besides, in many respects this teaching presents such striking correspondences with modern thought that, behind the incomparable language of our mystic, it sometimes appears as though we were listening to the halting accents of our contemporary philosophy of the spirit.

At all events, whether the doctrine rouse in us feelings of adherence or of reserve, this at least is certain: it stimulates thought. It brings us back from the state of dispersion in which we are living, right to the centre of the self. It reawakens the sense of mystery, of the divine. As we read these simple, artless books, studded with metaphors, something whispers to us that the soul's experience contained in these pages is valid for ourselves, certainly capable of being put in force once more.

We feel that the old mystic is speaking the truth when he proclaims with quiet assurance: "It is the infinite, the perfect, on which our souls are nourished." Then we momentarily forget the material cares and anxieties of life, and listen to this clear message ringing and expanding within us, like the vibrations of a fundamental tone.

To live a good life we must have a fixed centre in the invisible. Could but these pages, devoted to a long-forgotten fourteenth-century monk, at least point someone in the direction of that invisible which laves and envelops us all the time, we should not regret the labour expended in writing them. For the only way to acknowledge the debt of gratitude we owe to the masters of thought is *to think ourselves*, seeing that the whole of human dignity and worth also lies in the order of thought.

FINIS

Date Due